D0840258

Mark Edele is Associate Professor in History at the University of Western Australia. Born and raised between books and mountains in Bavaria's south, he received much of his education in Germany (MA, University of Tübingen), learned Russian in St. Petersburg, and earned an MA and PhD from the University of Chicago. In 2004, he moved to Perth, Western Australia, to teach continental European and Russian history. His research has been published, among others, in *Slavic Review, Kritika, Acta Slavica Iaponica*, the *Jahrbücher für Geschichte Osteuropas, Russian History* as well as in the collections *Late Stalinism: Society between Reinvention and Reconstruction* ed. Juliane Fürst (Routledge, 2006) and *Beyond Totalitarianism* ed. Sheila Fitzpatrick and Michael Geyer (Cambridge University Press, 2009). He is the author of *Soviet Veterans of the Second World War: A Popular Movement in an Authoritarian Society* (Oxford University Press, 2008). *Stalinist Society* is his second book.

Stalinist Society
1928–1953

MARK EDELE

OXFORD
UNIVERSITY PRESS

OXFORD

UNIVERSITY PRESS

Great Clarendon Street, Oxford OX2 6DP

Oxford University Press is a department of the University of Oxford.
It furthers the University's objective of excellence in research, scholarship,
and education by publishing worldwide in

Oxford New York

Auckland Cape Town Dar es Salaam Hong Kong Karachi
Kuala Lumpur Madrid Melbourne Mexico City Nairobi
New Delhi Shanghai Taipei Toronto

With offices in

Argentina Austria Brazil Chile Czech Republic France Greece
Guatemala Hungary Italy Japan Poland Portugal Singapore
South Korea Switzerland Thailand Turkey Ukraine Vietnam

Oxford is a registered trade mark of Oxford University Press
in the UK and in certain other countries

Published in the United States
by Oxford University Press Inc., New York

British Library Cataloguing in Publication Data
Data available

Library of Congress Cataloging in Publication Data
Data available

Typeset by SPI Publisher Services, Pondicherry, India
Printed in Great Britain
on acid-free paper by
MPG Books Group, Bodmin and King's Lynn

ISBN: 978-0-19-923640-4 (hbk.)
      978-0-19-923641-1 (pbk.)

1 3 5 7 9 10 8 6 4 2

Dedicated to the Memory of Marc Flament (1929–2010)

PREFACE

This book was written entirely in Western Australia, a place whose beauty, calm and relaxed way of life is in sharp contrast to the society I was immersed during reading and writing hours. I owe thanks not only to my home institution, the University of Western Australia (UWA), which allowed me to jump-start this new project during a six-month sabbatical in 2008, but also to many individuals without whom life outside the study would be lonely and boring.

First among them is my wife, Debra McDougall, who despite a busy schedule as a scholar, a mother, and a daughter, found time to not only listen to my preoccupations but also to serve as censor, copy-editor, and grammar police of the final product. Our daughter, Anna Dunateko Edele, emerged into this world about halfway through writing this book, and was a fabulous companion ever since. Anna decided after two months that sleeping through the night was what civilized beings did, thus freeing her parents from the burden of walking through life as red-eyed zombies. Without her cooperation, this book would never have been finished so relatively close to the deadline. With her enthusiasm for *Good Night, Gorilla* and the always elusive green sheep, Anna also opened up a whole new world of literature to me, bringing welcome change from my usual fare. My mother, Brigitte Edele, and my in-laws David and Carol McDougall, travelled at crucial points around the globe, in order to keep Anna company and her parents fed. Without their help the last year of this project would have been impossible. David van Mill helped enormously with another big project also underway simultaneously. Who would have thought that political philosophers could be so useful?

Several of the chapters of this book were written in Matt and Jane Davis's wonderful Gnarabup beach house, which they let us for unreasonably low rates. Together with their sons Harry and Sam, they were also crucial for companionship, encouragement, and sound advice ('attack! attack!') in all things recreational.

At UWA, David Medlen in the Humanities and Social Science Library, together with the hard working staff of the inter-library loan department, made my work possible in the first place. Sally Carlton provided research assistance early in the project, and the students in my honours course on Stalinism—James Curry, Aimee Lamatoa, and Jared Barnett—served as first critics to my ideas. Karina Diegel, a rare Russian native speaker out West, went to great lengths to ensure that her answer to my question about omelets and eggs was on a sound empirical basis. Thanks to her, I now know that 'you can't make an omelette without breaking eggs' is an idiomatic translation of 'if you chop wood, chips will fly' rather than a saying dear to axe-wielding Bolsheviks. Rebekah Moore insisted on the ethical dimension of historical writing despite her advisor's sceptical retorts and cynical jokes. She also commented on Chapter nine and shared her expertise on the 'Holodomor' debate, including a fine bibliography, which eased navigation of this literature significantly. Finally, she helped teaching two of my undergraduate courses, always asking the right questions, some of which I tried to answer in this book. Roderic Pitty the, for a while, somewhat hidden 'second Russianist' at UWA, continues to point me towards relevant literature while Ethan Blue helped teach an unprecedented number of first year students during the semester in which I finished the penultimate draft of this book. Although I would quibble, on historical grounds, with the notion that teaching with me is 'like working for Hitler', Ethan at times must have come close, Rudolf Hess-like, to board a plane and bail out. Instead, he cheerfully endured a rather Stalinist regime of forging hardened student cadres, which left his temporary 'boss' at least some hours every week to write.

Several chapters were read and critiqued by the UWA History Staff reading group. In particular, I would like to thank Susie Protschky, Sally Carlton, Rob Stuart, and David Barrie for their feedback, good cheer, and disagreement about whether or not Marxism was 'a religion'. The combined Russian Studies and Modern European History Workshop at the University of Chicago gave me a hard time about Chapters 1 and 9, which prompted further revisions. Michael Geyer's remarks about doughnut-shaped arguments and the absence of society were particularly pertinent. Sheila Fitzpatrick read and commented on the entire draft before it went to the workshop. While she did not agree with everything, particularly in the last chapter, her feedback was, as always, extremely helpful.

To anybody who knows him, Richard Bosworth's influence on my thought and prose will be obvious. Anybody who does not, should read his books. Richard took me under his wing from the moment I arrived in Western Australia, always commented very fast and frequently brutally on my writing, and commanded me to 'learn more words'. He also invited me to teach with him in several honours courses. Although we disagreed on nearly everything—one student described our seminar as the weekly 'Bosworth–Edele sparring contest'—they did something to change the way I think, in particular about historiography. Richard and Michal's hospitality punctuates the half of the year when they are 'out West' and was recently extended to hosting two opinionated academics and an inquisitive one-year-old in their small but fine Oxford apartment. The dinner parties chez Bosworth were always memorable, and I even managed, once, to get away sober.

Only a fool's thought is original. My own ideas, particularly the attempt to understand Stalinism as an economic system, were strongly formed by long years of discussions with Charles Hachten. While he would never have put it as crudely as I did, he influenced much of what follows, and well beyond what the footnotes reveal. I hope he will appreciate the results. I would also like to thank the editors of *Kritika* for opening the pages of their journal and its electronic drawing room e-kritika to a discussion of an article, which in some ways was a theoretical manifesto for this book. In particular, the comments of Michael David-Fox and Yoram Gorlizki nudged me in what was hopefully 'the right direction'. In the same discussion, Lewis Siegelbaum offered the metaphor of the 'force fields' which I made my own in this book.

Christopher Wheeler came up with the project, had faith in a young author who at that point still had no book under his belt, shepherded me through the proposal stage, suggested I needed more time than I had ambitiously first proposed, and showed great realism when I missed even that deadline. He has been an exceptional and supportive editor for both of my books, and his comments on the manuscript, uttered during a long and lavish luncheon, helped to polish the final version considerably. He probably also chose the peer reviewers, whose voices became part of my superego as I wrote and rewrote the manuscript. Two of them eventually revealed their identities and as Geoffrey Hosking and Susan Morrissey they added further commentary, which helped avoid some blunders. I wish I could blame them for the remaining mistakes.

CONTENTS

LIST OF TABLES & FIGURES

Tables

Figures

INTRODUCTION

❝ A society composed of an infinite number of unorganized individuals, that a hypertrophied State is forced to oppress and contain, constitutes a veritable sociological monstrosity. For collective activity is always too complex to be able to be expressed through the single and unique organ of the State. **❞**

Emile Durkheim, 1893 [1]

'Aspiring to write the total history of a totalitarian society is a delusion', writes a historian who tried.[2] In fact, this aspiration in many ways mirrors those of the rulers in revolutionary polities—total knowledge is the precondition to total reconstruction. Alas, recognizing the futility of the endeavour does not free us from longing to understand the social totality, unless we are ready to accept the bliss of ignorance. If we thus continue trying to know, we might be well served to adopt the attitude of the essayist rather than the boundless ambition of the scholar. This book, therefore, is an essay—a 'first tentative effort in learning' as the OED's always terse definers have it. It is a lengthy answer—shortened only by the prescribed word limit—to a simple question: 'What was Stalinist society?' Both terms raise a variety of conceptual issues, some of which will be addressed in chapters to come. For the moment, we shall accept two short definitions: By 'Stalinism', I mean the period of Soviet history when Iosif Stalin was, more or less, in control of its destiny, i.e. from the late 1920s to the dictator's death in 1953; 'society' will denote the system of formal and informal relations among people that existed during this period on the territory of the Soviet Union.[3]

The central premiss of this book is that Soviet society was complex and not completely 'totalized'. It was part of not only one, but multiple histories; it partook in not a single but a multitude of historical transformations. Soviet society was made up of dreamers and idealists, of cynical self-seekers, careerists, and butchers; they were capable of sincerity and longing, and of baseness and brutality; of heroism and unselfish work as well as cynicism, vicious cruelty, and utter depravity. The people who made up this society, the social ties they spun and cut, their ideas, ideals, and mores were not woven from one cloth. Many pasts and a multitude of presents weighed on their minds and deeds, both empowering and disempowering them. There were the many and contradictory legacies of Russian history—peasant and intelligentsia milieus, a specific urbanism, a multitude of nationalities, ethnicities, and regional cultures, a particular state tradition, as well as the general geographic and geo-strategic setting of a society scarce in resources and vulnerable to inhospitable elements and foreign conquest. There was a history of radicalism, political idealism, and militancy, which far exceeded the boundaries of what had become, long before we join the story, the Bolshevik party. There was the legacy of wars on social organization and on the expectations of elite and non-elite members of this society as well. There was the legacy of more generally European ideas and practices, including a belief in progress and the malleability of human nature and society, a modern patrimony also including Marxism and industrialism. And there was the immediate context of the first half of the twentieth century—a period of severe crisis of capitalism, the rise of fascism and Bolshevism, and the constant threat of world war.

The argument of this book revolves around the two major tendencies of communal life—social integration and social disintegration. The book looks at processes breaking ties between people as well as those which bound them back together. In real life, of course, cohesion and destruction were active at the same time and it is the logic of writing, rather than the logic of historical change, which dictates a focus on the one or the other in any given chapter. Writing about a society in flux has its own challenges. This was an unstable social formation made up of various, interdependent and overlapping, but often also mutually exclusive and contradictory, and—more confusingly—continuously changing entities. As a result of this complexity and lack of stability, a history of this social form can only be, in the literal sense of the word, an essay—or, more precisely, an interrelated collection of attempts at understanding, not fully integrated, and flaking at the edges. This book is meant as a general map to more detailed exploration, a guide to further reading, thinking, and daydreaming about a past that was as nightmarish as it was inspiring.

Our journey into Stalin's society starts with an exploration of the life, times, and recollections of Grigorii Chukhrai, a rank-and-file Stalinist in his youth who would become a central spokesman for the generation of Second World War lieutenants later in life. This chapter raises many of the themes to be explored throughout the remainder of this book: social upheaval, death and terror, ideological commitment, the impact of the Second World War, the centrality of family, informal social relations, and economic practices. Chapter 2 explores one central aspect of Stalinism—violent social change. The fuzzy notion of 'terror' is unpacked into its constituent parts and an estimate of the victim numbers for each of these forces of destruction are offered. Chapter 3 continues the exploration of upheaval by considering social and geographical mobility. The chapter also starts the line of thought about social integration, which runs as one of the red threads through the pages to follow: what were the social forces which held Soviet citizens together within the general flux and instability? This motif is further developed in the next two chapters, which cast light on two of the central force fields of this society: the family (Chapter 4) and the state (Chapter 5). Chapter 6 then discusses the ideas, ideologies, and world-views prevalent throughout Stalin's years in power. Like the rest of this study, the focus is on pluralism rather than monolithic singularity. Just as there were many histories criss-crossing the Soviet landscape, ideas about how society and the universe were supposed to be ordered, either in actuality or in the abstract and the ideal, were not monolithic, but multiple, fractured, and contradictory. Soviet society was not held together by one shared ideology, cosmology, or cultural system. The discourse of Socialism, which formed the backbone of the official way to see the world, was itself part and parcel of the history of Russian radicalism, which formed a broader ecosystem of revolutionary emotions, deeds, and thoughts which cannot be reduced to Bolshevism, Stalinism, or state propaganda.[4] As the regime could not erase personal and collective memories, Soviet citizens could do much more than just tactically appropriate the language of Bolshevism (although they did this, too). Rather, they could hark back to their own, or their family's or community's revolutionary past and the rich tradition of revolutionary socialism in Russia. They could also draw on a variety of alternative discourses, some of them religious, others secular, to make sense of their world. The inability to control the cultural universe, on the one hand, threw the radicals in power back, again and again, onto brute force and repression; on the other hand, it also meant that conformity with the regime's ideology required ceaseless effort and activity on the part of those attempting to belong. As a result of these obstacles, ideology never successfully bound this society together. Ideas, dogmas, world-views did function as integrative forces, but they did not necessarily tie citizens to Stalin's regime. They could also alienate them; push them out of the inner circle of believers, either into self-isolation or internal exile, or into the arms of other ideologues, in particular religious groups of various kinds. Ideology was both a centrifugal and a centripetal force.

The final two chapters of Part 2 then pick up the question of social integration of the totality, which earlier chapters deconstruct: if there were many and contradictory force fields pulling people into different directions, what, if anything, held the overall society together? Chapters 7 and 8 propose that the answer, rather than in the realm of ideas or stable institutions, can be found in the hard realities of economics. Chapter 7 explores how aspirations and the promise of material and ideal rewards helped foster the loyalty of the few and appeased the majority by providing escapes from the harsh world of Stalinism. Chapter 8 then demonstrates that the presently unfashionable economic interpretation of the Soviet system provides the best clues to understanding what held this society together and allowed it to survive the violent upheavals of the period under consideration. The final chapter, then, provides an intellectual genealogy of the approach taken, which is itself an amalgam of several layers of historical writing about the Soviet Union.

Overall, then, the interpretation offered could be characterized as a neo-totalitarian political economy of Stalinism.[5] It is rooted in the rather old notion that this was a regime which *attempted* to completely reconstruct society as well as human nature in a bid to build a Utopia; a regime which, moreover was ready to use all means necessary to this end. We cannot understand the extent of the violence and the suffering, but also the devotion and discipline of the dictator's agents, without taking into account this basic feature of the political order.[6] However, to have a goal is not the same as reaching it. The Stalinist ideological warriors never even got close to achieving their aims. This was partially due to the utopian nature of the enterprise itself, which in many ways was bound to fail. It was also due to the resilience and recalcitrance of social self-organization, even within a series of calamities and catastrophes. And it was partially due to the limits of state power governing over a vast, agrarian country with poor communications and low levels of education. Much of the best research in Soviet social history has pointed to this discrepancy between ends and means, to what one historian has called a 'Leviathan in bast shoes'.[7] This book adapts that image to a related monster, the 'limping Behemoth', able to thrash about, destroy, and spread fear, but not to control and engineer complex social change. The most powerful lever of control, indeed, was not police surveillance and terror, although these prevented organized opposition and fragmented resistance; it was also not ideological indoctrination and the manipulation of discourse but the management—by the carrot as well as the stick, in a process of trial and error—of the economy.[8] As the penultimate chapter will show, however, the regime's greatest asset was also yet another fetter on its power, as economic activity turned out to be as recalcitrant to totalitarian ambitions as any other aspect of social interactions. In 1941, in its greatest hour of need, the regime could do no more than decentralize much of its economy, while focusing coercion and ideological overdrive single-mindedly on military survival.[9]

This volume is not an archival monograph written exclusively for specialists. While my view of Soviet society is informed by extensive archival research conducted for my first book, this one is not overburdened by the detailed labour of what Stalin disparagingly called the 'archive rat'.[10] Rather, *Stalinist Society* is an attempt to step back and reassess what, after one and a half decades of meticulous scrutiny of piles and piles of folders by dozens of Russian and international scholars alike, we might now know about this social formation. I am standing, thus, on the shoulders, if not of a whole army, then at least a company of giants, particularly as far as the 1930s are concerned, since that decade received most attention from scholars so far. This book, then, tries to fill the middle ground between the focused research monograph trying to make sense of new primary data and the textbook summarizing what we know. In researching this book I consciously stayed out of the archives in order to avoid the tunnel vision often involved with the excitement of chasing down files and finding new documents. However, it is hard to keep a historian trained in the Rankean tradition (*sources, sources, sources*) away from primary evidence. In the course of my reading I found myself gravitating back to the documentation even as I tried to focus on synthetic reading of the rich scholarship we now have. As a result, what follows is not only one possible summary of the current state of knowledge, but also an investigation into three kinds of evidence. Extremely rich source collections have been assembled by some of the finest historians and archivists since the breakdown of the Soviet Union, and these tomes became, in some way, my archive away from the archives. In addition, memoirs and diaries, some of them known for a long time, others only discovered since *Perestroika*, provide often idiosyncratic, first-person views of Soviet society. Finally, fascinating transcripts of the largest interview projects ever conducted on Stalinism—the Harvard Project on the Soviet Social System—have recently become easily available through a searchable online database.[11]

I used these sources to tell a story that started long before the time we plunge into it. The prehistory of Stalinism reaches back at least to the end of serfdom in 1861 and the state-led industrial take-off in the 1890s. After a first attempt at revolution in 1905, a growing strike movement resumed in 1912 only to stop with the outbreak of the First World War in 1914. This military engagement overcharged the already instable Tsarist empire, which imploded in the two revolutions of 1917. A savage civil war followed, which devastated the country and secured the political power of the Bolshevik party by 1921. The 1920s are known as the years of the 'New Economic Policy' (NEP), when small-scale trade and free marketing of agricultural products allowed an economic recovery. This was also the time when savage factional fights within the Bolshevik Party finally brought the clique around Stalin to power.

Stalin was not elected into office to abolish civil liberties and establish a national security state (as some tried in the twenty-first century). He was not the leader of a mass movement who was elevated to power through the constitutional act of a senile president (the model of Hitler). He never directed his black clad strongmen to march on Moscow (the model of Mussolini), or led a military coup (the most common career path for aspiring dictators in the twentieth century). Rather, he came to power through institutional politics reminiscent of the rise of a corporate CEO or a machine politician. The institutional base from which he built his power throughout the 1920s was the position of General Secretary of the Party, a post he had gained in 1922. In the power vacuum left by the death of the undisputed leader of the Bolsheviks, Vladimir Il'ich Lenin, in 1924, Stalin used this starting point to gain predominance through clever tactics—first sidelining Trotsky and his associates of the left in 1924, then the 'Joint Opposition' of Trotsky, Zinoviev, and Kamenev in 1926 and 1927, and finally his former allies on the right, Rykov, Bukharin, and Tomsky in 1928–29. By April 1929, Stalin had managed to elevate his faction to the position of the Central Party Line—which meant that any opposition against it was illegal.[12]

It is here, at the end of the 1920s, where our story properly starts. The years of 'Stalinism' can be broken down into several rough segments.[13] It all started with what I will call the first revolution from above (1928–32), spanning the First Five-Year-Plan (1929–32) and forced collectivization (from 1929) as well as an onslaught on specialists of pre-revolutionary vintage, which is sometimes described as a 'cultural revolution' (1928–31). It was an attempt not at counter-revolution, as some of Stalin's enemies had it, but of completing what the revolution of 1917 had left unfinished. It aimed at transforming a backward agrarian country with little industry, run by elites of old regime vintage into an urbanized revolutionary superpower led by loyal 'red specialists' of good proletarian stock. The results of this directed turmoil were contradictory and often destructive, but these years nevertheless formed a watershed when a new society started to take shape. After this first cataclysm followed 'three good years' of relative calm, although behind the scenes the next radicalization began to gather force. In 1934, Stalin's close associate Sergei Kirov was murdered by a deluded but lone gunman. The dictator manipulated this event to trigger a search for the alleged conspiracy behind the shootings.[14] The resulting re-escalation of repression culminated in the blood-letting of the Great Terror, which this study treats as Stalin's second revolution from above (1937–38). It was during this second upheaval that Stalin eliminated perceived and actual enemies both within the Party and without, in order to consolidate his power in preparation for war against the counter-revolutionary forces menacing the Soviet Union from all sides.[15]

In a bid to lessen such hostile encirclement, the dictator, his power consolidated domestically through his bloody second revolution, exported his system in the 'Revolution from Abroad' to Poland (1939), Bessarabia, and the northern Bukovina, as well as the Baltic states Lithuania, Latvia, and Estonia (1940).[16] This expansion of the Soviet sphere of influence was followed by its contraction in the catastrophic first phase of the war with Germany in 1941. After a slow and painful turning of the tide in 1942, German forces were destroyed and Soviet lands reconquered, followed by further expansion westwards from 1944 until the war's end in 1945. Reconstruction had already started in many liberated areas in 1943 and continued until at least 1948, when after the overcoming of a post-war famine, the abolition of wartime rationing, and the end of mass demobilization life returned to its Stalinist normalcy. The final years of Stalin's life were marked by a slow recovery of consumption, remilitarization in the context of the burgeoning Cold War with the United States and continuing violent struggle against nationalist resistance in the newly acquired 'western borderlands' (formerly parts of Poland), and the Baltics. Better known is the internal witch hunt for 'rootless cosmopolitanists', a campaign attempting to subdue the intelligentsia, which soon acquired disturbingly anti-Semitic overtones. The official Jew-bashing culminated in the so-called 'doctors' plot' of 1953, when Kremlin medicos were arrested under the allegation they had conspired to kill the Soviet leadership.[17]

Stalin died in 1953 and his successor—the energetic Nikita Khrushchev—did much to blame all 'excesses' on the dictator. He did not, however, change the basics of the society that had emerged under the iron thumb of his former boss. Nor did anybody else until Gorbachev tried fundamental reforms, which quickly led to disintegration and breakdown. Until then, however, what Stalin had helped engender remained the building blocks of Soviet socialism. It is for this centrality in the history of the world's largest country, rather than for the mustachioed Georgian himself, that Stalinist society continues to deserve our attention.

PART I

CHAPTER 1
A STALINIST LIFE

66 The period I lived in was at the same time hungry, cruel, bloody—and great. **99**

Grigorii Chukhrai[1]

I

Beginnings need to be learned. There are rules about how to properly start a book about one's life, and those are given in the historical context in which writers find themselves. Grigorii Chukhrai's memoirs were published in Moscow in 2001, the year of the author's death, a decade after the Soviet Union fell apart.[2] They are torn between two cultures— the well-ordered, officially endorsed symbolic system of the Soviet Union, which in many ways had crystallized under Stalin; and the much more disjointed universe of the post-Soviet decade, still grappling for coherence. This tension between the old and the new is evident from the first page of *My War* (*Moia voina*). Despite its title it is much more than just a recollection about the war itself, but the story of a life which starts even before the author's birth. In Stalin's time, such a narrative, properly told, began with a description of the author's social background: When was he born? What did father and mother do for a living? What social class did they come from? What had they done during the Revolution? On which side had they fought during the Civil War? All these details were necessary to establish the citizen's credentials, his or her worthiness of state support, or—on the contrary—the likelihood of being treated as a potential enemy of the Bolshevik regime.[3] Chukhrai was part of the 'first Soviet generation', a result of the 'baby boom' when society recovered in the early 1920s from the ravages of the Civil War.[4] He was born in the year the Civil War ended, had grown up within the Bolshevik habitat, soon to transmogrify into Stalinism. He had learned to speak, think, read, and write in this ecosystem. No wonder that on the first page of his book he automatically reached for the code of the Bolshevik memoir:

> I was born on 23 May 1921 in the town of Melitopol in the Ukraine.
> This was a hungry year. The Civil War had ended only recently. My parents, my father Naum Sinov'evich Rubanov and my mother Klavdiia Petrovna Chukhrai, took part in it on the side of the Reds.[5]

Here, in a nutshell, the readers learn all they need to know: Chukhrai comes from solid Bolshevik stock—both parents had served in the Red Army. He does not need to write himself into the Soviet master narrative. His Bolshevism was inherited.

Alas, by 2001 such a heritage was no longer a blessing. In 1991 the Soviet Union had imploded unspectacularly. The former superpower had broken apart into fifteen new states and the entire project for which Chukhrai's parents—and Chukhrai himself—had gone hungry, fought, and nearly lost their lives—Soviet style communism—had been relegated to the dustbin of history. The decade and a half of open discussion about the past, which had started with Gorbachev's campaign for 'transparency' (*glasnost*) in the mid-1980s, had brought out into the open more and more grizzly details about Stalin's, but also of Lenin's crimes. The Bolshevik revolution looked increasingly like a totalitarian enterprise—the term, long declared useless by Western intellectuals, quickly became fashionable among former Soviets from the 1980s onwards.[6] The Party of Lenin and Stalin, once hailed as the heroic vanguard of the working class, began to appear as an organization of political gangsters, murderers, cynics, and self-seekers. Even the victorious war against Germany, which had been not only the major achievement of the Soviet regime as a whole but also of millions of ordinary citizens who had taken part in this most brutal of all Second World Wars, had lost its appeal to many. 'You victor', a gang of teenage thugs abused a bemedalled war veteran as they dragged the old man, face down, through a park in the final years of the Soviet Union. 'If you would not have won, we would now drink Bavarian beer'.[7]

Not ready to agree with those who denied all moral value to what much of his life had been dedicated to, Chukhrai tried to negotiate this new context by inserting a philosophical reflection of existentialist flavour (with a tinge of Great Russian nationalism) before the instinctively Stalinist beginning establishing his birth-credentials as a Bolshevik citizen:

> A person is not free to choose in what country and what epoch he is required to be born. He is [simply] born and all that surrounds him, he takes as a given. He learns to live in this given world and as he grows up, he tries to occupy not the last place in this, in his world. To be born in Soviet Russia is neither an achievement nor a sin, for which one needs to repent. It is fate.[8]

II

The world he was thrown into was the world of Bolshevism–Stalinism. Chukhrai would grow up and indeed he did not occupy 'the last place' in the society he was a part of. After fighting his war as a crack paratrooper he became one of the Soviet Union's most accomplished filmmakers and a major voice of his generation. Chukhrai was born in 1921—slightly more than a year before Stalin became General Secretary of the Communist Party (3 April 1922), the position, which evolved into the basis for his power; by the time of the dictator's death in 1953, Chukhrai was in the final leg of his studies at film school, which he completed that year. This section of his life can thus serve as a window to a world now gone forever, a world of violence but also of high hopes and great ideals; a world now foreign to us, but not unbridgeably so. This world—the society often called 'Stalinism'—was inhabited by real people like Grigorii Chukhrai. They were not only 'Stalinists' but also human beings; thus we can attempt to understand both them and their civilization, which, to a considerable extent, they themselves created.[9]

Chukhrai's was not the biography of an enemy of the regime, a resister or a victim. It was the life of a believing follower and a beneficiary of Bolshevism. Scrutinized closely, however, we also see that this life was again and again teetering on the brink of disaster. It could have taken a host of turns to the worse—as a boy he could have been killed during collectivization; in the early 1930s he could have died of starvation; during the Great Terror his mother might well have been arrested and shot; in the first months of the war against Germany he might have died; and during the battle of Stalingrad he came close to being arrested as a deserter. He was, thus, immensely lucky, but more than serendipity was involved. He managed to skirt past these precipices in part because his mother—a remarkably streetwise Communist—made the right decisions at the right time and later because he had learned from her how to get along in this society.

The start of this educational journey takes us back to the 1920s—not a time of stable relations between the sexes. The Bolsheviks saw the family as a 'bourgeois institution' as well as a haven of patriarchal values, due to 'wither away' as progress towards socialism deepened. To help history along, they fashioned the world's most permissive legal regime governing gender relations. The general upheaval of revolution, civil war, and the hard times that followed put enormous stress on many couples, and the ease with which they now could part did its own to produce Europe's highest divorce rates.[10] Chukhrai's parents were one such statistic—they broke up when Grigorii was three years old and the boy remained with his mother—a family-type widespread throughout the Soviet experience. Klavdiia Petrovna was an early and dedicated member of the Communist Party (Bolsheviks). Being a Communist entailed privileges, but also severe discipline and a host of duties. It was not an easy life choice. It meant hard work, both 'at oneself' and for 'the cause'. As a result, Grigorii was frequently left to his own devices, spending his days in the courtyard and the streets, while his mother devoted her time and energy to the Revolution. While he does not dwell on this early time as an unsupervised street kid (what the Soviets called a *beznadzornyi*), it must have taught him a lot about how to survive in a tough environment.[11]

The published memoirs thus do not tell us much about the 1920s, the time of the so-called 'New Economic Policy' (NEP), when the regime, in a tactical retreat, allowed a modicum of private enterprise after the years of 'War Communism'. This was a time of striking contradictions—some were recovering economically from the devastation of the Civil War, while others, Communists like Klavdiia Petrovna, were frustrated by this apparent return of bourgeois ways. What, they griped, had they shed their blood for?[12] This was also the time when far away from Chukhrai's native Ukraine, in Moscow, serious factional fights bubbled, conflicts both political and ideological, which eventually brought Stalin and his associates into a position from which they could control the Soviet state and the Bolshevik party. None of these events filtered through to the boy, although his mother, as a Party member, must certainly have been aware of these developments, since associating with the wrong faction could cause serious problems. She chose the right side, though, and in early 1930 she was one of those militant city dwellers who went to the countryside to enforce Stalin's policy of collectivization and 'liquidation of the kulaks as a class'. This campaign impressed itself deeply into the memory of the maybe ten-year old Grigorii.

My first childhood memories are linked to collectivization. I remember a Ukranian village, where mama and I had traveled 'to liquidate the kulak as a class'. I saw how some random people were led out of their hut, put into a peasant wagon, and carted away, who-knew-where to. Somebody was sobbing, somebody was swearing, somebody was cursing Soviet power under his breath. I felt sorry for those who cried. But mama said that this was necessary, that these people were kulaks, bloodsuckers. I did not understand what that was, a 'bloodsucker', but I believed mama that they were evil.[13]

In its campaign against the peasantry of the years 1930–31, just as during the Civil War, the Soviet regime tried to find allies in the village among those least powerful in peasant society—youth, women, and the poor. In 1918, the latter had been organized into Committees of the Poor (*kombedy*), an institution which survived in Ukraine 'into the 1920s'.[14] Klavdiia Petrovna and her little son lived with the (presumably former) chairman of one of these bodies—an old campaigner of class war in the village who, understandably, was disliked by those subject to expropriation and deportation as 'rich peasants' (*kulaki*—from the Russian word for 'fist'). Their resistance to dekulakization took many forms, including violence against the collectivizers, as Chukhrai experienced first hand, when one night shots were fired at the house of their host, 'uncle Prokhor', who was wounded. The response was swift. Soldiers were called into the village to hunt down the 'kulaks' responsible, who, it turned out, were Prokhor's neighbours. They were arrested and taken away.[15]

Chukhrai thus learned early that violence was part of life, but also that being on the right side in this ongoing civil war of the state against the majority of the population had its advantages. In fact, it soon saved his life. One of the results of the collectivization campaign was a serious famine in 1932–33. Historians estimate that nearly six million died of starvation and famine-related illness.[16] The Ukraine was particularly hard hit. Grigorii and his mother, who after the collectivization campaign had left the village and moved to Dnepropetrovsk, were affected as well. As city dwellers and state employees they were on better rations than others, but still suffered from serious hunger. Badly malnourished, the boy fell ill. His mother learned from a letter by a civil war comrade that life was a bit better in Kislovodsk, a resort town north of the Caucasus, and was invited to join her there. However, the regime reacted to the news of peasants leaving the Ukraine 'supposedly' in search of bread (a phenomenon that was allegedly 'organized by enemies of Soviet power') by closing off the Republic on 22 January 1933 to prevent population movement into other parts of the country.[17] This measure amounted to a death sentence to many thousands, who could not leave to find food elsewhere.[18] Communists like Klavdiia Petrovna, by contrast, could pull strings and receive special permission to leave. Thus Grigorii escaped what could well have been his untimely death.[19]

Arriving in Kislovodsk, the pair learned that their acquaintances had left for Baku. Unable to follow for lack of money, Grigorii's mother looked for work, to establish herself in Kislovodsk, but to no avail. Dragging her half-starved son on a suburban train, she tried once more in the nearby Piatigorsk. After two days of unsuccessful searches, she was desperate enough to beg for food—'bread for the child'—in the kitchen of a military sanatorium (the army tended to be better supplied even during times of famine). The cook, it turned out, was an Ukrainian, and felt obliged to help his country-folk (*zemliaki*). He also knew that the sanatorium had a job opening for a librarian. Thus she found food and a job.[20]

This episode takes us deep into the workings of Stalinist society. The practices we encounter—pulling strings (*blat*), relying on acquaintances and *zemliaki* to find a place to live or a job, and—if all else fails—begging for bread are typical of the ways people got along, made a living, and, while fortune smiled, survived in this harsh social environment. We will encounter them again and again throughout this book. For the moment, note simply that at the centre of people's lives were not only interactions with the dictatorial, maybe totalitarian, state and its institutions, but interactions with other Soviet people.[21]

Personal connections remained central to the path mother and son took. After an unspecified time living in the sanatorium, Klavdiia Petrovna fell for a holidaying Red Army commander. After he left, she tried to find him in Baku (he turned out to be a married man, which brought the relationship to a halt). Her first contacts in this city were her old comrades in arms (*odnopolchane*) from the Civil War—the same couple who had initially invited her to Kislovodsk, to escape death in the Ukraine. One of them was the police (or, in the Soviet term, 'militia') boss of the city and he employed her as an investigator (*sledovatel'*). She made a rapid career, soon becoming a 'big boss' (*bol'shoi nachal'nik*). His early 21st-century readers in mind, Chukhrai stresses that she was 'not a careerist' but simply worked hard and was a just officer. He also avoids using the feared acronym of the organization which employed his mother—until 1934 OGPU (United State Political Administration), from then on NKVD (People's Commissariat for Internal Affairs). Instead, he writes of 'the militia'.[22]

While life seemed to go upwards again, new storm clouds were gathering. From 1936 the possibly most famous episode of Soviet state violence gained momentum, culminating in the blood-letting of the 'Great Purges' of 1937–1938. Unlike earlier instances of state killings, these now also victimized the political and social elite within the Bolshevik party. Klavdiia Petrovna escaped only by the skin of her teeth and again because of the persistence of personal relationships. Her old lover—the Red Army man—learned that a major purge of the

Azerbaidzhan police forces was about to begin. Risking his own career and quite possibly his life, he arranged a meeting to warn her. She took her son and immediately left for the Ukraine, lying low as a rank-and-file member of a Machine-Tractor Station (MTS). There, she survived the Great Purges and also found a husband. Meanwhile, her patron from the Baku militia as well as her old lover were shot, while her other comrade from Civil War days disappeared into the GULAG, where she perished.[23] This story of escaping the Great Terror by simply leaving an area and a workplace affected might seem incredible, but it was not uncommon. The surveillance apparatus of the Stalinist state was quite rudimentary, as we shall see in Chapter 5. Many Communists fell victim to the purges exactly because they refused to believe that, as loyal followers of the Party and comrade Stalin, they might get accused of treason and damned as 'enemies of the people', Such pure-hearted communists smiled condescendingly when their peasant in-laws suggested making a run for it and hiding in a village—a lack of perspective they would come to regret.[24] Klavdiia Petrovna, clearly a convinced Communist, seems to have been nevertheless of a more realistic persuasion and not ready to risk her life and that of her son by insisting on ideological purity. (There was nothing un-Bolshevik about such realism. Already Lenin had known that 'he who believes every word is an idiot'.)[25]

Moving from a position as a 'big boss' to that of a rank-and-file MTS worker was a serious demotion in social standing, income, prestige, and life chances. However, it did not, in the long run, alter the tendency of Klavdiia Petrovna's life to move up in the world. Like tens of thousands of workers, she was destined to be promoted up the hierarchy in a regime eager to replace 'bourgeois specialists' with 'Red cadres' (see Chapter 7). Soon, she found herself in Moscow—city of cities—where she was sent with her new husband, Pavel Antonovich Litvinenko, to study in the Academy of Socialist Agriculture (*Akademiia sotszemledeliia*). These were two year courses to train qualified staff for the new collective and state farms. The family lived relatively comfortably by Stalinist standards—not in barracks or, as was common in places such as Magnitogorsk, a dugout (*zemlianka*) or a tent, but in a dorm (*obshchezhitie*), where they received their own room.[26]

Grigorii now experienced the social and cultural hierarchies of Stalinist society at very close quarters, slowly acculturating himself as he learned to behave as part of the elite. He struggled in school: 'I was a provincial; my, in comparison with the Moscovites, weak knowledge and my Ukrainian speech patterns prompted laughter from my class-mates'. The boy—he was now in sixth grade—decided not to attend this school any longer, drawing on his knowledge of street life acquired as a small child in Ukraine. He again became a *beznadzornyi*, using his lunch money to take the tram downtown, spending his days in the Politechnical Museum, a place where he was unlikely to be picked up by police, and which also had a cafe where he could buy sustenance. If any money was left, he spent it on the cinema. He counted this period as educational: 'The Politechnical Museum formed knowledge within me, knowledge of the kind no school could have given me; and the movies formed my worldview (*mirovozzrenie*)'. It was only at year's end that his parents learned of his antics and he was moved to a different school, where—being able to speak 'proper Russian' now—he had fewer problems. He befriended other students, largely sons and daughters of professors. The family of one of his new companions—Jewish mother and a Russian father, old Bolsheviks and intellectuals—served the youth as a model for a life well lived: 'This is how the Communists of the Leninist guard were: intelligent, modest, educated and hard working'.[27] Another friend and his family—from old aristocratic stock—also left deep impressions on him. They had, he writes, not just education, but 'what used to be called "culture"'.[28] And young Chukhrai, in the driven manner of the children of the upwardly mobile, worked hard to acquire both. His par-ents, too, encouraged him, leaving the youth in Moscow under the care of friends to continue his education while they returned to Ukraine.[29]

During his final years of school, Grigorii was unclear about where to go with his life, but it was clear that it was upwards—leaving the work-ing class behind. He dreamt of becoming a physician and was drawn to a higher technical education; or again, maybe it should be the cinema, via training in VGIK (All-Union State Institute of Cinematography)?[30] He finally made up his mind to sit the exams for the latter when mili-tary service intervened. The birth year 1921 was prepared for the draft, and the boys were told to return to their 'place of residence'—i.e. the city registered in their passports—to await the fatherland's call. Chukhrai took it in his stride—the one and a half years of service could be seen as 'life experience' necessary for the budding movie director. So he travelled back to Ukraine, residing with his parents, and waiting to be called up. His birth year was drafted in January 1940, which started a much longer stint in the army than Chukhrai had expected. He was released only in December 1945, a medical discharge, after the war with Germany had resulted in the victory of Soviet arms.[31]

III

The largest part of the first volume of his memoirs deals with his wartime experience. As the war broke out, Chukhrai was wounded in an encounter with a German paratrooper far behind the lines. This incident might have saved his life, since it took him out of action within the first twenty-four hours, during a time when whole armies were destroyed by the quickly advancing *Wehrmacht*. As he was recovering in a hospital in Kharkov, his entire unit was wiped out in the battles to save Ukraine. After his release from hospital sometime before the end of October 1941 (Kharkov, where his hospital was located, had not yet fallen to the Germans), he served for a short and unsuccessful period as commander of a platoon of terrified older men. He soon realized the danger this situation posed, because these recently mobilized and completely untrained soldiers were likely to panic and run if confronted with the enemy. Although this was well before Stalin's infamous order No. 227 ('Not a step back!' of 28 July 1942), he could reasonably expect that if his men refused to fight, he would end up facing a military tribunal.[32] Chukhrai, who had absorbed not only his mother's Bolshevism but also her survival skills, thus tried to get out of this commission, but his superior would not hear of it (there was nobody else available to replace him). What saved him this time was the chance to volunteer for the newly created paratroops—part of the of the maybe 20 per cent of increasingly mechanized elite forces within an army of footsloggers.[33]

Chukhrai thus escaped destruction once again. Instead of bleeding to death defending Kharkov, he travelled south-east to the city of Eisk, a town on the southern side of Taganrod Gulf at the Sea of Azov, where the new airborne corps he joined was being formed. As the *Wehrmacht* approached the town, the completely unarmed paratroopers in the making—there was one rifle for the entire corps, model 1891, supplemented by self-made wooden replicas—were evacuated to the Northern Caucasus. While at the front army after army was ground to a pulp, Chukhrai and his comrades learned how to parachute near the town of Essentuki. They were part of the replacement for the Soviet airborne forces, which had been wiped out in the first months of the war, fighting as infantry trying to stop the *Wehrmacht*. In September 1941, what remained of these crack troops was pulled out of battle, refitted and reinforced.[34]

The wartime Red Army is famous for the callous disregard with which it sent barely prepared and poorly armed soldiers into battle. The Soviets, however, took better care of their elite units, which had far superior equipment and were much better trained than the majority. Chukhrai, who volunteered for the airborne forces in the fall of 1941, was thus taken out of battle for another couple of months. When, in the spring of 1942, he returned to the front, the worst was not yet over, but the death rate had started to decrease, partially because of the end of the chaotic rout of the first months of war, partially because medical services began to work better. The half year of fighting in 1941 had yielded nearly 30 per cent of all 'irrecoverable losses' of the entire conflict, but only 7 per cent of the sick and wounded. No other period had such a staggering number of killed, missing in action, and captured as the first three months of the war (over two million). After 1941, the one million mark was again reached only in the third quarter of 1942.[35]

During the fighting in early 1942, Chukhrai was wounded for the second time, but not badly enough to be separated from his unit. When, in response to the German *Operation Blau*, the Soviets reorganized their airborne forces into rifle divisions and rifle brigades to support defences in the Stalingrad region, his corps was renamed 33rd rifle division, soon honoured by the title 'Guards division'. Heavy losses among lower-level commanders required the swift promotion of soldiers and NCOs, so he soon found himself elevated to officer rank (a junior lieutenant). A commander now, he participated in the retreat towards Stalingrad—during which his group had to fight its way out of

German encirclement—and in the epic battle for the completely destroyed city itself, before his unit was taken out of the frontline to be rested and reinforced for the next engagement. That he survived these episodes borders on the incredible. There was much luck involved, surely, but also determined action. The paratroopers had been taught how to escape encirclement in small groups, and they knew each other well, having learned to rely on their comrades, first in training, then in battle. But even they escaped only by the skin of their teeth, half starved and wounded.[36]

Chukhrai was even better prepared to deal with the constant threat of falling victim to the own side. Consider the following episodes. After reaching their lines, recovering for a little while and getting re-equipped, Chukhrai and his group were back in battle. In the chaos of the further fighting retreat towards Stalingrad, he was sent on a mission to head-quarters, itself in the process of relocation. As a result he lost his unit and feared—realistically—he would be treated as a deserter. To avoid this fate he asked if he could help with the evacuation of field HQ, and was assigned the task of looking after the telecom workers, a group of female soldiers. The trucks promised to get them failed to materialize. Chukhrai had to commandeer other vehicles, which he then abandoned just before German tanks blew them to pieces. The group finally made it to Soviet lines, only to be stopped by one of the fearsome blocking detachments (*zagraditel'nye otriady*)—the units instituted after Stalin's order No. 227 to stop further unauthorized retreats. The unit contacted HQ to verify his story, and somebody there tried to lay the blame for the botched evacuation on Chukhrai. 'I knew war, I know that the most dangerous people in it are panic-mongers and cowards.... They are always not to blame for anything and always right in everything.... "No", I decided, "I will not return to Headquarters"'. He managed, somehow, to get his charges to the river, where the women were taken across by a boat, while he set off back into the ruined city to find his own unit. He was now in the position of the isolated soldier, the potential deserter—the situation he had tried to avoid in the first place—and was promptly arrested. His prospects were not good; the penal battalion (*shtrafnoi batal'on*) beckoned. This time, he was plain lucky. As his group of arrested deserters was marched through the streets of Stalingrad, they happened upon part of his unit. The officers recognized him and, reaching for their handguns, demanded his release. He was let go.[37]

After a second stint in Stalingrad, which, if not less bloody, was much less chaotic than his first encounter with the city, his unit was sent to Rostov-on-Don to help encircle German troops there. In one of the ensuing battles, he was taken out of action with a splinter in his lung. An odyssey through various improvised medical facilities followed until he ended up in a hospital in Cheliabinsk, where he recovered well enough to be allowed back into the army, but not to the front. Pulling strings, he managed to be transferred back to the airborne forces, which were in the middle of one of their many re-formations of the wartime years. He again became the commander of a radio company, which, sometime in 1943, was sent on a disastrous mission behind German lines. A little later—it is hard to date this section of the memoirs, but the Battle of Kursk (July 1943) was already over—his 3rd Airborne Brigade was relocated to Belorussia, where, in early 1944, they were stationed in the town of Slutsk. From there, they marched south, through Romania and Hungary towards Austria, participating in the battle for Budapest. Chukhrai was wounded and taken out of action for the last time on the way to the Austrian border.[38]

He met Victory Day in hospital, was medically discharged in late 1945 and had to find his way back during the chaos of mass-demobilization.[39] Post-war life took a while to settle down, and like many Soviets, he remained on the move. He travelled back to Essentuki to meet his wife Irina (he had married during the war) and took her, now pregnant, to Ukraine, where his mother had returned after her own wartime dislocation. They found their pre-war cottage bombed out and his mother, who had fallen ill, living together with ten other families in the collective farm's henhouse. They somehow survived until early summer (1946), when makeshift repairs made some of the destroyed houses more or less habitable again. The family was joined in their new home by Chukhrai's stepfather, who turned up seriously wounded from the war. He did not manage to get his pre-war job back and instead was sent to work in Iaroslav region. The family decided to split up temporarily—Chukhrai would move to Moscow to study in VGIK, the others would transfer to Iaroslav region. Chukhrai was admitted to the institute and Irina joined him in Moscow at the end of 1946 or early 1947. These were hard times. The Soviet Union lay in ruins and a bad harvest triggered a post-war famine in 1946–47. The young family, now with a baby boy, lived outside Moscow, in a small weekend house (*dacha*), which they shared with Irina's aunt and uncle. Chukhrai had to study, work for a living, commute, and constantly struggle against his health problems. He still had a splinter in his lung and poor nutrition did its part—he developed TB, and was admitted to hospital. Ignoring medical advice, he continued to study, interrupted by stints of sickness. He wasted away—skin and bones, at one point weighing only 56 kilograms.[40]

Life was also hard for other reasons. In order to bring the intelligentsia back into line after the years of war, Stalin had his henchman Andrei Zhdanov unleash a campaign, starting in August 1946, against 'servility before the West' and 'rootless cosmopolitanism'. As a film student, Chukhrai experienced this campaign first hand, and he interpreted it as, in the first instance, directed against veterans who had seen the West. He was shocked by the ensuing witch-hunt but unintentionally profited from it. His professor—Sergei Osipovich Iutkevich—was sacked and the students this 'rootless cosmopolitan' had supervised were transferred to Mikhail Il'ich Romm, who became a generous patron of Grigorii. With his help, and despite continuing financial as well as health problems, Chukhrai managed to graduate in 1953, the year of Stalin's death.[41] He was still far from established, but would soon become a major cultural player in the Thaw and an important voice of his generation, the generation of 'lieutenants'.[42]

IV

The space the war occupies in his memoirs indicates the centrality of this experience. For the frontline generation—men born between 1923 and 1927—the war was, to adapt the words of one historian, an 'autobiographical point of reference and point of departure'.[43] But what was the war's impact on his life course? In his own estimation it changed a lot. The Great Patriotic War was a school of life and resulted in many long-lasting friendships. He met his wife, too, during the conflict, as the stint in Essentuki gave him time not only to properly learn to fight, but also to fall in love. The two married on 9 May 1944, after the town had been liberated from German occupation. (The newly-weds could not know that in the future their anniversary would fall on Victory Day). The war also made him a 'Communist' in the Soviet sense of the term—a member or candidate member of the Communist Party (the Bolsheviks). Like nearly four million other soldiers and sailors, Chukhrai was admitted to candidacy during the war. The experience of war also gave him the material for much of his work as a movie director. The war thus remained central to his identity and to his life. 'It coincided with my youth and was the most striking happening of my life. It taught me to not separate my fate from the fate of the Homeland and the people'. However, seen in the context of his pre-war life-trajectory, very little changed: he had been well on his way into the Party, even if the easing of admission standards in August 1941 might have smoothed the path. His march into the Soviet artistic elite also dated from prior to the 'Great Patriotic War'; he had already planned to become a movie director before his induction into the army. This upward mobility—writers and movie-makers were highly respected and richly privileged members of the Stalinist elite—continued his mother's consistent if partially aborted move up in the world. Viewed from this longer-term perspective, then, the war might have been a catalyst, but not a watershed. As far as one can tell from Chukhrai's own recollections—which are not always a good guide for changes in a person's understanding of the world—the war also did not change his basic adherence to Bolshevism and Stalinism.[44]

The question of ideology—a more or less coherent system of ideas about the world and about the way society should be ordered—deserves some more attention. The imaginaries and experience of capitalism, which suggest that self-interest makes the world go round, might seduce us to the assumption that historical subjects are both cynical and conformist to the core. We might assume that they will always present themselves in the best light possible, by adhering to the latest ideological mainstream, which is, of course, often enough the case. For Chukhrai, writing in the post-Soviet world where neo-liberalism and anti-Soviet-ness became dominant, this would have meant to present himself as a victim of the regime and as a more or less secret anti-Stalinist. He could well have fashioned such a self for the new times. He could have played down his mother's participation in dekulakization and stressed his near-victimization by the famine of 1932–33—a famine most scholars now see as a direct result of state action.[45] He could have stressed the moments when he was nearly victimized by suspicion against potential deserters or those who had been behind enemy lines. Stalingrad was not the only such incident. After one commando-operation into German-held territory, Chukhrai and one of his comrades were arrested by an over-vigilant sentry, taken for spies, beaten and locked up. They were lucky to escape alive after the intervention of an officer who happened to know them. Rather than taking this episode as an example of the lack of trust towards their own side and the spy-mania endemic to Stalinism, he took it philosophically (at least in retrospect): 'Idiots exist in every country and under any kind of social system'.[46]

These incidents could also have been interpreted by drawing on a developing discourse about the darker and more depressing sides of wartime conduct—the orders no. 270 and 227, of 1941 and 1942. The first of these introduced stiff penalties for surrender to the enemy, the second ordered the formation of penal units and blocking detachments to prevent further retreat without order. Both became major points of public discussion from the mid-1980s onwards.[47] Chukhrai could have chosen to construct his memoirs in a manner forging himself into a victim and an anti-Stalinist. Instead he fashioned a narrative that explicitly presents himself as a former Stalinist and as a continuing Leninist. The moments of victimization he stresses—trouble he got into because of his movies later in life—all refer to the post-Stalin years.[48] For the years of Stalin's rule, he presents himself as a victor, not a victim, and as a dedicated follower of the regime. He reserves for himself what deconstructivists and cynics alike lampoon—honesty and self-criticism (as we shall see in Chapter 6, Stalinist virtues). His goal, he writes in the first volume of the memoirs, is a 'truthful' (*pravdivo*) description of his life, including what in retrospect appear as mistakes and even 'crimes' (*prestupleniia*), but also recounting 'achievements' (*dostizheniia*). By using these terms, Chukhrai again put his life into the context of the past and of the present: 'achievements' were what was hailed by the regime and its followers; 'crimes' were at the centre of the discussion from perestroika onwards. While writing for the present,

Chukhrai remained thoroughly rooted in the past. He did not refash-
ion himself as an anti-Stalinist to accord to the latest trends; rather, he
tried to communicate his experience—'truth (*pravda*), about which
contemporary youth has no understanding'.[49] Rather than self-serving
constructions, these memoirs might also be seen as desperate attempts
at communication with a generation and a society far removed from
the experience of Stalinism.

Memories and self-understandings as well as the way they are presented in public are thus not completely 'presentist'.[50] While always
somewhat anachronistic, they also partake of the past and bear history.
Ideologies are part of these histories and they give coherence to lives.
Chukhrai wants his readers to understand that what he did was not just
cynical self-seeking, but an active attempt to participate in socialist society as well as he could. You are thrown into a world not of your making
and then you endeavour to get ahead, he wrote, paraphrasing a celebrated Marx quotation from *The Eighteenth Brumaire*. For Chukhrai,
ideological conformity and self-advancement were not two opposed
aspects of his life; idealism and realism were not battling each other;
ideological motivation and self-interest were not diametrically opposed.
They reinforced each other: to get ahead in life one needed to be a
Stalinist; Stalinists got ahead in life.

V

The unwitting traces of Stalinist language in Chukhrai's memoirs are
telling evidence of a long-gone ideological world. Closer to the text's
surface are his overt support for dictatorship—not for a new Stalin, he
concedes, but a Russian Franco or Pinochet ('dictatorship...as a small
step to democracy'). Likewise, his organic understanding of society ('If
a person has cancer, one needs to perform a surgical operation. That's
connected to pain and blood, but is inevitable'); his polemics with the
present (then we could walk on the street at night, now we can't; then
education was free, now its not; even 'hooligans' were better behaved
under Stalin); and his sophisticated understanding of the crimes of
Stalinism as a necessary historical step on the march to Communism, all
witness how deeply his thought patterns are beholden to this past.[51] We

should be more careful, however, with his explanations and extrapolations. One of the basic patterns of the Stalinist approach to reality was typification—the actions and beliefs of individuals were seen as tokens of a type, particular and concrete instances of more general phenomena.[52] Chukhrai used this technique when reflecting on and explaining his own ideological past: it was just one instance of a universal pattern. 'It was not necessary to wash our brains,' he writes about his pre-war life, 'there was nothing else in them than Soviet ideology.'[53] The collective subject here is not just people of his background—upwardly mobile sons and daughters of committed Communists, members of the Communist Youth League (Komsomol), who went to elite Moscow schools before 1941, were already in the Party in their early twenties, fought in elite units during the war, and made high-powered careers after war's end. The 'we-group' of loyal Stalinists is much larger in Chukhrai's mind:

> My generation infinitely believed in Stalin. All the best which was in us was related to our communist ideals, with our fight for communism. Stalin who led this fight, we imagined as a person of crystal-clear honor and justice. The disillusionment about him [after Khrushchev's revelations at the Twentieth Party Congress in 1956] hit us hard. And nevertheless this hit did not shatter our beliefs. As before we remained faithful to our ideals and were ready to go on with the fight for them.[54]

Such generational analysis makes some sense. The first Soviet generation—those born after the Revolution of 1917, in particular during the baby boom after the Civil War ended in most regions of the country in 1921—grew up without personal memories of pre-Soviet times and were subject to a concerted education, acculturation, and indoctrination campaign from the Bolshevik state.[55] Nevertheless, these youths were not blank slates that could be inscribed with whatever the regime wanted. These were children who had mothers and (sometimes) fathers, and, more importantly, grandmothers, who were often in charge of their care, as Stalin knew well.[56]

The adherence to Stalinist values—acceptance of the Party line as a priori correct, subordination of oneself to the collective, duty, service, discipline—was patchy and uneven among Chukhrai's coevals. He recalls a former schoolmate who managed to shirk military service by finding a cushy job in an institute and who took his refusal to do the same as a sign of mental illness (*on...poschital menia psikhom*)—an attitude which at different points he ascribes to contemporary youth (who have no ideals) but declares completely foreign to his own generation of idealists.[57] Further contradicting such generalizations, he also reports that one of his closest friends in the airborne unit deserted,[58] and remembers a conversation with another frontline buddy, while in encirclement and expecting not to get away alive: 'I agree with everything Stalin did, with the exception of the kolkhozes.' Slipping in and out of the plural, Chukhrai writes: 'At that time there was a lot we did not know, and this seemed savage to me.... '[59] Desertion, pulling strings to escape army service, and bitter commentary on the collective farms are not part of his notion of 'my generation', but did happen among his cohort. If such thoughts and practices were current even in an elite military unit—which recruited from among the most committed and best educated sectors of youth and which had a very high incidence of Party membership—we can imagine what happened outside this ideological core.[60]

Again, the text gives clues. It mentions desertion and self-mutilation to escape the army as well as the more ingenious attempt to survive by joining a 'Red Army song and dance ensemble of the airborne troops'.[61] There are at least two glimpses into the world of the majority of Soviets, which point to the exclusivity of Chukhrai's Stalinist social sphere. Whenever he came into contact with the peasantry—the vast bulk of the population—he heard and saw things that had little to do with the official view of the world. The first of these instances has already been quoted—collectivization—and his recollection of mumbled curses against Soviet power. Later, he had an even more destabilizing experience. During one of his wartime hospital stints, Grigorii found himself in the room reserved to 'goners'—hopeless cases. His room-mate was an older man, who—knowing he would die soon—did not hold back.

The main theme of his monologues were the collective farms. Many preferred to be silent about them. They were afraid. But he no longer feared anything. He said what he thought.... 'Stalin is a demon. I believe that he's the anti-Christ. People only do not know that. Where his toes should be he has grown hoofs!'[62]

This man was at the other end of the political spectrum: he was older than Chukhrai; he was probably poorly educated and more beholden to peasant ways than to a 'scientific world-view' (as Bolsheviks called their own superstitions); he had not been among the collectivizers like Grigorii's mother, but among those who fell victim to dekulakization. Exiled to Siberia, both parents starved to death and the son ran away, hiding his identity as a 'son of a kulak'. The Soviet regime had given him nothing but grief, and during the last moments of his life he communicated his anger to a stunned supporter of Stalin.[63]

Chukhrai even encountered open resistance to the Red Army, which troubled him deeply. While marching from Stalingrad to Rostov, his group rested at a farmhouse (*khutor*) and the peasants offered them freshly baked rolls for the way, telling the soldiers to wait for a while to let them cool down. Breaking the bread later on, they found them full of sharp pieces of glass. Shortly after this incident, their unit was prevented from entering a Cossack village (*stanitsa*). 'They put women and children in front of them and said: we won't let you in!... "We'll die with the women and children, but we won't let the godless enter our village!"' Chukhrai's commander refused to fire on civilians, so army HQ sent two 'Katiusha' rocket launchers, which obliterated the village and its inhabitants. Chukhrai did not seem to have known what to do with these incidents, which stand squarely in the way of his interpretation of the war as a just fight of 'us, the people' against 'them, the German fascists'. He simply recounted the matter, without explanation or elaboration. It seems that these experiences were bothering him and that he could not forget about them, but that he could also not completely make sense of this war from within the Soviet master narrative.[64]

VI

Chukhrai's memoirs are thus a historical source of great depth and complexity. They provide us a glimpse into the world of Stalinism, seen from the perspective of one who at the time supported the regime and later continued to support the system but criticized the past leader.[65] As we have seen, the gaze back from the twenty-first century put the ideological nature of this Stalinist life into sharper focus, rather than, as one might expect, obscuring it. A close reading of the same memoir also allows a critical—if respectful—approach to the witness's interpretation of himself as 'typical' of his 'generation'. But the usefulness of this memoir as a source for the Stalinist past goes well beyond the preoccupations of the author himself. It is not only a good guide to the ideological complexities of this society, but also to other complications. Social mobility and social hierarchies are a constant background theme; so is the fluidity of this society. Note, for example, that his mother was enforcing the Party line one day and begging for bread the next; note that Grigorii lived as a street kid one day and as a son of the elite the next. The problem of victims of the regime and the perpetrators engaged in this victimization also displays this fluidity, making it very hard to draw a clear line between the two groups. Chukhrai's mother was, during collectivization and—one suspects—during the Terror, on the side of the perpetrators. Had she been less persistent during the famine and less quick-witted during the terror, she would have become part of the appalling statistic of victims of the regime.[66]

But there was also remarkable stability within this flux. In fact, what comes across most strongly in the memoirs is the centrality of the family to the survival of Soviet citizens—but also of friends, *zemliaki*, patrons, and acquaintances. Their role has already been stressed in the discussion of Chukhrai's pre-war life: his rescue from the famine, his mother's career, her escape from the purges—they all relied on ties with other citizens. During the war, his very survival often depended on his frontline friends, and he managed to stay in the line of fire because he had patrons within the army, who could pull strings. After the war, such informal connections and practices remained central. Housing in Moscow was first provided by a childhood friend, then by the family of his wife.[67] Without the help of Mikhail Romm—a major supporter of promising young directors—Chukhrai's career in the movie industry would have never taken off.[68] The importance of ties to other citizens in the lives of ordinary Soviets will be one of the major topics of the investigation to come. This book will argue for a decentralization and pluralization of our view of the Stalinist dictatorship. But before we can do this, we need to have a closer look at one central feature of this society—terror.

PART II

CHAPTER 2
FORCES OF DESTRUCTION

> **❝** The cleansing (*chistka*) was implemented radically and thoroughly. As befits Bolsheviks, we purged (*chistili*) all that was subject to the cleanup (*ochishchenie*), starting from the very top and finishing at the very bottom. **❞**
>
> **K. E. Voroshilov[1]**

I

Much has been made of the Soviet Union as a 'gardening state'. In such polities those in power want to create a better, purer, healthier, and prettier society. As gardeners do in their rose beds, they weed and prune the 'human garden', killing off many 'weeds' in the process.[2] There is gardening, to be sure, and gardening; and the alternative might not be to either destroy or let things grow.[3] Stalin did enjoy pruning his roses when on holiday,[4] and in 1934 he noted that 'people must be cultivated as tenderly and carefully as a gardener cultivates a favourite fruit tree.'[5] But generally he and his entourage were less interested in careful horticulture than in forceful clearing of the underbrush. 'If you chop wood,' they would say, 'chips will fly.'[6] One of Stalin's most enthusiastic enforcers, Lavrenti Beria, recommended himself to the leader during a gardening session by taking an axe, exclaiming 'I can chop under the roots of any bush which the owner of this garden, Joseph Vissarionovich, might point to.'[7] Why such love for wielding axes?

At the end of the 1920s, the Bolsheviks were despondent victors. On the one hand, they had been successful beyond anybody's expectations.

Not only had Lenin's party made a revolution for which—in the mind of most Marxists, including themselves—their country was not yet 'ripe'. They had also won a bloody struggle against what they saw as the forces of reaction and foreign intervention and managed to survive peasant uprisings, revolutionary mutinies, and anti-regime strikes during the Civil War. However, their hope to be catapulted towards Communism by the forces of History turned out to be delusional. The predicted world revolution petered out and the self-proclaimed vanguard of the proletariat found itself in a peasant country surrounded by unfriendly, well-armed, and much more industrialized capitalist countries.[8]

Internally, the revolutionaries seemed to be beleaguered by the forces of the past, too. The social group they claimed to rule for—the industrial working class—had all but disappeared during the Civil War, and even by the end of the 1920s not much more than pre-revolutionary levels of industrial development had been regained. The New Economic Policy—a partial return to small-business and market relations introduced in 1921—had revived petty trade, resulting in the visible presence of a group of small-time entrepreneurs (the so-called NEP-men or *nepmeny*) and a night-life bustling enough to have historians speak of the Soviet roaring twenties. Some youth preferred to snort cocaine, embrace the analogy between sexual intercourse and a glass of water (if you are thirsty, you have a drink, a theory the sublimated Lenin had strongly condemned in his day) and even—summit of all decadence—shake their bodies to the rhythms of the foxtrot.[9]

For many believers in the Bolshevik party and its youth wing, the Komsomol, the 1920s were thus a period of hightened anxiety. Bourgeois ways seemed to have returned to the cities, the countryside remained a hostile territory inhabited by aliens, and industry was developing slowly, manifestly strangled by economic imbalances between the city and the village, a situation which made peasants consume their produce rather than market it. In the North and the East, hunter-gatherers and nomads roamed the taiga and the steppe, too backward, it seemed, to even have national consciousness, and impossible to properly exploit as 'they'll just migrate out of sight', as one distressed official put it. In the western borderlands, too, people were too primitive to understand that moderns needed a nationality (they insisted that they spoke 'Catholic', for example), and the poor roads and long distances made it nearly impossible for the revolution-ary bureaucrats to properly map these territories and uncover the true national essence of each rustic. Religion, which was a dangerous and coun-ter-revolutionary 'people's opiate' as any rational follower of Marx knew well, was all around in this deeply devout country.[10]

Another headache was the prevalence of ethnic and nationalist think-ing instead of an abstract commitment to 'Socialist internationalism'. The 'Russia' that Lenin's party had taken over had been a multi-ethnic empire for centuries, and nationalism was one of the fateful political innovations in the final decades of the Tsar's rule. Unable to simply deny this reality, the Bolsheviks tried to accommodate it with 'a commitment to ethnic proliferation' leading to 'a byzantine network of national territories, servicing around one hundred different nationalities'. Notwithstanding this 'affirmative action empire', some non-Russian ethnicities remained hostile to the revolutionary regime and nationalists of all stripes were one of the major competitors to socialists as far as popular support was concerned. Guerilla warfare continued throughout the 1920s in Central Asia (giving the newly created paratroops their bap-tism of fire in 1929); there were major uprisings in the Caucasus, Karelia, and Yakutia as well as sustained 'political banditry' along the western borderlands. Put this political instability into the context of a hostile international environment and we might be able to appreciate why it seemed to many committed revolutionaries that the revolution had stalled, failed, or was in danger of collapsing.[11]

In retrospect, then, the launching of Stalin's revolutions from above appears not so much as an unlikely outcome or a fundamental break, but rather a logical radicalization of the revolutionary programme of the Bolshevik party. Of course there were not only hardliners in this party, but the support for moderates among the rank-and-file—who had often joined during the Civil War, which was their blueprint for revolutionary action—was tenuous at best and nonexistent at worst.[12] Still, there might have been alternatives, and the 1960s and 1970s saw a fierce debate among Western intellectuals about what they might have been and if they had a chance. Like much counter-factual history, this debate often boils down to philosophical questions about contingency and determinism.[13] We do not need to embrace the latter to note that there was nothing un-Bolshevik about trying to force Minerva's wing, to charge ahead military style, to will the future into being, cost it what it may. We might follow the economic historian who likened the choice the Bolsheviks faced at the end of the 1920s to the dilemma of a rabbi confronted with the alternative of eating either a ham or a cheese sandwich. He could of course reach for pork, but would we find this choice likely?[14] Similarly, the Bolsheviks could have transformed into Mensheviks, the other wing of Russian social democracy, humbly accepting the dialectical unfolding of History, waiting for preordained tipping points to intervene gently to push it into the right direction. This was an altogether too professorial approach to politics for many who knew they were made of different cloth. 'There are no fortresses that Bolsheviks cannot capture', Stalin said in 1931. Many in the Party agreed and followed his lead which promised heroism, struggle, change.[15]

II

Chopping down trees or storming fortresses—both activities leave debris in their wake, be it flying chips or exploded bastions. There was more rubble in some periods than in others. We can distinguish three large waves of terror and repression—the two revolutions from above (1928–32 and 1937–38, the latter better known as the 'Great Terror') and the years of the war with Germany, designated the Great Patriotic War within the Soviet context (1941–1945). A fourth wave of misery occurred in the post-war years. What was the dynamic of terror and repression? How do the numbers change from wave to wave? Did Stalinist terror escalate or de-escalate? As 'terror' cannot be quantified, we need to unpack the category into its constituting parts before we can answer such questions. What can be counted are executions, other forms of man-made mass death, detention, and deportation.[16]

To begin our enumeration with physical annihilation: of the 874,074 death sentences registered by the security organs between 1928 and the first half of 1953, the vast majority fell on the second of these waves (the Great Terror, with 78 per cent), followed by 15 per cent in the first revolution from above and 5 per cent during the war. The other years (1933–36, 1939–40, 1946–1953) saw only two per cent of all cases of the 'highest measure of punishment'.[17] However, the executed were only the tip of the mountain of corpses produced during Stalin's years in power. Historians have calculated that between the censuses of 1926 and 1939 some ten million people died 'in excess' of what could have been expected under peaceful conditions. The Great Terror nearly disappears in this macabre reconstruction as it 'only' cost between one and one and a half million lives (that is, the equivalent of the entire population of the city I reside in while writing this chapter), while the years 1927 to 1936 saw the production of around 8.5 million extra corpses, largely during the famine of 1932–33. These staggering numbers compare to about 16 million excess deaths during war, revolution, and Civil War (1914–21) and between 25 and 27 million during the Great Patriotic War.[18] The latter, of course, should be credited largely to the German aggressors, if we want to practise history as moral accounting. While the post-war famine of 1946–47 could surely have been handled more competently by the government, the at least 1 million and maybe even 1.5 to two million excess deaths it caused are probably also best ascribed to the results of the war.[19] Compared to what had happened since the end of the 1920s, such post-war accumulation of dead bodies nearly appears 'small'.

Beyond the dead, we need to also enumerate the millions who found themselves—temporarily or for prolonged periods—behind barbed wire or in 'special settlements'. In these numbers, the post-war years rather than the thirties stand out (see Table 1).

Table 1 Inmates of the forced labour system, 1933–1953, as of 1 Jan. (thousands)

	1933	1937	1941	1953
Prisons	800	545	488	276
Camps	334	821	1501	1728
Colonies	240	375	420	741
Special Settlements	1142	917	930	2754
Total	**2516**	**2658**	**3339**	**5499**

Source: R. W. Davies. *Soviet Economic Development from Lenin to Khrushchev* (Cambridge and New York: Cambridge UP, 1998), 49.

These yearly snapshots do not tell us the whole story of the forced population movements of the Stalin years. The GULAG had a 'revolving door', constantly releasing prisoners as it added others. As a result, many more people had 'camp experience' than the annual numbers suggest.[20] Moreover, the mass deportations of the Stalin years also caused many of the excess deaths during the period, as people died on the way and after being dumped, often without adequate shelter or supplies, somewhere in the middle of nowhere.[21] They are therefore not accounted for in the statistics of Table 1. We need to, thus, look at the numbers of people relocated during the many forced population movements to add another indicator for the waves of slashing and burning of the Stalinist gardeners.

As in the case of excess deaths, the first revolution from above stands out in this statistical series. Between the start of 1930 and the end of 1936 a total of 2.4 million people were deported as part of anti-kulak operations. These deportations were flanked by the forced settlement of nomadic Kazakhs (with highly lethal consequences) and the 'cleansing' of the frontier regions of people of perceived dubious loyalty (ethnic Poles, Finns, and Germans from the Ukrainian western border, 'counterrevolutionary elements' from Leningrad and its surrounds, ethnic Finns from the northern border, Koreans in the East), bringing the tally of persons subject to forced (re-)settlement during the years 1929 to 1936 to at least 2.7 million.[22] In comparison with this first wave, the years of the Great Terror again appear rather minor, even if we include the years leading up to the war with Germany. To be sure, forced relocations of population groups continued after the great kulak operations were over. In 1937 the southern border zones were cleared of Kurds and the eastern borders of Koreans; in 1938 the southern borders were cleansed of Iranians and Iranian Jews; in 1940, after the acquisition of Eastern Poland as a result of the Hitler–Stalin pact, followed the 'sovietization' of these now Ukrainian territories as well as the removal of 'other nationalities' (*inonatsional'nostei*) from the northern border; and in 1941 deportations from the new territories in the Baltics, Western Ukraine, and Western Belorussia as well as Moldavia continued. Together, these operations uprooted between half a million and a million people.[23] After this relative lull followed another period of immense forced population movement, the years of the so-called 'Great Patriotic War'. By the time the Germans attacked in mid-1941, mass deportations had already become a major tool of Stalinist population management, which could now be applied to potential collaborators with the enemy. During the war the Soviet regime deported ethnic Germans, Finns, Italians, Greeks, Rumanians, Chechens, Ingush, Kalmyks, Balkarians, Kurds, Azeri, Ukrainian nationalists, and their families, Crimean Tatars, members of the sect of 'Truely Orthodox Christians' (*istinno-pravoslavnye khristian*) and others—a total of more than 2.5 million, nearly equal to the first wave in the early 1930s.[24]

Forced population movement continued after the war, then including also the repatriation of various groups of Soviet citizens who found themselves abroad (former slave labourers, former prisoners of war, and some others), and adding some categories of German citizens who were coerced to move to the Soviet Union, while their non-working co-nationals were deported to Eastern Germany. A major innovation was the deportation of 'idlers' and 'parasites' from collective farms from 1948 onward. In addition, the removal of the usual suspects continued—Ukrainian nationalists and their families, Greeks, Turks, and Iranians from border regions, 'kulaks' from the newly acquired and to-be-sovietized western regions, and certain religious sectarians, etc. Together, these groups constituted more than 5.8 million people![25]

Bringing the distinct statistical series for executions, excess deaths, detained populations, and deportations back together does not reveal a universal pattern. Some indicators show a tendency of escalation over time. The number of detained dipped temporarily during the war—an occurrence not visible in Table 1—but otherwise constantly rose, reaching its largest tally in the post-war years. The related category of deportations shows a decline in the 1930s, but then conforms to the tendency of intensification, likewise reaching its apex in the post-war years. Mass killings, by contrast, came and went. Executions reached their climax during the Great Terror, to drop off significantly thereafter. Excess deaths reached a first high point during Stalin's first revolution from above, then declined, despite the shooting spree of 1937 and 1938. Only the apocalyptic war against Hitler's Germany destroyed more lives than the war with the peasantry had a decade earlier, but for different and largely external reasons. Mass killing—either by famine as in the early 1930s or, more clearly intentionally by bullets during the Great Terror—remained episodes which were, if possible, avoided later. The Stalinist gardeners began to favour the tools of deportation and detention over extermination—the opposite pattern to the process of cumulative radicalization their Nazi counterparts went through, who started with deportation and ended by constructing death factories like Auschwitz.[26]

III

That the first revolution from above impresses in terms of excess deaths as well as deportations is not surprising, as these years saw a civil war fought with the majority of the population, a war against the peasantry.[27] It was Stalin, first of all, who radicalized the approach to collectivization. There were, indeed, attempts to run the operation less as a military campaign against an internal enemy than as a careful social engineering project (or, to stay with the metaphor which started this chapter—a 'gardening' enterprise).[28] Stalin would have none of it, however, pushing for civil war, the only valid revolutionary action, as he had learned from his old mentor Lenin.[29] Any resistance was seen immediately as hostile enemy activity, to be opposed by overwhelming force. Kulak 'resistance' (*soprotivlenie*) had to be broken, as one of Stalin's Lieutenants put it, 'with a quick, decisive blow' in order to 'break his spine once and for all.'[30]

To view collectivization as war is thus not a rhetorical trick of anti-Soviet historians. The subjects of this history saw it in similar terms. Stalin, for one, conceived of resistance to grain procurements as 'a "quiet" war with Soviet power'.[31] At times the military operation against the peasantry was fought with regular troops, although the authorities were worried peasant recruits might mutiny and therefore kept the army out of the operation as much as possible. Instead, the violence was administered by the shock troops of the 25,000ers—industrial workers with close ties to Bolshevism and a distaste for village life mobilized in 1929 to enforce class war in the village. They were assisted, where necessary, by the security forces of the OGPU, who took charge of much of dekulakization.[32]

The operation to forcibly collectivize the peasantry started in late 1929 after Stalin had given out the slogan to 'liquidate the kulaks as a class' and gathered pace in early 1930 once the slogan became policy. Violence and mass unrest soon escalated in the countryside.[33] In the first two months of 1930 alone, 7,257 security troopers, assisted by an unknown number of border troops, were sent to enforce dekulakization, put down mass resistance and fight 'banditism'.[34] By March the situation was so out of control that the leadership sounded a tactical retreat. In a famous article, Stalin first declared victory ('*a radical turn of the countryside towards socialism may be considered as already achieved*') and then laid the blame for all that might have gone wrong at the feet of local activists, ignoring the fact that he had consciously framed the policies in a way which made escalation a completely logical result. The successes, he said, 'induce a spirit of vanity and conceit' and the local communists had 'become intoxicated', 'dizzy with success.' As a result, they lost 'all sense of proportion and the capacity to understand realities.' Referring to attempts to socialize poultry and private houses, the leader lambasted 'such blockheaded exercises' and 'ludicrous attempts to overleap oneself.'[35]

The article was widely read and the peasants generally liked it. Quickly, much of the collectivization that had been achieved by threats and violence since January was undone. Peasants organized demonstrations in the villages, waving Stalin's article like a banner.[36] 'Dizzy with Success', intended to calm the waves and move the Moscow leadership out of the line of fire, instead fuelled peasant unrest.[37] The number of officially recorded mass disturbances in the month of March alone exceeded by three times those of 1928 and 1929 combined![38] Particularly forceful was resistance in the Muslim regions of the Northern Caucasus, where armed bands of between 200 and 600 men roamed the mountains and took control of regional centres. Standing in a long tradition of resistance against Russian imperialism going back to the nineteenth century, they marched under the motto 'Down with the collectives and state farms,...down with Soviet power, long live the Sharia'.[39] Throughout the Soviet Union the wave of peasant unrest continued on a lower level through April and May 1930 and then slowly petered out (see Figure. 1). Altogether, according to the OGPU's estimates, 2.5 million peasants participated in these uprisings.[40]

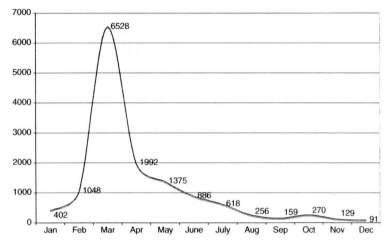

Figure 1 Dynamic of mass disturbances, 1930
Source: Viola, *Peasant Rebels*, 136.

The partial retreat of the Bolshevik Party-State when confronted with the spectre of a peasant war, which threatened to draw in the army, was more than just rhetorical. Stalin's article was flanked in the same issue of *Pravda* by the publication of the Collective Farm Charter (issued 1 March), which allowed peasants to keep one cow, some small animals, and a garden plot per household.[41] The peasantry had won the first round against the state, which paradoxically might have contributed to the long-term victory of the latter in the war over the countryside. The concessions made in early 1930 in effect allowed the beginning accommodation of the majority of the peasantry with the new political economy of agriculture. Exhausted from a year of struggle against collectivization and faced with the choice between confronting overwhelming force, arranging themselves with the collective farm regime, or leaving the countryside, most chose one of the latter two options. With alternatives to outright upheaval now open to peasants, OGPU troops had little trouble breaking the resistance in the villages and collectivization advanced again in the fall of 1930. The share of collectivized households now steadily increased, reaching 53 per cent in the summer of 1931 and 97 per cent in 1940.[42] The pacification of the countryside was also eased by a de-facto decapitation of village society from the most enterprising farmers and community leaders. The *kulak*, or rich peasant, was supposed to be a scientifically defined sociological category but, de facto, anybody who opposed collectivization and dekulakization could be branded with this name, leading to confiscation of property and deportation.[43]

The forced exile of 'kulaks' in 1930 and 1931 was a major innovation in the techniques for clearing the social underbrush. It became the blueprint to the series of resettlements of the Stalin years. The apparent success of this exercise in terms of controlling the countryside might well explain why deportations became a favourite tool of the Stalinist gardeners: it turned out that ripping potential enemies out of the social soil they were rooted in decreased the power of social groups uncontrollable by the Party-State.[44] Overall, as many as 337,563 families were 'dekulakized' with or without excile in 1930. Over half a million people were deported to the Northern Territory, the Urals, and Siberia. In addition, 20,201 persons were sentenced to death by the OGPU. In the following year, as many as 1.2 million peasants were deported and over 10,000 shot.[45]

Stalin's state thus ultimately won its campaign against village society. The price of victory was horrendous. The largest toll in excess deaths came from the famine of 1932–33. There is some controversy about this episode, in particular regarding the extent to which Stalin and his regime had planned mass death by starvation (as opposed to callously accepting it once it happened as an unintended consequence of their actions), and of course the numbers, shaky as they are, are in dispute. What is less controversial, however, is that this famine was in large part the result of excessive grain procurements and that it caused a large share of the excess deaths during the early 1930s. Three regions were hit particularly hard: the Ukraine, the settlements of Volga Germans, and Kazakhstan.[46]

If collectivization was a war with the forces of the past in the village, the equivalent in the cities was an assault on 'bourgeois specialists'. Again, this was less careful gardening than smashing things up. In the factories, the main targets were engineers of pre-revolutionary training; in the universities, professors were harassed by their students—in all fields of culture: attacks on the old intelligentsia. The years 1928–31 were years not only of industrial and agricultural, but also of 'cultural revolution'.[47] Finally, the struggle with old Russia of 1928–1932 had to include a fight with religion, too and the war against the peasantry was accompanied by a wave of anti-religious campaigning.[48] This assault on all transcendent systems other than Bolshevism bridges the first and the second revolutions from above, as violence against religious leaders as well as believers returned with a vengeance in 1937 and 1938. It did so at a time when suspicion against internal enemies had reached a fever pitch, the culmination of a process of escalation which started in the late summer of 1936, after three relatively quiet years since the end of the great famine of 1932–33.[49]

IV

The so-called Great Terror went through several stages of cumulative radicalization—first of means, then of the size of the targeted groups. All started with an attempt to get rid of old rivals of Stalin, who had been sidelined since the late 1920s but continued to irritate the leader with their presence in the ranks of the Bolshevik party. A non-violent purge of the Party membership had been going on since 1933 but now things moved to a new level, eventually spiralling into a second revolution from above. The stage where Stalin's regime went from sidelining and marginalizing potential enemies to killing them was reached with the first Moscow show trial of August 1936, resulting in the execution of Kamenev and Zinovev and fourteen others; in January 1937 and March 1938 the second and third Moscow show trials followed, victimizing Radek, Piatakov, Bukharin, and others; and in May and June 1937 the officer corps was decimated, too. These spectacular executions of high-level Bolsheviks and military men were only the context of a country-wide search for 'enemies of the people', who were quickly found. A complete lack of restraint by due process made the security organs take any denunciation at face value, allowing citizens to settle scores and remove competitors, or simply indulge in their resentments and enmities.[50]

In June 1937, the terror moved from cleansing the elite to eliminating potential enemies in the general population. A 'counter-revolutionary insurrectionary organization amongst exiled kulaks' was 'uncovered' in West Siberia and the Politburo ordered the execution of this organization's 'activists'. A Politburo resolution (2 July 1937) 'Concerning anti-Soviet elements' widened the search for 'former kulaks and criminals' to the entire Soviet Union. On 31 July the Politburo approved the NKVD order No. 00447 'Concerning the operation for repressing former kulaks, criminals and other anti-Soviet elements', which set targets for executions and arrests by region. As this mass operation got under way, local leaders quickly requested an increase in these quotas, which were granted.[51]

As the terror unfolded a significant shift occurred as well. Until the early 1930s, repression had been based, by and large, on 'class' as well as political affiliation with opponents of Stalin's rule. Slowly, nationality was added as a marker for potential enemies and by the mid-decade ethnic cleansing started with the partial removal of groups of dubious political loyalty from the western borderlands. By the summer of 1937 'it had escalated into total removal, which would remain the typical pattern . . . until Stalin's death'.[52] First came, on 20 July 1937, the order to arrest all Germans working in factories; on 9 August 'Polish diversionists' were added, followed by 'Japanese agents of the so-called Harbintsy' (railroad workers resettled from China in 1935) on 19 September. The second half of 1937 saw mass expulsions of 'unreliable elements' from frontier region, including the entire Korean population from the Far Eastern krai to Kazakhstan and Uzbekistan.[53] Within the killing frenzy of the Great Purges, this shift was further radicalized by moving from deportation to extermination in the so-called 'national operations'. Members of nationalities that had been deported since 1935 were executed in 1937 and 1938 to a degree that, writes one authority on this topic, 'verged on the genocidal'.[54]

V

Stalin has rightly been blamed for the readiness to embrace the most extreme 'solutions', but they were not, in themselves, radical departures from the Bolshevik repertoire of acceptable action. Eager students of the French prototype, the Bolsheviks knew that a revolution meant killing people. Already in 1908 Lenin had noted that a proletarian revolution could only succeed if it '*exterminated its enemies*'.[55] A day after the Bolsheviks had taken power, he admonished his associates that the mere thought that one could accomplish a revolution 'without shooting' was 'an inadmissible weakness'. A little later, in early 1918, he growled in response to hesitations to order on-the-spot executions: 'If we are not ready to shoot a saboteur or White Guardist,... what sort of revolution is that?'[56] This rhetoric was meant quite literally. During the Civil War, the Bolsheviks—a minority party which had taken power by military means in a few urban centres—unleashed what in memory of the similarly named episode of the French Revolution they called the 'Red Terror'. Between 1918 and 1919, according to their own proud figures, the Bolsheviks shot at least 8,389 persons without trial and arrested 87,000.[57] The total number of death sentences during the Civil War is today estimated at 51,000, or 200 per every million inhabitants—an extremely high rate by international comparison.[58]

What was new and unprecedented in the second revolution from above was both the sheer number involved and the universality of the targets. Lethal violence now engulfed the Party itself, including members of the highest level, which formerly had been sacrosanct. Under Lenin, terror had been what Bolsheviks did to others; under Stalin, they turned on themselves, too. The over-representation of the elite among the victims of the years 1937 and 1938 can be clearly seen from the data presented in Table 2.[59] More than 16 per cent of all arrested by the NKVD between 1 October 1936 and 1 January 1938 were white collar employees (*sluzhashchie*), who comprised less than 14 per cent of the population in 1937.[60] But the Terror was not restricted to the top level of Soviet society as the same data set makes clear.[61] The largest single victim group listed in Table 2—over half a million—are 'former kulaks'.[62] Add other 'declassed elements' and 'former people' and the vast majority of victims come from the group of usual suspects and assumed enemies of Soviet power, not from the elite in party, government or the army. Many members of this group made a living in cities, which turned the Terror into the urban equivalent of the war with the peasantry half a decade before. It would be wrong, however, to suppose that the village was completely untouched. For one, many former kulaks lived in the countryside, which meant that some of these arrests took place outside of the urban centres.[63] Between 1935 and 1937, for example, 13,747 villagers were arrested or otherwise 'brought to responsibility' (*privlecheno*) for 'terror'.[64] And the 8 per cent collective and single farmers listed in Table 2—while a severe under-representation if compared to the share of peasants in the population—still add up to 112,958 victims.[65]

Table 2 Social background ('*sotsial'nyi sostav*') of people arrested by NKVD SSSR, 1937–1938 (per cent)

Social category	Total	1 October 1936 to 1 January 1937	1 January 1937 to 1 January 1938	1 January 1938 to 1 July 1938
Former kulaks	36.8	10.3	40.2	32.1
"Former people" (gentry, aristocracy, traders, gendarmes, etc.)	13.5	9.5	12.4	15.7
Without clear occupation and other declassed elements	11.8	9.9	13.9	8.0
Servants of religious cults	3.2	1.9	3.6	2.4
Handicraftsmen	1.1	1.5	0.8	1.8
Housewives, dependents, pensioners	1.5	1.7	1.4	1.8
White collar workers	16.2	31.6	14.1	19.1
Independent farmers	2.9	6.1	2.8	2.8
Kolkhoz peasants	5.1	10.1	4.4	6.0
Workers	6.1	13.7	4.7	8.3
Red Army soldiers and junior commanders	0.6	1.9	0.6	0.4
Commanders	0.7	0.2	0.6	0.9
NKVD personnell	0.5	1.6	0.4	0.7
Total arrests	100.0	100.0	100.0	100.0
Among them				
Former members of the Bolshevik Party	7.0	11.9	5.8	9.0
Former members of the Komsomol	1.1	3.1	0.8	1.4

Source: Calculated from raw data in Svodka 1 spetsotdela NKVD SSSR 'O kolichestve arestovannykh i osuzhdennykh organami NKVD SSSR za vremia s 1 Oktiabria 1936 g. po 1 iiulia 1938 g.', reprinted in *Tragediia Sovetskoi derevni*, vol. 5.2, 156–64, here: 158–9.

VI

The Great Terror represented the apex of the first process of cumulative radicalization of means—from individual to mass arrests, from individual executions to mass shootings, from deportations of 'class enemies' to the forced relocation of entire peoples. The destructive consequences of the killing operations in 1937 and 1938 seem to have stopped further escalation. 'There is no doubt,' Stalin declared in 1939, 'that we will not use again the method of the mass purge.'[66] It seems the leader had been 'unnerved by the Great Purges and was wary of embarking on a new round of bloodletting on such a scale'.[67] This did not mean that the Stalinist gardeners stopped 'weeding', but they used by and large different tools now. The preferred methods of population management became mass deportations—a practice perfected since the kulak operations—and criminal law.[68]

There were exceptions, to be sure. In the newly acquired territories, a terror regime bordering on genocide was part of the 'Revolution from Abroad' of 1939 and 1940, when the Soviet Union acquired parts of Poland, the Baltics, and Bessarabia. The massacre of 21,857 Polish citizens in 1940 in the forest of Katyn, the camps of Starobelsk and Ostashkov, and other places of detention in the Western, formerly Polish, regions of Belorussia and the Ukraine is only the most notorious example.[69] When, in 1941, Soviet troops were forced to retreat in haste and often in panic, NKVD troops slaughtered at the very least 8,789 prisoners in Polish (or 'Western Ukrainian' and 'Western Belorussian') prisons—actions strongly reminiscent of the 1937–38 mass operations.[70] The catastrophe of the first weeks of war also led to a general relapse into the mindset of the Terror: scapegoats had to be found and their arrest and execution triggered the down-fall of others, with whom they had been associated in a 'defeatist conspiracy'. In this context, 157 high-profile political prisoners were executed in what came to be known as the 'Orel massacres' of 11 September 1941. The witch-hunt, however, soon petered out once the front stabilized and ended by July 1942.[71] During the entire war, military tribunals sentenced 'only' 157,593 and the NKVD 40,139 people to death—compared to the killings before the war this toll within the wartime state of exception appears perversely small.[72] After the war, too, there were some lapses into execution-frenzy—the Aviators', Leningrad, and Mingrelian affairs—but they were concentrated on specific groups of elites and apparently intended to keep Stalin's henchmen on their toes.[73]

By and large, however, we see a dual shift taking place throughout the 1930s, gathering steam during the war, and coming into its own in the post-war years: from execution to detention, deportation, or criminal prosecution; and from class based to nation or ethnic based operations. The practice of deporting whole peoples had already reared its ugly head in 1935 but the German attack 'led to a massive escalation in Soviet ethnic cleansing'.[74] While the war and the post-war years are thus rightly seen as a high point in deportations and GULAG numbers,[75] these years also involved a de-escalation in the means of destruction—a 'normalization' of Bolshevik social engineering; the end of slash and burn and its replacement by less overtly bloody (although not always less lethal) gardening methods.[76]

If there ever was a 'gardening state' weeding and pruning away in the Soviet Union, it emerged in the post-war years. Compared with the Great Purges, for example, the treatment of returning POWs and other displaced persons can nearly be called discriminate. Rather than sentencing them to death or simply shipping them off for decades for their contamination with foreign influence, these 'dangerous populations' were detained in camps and underwent 'screening' (*filtratsiia*), where good weeds were supposed to be separated from bad. The outcome of such investigations was by no means preordained, and the vast majority was either sent home or drafted back into the army, although often into highly lethal storm battalions.[77] While the security organs thus remained suspicious of much of the population, such tactics are more reminiscent of other 'national security states' than of the hysteric killing spree of 1937–38.[78] This normalization also increased the importance of criminal justice as a means of social control. Theft became the most likely reason to end up behind barbed wire. Legal changes introduced in 1947 meant that even minor acquisitions (a scarf picked up on the street, a piece of bread slipped into a pocket, some nails needed for home-repairs purloined from the work place) could lead to lengthy sentences. The result of this zero-tolerance approach was that nearly half of the unprecedented number of citizens in detention in

1953 were serving sentences for theft.[79] Moreover, in contrast to the political prisoners of the 1930s, who could expect to be locked away for decades, the 1940s and 1950s saw large populations entering and leaving the GULAG, which—like most detention regimes—was connected to the outside world through a 'revolving door'.[80]

What are we to make of the various transformations of Stalinist population management? It is sometimes suggested that modern states, once they start the process of categorizing people with the goal of social engineering, initiate a destruction process which tends to drift towards extermination of ever larger categories.[81] The Soviet example can be accommodated to such a narrative linking modernity and mass death.[82] Once we look at the larger context, however, we see not only a process relatively independent of individual action. Decisions made at the top—'by comrade Stalin personally', to use the jargon of the time—led the Soviet destruction process first to drift in the direction the Nazis would take a little later: towards the physical extermination of perceived enemies, a final solution; decisions taken at the top then caused it to veer off this twisted path and towards the high road of the security state and detention regimes. The forces of destruction, once unleashed, could be checked and reigned in if this was politically (and ideologically) expedient.[83]

CHAPTER 3
PATTERNS OF CHAOS

❝ Millions of people were moving from place to place: one in search of better conditions; another on a business trip; a third going to a different job. Peasants went to the city to buy products; echelons of prisoners travelled under convoy to labour camps. Crowds besieged the train stations, and lines of hundreds or thousands stood at ticket windows. **❞**
A memoirist describing Stalinist normalcy[1]

I

The forces of Stalinist destruction caused immense upheaval in a society used to it. Already nineteenth-century historians diagnosed a kind of 'Wanderlust' (*brodiachii instinkt*) in Russian peasants, who were in fact often on the move, searching for better living conditions and taking advantage of newly opened spaces at the frontier of the empire. Mobility increased with the end of serfdom in 1861 and now more often meant movement not only between agricultural regions but from village to town, between cities, and back to rural areas. Such nomadism grew further during the industrial take-off in the 1890s and reached unprecedented proportions during the first Russian age of violence (1914–1921) when 'a whole empire' was 'walking'.[2] The corollary of such movement across space was elevation or depression of economic position and status—what sociologists call 'social mobility'. By the time the Revolution of 1917 promised to create a dictatorship of one class over all the others, the rise and fall through society's strata was so pervasive and social identity as a result so complex that historians speak of a 'sedimentary society' where old and new markers were layered to such an extent that the Bolsheviks had considerable trouble defining who belonged to what class.[3] Was the son of a peasant-worker who had become a factory owner a peasant, a worker, or a capitalist? Were the new rulers to discriminate against the impoverished daughter of a bourgeois, who sold her body in the sex trade? Was she a 'class enemy'? Or should they instead assist her as a victim of capitalism in general and patriarchy in particular?

Despite the Bolsheviks' conviction that society and politics were neatly ordered according to exploiters and exploited, bourgeois and proletarians, class exploitation and class war, the Soviet population remained mobile both socially and geographically. Once Stalin's first revolution from above was launched, this fluidity increased even further. In what one historian has termed the 'Great Departure' from the village, more than forty-four million people arrived in cities during the period 1928–32. Most were temporary city dwellers who would circle back to rural regions, although not necessarily to the villages they had come from. About twelve million, however, remained as 'surplus' in the cities.[4] Concerted state efforts to police, control, and channel these internal population transfers were largely unsuccessful. They included residency restrictions, a residence permit system for cities, internal passports introduced from 1932, the introduction of workbooks and the new rule that Party members could only leave a region after explicit permission from the City Committee in 1938, as well as draconian labour laws criminalizing self-directed departure from workplaces in 1940. Despite such attempts to control who was moving where, labour turnover remained high and the rural population continued to decline at an accelerated rate. If in the mid-1920s 82 per cent of the population had lived in the countryside, by 1937 this share had shrunk to 68 per cent, only to decline further to 56 per cent in the year after Stalin's death.[5]

Following centuries-old routes of temporary peasant migration to towns, millions of peasants transformed Soviet cities into a strange bastardization of the urban and the rural—ruralized cities with a peasantized workforce. In these new peasant metropoles many lived in dugouts or tents, and even if they found a corner in one of the new barracks or the old apartments now transformed by necessity into 'communal apartments' (*kommunalki*), they often tried to raise livestock and tend gardens, continuing to act like peasants more than proletarians. Indeed, to keep farm animals in town was often a matter of life or death during the years of hunger, even for white collar employees.[6] 'Comrade Editor', wrote a distressed citizen from Akiubinsk in Kazakhstan to the party organ *Pravda* in 1932,

> do the local authorities have the right to forcibly take away the only cow of industrial and office workers?...How can you live when the cooperative distributes only black bread and at the market goods have the prices of 1919 and 1920? Lice have eaten us to death, and soap is given only to railroad workers. From hunger and filth we have a massive outbreak of spotted fever.[7]

The problem persisted, though. In 1936, a factory's deputy director complained to one of his underlings that he had 'put a comrade from your shop into the dormitory, and he immediately brought a chicken into his room'. Such behaviour was not permissible for Soviet workers. 'Perhaps it is possible to bring in chickens, cows and pigs. But then it will be a barn, and not only in the room because the chickens also block up the corridor. It's not necessary to have chickens walking around in the corridor'.[8] Nevertheless, such attempts to stop the idiocy of rural life taking root in the very centre of enlightened progress—the city and the factory—were doomed to failure. Magnitogorsk, the Stalinist city par excellence, built in the middle of nowhere during the First Five-Year Plan, hosted over ten thousand farm animals—goats, pigs, and cows.[9] In 1940, the government finally caved in to the inevitable and regulated the distribution of land for garden plots in urban places. Some of these were attached to enterprises, but much of this subsistence farming was done by individuals and families. Already in 1939 more than one million people had been engaged in this activity, nurturing on their plots close to one third of all Soviet cows and pigs.[10] The German attack in 1941 further intensified such localized efforts, forcing the limping Behemoth to give up even the pretense of managing the population's provisioning. Transforming itself into a more literal 'gardening state' than one historians construct *ex post facto*, the authorities now openly promoted growing food as a strategy of survival. As towns, enterprises, and individual citizens and their households ploughed much of public parks and surrounding land into vegetable plots, they effectively reinforced Soviet citizens' ties to the land, laying the groundwork for the dacha socialism of later years. The continuing dirt under many urbanites' finger nails would, decades later, also guarantee their survival when, in the 1980s and early 1990s, state provisioning broke down again without the unregulated market economy taking over the complicated business of producing and distributing food.[11]

Many of the inhabitants of these huge and incredibly dirty villages claiming to be cities also remained rather tentatively attached to the urban landscape. As the migration statistics above imply, in the short and medium term many millions were temporary workers only—part-time peasants and seasonal migrants. They remained, as an analysis of the state planning agency put it in late 1932, 'nomadic between village and town depending on which has the best food and other material conditions at a particular time.'[12] Some lived in the village to begin with, commuting to nearby factories. This practice was so contrary to the official view of what a 'worker' was, that the statistical agencies made the phenomenon disappear in their budget and consumption studies.[13] Those who did, as was proper for a member of the working class, live in cities, continued to skip the factories come harvest time. Behaving like their forefathers, they came to the city as temporary migrants during the agricultural off-season—*otkhodniki*, as they were called. These men—and most of them were male—had a life centred in the village, where their spouse remained. They went, as it were, harvesting in the city, when there was little to do in the countryside but returned when their labour was necessary to keep the family economy running. This practice proved remarkably tenacious—historians found *otkhodniki* throughout the 1930s—about four million per annum in the second half of the decade—and well into the post-war years. From the perspective of the worker-peasants themselves, seasonal migration was not just a transitional phenomenon of incomplete modernization but a strategy of villagers living in a world dominated by the city boys.[14]

Over the long term, however, more and more peasants were leaving the village for good.[15] The cities might have lured some, particularly the young, with their promise of modernity. The vast majority of peasant migrants, however, were pushed out of the village by the regime's callous exploitation, rather than won over by the alluring lights of the city. As a typical outburst of a kolkhoznitsa put it in 1938: 'We now will all die of hunger... Soviet power provides no help, we all need to leave the collectives, it's better to go into industry, there we will earn money and there will be bread.' Or, more generally: 'It is necessary to quit work in the kolkhoz and leave somewhere, to the city, into industry, because the entire grain of the new harvest will be given to the government, while they don't give any to the kolkhozniks.'[16] That city life was not necessarily the preferred option, but that the continuing greater misery of living standards in the countryside was the main reason for moving to the cities, is illustrated by what happened after the war. When rumour as well as official propaganda implied that life would be better in the post-war village, millions of demobilized servicemen initially returned 'to mud and cockroaches again'.[17] As their hopes were quickly quashed by a post-war campaign to undo the reprivatization of kolkhoz lands which had taken place during the war, most of them turned around and left.[18] The reasons echoed those of pre-war times: 'One needs to run away,' concluded one grumpy peasant-veteran after realizing that the promised good life was not eventuating even after Victory, 'only slaves work in the kolkhoz, they don't give out grain.'[19]

In fact, any improvement, however slight, of conditions in the countryside slowed outmigration. As the state's statistical agency noted in August 1932: 'the development of kolkhoz trade and the new conditions for artisan cooperative have affected the rate of recruitment of labour for the building sites.'[20] The alternative to leaving was trying to circumvent the kolkhoz regime: 'There's no benefit to working in the kolkhoz,' noted one peasant woman. 'Better work in your own household [garden] or on the side, as I do.'[21] She was not alone. Throughout the 1930s and well into the post-war years, peasants found ways to live in the countryside while avoiding the collective farms.[22]

Most Soviets were not only tentatively attached to urbanity at best; they were even less likely to stay in any particular city or enterprise. The horrible exploitation of the industrial workforce led millions upon millions to vote with their feet, looking for bearable living conditions, housing, enough pay and food to raise their families or to simply survive as individuals. Despite the increasingly tough labour laws designed to keep workers in place, turnover remained massive.[23] Following family members, acquaintances, and regional networks (*zemliaki*), the Soviet workforce, in a pattern reminiscent of the turn of the century, was constantly on the move from factory to factory, city to city, town to country, and back. And it was not only the exploited and the powerless who were constantly on the move. Much of the ruling elite remained nomadic as well. 'At all levels of the local administration and party *apparat*', writes one of the pioneers of Soviet social history,

> **people adopted the habit of leaving in good time, before they were penalized, recalled, brought in for questioning, downgraded, fired, or arrested.**
>
> **Thus workers, administrators, specialists, officials, party apparatus men and, in great masses, peasants were all moving around and changing jobs, creating unwanted surpluses in some places and dearths in others, losing skills or failing to acquire them, creating streams and floods in which families were destroyed, children lost, and morality dissolved. Social, administrative, industrial, and political structures were all in flux. The mighty dictatorial government found itself, as a result of its impetuous activity during those early years of accelerated industrialization, presiding over a 'quicksand' society.[24]**

These currents of humanity on the move formed the waves on which the state-run deportations, resettlements, and detentions discussed in the previous chapter crested and foamed. During and after the war, new tides occurred—people fleeing the Nazi invasion; workers and employees evacuated together with their factories behind the Urals or without them somewhere to safety, often returning the other direction once the tide of war had turned; prisoners of war and slave labourers of the Germans (the so-called *Ostarbeiter*) repatriated with or without their consent and subjected to an often lengthy screening process in hastily constructed 'filtration camps'; demobilized soldiers returning either on their own or in organized echelons after victory in 1945.[25]

II

Many Soviet citizens were thus unsettled by the events of the time, had been deported, called-up, mobilized, or fled invasion. They often tried, once a chance presented itself, to escape, to return, to find a better place to live. Siberia, the human waste-dump of Tsarist and Soviet rulers alike, had long seen large numbers of escapees from the prisons and camps roaming the countryside. In the late nineteenth century, there were maybe 50,000 such *brodiagi* at large at any moment, reined in only by an insignificant police force and the locals' 'lynch law'.[26] Such community policing continued as the problem escalated, when the mass deportations of kulaks and the cleansing of cities from 'criminal, socially dangerous, and parasitic elements' in the early 1930s dumped hundreds of thousands in the tundra. The most vigorous of these so-called 'special settlers' ran away as soon as they could. In 1932, the authorities registered 207,000 such people as 'escaped'. As detained and exiled populations grew during the Great Terror, so did the ranks of the runaways. Eleven per cent of the inmates of one camp in 1937 had absconded, for example. Officially registered numbers of getaways from camps alone reached 58,200 in 1937 and 32,000 in 1938.[27]

As before the revolution, Siberia remained haunted by these fugitives. Police forces for the entire western part of the region numbered 'no more then 2,200 men', supplemented by 2,000 OGPU officers in 1933. Together with hastily recruited paramilitary units, these agents of central power had to contend with masses of 'criminals and deported elements who have fled the places of residence assigned to them'. A rising tide of banditry with deep roots in the history of this frontier region, which had long been a haven for marginals, outlaws, and jailbreakers, added to their workload. The upheavals of collectivization and dekulakization strengthened the pre-existing gangs, terrorizing 'representatives of Soviet power', attacking kolkhozes and burning them to the ground. At least 880 such bands were in existence in 1930, since these numbers included only those 'we know about', as an official report stated. Despite an aggressive campaign against such groups, crime remained endemic in Siberia.[28]

As in the nineteenth century, the locals reacted to the escape of 'socially dangerous elements' with self-help. An upset official, a comrade Shpek, reported in early 1932:

> When the peasants saw that the militia did not do anything [to protect them from freshly arrived deportees], they decided to organize a night-time ambush and to take the law into their own hands in order to deal with the criminal element.
>
> One night in September [of 1931], I do not remember what date, between ten and eleven at night,... I heard gunfire break out and a heavy firefight continued for two or three hours. I thought that some kind of uprising had started, but in the morning I learned that these had been the peasants making short work of the exiled criminals. In the morning many corpses were found in the gardens – how many I do not know exactly, but I was told ....about 18 dead, four I saw with my own eyes.[29]

Given the violent history of the region, the extreme breakdown of social order and policing, and the large number of exiles dumped on them, it is little wonder that local officials soon followed suit, reaching for more final solutions. 'You seem to think,' a party secretary reportedly told Shpek, 'that they were really sent here to be re-educated? No, Comrade, we should make sure that by spring they have all died out.'[30]

The best way to avoid such a fate was for those stigmatized and victimized by the regime to stay on the move in order to keep below the radar screen of the security agencies. Maybe two or three million peasants escaped the peasant war by 'self-dekulakization'. They sold their property ahead of time and went to the cities or the new construction sites.[31] A secret OGPU report knew by 25 April 1930, of '20,433 kulaks, among them 3,184 together with their families' who had run away 'from their places of permanent residence' since the beginning of dekulakization, while only 8,305 of them were detained 'including 642 with families'.[32]

In this context, we might also recall Chukhrai's childhood experience, related in Chapter 1, of escaping arrest by simply staying on the move. We might add more stories here. In the summer of 1937, for example, Stepan Podlubnyi, a son of a 'kulak' who was hiding his social background in order to make a career in Moscow, was visiting his home-region when the local NKVD decided to arrest him. Like Chukhrai's mother, he was warned and escaped—by walking 30 kilometres to the next village. Lacking as basic communication equipment as a telephone or a two-way radio, Stalin's feared policemen could only have jumped on a horse to catch him (if one had survived the mass slaughter of livestock during collectivization). Even in Moscow, the many city dwellers who lived either illegally or under fabricated identities in the city routinely escaped by simply sleeping away from home during the most likely times for mass arrests (such as close to holidays), or by leaving the house when they learned through the rumour mill of an impending round-up.[33] People denied residence permits moved in and out of temporary accommodation to escape eviction from the centre. Sergei Rybin-Lugovskoy, a former Socialist Revolutionary, who spent three years in Siberian exile before his return to Moscow in 1932, had his permission to reside in the capital rescinded in early 1933. While his family remained in their apartment, he stayed outside the residency zone or with friends in the city, visiting his wife and children only intermittently. Thus he managed to evade arrest until 1935.[34] He might well have escaped altogether, had he not been tied to Moscow by his family. Unattached citizens had the best chance to dodge the worst by staying mobile. 'In general,' writes an eminent historian of the Great Terror, 'moving frequently was a certain protection' against arrest. Surveillance files had to be forwarded from one local NKVD agency to another; papers sometimes were lost; and it took the local chekists some time—often six months to a year—to collect enough 'evidence' to go after a newly arrived victim.[35] 'When I was threatened with arrest I had to pack my bag and go,' a skilled worker from a pre-revolutionary 'petty bourgeois' family explained his itinerant lifestyle. This man had fought against the Bolsheviks during the Civil War and remained on guard: 'I worked at each place for about two years, and then left because it was impossible...for me to work too long at one place, since I had to hide my background.'[36]

III

Many Soviet citizens would thus have felt with Hannah Arendt, who in 1950 wrote about the 'chaos produced by the violence of wars and revolutions and the growing decay of all that still has been spared. Under the most diverse conditions,' this great pessimist continued, 'we watch the development of the same phenomena—homelessness on an unprecedented scale, rootlessness to an unprecedented depth.'[37] One group stands out as a symbol of this quicksand society: 'One gets the impression,' wrote one enraged citizen in 1947, 'that our country is a land of beggars.'[38] For many, this was a temporary occupation, when things got particularly tough. For others, it was a longer-term way of making do. War invalids, in particular, often settled into a life of begging and small-scale trade when they found it impossible to adapt to civilian existence in a society where life was hard for the physically fit.[39] 'The begging of cripples around bazaars and railroad stations,' writes one historian, 'became a characteristic feature of the time.'[40] The obvious connection of this phenomenon with the Second World War should not seduce us into believing that it was new, unprecedented, or solely connected to wartime destruction. Before 1941, state policies caused the social dislocation and unsettlement of many, creating social problems to which the state reacted with ever increasing levels of repression.

Consider child-homelessness. Forced collectivization, dekulakization, and the great famine resulted in a sharp increase in the number of street children, who often organized themselves into gangs and survived by begging, theft, and violent crime. Soon, the police started ambitious but futile campaigns against the problem. In March 1935 a letter from Voroshilov brought the phenomenon to the attention of the highest Party leadership (Stalin, Molotov, and Kalinin). Referring to two cases of particularly violent conduct by juveniles, committed in Moscow itself, Voroshilov wrote: 'I think that the Central Committee should instruct the NKVD to organize a settlement of not only homeless but also neglected children and thus protect the capital from the growing problem of juvenile hooliganism. As to this particular case, I do not understand why we cannot just shoot these scoundrels. Do we have to wait until they grow up to be even greater thugs?' After Stalin personally had toughened up a draft resolution, new regulations came into effect in April 1935, which allowed 'all forms of punishment', including shooting, of violent offenders from the age of twelve. The resulting campaign against homeless and unattended children saw apprehensions in the hundreds of thousands. In 1935 and 1936 the courts sentenced over twenty thousand youth of sixteen or younger, creating a whole subset of camps for juveniles in the process.[41]

The masses of homeless youth, however, refused to disappear, as again and again lives were shattered by events. The Great Terror created the next wave of waifs and runaway youth and their numbers simply exploded during the war. In the mid- and late 1940s, the authorities were confronted with a public order problem of roaming youth gangs of frightening proportions.[42] Their internal loyalties allowed them to function as economic units engaged in pick-pocketing and begging, burglary and theft. The thieves, in particular, sometimes resorted to vicious violence, when necessary, both with regards to the outside world and in order to police their own ranks. They felt contempt for the 'soft' beggars and often attempted to remain separate from them. The regime's clampdown on juvenile delinquency only meant that many of them were hardened into professional criminals as they grew up between children's homes, prisons and labour camps, and the streets, markets, trains and stations to which they returned to, again and again, to do 'jobs', to steal and mug, pilfer and rob, or, if illness or injury prevented such 'honourable' work, to beg and sing for their supper.[43] Their life proved attractive to many other youngsters, who, according to police reports, saw it 'surrounded by a "romantic oreole"', attended drinking parties of the *besprizornye* and 'started to leave their parents to go and live with the homeless children.'[44]

It might well have been more than just romanticism which drew children to this world. 'Well,' responded one former Soviet citizen interviewed by American sociologists after the war,

> there are lots of homeless children in the stations, and I then was 11 years old and I felt that even though we did live better than some other people it was quite a strain for father to pay for me, and to supply my clothes. And I tried to tag on to this gang. I was the smallest and the youngest one of the gang which had a very strict hierarchy. And my job was to look around and tell them if there were soft pickings any place. If they ordered me to steal and if I was caught they would have beaten me up until I learned how to steal properly.[45]

Like many others, this boy joined a by now large and frequently violent subculture of beggars, thieves, con men, and other criminals who had made the markets, the trains, and the streets their habitat. This world was fuelled by the state's destructive policies followed by the ravages of war, which together produced a continuous stream of new recruits. But this shadow society also proved resilient because it had its own history, its own path of transformation, its own songs, stories, argot, and iconography (inscribed as tattoos onto many of the participating bodies), its own memories, which reached back through the underbelly of the NEP, through the hard world of the Civil War to the back alleys of Tsarist society, its slums, markets, prisons, and Siberian exile. It now included itinerant preachers, roaming bandits, and con men, populations frequently entering and re-entering the world this side and that side of the barbed wire. At its hard core, this was a sociality with its own code of morality, behaviour, language, and aesthetics. Begging, too, had a long and involved history, both as a practice of asking and giving and as a whole system of gestures, utterances, and symbols. As living history it was at the disposal of disabled veterans, who knew exactly how to behave when, re-enacting a long-standing pattern, they entered train compartments in 1947 singing psalms and asking for God's help, which of course meant the help of others. Similarly, newly minted wartime street children knew the songs *bezprizorniki* had sung during the Civil War.[46]

The world of thieves, beggars, bandits, hooligans, and con men, living at the intersection of the GULAG and the nominally free population, was not a subculture hermetically sealed from respectable society. Many of the violent assaults summarized under the label of 'malicious hooliganism' were committed by young men, often temporary or seasonal workers from the countryside.[47] Even communists could be reduced to begging at times, as we have seen in Chapter 1. Literary con men were so popular that historians have interpreted them as impersonations of what it meant to be Soviet (everybody had to hide some aspect of the past, and impersonate the perfect Soviet citizen, that is, play a con artist's game).[48] The GULAG's doors were indeed revolving, constantly releasing prisoners as new ones were added (see Table 3). At least six million inmates were 'officially freed' from detention during Stalinism, re-entering the world outside the labour camps, but often bringing prison culture with them.[49] One result of this pervasive shadow world was that plebeian youth culture after the war was less influenced by foreign models—as their more prosperous peers, the

Table 3 Releases and escapes from NKVD camps, 1934–1941

	freed	escaped
1934	147,272	83,490
1935	211,035	67,493
1936	369,544	58,313
1937	364,437	58,264
1938	279,966	32,033
1939	223,622	12,333
1940	316,825	11,813
1941	624,276	10,592

Source: Khlevniuk, *History of the Gulag*, 308.

stiliagi, were—than by the style, argot and behaviour of the criminal underworld.[50] The GULAG thus spread 'beyond the barbed wire', as one historian noted. 'Society absorbed the criminal mindset, the reliance on violence, and the prison culture.'[51]

Given such behavioural models and the continuing work of the forces of destruction—Civil War, terror, war—youth delinquency, child homelessness, and child begging continued to plague Stalinism. During the war, the number of youth in prison camps (ITL) more than doubled, only to further expand by a factor of 2.3 between 1945 and 1947, and 2.4 between then and the year of Stalin's death. From 1943, a special department of the NKVD was in charge of 'the fight against child-homelessness and lack of supervision'.[52] Eventually, in the early 1950s, the struggle against the *besprizornye* turned into a concerted campaign against beggars more generally, a police action often remembered as a clean-up of the cities from war invalids.[53] But repression was only one side of the state's attempt to impose order on the commons. It was flanked by efforts to get children off the street and to reintegrate war invalids into productive work, campaigns which included all branches of the official structure—state institutions, local leaders, trade unions, places of employment, the Komsomol, and the security organs. In the case of street children and waifs, foster care and adoption by regular citizens were as common solutions as institutionalization. In the case of war invalids, too, families and partners provided much of the welfare, as, despite official announcements to the contrary, the Soviet welfare state remained most developed in the realm of political rhetoric.[54]

IV

Movement was not restricted to change of position across physical space. Soviet society was fluid in terms of social position as well. Analyses ever since Trotsky have revealed extreme differences in life chances between different levels of society. At the bottom were the slave labourers in the GULAG, followed by those subjected to the new serfdom of the collective farms. Above them were workers, internally stratified themselves according to skill, productivity, and branch of industry. On top was the new elite of Party functionaries, engineers, writers, artists, and scientists.[55] Such class analysis, however, is not more than a snapshot, freezing the Soviet system of stratification at a moment in time. In the 1930s, 1940s, and 1950s, people and groups moved constantly between the different strata, resulting in a hierarchy which itself remained intact, while many of the people inhabiting its positions constantly changed.

Upward social mobility was extremely widespread in Stalin's time.[56] We have already encountered the masses of peasants leaving the village to become temporary or permanent workers. This movement to urbanity did constitute social mobility, even if the progress here was from a form of serfdom to an extreme form of exploited wage labour. In the cities, the recruitment and training of 'red cadres' from the working class during the First Five-Year Plan catapulted many upwards. It was not uncommon for illiterate peasant girls to move to the mines, graduating from backbreaking unskilled labour underground into the new elite through training in a technological institute.[57] Stalin's attempts to rid the Party of critics and old-timers, culminating in the blood-letting of 1937–1938, removed many cadres from leading positions, leaving it up to these newly trained men and women to quickly fall up the ladder. The war opened more doors, particularly for women, who now took over many of the positions from the men who left for the front. Demobilization did return men to these posts, but the immense losses meant that women were not pushed out of the workforce to the same extent as elsewhere.

Upward mobility continued in the 1940s, but, compared to the 1930s, it slowed considerably. The new elite consolidated its position, surviving cadres returned to their pre-war life, and only a small share of peasants became comrades during the war and after. The absence of a second Great Terror after 1945 resulted in a much slower movement into power of the political generation which had come of age in the Great Patriotic War. Nevertheless, the society of the 1940s and early 1950s was still a far cry from the ossified social structure of the Brezhnev years.[58]

The high turnover of personnel within the elite led to a severe disjuncture between the objective existence of a ruling elite and the subjective apprehension of this fact by its constituents. Subjectively, most members of the 'new class' did not feel that they, in fact, were the beneficiaries of the exploitation of others.[59] Such misrecognition was enhanced by an all-pervading sense of insecurity, particularly during the second half of the 1930s. 'Few of those who envied their well-paid . . . new masters, or caught a glimpse of the sorry splendours of our life,' wrote the high-level defector Victor Kravchenko in the 1940s, 'realized the weight of fear, lack of personal freedom and professional independence, the torment of uncertain tenure under which we enjoyed our advantages.'[60] This uncertainty started to fade after the war, when the new elite was confirmed in its status, managed to escape a renewal of the horror of 1937–38, and increasingly settled into a life of orange lamp shades, rubber trees, and respectable domesticity.[61]

Like the movement in space, the mobility in social position was ordered by a mixture of state policies on the one hand and spontaneous action of individuals, their friends, and their families on the other. Historians have often focused on the former, but the latter require attention as well. Social mobility, both as an ambition and as a reality, was not an unprecedented phenomenon, but had a history. Among the many peasant lads who in the late nineteenth and early twentieth century moved between village and city was a distinct minority who were fascinated by the possibilities of urban life and who quickly shunned their background of smoky huts and cow dung. Apprenticeships opened the world of skilled labour, and they distinguished themselves from the unskilled peasant workers by their clothes, speech, and mannerisms. Some became worker-radicals, while many others preferred the model of the working-class dandy. Both types, however, were distinctly urban and oriented towards self-improvement and getting ahead in life.[62] Read against such precursors, the life stories of peasants turned skilled workers, or working-class youth studying to become engineers, appear strikingly similar. In many cases, the resemblance is more than phenomenological. Nikita Khrushchev, for example, came from a peasant-worker family from the Ukraine, made it as a metal worker before the revolution, and started to attain the trappings of working-class respectability. He dreamt of further advancement into the ranks of engineers. After the revolution, his life trajectory continued upwards, but in the new environment this meant political engagement rather than simply self-improvement. He joined the Bolshevik party, fought in the Civil War, worked in the Ukrainian party apparatus in the 1920s, entered the Industrial Academy in Moscow in 1929, became a member of the Central Committee in 1934, First Secretary of the Moscow Party organization in 1935, First Secretary of Ukraine in 1938, only to continue his high-powered career after the war, avoiding demotion by the erratic Stalin and winning the succession struggles after his patron's death.[63]

Often, upward mobility was a cross-generational affair encompassing an entire family. We have already seen, how Grigorii Chukhrai's advancement continued his mother's mobility, extending it further into the elite. There are other examples of such long-term, intergenerational mobility in the making of Stalin's new class. The fathers and mothers would move from the working bench or the tractor into the political elite, through quick training as red specialists during the Stalin revolution; they would then fall up the steps as a result of the Great Terror, which removed many office holders and thus freed up positions for ambitious newcomers.[64] Their sons and daughters, in turn, tended to move from politics into arts and science—fields both prestigious and very well paid in the Soviet context. Parents, who twenty or twenty-five years ago 'worked at fitters' benches and textile machines, as dockers in the ports, ploughed and sowed on the land and sang wonderful songs about blacksmiths forging the keys of happiness,' complained the *Literary Gazette* in the year after Stalin's death, 'have suddenly taken fright that their children too might have to work at benches and machines.' These parents might well have answered, under their breath, that it was their very knowledge of what life was like for the Soviet working class which enticed them to pull strings and pay for private tutors to get 'Mitya', 'Borya', and 'Tamara' into tertiary education.[65] Moreover, they also knew the cut-throat world of Soviet politics, and thus hoped that their offspring could find a niche in the creative and scientific intelligentsia instead.

Social mobility, however, was not a one-way street. Every purge of the Party, in fact, stopped hundreds of thousands in their tracks, reversing fortunes over night. The first of these small-p purges (as opposed to the capital-P Purge of the Great Terror) was conducted in 1933–34, after the recruitment drive during the Stalin revolution had swelled the Party's ranks and the brutality of collectivization had increased internal criticism of the party line. New screening campaigns followed in 1935 and 1936. The first of these cleansing operations excluded at least 450,000 people from the party, followed by the expulsion of 177,000, or 9 per cent of the membership in 1935 (15,218 of them were arrested as well). On the eve of the Great Purges some regions and enterprises counted more ex-communists than actual Party members. In early 1937, the authorities knew of 1.5 million former Communists, and a year later the number for Ukraine alone was as high as 10,000.[66] All of these broken lives did not yet include the victims of the Great Terror or of the renewed 'cleansing' of the Party's ranks after the successful war against Germany. In the Ukraine alone, by early 1949 this latest purge had cost 68,032 Communists their Party-card.[67]

Many of those who had their career destroyed during these witch-hunts were in fact the same people who had benefited from Bolshevik takeover, new regime, and Stalin's top-down revolutions. A son of a peasant, who had moved from factory lathe hand to higher education, research work, and finally teaching might be excluded because he was once associated with Trotskyist ideas; a Civil War veteran with a long career as a factory official who was promoted to technical training in his late thirties fell because he found the business of 'liquidating the kulaks as a class' unpleasant, and said so, while continuing to enforce the policy himself; a daughter of a carpenter who started factory work in her early teens, studied in the evening and made it to the institute by the early 1930s could be excluded because she failed to divorce her husband, who had already been arrested as an enemy; the list could go on.[68] We should

thus not be tempted to take the very clear examples of upward movement—such as Khrushchev or Brezhnev—as the only way mobility
could play itself out. As elsewhere, in Stalin's Russia, too, what went up
often had to come down again. And former Party members were only
the tip of the iceberg of those whose life chances, income, and status
plunged throughout Stalin's tenure. Consider, for example, the probably
5 to 6 million 'dekulakized elements' produced in the years 1930–1933;[69]
add family members and surviving victims of the Great Terror of 1937–
1938 and the Revolution from Abroad in 1939–1941; add further those
accused of collaboration with the Germans and those stigmatized as
Ostarbeiter and POWs; add finally those whose lives were destroyed in
the post-war campaign against 'rootless cosmopolitanists'—Stalin's
regime was as good at making enemies as it was promoting friends.

V

While popular notions of dictatorship might suggest that Soviet society
was stable in some fundamental way—whether as the totalitarian dictatorship of one man or the rule of a new class—in actuality, the overwhelming sense of life in the period was of great fluidity. Being on the
move was the normal state of affairs, both in economic and in geographic terms. People moved to escape disaster, to try to find marginally
better living conditions, to avoid repression, or because the state forced
them. People also moved up and down in the social hierarchy, confusing
any attempts to ascribe stable categories to them. The political leaders
reacted to this fluidity with ever more rigid residency and labour laws
and with a constant attempt to police and uncover people's 'real selves'.
During the mass operations of the Great Terror, these attempts to impose
order lapsed into mass killings to solve the problem once and for all, but
they had to fail, as fluidity was at the very core of the life under Stalin.

Nevertheless, the metaphor of the 'quicksand society' is also misleading. There was considerable order to this chaos, which was not imposed
by the state, but emerged spontaneously as people tried to make do and
survive. These patterns were not accidental, but they followed the lead
of precedent. They had, in other words, their own histories which were
of considerably longer term than either the regime we call Stalinism, or

the Bolshevik project of which it was a part. The history of begging and beggars, the subcultures of thieves, con men, and homeless youth, the networks of fellow countrymen and the pathways of migration to, from, and between cities, even the trajectories of upward mobility are only examples for many long and deep histories which guided people's actions, reactions, thoughts and solutions to a world of severe flux, uncertainty, and violence. It was these many tenacious pasts which imposed some order on the 'chaos produced by the violence of wars and revolutions' and allowed people to survive and live.

CHAPTER 4
FAMILY CHRONICLES

" A Russian cannot live without relatives. **"**

proverb[1]

" Under the Soviet regime we became slaves. And it was only natural that at home, we felt secure and safe. At home, we wept, we smiled, we criticized or cursed those who made us poor and hungry. **"**

a Soviet citizen about the centre of Soviet life[2]

" If I had known it [her character] I might not have married her, but if I wanted to divorce [,] my father would not have permitted it, and I respected my father. (Why would your father not have permitted it?) Because he was religious and did not want people to divorce. 'Marry once,' he always said, 'even if she's an onion and you your tears will flow.' **"**

Ukrainian peasant about who defined divorce procedures[3]

I

Many of the histories criss-crossing the Soviet landscape in the 1930s, 1940s, and 1950s proved remarkably resilient to the onslaught of the forces of destruction. They were not, however, static. There are no unchanging traditions without an internal dynamic of their own; there are no customs unresponsive to their social, cultural, political, and physical environment; there are no institutions which can remain unaffected by the assault of industrialization, urbanization, war, revolution, and a totalitarian government. The dialectic of continuity and change, tenacity and fluidity can be studied through several sites—the family, gender relations, and ethnic particularism. All social formations have to deal with the challenges posed by biological reproduction; groups centred around ancestry and procreation—families, in short—are universals in the social organization of humans. So is the preoccupation with the roles men and women are expected to play, a topic we will return to in Chapter 7. Finally, all societies have to come to terms in one way or another with inclusion and exclusion, with differences in language, custom, cultural heritage, or complexion. As an impressive library of empirical research demonstrates, however, none of these patterns is fixed. Kinship, sex-roles, and nationalities have their histories, are subject to evolution, transformation, adaptation to the changing world around them. But families, gender relations, or ethnicities are not only acted upon by forces outside of them. They are themselves part of the historical process in which they impact on their environment. This environment, in turn, is complex and contradictory. In order to better understand these interdependencies and to further focus our analysis, this chapter concentrates on the family—as we shall see, a central institution of Stalinist society.

The general outline of the history of the family can be sketched as a tale of state regulation.[4] Under the old regime, from the middle of the 18th century, marriage and divorce had been religious affairs, with the law allowing each of the many religions of the empire to formulate its own rules, which were, in turn, incorporated into the legal code. The state's law was classically patriarchal, subjecting the obedient wife to the power of the husband, whose name, place of residence, and social status determined hers. Women did have the right to own property, but obtaining an internal passport, taking a job, enrolling in educational institutions, or executing a bill of exchange required the patriarch's consent. Divorce, which before the beginning of the 18th century had been quite common, was now possible only with the permission of the church, in cases of sexual impotence or its opposite, adultery, the exile of one partner or an unexplained absence over a long period of time. It was seldom granted—in 1913 there were less than three divorces per 100,000 population, a very low proportion by international comparison. Only in 1914 did legal reform allow women to separate from their spouses under certain conditions, legalizing what in practice had happened under the law's surface for quite some time.[5]

The Revolution of 1917 secularized marriage, recognized common-law bonds as equal to their more formalized equivalents, and simplified divorce. In December 1917 the Bolsheviks replaced religious by civil marriage and allowed divorce initiated by either partner. Less than a year later, already during the Civil War, the Code on Marriage, the Family, and Guardianship (October 1918), 'swept away centuries of patriarchal and ecclesiastical power and established a new doctrine based on individual rights and gender equality'. The code put men and women on an equal legal footing and recognized civil marriage only. Divorce proceedings could be initiated by either spouse and without having to state a reason. Property was to remain separate, but both partners could claim alimony, if necessary, after divorce. All children were now treated equally, had the same right to parental support, no matter if born in or out of wedlock—the revolution thus abolished the lowly status of the 'rightless bastard'. Adoption, once a major way to reintegrate orphans, was outlawed on the belief that the state would be a better guardian than potentially exploitative adoptive parents.[6]

In January 1927, despite considerable controversy over these revisions to the family code, divorce procedures were further simplified, and alimony was granted to women in de facto relationships, even if the 'husband' was also legally married. From the mid-1930s, in what has sometimes been called the 'Great Retreat' from revolutionary values, much of this far-reaching legalization was undone. The June 1936 family law made divorce more complicated again, introduced higher penalties for the non-payment of alimony, and outlawed abortions (which had been legal since 1920).[7] The new pro-natalism became more pronounced during the war when the staggering wartime losses put replacing the dead on the top of the agenda. A tax on bachelors was introduced in November 1941 and in 1944 child subsidies were increased. In a bid to increase male promiscuity and raise the birthrate, men were absolved of financial responsibility for children born out of registered marriage. The 'single mothers' of these babies were granted state support instead.[8]

II

The reaffirmation of the family in the 1930s did not mean an end to policies destabilizing it. A central icon of official rhetoric can illustrate the point. In 1932, just as the Communist Youth League's childhood branch—the Pioneers—celebrated its tenth anniversary, a boy was killed and a hero was born. Pavel ('Pavlik') Morozov and his brother Fedor were found brutally murdered, lying in the woods adjacent to their village where Siberia borders on the Urals region. Soon the press claimed that they had been slaughtered by 'kulaks' against whom he, the vigilant and upstanding child Communist, had allegedly waged his own mini-campaign. He had even, or so the story went, stood up in court against his own father, whom he denounced as helping the class enemy. And he was killed by his own relatives, allegedly in an act of 'class revenge'. Nearly nothing about this story was actually true, but this did not matter. Over the next three years, Pavlik was built up as a major role model for Soviet youth—the boy whose allegiance to the regime was stronger than the call of blood. In 1935, the Politburo decided even to build him a monument in Red Square in Moscow, enshrining him in the pantheon of Soviet saints, close to the holiest, Lenin, whose body lay nearby. This monument was never built, but countless others were, all around the country. The official rehabilitation of the family as a central institution of Soviet life in the mid-1930s demanded some adjustments to the Pavlik myth. Now, Morozov was said to have been tormented by the knowledge of his father's betrayal of the revolution, and only after another adult, a teacher or a secret policeman, depending on the version of the story, had reassured him, did he come forward with the denunciation. The message was that the family was sacred, but only as long as it was in alliance with the *Über*-family, the Soviet collective. Where the different levels of patriarchal authority clashed (as in real life they inevitably did), the higher level won out. In the final analysis, family loyalty could not be stronger than loyalty to Comrade Stalin. Or as the journal *Our Achievements* put it in 1936: 'The family should not be comprised merely of blood ties. We will pay for such blood ties in blood.'[9]

Despite the law's new protection of the family, then, actually existing kin structures continued to be eyed with suspicion. Throughout Stalin's time genetic connections were seen as dangerous and potentially subversive. Most notable was this anti-family thrust when relatives of those 'repressed' regularly fell victim as well, on the assumption that, as relatives, they must share the 'enemy's' beliefs or, at the least, would be likely to hold a grudge against a state which destroyed their near and dear.[10] This premiss was, of course, not too far off the mark. As one schoolgirl noted in her diary on 24 March 1933, after her father, who had just returned from a stint in exile, was not allowed residency in Moscow, again separating him from his daughter:

> I didn't know what to do. I was filled with rage, helpless rage. I began to cry. I ran around the room swearing. *I decided that I had to kill the bastards.* Ridiculous as that sounds, but it's no joke. For several days I dreamed for hours while lying in bed about *how I'd kill him. His promises, his dictatorship, the vile Georgian who has crippled Russia.*...I must kill him *as soon as possible! I must avenge myself and my father.*[11]

Of course she did no such thing, but when the young woman was arrested in 1937 as a consequence of her father's renewed detention, the secret police marked this passage, like many others, as proof of her 'anti-Soviet activities'.

The time to pay for blood ties in blood thus soon came. In June 1937, Minister of Internal Affairs, Ezhov, ordered that family members of repressed Communists were to be expelled from the big cities, and in July the Politburo decided to round up and intern the family members of purge victims as well.[12] As Stalin explained in a toast to his closest circle at a dinner party on the anniversary of the October revolution, on 7 November 1937:

> And we will destroy every such enemy, even if he's an old Bolshevik. We will destroy his entire clan (*rod*), his family (*sem'ia*). We will destroy without mercy anybody who, with deeds or thoughts, (yes, even with thoughts), infringes on the unity of the socialist state (*gosudarstvo*). For the destruction of all enemies to the end, [to the destruction of] their own, their clan![13]

This programme of exterminating enemies together with their kin in the Great Terror was the most radical incarnation of policies that were in place throughout the Stalin years. Before and after this climax of terror the same flame burned, just less brightly. Already in 1934, the families of 'traitors of the homeland' and deserters were made criminally liable, even if they had known nothing about the intentions of their relative.[14] During the war, the habit of victimizing the whole family for the real or imagined deeds of one of its members re-emerged in the notorious order No. 270. It stipulated that officers who 'gave themselves over to the enemy' (as falling captive was misleadingly labelled) were to be punished as deserters (that is, shot on the spot, if recovered), while their families were 'liable to arrest as families of deserters'. Rank-and-file soldiers were treated somewhat more leniently, but their families suffered as well, by being deprived of support payments military kin otherwise received.[15]

Such threats to the near and dear of potential enemies or deserters were, as one historian of the practice points out, a form of hostage taking. The NKVD further perfected the method, by detaining relatives of those accused, in order to pressure them to confess to often ludicrous crimes. Stalin, too, terrorized his closest circle by arresting family members, both as hostages and as punishment. 'No one who contradicts Stalin,' claimed Beria, 'keeps his wife.' Marshal Budennyi was one of the first victims of this practice in 1937, followed by President Kalinin, (whose spouse was arrested in 1938), Stalin's secretary Poskrebyshev (1939), and Party Control Commission Chairman Andreev (late 1940s). The most celebrated example is Molotov's wife, Polina Zhemchuzhina. Stalin had her arrested in 1949 for her warm welcome of Golda Meir, the representative of the new state of Israel. Molotov was forced to humiliate himself, demonstrating that his love for the leader was stronger than for his wife, by voting for her expulsion from the Party and confessing 'my heavy guilt in not restraining Zhemchuzhina, a person close to me, from erroneous steps and link with anti-Soviet Jewish nationalists.'[16]

III

The family thus loomed large in the suspicious mind of Stalin and his perverse strategies of rule. But there is more to this history than the paranoia of the leader or cynical instrumentalization of a social institution by those in power. The historical record is abundant with examples of the centrality of the family in the life of Soviet citizens. The strength of kinship ties can be gauged by instances where people took the risk of showing solidarity with repressed relations. Consider, for example, cases of children orphaned by the Great Purges. Many of them ended up in state institutions or on the streets, but many others were adopted by their kinsfolk, despite the clear and present danger such an association with the offspring of an 'enemy of the people' posed.[17] Or consider the following statistic about yet another repression wave a decade later: The 33,266 peasants who were deported as 'parasites' from collective farms between June 1948 and March 1953 were followed, voluntarily, by 13,598 members of their families. On average, then, about 41 per cent of these unfortunates were joined by one family member into a life of increased hardship somewhere at the periphery of the empire.[18]

Likewise, a decade and a half earlier, the tides of peasants floating back and forth across the Soviet lands in search of bearable living conditions was guided by information provided by their kinfolk. 'The tendency to migrate is caused, besides by the lack of bread, also by relatives living in the Northern Caucasus,' the secret police reported, confusing solutions with causes during the famine year 1933. 'In letters and during personal encounters, they praise the life in the Northern Caucasus and agitate the migrants to move'.[19] Those who stayed in the collectives (or returned to them after finding life elsewhere not much better), often used family strategies to circumvent the kolkhoz order, to live at its margins and make the best of the privileges of the kolkhoznik while sidestepping to the best of their abilities the attached exploitation. The trick was to keep the garden plot and a few private farm animals, as well as the right to trade surplus produce on the market, while working outside the collectives, where monetary wages were paid, and avoiding the heavy taxes imposed on collective farmers' private plots. 'Collective farmers,' complained Stalin's gendarmes in early 1937, 'who have managed to find [non-agricultural] work, forbid their families to work in the collective farms. They explain to them, that they should see themselves as families of workers who are freed from milk and meat deliveries and other obligations towards the state.'[20] Once the kolkhoz regime settled down in the second half of the 1930s, many families registered only the head of household as a member, which meant that the rest of the family could refuse to work the collective farm's fields, focusing on their private plot and their private animals instead—which they frequently owned in larger quantities than allowed.[21] As late as 1937, some regions of the Ukraine counted even substantial shares of single farmers (*edinolichniki*), i.e. families which refused to enter the collectives—reaching 10 to 20 per cent in some areas.[22]

Families were not only central institutions in the under-governed countryside and the empire's periphery, where 'years of Sovietization did not eradicate the important social functions of kinship'.[23] In the very centre of Bolshevik civilization, the large cities in the Slavic heartland, families were not squeezed out of people's lives either. City dwellers also relied on family support to satisfy many of their most basic needs. The ever tight housing supply meant that recent arrivals in the cities often relied on kin to provide shelter. The urban housing shortage as well as the necessity for both spouses to work to make ends meet enforced extended, multigenerational families sharing one household, centred around one room in a communal apartment in many cases, if the family managed to escape even more basic accommodation in tents, dugouts, or barracks. A thus privileged couple with a child might have to cram into a sixteen square metre room together with the wife's mother and an uncle damaged by the war. 'It was very difficult to live so crowded,' Elena told a historian decades later, 'and even more so with my mother who was always aggravating.'[24]

Such conditions also counteracted the aggressive attempts to accelerate the birth rate, although they did not completely cancel them.[25] As one memoirist describes her post war life:

> ...life was hard and bothersome, disorderly and cruel in all respects. How could we have loved one another in a room, which also contained mama, Lesha and the houseworker Dusia? When those in power completely outlawed abortions and every pregnancy became a tragedy, leading to a search for a private doctor, who under some pretext or other would admit you to hospital and whom you would have to pay large sums of money? All this degraded people, in particular the women, reduced them to an animal like condition. After all, having yet another child in our circumstances

would have been impossible. It would have meant to completely transform our life into hell, would have forced mama or myself to stop working.[26]

In its most intimate aspects, then, Soviet citizens' daily lives were constrained by the family as much as by the effects of government policy. At both ends of the life cycle, kin rather than the state was the central caring institution. 'The position of the old folks is desperate,' complained a former Soviet citizen after the war. 'No one wants them, there is no one to take care of them. Until 1937, there was no old folks home in Kherson. Old people went around like beggars, and they died like flies. Finally the municipal administration organized a home, which had place for forty old people, but this is just a drop in the bucket as it takes care of only a tiny part of those who need help.'[27] Given such lack of facilities, many elderly lived with their children.

This relationship was not just one of reliance of the old on the young. It was, rather, a symbiosis, a relationship of mutual dependency. Somebody needed to run the household, after all. 'It is good,' evaluated one worker the usefulness of a grandmother in the house, 'when both spouses work and have someone to do the laundry and cooking, etc.' 'This important and thankless duty lay mostly upon my wife's mother,' reported another informant the typical pattern. And somebody needed to raise the children and even educate the grownups, too. 'With me lived only my wife's mother,' noted an engineer. 'She was most useful. She educated the children. She taught her daughter things, that is, how to behave and do things better.'[28] As more and more women chose to work (or were forced to by necessity), it became the grandmothers who cared for their children and ran the household. To take charge of grandchildren when their parents disappeared in the GULAG was just the extreme form of this widespread child-rearing pattern.[29]

The result was that many of the values of the oldest generation were passed on to the youngest—one of the chief sources for enduring traditionalism in many societies.[30] The force of the grandmother remained strong, even for those growing up breathing, eating, and drinking Stalinism in school. As one of them, born in 1927, remarked:

I don't know if Comrade Stalin understood this, but the New Socialist Man—the new kind of man who would be free from vestiges of bourgeois

individualism—was being raised by a legion of grandmothers. As our mothers spent their time at the universities and Komsomol meetings, the grandmothers gently rocked our cradles, singing the songs they had heard from their mothers back in the days when the Bolsheviks were just being born.

Whether Comrade Stalin liked it or not, traditional values were being instilled alongside the icons of the new era. And sometimes, as in the case of my instinctive rejection of Pavlik Morozov, old values directly contradicted the new icons.[31]

The story of little Pavlik, as many other aspects of Stalinist education, scraped against the rough surface of familial ties:

I loved my grandmother. I loved my parents, I felt good walking outside in a starched, white dress. These were real people and real objects that constituted my world. Compared to them, Pavlik Morozov was a two-dimensional icon and the 'collective' was something so abstract that it defied my imagination.

A child brought up by the undivided attention of Anetta Marietta Rozalia Yanovna Sinberg could never grow up to become a cog in the machine of state. Nor could thousands upon thousands of other children raised under the close supervision of other grandmothers. No matter how hard we would try to fit into the system, each of us would be different. And, eventually, we would stop trying to fit in and would instead become ourselves.[32]

Comrade Stalin, by the way, was well aware of the force of primary socialization. 'The working women and the peasant women are mothers,' he gravely stated the obvious in 1923; 'they are rearing our youth—the future of our country.' Their influence was politically problematic as they could 'either warp a child's soul or rear for us a younger generation that will be of healthy mind and capable of promoting our country's progress, depending upon whether the mothers sympathise with the Soviet system or whether they follow in the wake of the priests, the kulaks, the bourgeoisie.'[33]

Peasant women were, moreover, not only central to child-rearing in the village, but they strongly influenced the offspring of the elite. More often than not, children of party functionaries were raised not only by their grandmothers (often less beholden to the Party's gospel than their children), but also by nannies or domestic servants, even when, as in the case cited above, the whole family had to share one single room in a communal apartment. The latter were, in most cases, peasant women who took the job to escape the collective farms and eke out a living in the metropole.[34] Such 'houseworkers' (*domrabotnitsy*) could become very close to their charges, and they often became part of the family.

> I don't know what would have happened to me, were it not for her. After mama and papa she was the person closest to me. She knew all my sorrows and all my joys. Natasha raised and educated (*vospityvala*) not only me, but also my daughters. She even lived to see my grandchildren, who became her great-grandchildren. She died with 87 years in my arms, in my house.[35]

The influence of the family on the lives of Soviet citizens went far beyond its reach as an organization within daily life. Even apparently single, unattached citizens carried their kin with them and the merely psychological presence of parents (and frequently grandparents) was a powerful force, shaping people's lives. For the defector Victor Kravchenko, to quote a particularly impressive example for this phenomenon, the family remained a moral and political reference point in his struggle to make sense of the Soviet experience. His father in particular served as his bad conscience, but his mother and brother remained central with critical commentary on his career within a dictatorial regime. The huge role his father played in his superego is such a striking feature of his memoirs that only current intellectual fashion prevents a Freudian reading. *I Chose Freedom* (composed after his wartime defection and published at the beginning of the Cold War, in 1947) is at its core a triple dialogue— with Soviet reality, which constantly fell short of the proclamations of official rhetoric; with the Western reader, who needs to be convinced of the evil of Stalinism; and with Kravchenko's father, who plays the role of the humanist conscience. The conversation with the father could be actual, when the old idealistic revolutionary challenged his Stalinist son whenever he visited. But more importantly, this dialogue continued as an internal struggle. 'It was as if my father was watching and judging—looking at the facts and deeds behind the slogans.'[36] Even those whose allegiance to the regime became a way to transcend the own heritage—as it did for many assimilated and 'bourgeois' Jews—carried the influence of their family deep inside themselves, 'as a turbid sediment of memory,' as one of them put it. Despite all 'consciousness', all 'ideology', and despite the constant pains of 'working on the self'—a technique with which the Party-faithful tried to purge their inner beings of sinful thoughts in order to align themselves with the sacred collective—there remained 'in my subconscious, in the roots of my way of sensing the world, on the level of conditioned reflexes... irrational but close ties to my grandmother and grandfather, my great-grandfather, my relatives and relations, their fears and hopes, their sufferings and joys.'[37]

IV

The family, then, remained a central focus of social integration, a force field organizing the Soviet citizens' lives. One of many reasons were state attempts to regulate these very lives, although we should avoid the caricature of the all-powerful and all-knowing apparatus, reconstructing society at will, here destroying families if necessary, here rebuilding them when convenient. Mostly, the state had to retreat from policies which simply proved destructive, counter-productive as well as unpopular, particularly as the state was unable to make good on the promise that it would replace the family in the realm of child rearing and welfare. To some extent, then, a measure of realism replaced the utopianism of the earlier period.[38]

To reconstruct this history, we need to go back to the beginning of the Soviet experience. By the time of the October revolution the family had often been discussed as a doomed institution, soon to be chucked into the dustbin of history (along with other annoyances of the past, such as money, housework, religion, law, or the state). As the author of one learned tract, published in 1929, paraphrased Friedrich Engels: the family would 'be sent to a museum of antiquities so that it can rest next to the spinning wheel and the bronze axe, by the horsedrawn carriage, the steam engine, and the wired telephone.'[39] In real life, however, the state's inability to supplant the family from its economic and welfare roles meant that the revolutionaries needed to make compromises. What one commentator on the 1918 family code noted with regards to alimony has wider validity. Such payments were, wrote this expert, permissible only because of the 'present inability to organize a comprehensive program of social welfare'. Once the 'shining new world where all society will be one family' was reached, such 'transitional' arrangements which relied on the family as a unit of social (self-)organization would, quite naturally, disappear.[40]

Alas, the path to such a welfare society was so long and twisted that it led elsewhere in the end. Rather than withering away, the family provided ready-made answers for many problems of social organization not foreseen in Marxist theology. By the mid-1920s, it had become clear, for example, that to communalize child-rearing was prohibitively expensive, and state support of struggling families was much more effective. Faced with child homelessness of crisis proportions and a completely inadequate welfare system, which, moreover, seemed to contribute to the growth of the problem in the first place, the state quietly reintroduced adoption 'as a temporary measure' in 1925, only to abolish the prohibition against this practice in the following year. To draft families into solving the problem of child homelessness proved much more effective than state-run children's homes—a solution which continued to be used for the new waves of besprizorniki produced by collectivization, terror, and war.[41]

Similarly, property law quickly re-established the family as a central institution of managing resources. Inheritance was legally abolished in 1918. 'Property of an owner (movable as well as immovable)', a 27 April decree announced grandly, 'becomes after his death the domain of the Russian Socialist Federated Soviet Republic'. However, this radical statement was watered down immediately, by allowing relatives who had cohabited with the deceased to inherit estates up to 10,000 rubles. Soon, further weakening of the revolutionary zeal of the law occurred. In 1919, peasants' farmsteads were excluded from the 10,000 ruble limit, in 1922, inheritance up to the magical 10,000 was explicitly permitted, and in 1926 the limit was abolished altogether.[42] Inheritance was allowed not only because it was unclear what the state should do with the pots and pans, underwear and sheepskin coats of a dead citizen, but also because incentives were needed to encourage the reverse of this policy: the expectation of mutual care within the family circle. Soviet property laws, as one historian has put it, 'strongly emphasized the mutual responsibility of family members for each other's financial welfare; the consensus of Soviet legal experts was that, since the state lacked the resources for a full social welfare system for the time being, the family remained the basic institution of social welfare for Soviet citizens.'[43] By the mid-1930s, what once started as temporary measures had become stable solutions. Just as it had become plain that the state would not wither away any time soon, it had become clear that neither the Bolshevik nor the Stalinist state could do without the support of families and the unpaid work performed in them, first of all, by women.[44]

The war only reinforced the central role of the family and the household economy in Soviet society. Faced with the enormity of the German onslaught, the central government gave up most pretensions to managing food, housing, and other necessities for the civilian population. Responsibility for civilian supply now devolved down the chain of command, to the level of local government, further to the factory, and ultimately to the smallest available unit of social organization, the household. Food production in the cities now depended, as in the village, on gardening by individuals and their families, as well as on the subsidiary plots where enterprises raised their own food. As a result, families emerged from the war as more self-reliant entities than before, and were soon to face the brunt of the reconstruction effort. The reintegration of returning veterans and the care for those among them, who returned mentally or physically damaged, relied to a large extent on the work of kin, in particularly women—mothers, sisters, wives. As the state proved both incapable of providing for the welfare of its subjects and preoccupied with preparing for and executing warfare instead, the family thus continued to be relevant. Rather than a residual social unit for a transition period due to 'wither away', it turned out to be a necessary evil, the welfare helpmate to the warfare state.[45]

But the family reasserted itself after the upheaval of revolution in part also because of its own resilience as an institution, deeply rooted within the psyche of historical actors, however radical they professed to be. In many cases, the dangerous environment of the 1930s strengthened families, just as usually quarrelling academics are drawn together when their departments are confronted with rationalizing administrators, or as the threat of outside aggression can override internal contradictions in otherwise divided nations. 'The Soviet Union,' claimed a respondent of Harvard University's post war study of Soviet citizens, 'is a mass of individual family units isolated from each other.... Families are not broken up, rather, they try to draw close to each other.'[46] Even without threat, the simple tendency to re-enact the well-known played a role. The new elite, certainly, took many of the rules and obligations of kinship with them into their new positions. Nikita Khrushchev, for example, a freshly minted Party stalwart, brought his parents to live with him in early 1930s Moscow—not because they so desired or because he needed them, but because it seemed natural. According to his son-in-law, he 'had preserved the traditional Russian respect for and attachment to his parents, and they, in their turn, knew that Nikita was a good son who had invited them out of a pure heart.'[47] Quite spontaneously, too, intermarriage among the members of the new political elite occurred, assisting in its consolidation. The Stalins, Timoshenkos and Zhdanovs, the Kamenevs and the Trotskys, the Gorkys and Berias, the Mikoyans and the Kuznetsovs—all these elite families were connected by kinship ties as the offspring of the leaders married each other.[48] The leading Bolsheviks might have professed their Marxist disdain for 'the bourgeois family' in theory, but in practice they were as much family men as had been their bearded patriarchal prophet. It is in this context that the repressive urge to go after family members starts to make sense—hostage taking only works if somebody cares about the hostage; and, if one can assume that people care about their kin, wiping out the relatives of enemies along with these enemies might appear as a sensible strategy to a leader surrounded by perceived foes.

The new bosses' valuation of kinship reflected widespread emotional attachments within the milieu they had come from—the labouring classes of the Tsarist *fin-de-siècle*. At the turn of the century, 'free love' and anti-marriage views were largely confined to a minority among the highly educated and the privileged. To working women, marriage tended to connote security rather than domestic slavery. Worker-authors, the literate as well as literary avant-garde of the self-conscious working class, were firmly committed to a clear sense of sexual respectability, continually preaching against such vices as drunkenness, obscenity, lying to wives, or lustful objectifying of women. The struggle to define 'respectable behaviour', in sexual as in other matters, pervaded popular as much as elite culture in the last years of the old regime. The Revolution did not end the quest for morality, even if it seemed to many that the forces of order were on the defensive. Throughout the 1920s, peasants of both sexes expressed their dislike of the libertarian family laws introduced by the revolutionary intellectuals, and even radical students were, at best, disoriented and searched for clear moral guidelines in the confusion of NEP. Eventually, the exceptionally high divorce rates of the 1920s (three times above Germany, twenty-six times England and Wales, and approximated only by the exceptionally transient USA) had to become cause for concern for a regime increasingly made up of former workers and peasants, who were not suddenly transformed into bohemians once they left the workbench for the desk. The 1936 law, with its attempt to 'struggle with a frivolous attitude toward the family and family responsibility', in fact reflected widely held attitudes towards this social institution. Three quarters of displaced persons interviewed after the war by American sociologists 'recorded their approval of the legislation which made the procurement of divorce considerably more difficult'.[49]

That the 'sexual respectability' of the Tsarist turn of the century rose to power with the new elite under Stalin also explains why the mid-1930s 'retreat' from the permissiveness of the revolution was both so all-encompassing and so contradictory. There is no logical reason, for example, why the strengthening of the family should be flanked with outlawing of homosexuality. If it would only have been a question of entrenching households capable of providing welfare and organizing the reproduction of their members' labour power, homosexuality could have been left out of the equation. In reality, however, it was one of the first targets of the Great Retreat, long before the family was rehabilitated. The homosexual subculture, which had emerged at the turn of the century and reconstructed itself in the cities during NEP, was swept up in the police operations against undesirables of 1933. The cleansing of the cities during the 'passportization campaign', which started in January, was, in the first place, targeted at the masses of peasants who lived, often illegally, in cities—the beggars, prostitutes, and small time criminals. However, once they started 'purifying' the cities of 'parasites', 'socially dangerous' and 'socially harmful' elements, raids on 'salons...dens, groups, and other organized formations of pederasts' (as the police called men engaged in same-sex practices) seemed quite natural to the guardians of order. Legal change followed repressive practice. After one hundred and thirty men had been detained in Moscow and Leningrad, deputy OGPU chief G. G. Iagoda wrote to Stalin in September 1933, requesting a new law, since these 'pederasts' were soiling the moral landscape of Socialism. They operated 'salons', organized 'orgies', recruited and corrupted 'totally healthy young people, Red Army soldiers, sailors, and students'. Stalin agreed that this perversion needed to stop. The new law was quickly drafted, approved by the Politburo in December 1933 and enacted in March 1934. From now on 'voluntary sodomy' incurred a minimum sentence of three years; if force or the exploitation of a dependent was involved five to eight years loomed. Stalin's reaction to a spirited critique of this new law on Marxist grounds reveals his emotional attachment to a particular order of sexualities. The author, he scribbled at the margins of the letter in May 1934, was 'an idiot and a degenerate'.[50] Not surprisingly, then, the criminalization of same-sex relationships went hand in glove with a general campaign in 1934, 1935, and 1936 against 'sexual promiscuity, quick and easy marriage, bigamy, adultery, and the exploitative approach toward women'. The retreat from *laissez-faire* divorce law and the new valuation of the family was part and parcel of this reassertion of respectability.[51]

V

That families remained central institutions in Soviet society does not mean that all was well within them, that they did not change, or that all Soviet citizens were tightly integrated into kinship networks. The masses of homeless children alone, discussed in the previous chapter, illustrate the extent of social breakdown throughout the years of Stalin's domination. Political repression and the discrimination against certain groups of 'former people' created strong incentives to disown one's parents, to make up a new identity, to hide one's 'real self'. The upheavals of the time—the two revolutions from above, the war, post war re-evacuation, the persistent flight from the village and continuing labour turnover—pulled people apart, destroying families, breaking up households. In Russian cities in 1936, for every thousand marriages came 213 divorces, and 178 in the following year. Most of these had lasted only a couple of years; some collapsed after a few months.[52] Following the war, as a result of the changes in divorce procedures in 1936 and 1944, the corresponding numbers were much lower, but still considerable. Moreover, their tendency was rising, pointing to the continuing fluidity of post-war life: 13.8 per thousand in 1946, and 86.8 in 1952. These numbers compare with 16.5 in England and Wales or 80.3 in France. Only the USA, prone as it is to superlatives, could boast higher numbers—165 per thousand in 1940.[53] Few, however, separated in order to stay alone. Even if many individual entities were crushed, the institutions of the family and the household based on sexual division of labour survived. From the rubble of broken social ties new ones emerged. 91 per cent of men and 82 per cent of women between the ages of 30 and 39 declared themselves married in 1937, a number probably underreporting unregistered unions.[54] In the countryside in particular, most people were married—92 per cent of adults in both the censuses of 1939 and 1959.[55]

New connections, based as they were 'upon sexual or emotional affinity, practical necessity, or mere accident',[56] more or less by default re-enacted patterns which were known, consciously or unconsciously, to the people involved. The past, which to revolutionaries—priests of the cult of the totally new—appeared as a nightmare, thus weighed on the minds of contemporaries (including the revolutionaries themselves) in productive ways, allowing them to live in the present and face the future. Take the particularly Stalinist form of the trophy wife: In a perverse twist, the repression of 'former people' (that is, those discriminated against as members of the now abolished bourgeoisie or other undesirable social groups) got tangled around the newly minted functionaries' aspirations to the trappings of respectability and upper-classness. Like many social climbers, they tried to marry 'up'. That 'up' in symbolic terms really meant 'down' in the official hierarchy mattered less than the dizzying fact that these former working men could now marry the daughters of yesteryear's upper classes, good manners and all. The latter were more inclined than usual to attach themselves to such men, and to teach them how to properly dress, talk, feel, eat and live, as this proved the only way to both gain some protection and to continue a life of relative privilege and prosperity. For some, such purely pragmatic reasons combined with the romance of the Russian intelligentsia since the nineteenth century—to connect with 'the people' and to immerse and thus lose the alienated intellectual self in the deep truth of 'the masses'.[57]

In the final decades of Tsarism, similarly high-placed wives had frequently engaged in volunteer and philanthropical work, bringing culture and morality as well as soup and soap to the hungry great unwashed.[58] Old habits die hard. The reborn elite wives were sometimes the daughters of late Tsarist lady-activists, and at times old enough to have been involved in charity work before the revolution themselves. After adjusting their husbands' poorly wound ties (leather jackets and boots, the uniform of militant Bolsheviks ever since the Civil War, had gone out of fashion with Stalin's new men), they left the house in their own attempts to lift up the plebs. They policed working-class dwellings (where was the white table cloth?), planted flower beds, ran clinics or cafeterias for their husband's underlings (and sometimes cultured cafes for themselves)—in a word, they brought the blessings of civilization to the people. Taking local precedent as a model, the government systematized such spontaneously emerging activities, starting a campaign, a 'war for cosiness, for culture in daily life', known as the 'wife-activist' (*obshchestvennitsy*) movement of the years 1934 to 1941. As in the olden days, local first ladies provided respectable entertainment (concerts, lectures, literature readings), beautified public as well as private space, but now discussion and education circles were added to the repertoire of activities meant to distract the exploited from cursing and drinking, fornicating and fighting. At their best, then, the *obshchestvennitsy* combined two pre-revolutionary role models in a new, Stalinist synthesis—the lady philanthropist became fused with the intelligentsia radical running political cirlces (*kruzhki*) for self-improving proletarians. Down the social hierarchy, the movement was echoed by the spouses of overachieving labourers, the shock workers (*udarniki*) and Stakhanovites, working-class aristocrats named after their role model, the famous miner Aleksei Stakhanov. The expectations were only slightly lower for the plebeians, who were sometimes tutored by the *obshchestvennitsy*. Nagging husbands into norm-busting and providing them with a harmonious family live were not enough—even if hard enough to achieve in the economy of scarcity, where most of these women had to work themselves as well. 'Now if a wife welcomes her husband home with love and tenderness,' M. A. Poliakova explained the 'general conditions' she created for her blacksmith husband, 'if she respects him and talks to him, then the husband will go back to work in a good mood and think only about his work.' Volunteer work ('I check the consumer goods we get for the workers,' reported another working-wife activist) as well as raising a husband's cultural level were equally part of the package—selecting books, reading them to the husband-student, dragging him to the movies and the theatre after work, and quizzing the spouse afterwards about the contents of the evening, to make sure 'he had been paying attention' and did not fall asleep. Re-enacting the model of their upper-class tutors, Stakhanovites' wives also scolded other working-class women into emulating their example and 'encouraging' their men to work harder.[59]

The rise of the activist-housewives was not the only instance where the new begot the old to bear a weird present. A second intriguing example of the past becoming the new future is encapsulated in the strange history of the veil in Central Asia. The thick, full-body veil was not a widespread or very old fashion—it had become popular for elite urban women in the nineteenth century, as a way to distinguish their own morality from the infidel Slav colonizers with their shamelessly exposed faces. For largely symbolic reasons, the Bolsheviks decided that this veil should be the centre of a campaign of enlightenment—as ripping it off Muslim faces would expose them to the sun of reason and the fresh air of progress. The campaign, started in 1927, was spectacularly successful, but in the opposite direction from the one intended. As the Bolsheviks, perceived as they were as religious, social, and cultural outsiders, tried to enforce the modernization of local women by 'unveiling' them, they in fact popularized the veil as a new tradition as local society closed ranks against the intrusion by the godless city people.[60]

VI

The morphology of families changed not only in interaction with the policies of the revolutionary (or post-revolutionary) state and the adaptation of men and women of various classes to the phenomenon of massive social and geographic mobility. They also transmogrified in reaction to the drastically changed ratio between the sexes, the severe shortage of men created by the upheavals of wars, revolutions, and terror. In the Russian Empire of 1897, nearly half of the population (49.7 per cent) was male. By 1926, as a result of the First World War, a year of revolutionary upheaval in 1917, the Civil War of 1918–1921, followed by the famine of 1921–22, this share had declined to 48 per cent. By 1937, the Stalin Revolutions had reduced this figure further, to 47 per cent. Germany's war of extermination together with the often suicidal tactics of the Red Army caused the largest decline yet. If by mid-1941, maybe 48 per cent of the population of the Soviet Union was male, by early 1946, only 44 per cent was. The next thirteen years increased the share only slowly to 45 per cent but this recovery did little for the millions of women whose coevals had bled to death on the barbed wire outside of Moscow, in the trenches of Stalingrad, or the ruins of Berlin, if they had not died less spectacularly but equally effectively of dystrophy, typhus, or malnutrition on the home front. By 1959, twenty four million women between twenty and fifty-nine were without a spouse.[61]

In reaction to this changed environment, new forms of unions took shape. Serial monogamy was frequent as divorce rates remained high and men tended to remarry more frequently than women.[62] More spectacularly, polygamy was not uncommon, again mostly among men and not only in the Muslim regions of the country.[63] The 1937 census reported nearly 1.5 million more married women than men. This might be because some men were in relationships with women they did not consider their wives (while their partners did believe themselves to be married), but it might also indicate that many of these men had more than one long-term partner.[64] Among non-Muslim populations, women often did not know that their husband had several families at the same time and often enough these arrangements were rather unstable, particularly once they became known to the women involved. As the newspaper *Trud* reported in 1936:

> A. V. Malodetkin, a worker at Moscow Instruments Plant, in a short period made the acquaintance of three young female workers, Petrova, Orlova and Matina. He proposed marriage to each of them in turn, and, receiving their agreement, began affairs with them. They all considered themselves his wives, since they did not know of his cheating.... [In addition], it turned out that Malodetkin had married back home in his village.

This philanderer was sentenced 'for deception and insult to women' to two years imprisonment,[65] but not always was as much trickery involved. One former prisoner of war, who by the discrimination against his kind after the war was not allowed to settle back in his home region, lived with a widow and her son in his place of exile, while carrying on an open correspondence with his original wife and children to whom he hoped, eventually, to return.[66]

Given the growing scarcity of men, all-female families became more common. In one village studied by Soviet ethnographers in the 1950s, nearly 46 per cent of the households were headed by a woman.[67] Before the war and in the cities, this share was lower but still substantial—23 per cent in 1939, rising to 28 per cent in 1959.[68] Some of these women were mothers of children born out of wedlock, a practice encouraged by the 1944 family law, and entitled to welfare payments by the paternal state. In practice, many of these 'single mothers' were not in fact single, but, like many widows or abandoned wives, supported by their own mothers. A typical family of the time—and of the decades to come—was a mother as the chief breadwinner, 'one or two children, and the irreplaceable *babushka* (grandmother) who ran the household'. This core was often joined by other women, particularly sisters, cousins, or other kin.[69] Although much rarer, there were also rump families headed by men. One former peasant whose wife, father, and two youngest children had died in the 1932–33 famine took his surviving daughter to live with him in a workers' barracks.

> I just asked the manager of the barracks to give me a bed in the corner, so she slept in the upper bunk and I slept down. I hung a sheet up between the corner and the rest of the barracks.... They proposed sending her to a

childrens home…But it was terrible there.…I did not want to send her to a childrens home. She would have gone from one to another and all around. I did not want to part with my last child.

There was at least a second such father-daughter family in these barracks.[70]

Another adaptation to the changing environment was a reduction in the size of cohabiting families. In 1916, the average size of a Russian peasant household had been 5.7 souls. In 1928, this number had decreased to 5.1, reaching 4.4 in 1940 and 3.5 in 1945. Due to demobilization of the army this indicator grew back to 3.8 in 1948 only to then fall steadily to drop to 3.6 in 1954.[71] This decline was partially due to the persistent outmigration from the village, but it was also, in part, a result of complex patterns of separation and cohabitation which emerged in order to secure the best results from a situation set up to utterly exploit

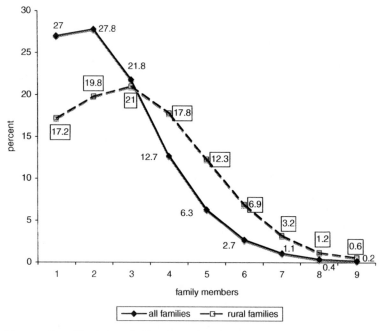

Figure 2 Size of family household, urban and rural, 1939
Source: Naselenie Rossii v XX veke, vol. 1: 188, 216

the peasantry. Collective farmers could profit from artificially separating the family into several households in order to maximize private garden space (which was allotted per household)—one of the reasons for the more dramatic decline in household size in the village. As an ethnographic study of a village of 1953 reported one such case, although the Soviet authors carefully avoided interpreting what they saw:

> A large family of a collective farm stableman…His mother-in-law, an old widow, has her own house and property and is considered to be an independent housekeeper. During the winter, though, she lives with her married daughter's family, looks after the house, and takes care of her grand-children. In the summer because of seasonal agricultural work she returns to her own house.[72]

Generally, as of the late 1930s, rural families nevertheless remained larger than their urban equivalent, as Figure 2 illustrates.

Urban households, while smaller than their rural equivalents, meanwhile did not change much in size, declining only slightly from 3.9 in 1926 to 3.5 in 1959.[73] The housing shortage as well as the need for the support from grandmothers and nannies worked against further reduction. Moreover, urban households seem to have become more family centred and more prominent as the focal point of the family's economic activity. Census figures imply that fewer and fewer household members were non-kin: the share of family members living in the average household increased between 1939 and 1959, while the number of kin living separately but on joint accounting decreased.[74] This 'familiarization' of the domestic sphere might have been an adaptation to the environment of terror, where too close connections to friends might prove highly dangerous. Family members, by contrast, were a liability anyway; moreover, they also might be trusted more than strangers, however friendly. Given that separate living was not much of an option because of the housing shortage, bunking down with blood relations was the next best option. Thus, in one of the many paradoxes of Stalinist society, anti-family violence and appalling living conditions strengthened rather than weakened the institution under stress. Whether or not Soviet citizens always felt secure and safe in their families, they certainly could not live without them.

CHAPTER 5
LIMPING BEHEMOTH

    66 In the Jewish eschatology—of Babylonian origin—Behemoth and Leviathan designate two...monsters of the Chaos. According to the apocalyptic writings, Behemoth and Leviathan will reappear shortly before the end of the world. They will establish a rule of terror—but will be destroyed by God. In other versions, Behemoth and Leviathan will fight each other incessantly, and finally will destroy each other. **99**

                                       Franz Neumann, 1944[1]

Like the family, gender inequality, or nationalism, the state was one of the annoyances which was supposed to 'wither away' as society marched towards Communism. Like these other pasts, however, it refused to do so. Instead, it did the exact opposite of what the revolutionaries had expected—it grew stronger, more repressive, more intrusive than it had ever been before. By the end of the Civil War, the Soviet bureaucracy was already ten times bigger than its Tsarist predecessor, and the growing Behemoth was staffed by 2.4 million officials, a number more than twice the size of the industrial working class, in whose name it allegedly ruled.[2] Asked to distinguish between 'Bolshevism' more broadly and 'Stalinism' in particular, most analysts would therefore stress 'the state' as a defining characteristic. Stalinism was that strain of Bolshevism which had emerged from the Civil War having abandoned the original hope that the state would 'wither away' once its 'objective base' was removed by revolutionary means. For this small, beleaguered but militant minority in a country of peasants, the apparatus of coercion and bureaucratic governance was, indeed, the only real source of power, support, and 'objective base'. Under Stalin's leadership, they put this apparatus to work to launch revolutions from above which, it was hoped, would overcome Russian backwardness and push the country towards socialism, whatever that might mean in practice.[3]

I

The Soviet state rose out of the ashes of war, revolution, and civil war.[4] Its central institutions developed step by step, to be slowly systematized into the dictatorship of the Bolshevik party and, eventually, first 'team Stalin' and then Stalin himself.[5] The Revolution of 1905 saw the emergence of two new institutions, which promised different types of democracy. On the one hand was the Duma, a pseudo-parliament, which for some represented the beginning of liberal democracy in Russia. On the other hand were the 'soviets', councils of worker deputies, which emerged in 1905 on the model of the Paris Commune of 1871. They pointed towards a different, more plebeian type of rule. As institutions they did not survive this first Russian Revolution but remained available as a model of insurrectionary organization, and thus quickly reappeared once conditions were right in the First World War. These two institutions would, slightly transformed, face each other throughout the revolutionary year of 1917, once the old authority of Tsarism had collapsed. After February, the Duma gave birth to the Provisional Government which tried to continue the war while guiding Russia towards a constitutional order; it was confronted with the increasingly muscular Petrograd Soviet, the epicentre of the Bolshevik party's strength. The stalemate was broken by Lenin's coup in October, which eliminated the Provisional Government and with it the historical alternative to revolutionary democracy. The path towards parliamentarism was effectively blocked.[6]

Instead of revolutionary, plebeian democracy focusing on the institution of the Soviets, however, Russia got civil war. Throughout the vicious campaigns of 1918–21 the Bolshevik party built its organizational reach through networks of underground fighters, who worked hard at taking control of the local and regional councils, sometimes founding them in the first place. Other revolutionary parties—the Socialist Revolutionaries and the Mensheviks, as well as anarchists—were either sidelined politically or defeated militarily. Lenin's men also took over the older bureaucracies, rather than destroying them and rebuilding a completely new administrative structure. At times they only added red paint to old institutions, but they also restructured what they found, breaking old ministries into more functional (and more technocratic) bodies. Now, technical experts (doctors, economists, statisticians, engineers) were often in charge of more specialized organs like the Commissariat of Health or the Supreme Council for the National Economy (VSNKh). While the Tsarist top administrators lost their jobs, the vast majority of these experts had been trained under the old regime and were, at best, of dubious loyalty towards the new rulers. It is here that we can find the origin of the peculiar system of the parallelism of Party and government: it was a means of controlling what, like the Soviets, had emerged or, like the ministries and the 'bourgeois specialists', survived outside Bolshevik oversight. By the end of the Civil War, the Soviets were in Bolshevik hands; at the top of the political system they had been subordinated to the Council of People's Commissars (Sovnarkom), which in turn oversaw the 'commissariats', as the Bolshevized ministries were called until 1946; and the formal destruction of alternative parties also proceeded apace.[7]

The authority to make decisions was increasingly centralized in the leadership of the Bolshevik Party, which in turn controlled the government. This takeover was a sliding process which started with the October 1917 coup. Originally, the central government (Sovnarkom) was responsible to the Central Executive Committee of Soviets (VTsIK), a body which stood at the top of a pyramid of councils, each electing the next higher body. At the bottom were the local and regional Soviets, once improvised expressions of 'revolutionary democracy', after October 1917 increasingly turned into Bolshevik organs to 'guide the masses'. They were largely confined to the cities, and sent delegates to the Congress of Soviets, which then elected VTsIK as its executive body. Formally, VTsIK controlled the government, but in practice Lenin soon made sure of emancipating himself from such checks. By the early 1920s, Sovnarkom was no longer held accountable to anyone but the Politburo of the Party. VTsIK still existed as a formal body, but it had lost most of its competencies and its bureaucratic apparatus had been subsumed into the commissariats. The local Soviets, which often had ceased to function as a result of the Civil War, were recreated 'from above' and functioned now as administrative bodies in the localities.[8]

At the top of the political system, then, initially three hierarchies converged—the government with Sovnarkom, the Bolshevik Party with its Politburo, and the Soviets with VTsIK. The latter hierarchy would increasingly wither while the Party-government duality overshadowed everything else, with power more and more centralized in the Politburo. When the Union of Soviet Socialist Republics reunited the revolutionary republics of the former Tsarist Empire after the end of the Civil War, the Sovnarkoms of the republics were kept as regional government and an all-Union Sovnarkom was created. Meanwhile, control over personnel decisions moved to the Party's new secretariat, with Stalin at its head. The institutional evolution of the Soviet political system thus put more and more weight on the Party and the Party-controlled government, a development acknowledged partially in the 1936 constitution. It abolished the old hierarchy of Soviets and replaced the Congress of Soviets with a directly elected Supreme Soviet, formally the legislature. The Party was defined as the *avant garde* of the working population and received the *de jure* right of controlling the candidates for the elections to the Supreme Soviet.[9]

The Party, too, became more and more centralized. Formally, the highest decision making body was the Party Congress, an institution, which grew from 106 members (VII Congress, 1918) to 1135 (X Congress, 1921) and on to 1669 (XV Congress, 1927), in the process transforming from a vigorous debating institution into an acclamatory mammoth. Real power moved upwards, via the Central Committee (CC), to the Politburo. The former, elected by the Congress, was originally meant to continue the business of the Congresses between their sessions. Like most institutions allowed to evolve on their own, it quickly grew, doubling its size from 23 members in 1918 to 46 in 1922. Its authority leaked to a smaller body, the Politburo, established in 1919, and intended, initially, to simply take decisions which could not be delayed until the next CC meeting. In the conditions of Civil War these were, of course, many, and soon the Politburo emancipated itself from its parent organization. Already in 1922 a delegate at the Eleventh Congress complained 'that the Politburo had escaped CC control to such an extent that it was often impossible to discover such elementary facts as the agenda of Politburo meetings'. More and more, backroom politics became the deciding factor in who would control the central Party line. Whoever won out in such struggles—and Stalin was particularly good at this kind of politicking—could declare his own faction to represent 'the central Party line', as opposition within the Party ('factions') had been outlawed at the Tenth Congress of 1921.[10]

This centralization of power in and within the Party was reinforced by the attention the leadership put on the development of the means of combat and repression. One arm of this new state apparatus was the Red Army, a conventional military force dependent on strict subordination and severe discipline, whose only 'revolutionary' aspects were the symbols on the soldiers' hats, the fact that officers were called 'commanders' and wore no insignia, and the institution of the military commissars— Party people who were supposed to keep the 'bourgeois specialists' of the old Tsarist officer corps in check. If the Red Army was the Bolshevik party's sword, then the Extraordinary Commission, or Cheka, was its shield. What would be renamed and reorganized frequently throughout the decades to follow—figuring under such feared acronyms as GPU, OGPU, NKVD, NKGB, MVD, MGB, SMERSh, or KGB—was one of the centres of the new state. The secret police apparatus, indeed, would become a mainstay of Stalin's power, and the arm with which he would strike at any potential foe in 1937 and 1938. Initially, the secret police were separate from the ordinary police forces, or *militsiia*, which had emerged out of volunteer militias during revolution and civil war, and which replaced the old Tsarist police as the guardian of law and order on the ground. Throughout the 1920s, this two-tiered system of regular and secret police was maintained, and only united at the beginning of the Stalinist decades, in 1930.[11]

The Bolshevik Behemoth was thus a curious mix of old and new, tempered by the experience of internal and external warfare. New were the dual structure of party and government, the Cheka and the militia as a regular police force; but much of the bureaucracy was taken over from Tsarism and 'slightly anointed with Soviet oil', as Lenin complained in 1922.[12] The major dispenser of the oil was the Bolshevik Party, which was inserted as a parallel structure into the governmental apparatus in order to keep the bureaucracy, staffed as it was by 'bourgeois specialists', under control. The Party, however, was never the centralized association of disciplined revolutionaries Lenin had dreamt about in 1901–02. His famous pamphlet *What Is To Be Done* was not a description of actuality but the daydream of an intellectual authoritarian longing to command others.[13] Lacking a coherent organization by the time of the Revolution, Lenin's men mobilized their personal friends and comrades from underground years to take over local administration and gather resources for the fight against political enemies. The years of the Civil War further bonded such cliques of regional 'committee-men' (*komitetchiki*)—the Stalin-team among them. As Bolshevik power consolidated itself, members of such networks of revolutionaries were co-opted into the central leadership, which allowed the Moscow rulers to control policy implementation through the personal networks thus radiating out from the capital. By the time the first revolution from above was launched, such personalism thus had become routinized to a significant degree: the only way to get things done was through personal networks and local strongmen; in order to achieve any progress, the centre thus had to further empower particularly well-connected individuals as 'plenipotentiary representatives of the central committee'; such *carte blanche* reinforced the authority of the cliques around these individuals.[14]

II

By the early 1930s, thus, Stalin's personal dictatorship was checked by several tenacious histories within the state itself: there was the old technical elite, the 'bourgeois specialists' within bureaucracies and the army, in education and industry, people who had been trained under the old regime and often had attachments to values inimical to Bolshevism; there was the history of the Party as an amalgamation of cliques of Civil

War veterans and underground fighters; there were the leftovers of the old party of intellectuals of pre-revolutionary vintage, the 'Old Bolsheviks' who had minds, politics, and connections of their own; and there was his own entourage, his 'team', which also needed careful handling. Over time, Stalin managed to knock each of them out of his way at least for a short time, streamlining the state in the process, concentrating power in his own hands and eliminating competing sources of authority.

Before the archives opened, historians sceptical of giving too much credence to an individual actor could still speculate that Stalin was simply the impersonation of larger social forces, the face, as it were, of the governing elite or ruling class.[15] However, with what we now know, such a view is harder and harder to maintain. Of course, Stalin did not act on his own, but was surrounded by his courtiers or, as he would have called them, 'comrades'. He was not an unlikely leader to them, however, and the story of the 1930s is not a tragedy, in which perfectly reasonable social democrats became afraid of their own shadows by forces of circumstance completely beyond their control. Bolsheviks were not Mensheviks and we should not be too surprised that a party which celebrated conspiracy, class war, revolutionary violence and 'toughness' ended up with a callous leader with paranoid tendencies. A small, radical and militant minority in power waging war on the majority of its population soon felt itself surrounded by enemies and their agents, growing frightened of this omnipresent conspiracy, which was all the more real since it was only partially a figment of the leaders' imagination.[16]

Stalin was central to this process of self-radicalization. He was a man clearly 'devious, deceitful, secretive, suspicious, treacherous, vindictive, totally manipulative in his relations with others and never happy unless *he* had the whip hand'.[17] He consistently thwarted plans for a more gradual pace in collectivization, and always pushed for the most extreme measures.[18] The Great Terror, which eliminated any potential opposition to the dictator, was also driven by Stalin at the top.[19] We do not need to delve into psychoanalysis or dissect Stalin's childhood to see that a different man, as Rudolf Schlesinger reportedly noted, could have sent Bukharin 'to teach in school in Omsk', rather than humiliate and murder him. Likewise, a different leader would not have prepared for war by killing large sections of the officer corps, or to push for ever harsher conditions in concentration camps.[20]

Meanwhile, the relationship between the dictator and his entourage as well as with the state-apparatus as a whole continued to change.[21] First, he was *primus inter pares* of 'team-Stalin'—a group relatively securely in power by 1929. During the initial revolution from above, this first among equals functioned somewhat like a prime minister, even if a comparison with Margaret Thatcher might be flattering to neither. Commanding respect and admiration akin to an 'authoritative "older brother"', he could not yet expect that his surrounding would obey his commands or even work towards him in anticipation of his likely wishes. Throughout the first half of the 1930s, Stalin had to labour to get his way, bullying, coaxing, flattering, and charming his retainers into line. There were setbacks, too. The upheaval of the First Five-Year Plan and the peasant war the Stalinists called 'collectivization' weakened whatever control they might have had over the country and increased resistance to the new course within the Party. The worsening international situation with the rise of National Socialism also suggested that internal relaxa-tion would be useful to gain support from liberal democracies. The result was a partial retreat in 1934 in order to consolidate whatever gains had been made—a partial and temporary suspension of the revolution from above.[22]

After the shock of Kirov's murder in 1934, Stalin pushed the leader-ship more and more into a return to militant policies, this time directed not against 'class enemies' in society at large, but against 'enemies of the people' within the Bolshevik ranks themselves. What this study calls the second revolution from above—generally known as the Great Terror—started with the execution of old comrades: Kamenev and Zinoviev in 1936, Piatakov, Bukharin and others in 1937 and 1938. It proceeded to draw in ever wider circles within the state and Party elite. After the blood-letting had swept through the officer corps in the first half of 1937 it moved outward, into the rest of society. In 1937 and 1938 the 'mass operations' exterminated or exiled hundreds of thousands of 'hostile elements' or what the security organs branded with this label. This second revolution from above was initiated and stopped by Stalin, who gained much from this upheaval. Now Stalin was really 'in power', his old associates terrified to death and a new group of loyal Stalinists promoted into the administration from the ranks of former workers and peasants. During the years 1938 to 1941, the Soviet system came closest to the model of 'totalitarianism' where the dictator rules over an otherwise fluid society, controlled by terror on the one hand and ideology on the other. Stalin now stood at the apex of both the government and the Party hierarchies, while formal procedures became less important, as the dictator could now ignore them with impunity.[23]

This period of 'high dictatorship' lasted until 1941, when Soviet society paid a bitter price for the over-centralization of its political system. The catastrophe of the first phase of the war with Germany was 'the ultimate proof of the failure of the Soviet system', as a recent account has it.[24] The enormity of the challenge forced Stalin to give up control to his deputies, who became semi-independent entrepreneurs with plenipotentiary powers. Indeed, it was this system of 'fully empowered representatives', rather than a centralized or regularized bureaucracy which explains the flexible adaptation to wartime circumstances. The institution of plenipotentiaries had been field tested in the Civil War and the first revolution from above, and now came into its own again during the state of exception of 1941–45. In practice, it meant considerable decentralization, despite the centralization of decision making at the top in the new State Defence Committee (GKO). Such loosening of oversight also extended to the central administrations, which were allowed to work more independently. This new freedom of action greatly enhanced their process of professionalization. Much control over the civilian economy was given up and devolved to lower and lower levels—to the regions at least, mostly as far down as enterprises and factories on the one hand and families and households on the other. That after the war much of this decentralization was undone and Stalin's henchmen again put on notice, did not signal a complete return to the totalitarian dictatorship of the pre-war years. Tired from old age and the exertions of the war years Stalin meddled less in domestic politics and focused on his new role as chief foreign policymaker and philosopher-king, who intervened into major intellectual, artistic, and academic discussions. The wartime learning curve of administrators on all levels and the new disinterest of

Stalin towards their work led to a political system that one historian has termed 'neo-patrimonial'—a combination of a dictator treating the country as his personal property whenever he wished, with the routine operations of a relatively modern, 'Weberian', bureaucracy, functioning on its own unless interrupted by the leader's erratic moods.[25]

In a perverse way, the Great Terror was essential in initiating this shift towards a bureaucratic system of centralized government. The Terror destroyed the local networks, which had underpinned Bolshevik rule ever since the Revolution; it eliminated the power of the Civil War veterans in the localities and replaced them by newly trained cadres. The old 'Red Directors'—revolutionaries who had become managers 'only by the accident of history'—were now gone, many of them indeed dead. They were replaced by very different men, technocrats who had been trained in Soviet schools, technical colleges, and universities and who were revolutionaries in name only. The old conflicts between Red Directors and 'bourgeois' engineers, too, disappeared: after the terror, officials in central administrations and those in the enterprises were, by and large, people of similar background. Once central control was lifted as a result of the war, these Stalinist managers could, for the first time, work relatively unsupervised from the centre. The greater authority they were now forced to wield further advanced their professionalization and opened space for a systematization of governance. Without the terror, the wartime weakening of central authority would simply have reasserted the power of the old networks; given the terror, it only expanded the reach of Stalin's governmental apparatus, without reigning in his personal dictatorship.[26]

III

If Stalin's position thus kept changing—from first among equals, to feared totalitarian dictator, to neo-patrimonial overlord—and the state's structure continued to evolve, there were many aspects which continued relatively unchanged or transmogrified only in their details. Many of these continuing features were not intentional facets of state power but rather systemic effects of a dictatorship which attempted to yank old Russia into modernity, cost it what it may. Despite Stalin's attempt to terrorize even those closest to him, the political elite remained remarkably stable after the Great Terror—and the more so the closer we move to the dictator himself. At the top of the political system, the Politburo had been decimated by the purges by less than half—a relatively low attrition rate if compared to other state institutions. Second-tier leaders were victimized more frequently, while most of Stalin's most prominent retainers were spared. Those of the despot's closest associates who survived the years 1937 and 1938 were allowed to live out their lives to their natural ends. 'The Soviet political elite', writes one specialist on the subject, 'had never had greater security of tenure than they had under Stalin at the height of his power'.[27]

Under-government was another constant—a continuing disconnect between the tools at the administrators' disposal and the tasks the existing structures were expected to perform. Much of the upheaval, the excess deaths, and the predilection to run everything as a voluntaristic 'campaign' can be explained by this disjuncture between means and ends. If we break down the Soviet Behemoth into its constituting parts—the Bolshevik Party, the government apparatus, and the police—we see the same problem in each of them. The government apparatus was supposed to run a planned economy, but did so only on paper.[28] Some officials did not even have that much. In 1933, Siberian bureaucrats scribbled their budgets on birch bark.[29] Notaries and judges were so poorly educated that they 'could not be expected to make "legal" decisions'.[30] Despite its size, the OGPU was seriously understaffed, given that it was meant to keep society in its grip. In 1924, more than one in five secret police personnel served in and around the capital, 'and a significant percentage of the remainder was in Leningrad and Ukraine'.[31] At around the same time an average of one policeman served five village administrations.[32] Change was slow. In 1930, the regular force was still four times smaller than its equivalent in 1913, and most of these thinly spread officers served in the cities. Early in the decade, rural coppers had no automobiles and horses were also in short supply. By and large, the guardians of law and order were reduced to walking.[33] Even the secret police was understaffed. In late 1930, the Urals Regional Committee ordered its district counterparts to not send chekists on tours of duty into villages, in order to avoid over-stretch: 'Bearing in mind the disadvantages of OGPU operatives, their extreme overload of basic duties...sending OGPU operatives on campaigns to the village at the expense of their basic duties is to cease forthwith.'[34] In August 1931, the West Siberian OGPU complained in a long report about the impossibility of fighting brigandage in the Siberian hinterland, which remained, essentially, non-policed. The report noted the 'weakness, indeed the total absence, of Soviet power' in these areas. In fact, in 1932 there were only 2,200 policemen in the entire Western Siberia, plus some 2,000 plain-cloth agents of the political police. Mob violence, rather than state power, enforced law and order in this region.[35]

This basic situation changed only in degree throughout the following decades.[36] We have already seen in earlier chapters that it was perfectly possible to escape repression during the Great Terror by simply packing up and leaving, sometimes by simply walking to the next village, or sleeping away from home.[37] And these instances took place after several reforms attempted to strengthened the powers of repression. In 1930, the regular police (or 'militia') was unified with the secret police (or OGPU) in the middle of the upheaval of collectivization and the First Five-Year Plan. The result was the opposite from the intention, decreasing the ability of the security organs to organize policing work. The regular police in particular continued to suffer from understaffing, underfunding, lack of firearms, uniforms, or automobiles, poor training, slack discipline, drunkenness, nepotism, brutality, and at times extremely high turnover of personnel. In 1934, the political and regular police, as well as border guards, fire departments, foreign intelligence, and even the highway patrol were united in a newly created union level Commissariat of Internal Affairs, or NKVD. This centralization of police powers was sold as part of a normalization of the security apparatus: instead of extra-legal violence of the OGPU there would now be routinized and regularized policing according to clear legal rules. In actuality, however, this reorganization 'consolidated under a single administrative framework every coercive organ in the state, except the Red Army'.[38]

The continuing efforts at expansion of the force and centralization of its work bore some fruits. The total number of police grew from 87,000 in 1930 to 182,000 in 1938 and on to 213,439 in 1940. While exact implementation of central directives remained a problem, by 1937 central police officials could reasonably expect 'that local police would carry out central directives more or less within the parameters set by the center'. The police thus reached a level of institutional development at the eve of the Great Purges, which other arms of the state system only approached in the post-war years. Nevertheless, police control was still far from perfect. By the middle of the pre-war decade, the increased police numbers were still only half of what they had been at the end of Tsarism. What one historian calls 'regularized policing methods' continued to be beyond the ability of Stalin's coppers and 'citizen vigilante groups continued to grow' in the void.[39]

Despite all efforts at tightly policing the country it thus continued to be possible to escape repression and hide under assumed identities. The internal passport system was subverted constantly. Documents could be forged relatively easily and such falsifications continued to be available throughout the period. People managed to hide for prolonged periods of time. One 'kulak' remained underground from 1932 to 1937 when, after he read the Stalin constitution, he returned to his village and demanded his house back. (He argued his case so forcefully to the local authorities, that his property was indeed returned to him and the new owner evicted!) Even high-profile suspects could disappear and cause the all-powerful secret police massive headaches. In 1938, the Ukrainian Commissar of Internal Affairs, Alexander Uspensky, saw the writing on the wall and tried to escape his imminent arrest as the next victim of the Great Purges. Despite great efforts of the NKVD to find him, he managed to remain hidden in the comparatively well-policed cities of the empire for five months.[40]

The war only exacerbated this situation, as documents were lost, burnt, or captured by the enemy and the fog of war allowed many to change their stories at least temporarily. Con men, long accustomed to fooling gullible provincial bureaucrats, now dared to target central administrators instead; the authorities were unable to track down servicemen who had abandoned their families and shirked their child-support payments; and the police more than once had to wonder if an escaped hoodwinker was 'only a con man or a spy'. Because the security forces were unable to live up to the image of totalitarian control they themselves projected, tricksters surveying the Soviet landscape saw 'an expansive frontier of possibility' rather than 'threats, prescriptions, and constraints'. The impotent guardians of law and order, in turn, soon adopted the heavy-handed methods of mass checking of passports and deporting anybody from the cities who did not hold a valid (or apparently valid) document. Such 'cleansing' of urban areas from undesirables first emerged when internal passports were introduced in 1932, became 'the basic method of Soviet policing' by 1935, was radicalized during the mass shooting-operations of the Great Terror in 1937 and 1938, reappeared in less brutal form in the post-war years and indeed would remain a favourite tool of population control far into the post-Soviet years.[41]

The Party, like the police, was concentrated in the cities. In 1928, one in every ten urban workers and one in every 25 urban inhabitants more generally was a Party member, while there was only one Party member per every 125 peasant households. Those Party organizations which did exist in rural areas, were isolated in a hostile peasant environment. During the collectivization campaign more than one in three district Party organizations in the North Caucasus 'had no direct telephone or telegraph connection to the regional capital in Rostov', and the situation in Western Siberia or Kazakhstan was similar. The central government knew well, in 1930, that it was 'incapable of knowing whether local organizations were even aware of its decisions, let alone fulfilling them'. The problem was paralleled in the rural state apparatus. We can take communication as an index of the state's penetration of the countryside. As a rule, there were no phone connections to collective farms. Only two out of three rural Soviets (which would administer between three and ten collectives and about 2,000 inhabitants) could be reached by phone by their next higher level, the raion, in the mid-1930s. Only four in five raions, in turn, could be reached by the regional (*oblast*) administration. Often, even those connections broke down, as phone lines worked notoriously poorly.[42]

The hold over the countryside thus remained tenuous at best. As late as 1938, in the middle of the 'mass operations', the NKVD complained that the 'attack on anti-Soviet elements' was only effective in rural areas close to bases of security forces, while in more remote regions their 'repression was patently insufficient'. Rural councils (*sel'sovety*) were poorly organized, struggled with abysmal remuneration of frequently inebriated officials and a very high level of staff turnover.[43] Chairmen of these bodies often stood with one foot in jail, as they needed to break laws left and right in order to fulfil plan figures. This situation did not increase their morale. 'I will only bring up the fact,' wrote one rural chairman in late 1933,

> that out of eight rural soviet chairmen working in 1932, four were given sentences of two to three years for misappropriation, theft, and embezzlement.... I always ask myself if in the end I'll be tried.... You're between the devil and the deep blue sea. If you add taxes, you're violating revolutionary legality, and you're put on trial. And if you don't fulfill the raion's assignments, you're tried all the same, and besides that you'll be shamed and so forth.[44]

The vast majority of administrative personnel working outside the capital continued to be, moreover, extremely poorly trained. In 1953 Kazakhstan, for example, 91 per cent of district planning commission chairmen and 87 per cent of senior economists had not benefited from higher education. The rural underdevelopment, however, was only the extreme end of a more general problem. Even in cities the Party 'was astoundingly disorganized at every level' by 1936.[45]

Attempts to increase the Party's grip on society by expanding membership were again and again undermined by suspicion of 'self-seekers' and 'enemies' finding their way into the proletariat's vanguard. First, membership expanded: from 1.5 million Communists (i.e. full members and candidates) in 1929 to 3.5 in 1933, but a series of attempts to 'cleanse' the Party from 'foreign elements' reduced this number. By 1936 only 2.1 million were left, a figure which further fell during the Great Terror to reach 1.9 million in 1937. After this blood-letting, the Party again grew, reaching 3.8 million in 1941 and 5.8 million in 1945. Despite a smaller post-war purge of 'unworthy elements' the general trend was towards more stable growth after the war. In 1947 the Party tallied 6.1 million, reaching 6.9 million by 1953. This augmentation of Party membership was paralleled by a growth of the administrative apparatus. Rural regions saw an immense increase in the number of higher bureaucrats at a time when the population declined to 91 per cent of its 1926 level (see Table 4). However, this still meant that by 1937 less than half of the bureaucratic personnel worked in rural regions, which at the time still contained

68 per cent of the population. It was not until the post-war years that the growth and professionalization of the administrative apparatus had evolved to an extent that the centre could expect to find its orders implemented on the ground.[46]

Administrators on all levels thus had to find ways to cope with the institutional underdevelopment of the system of which they were a part. Officials tried to compensate with exhausting work schedules that wrecked their health. At the top of the political system, the effects of overwork were further exacerbated by the dictator's habit of working at night and sleeping in the morning, which forced not only his entourage, but also the top administrators to stay in their offices until comrade Stalin had gone to bed.[47] But overwork alone could not make up for lacking routinization of administration. In order to get things done, one had to find people one could rely on: patrons and clients, friends and comrades. Only personal connections could produce results. The cliquishness of the Party and the state greatly annoyed Stalin, as it limited his own power and control, but also undermined attempts to put both on a more rational footing. 'So-called acquaintances and personal friends,' he griped in *Pravda* in 1937,

> are selected regardless of their suitability from a political or practical standpoint. It is not difficult to understand that such family circles allow no place for criticism of shortcomings in performance. Such family circles create a favorable environment for raising toadies. In selecting cadres for their personal devotion, these comrades evidently want to create conditions which make them independent from the locality as well as from the center.[48]

One of the aspects of the Great Terror was an attempt to break up such networks, indeed destroy them once and for all. As far as the old networks

Table 4 Number of higher-level administrators

	1926 (thousands)	1937 (thousands)	1937 in % of 1926
Rural regions	93	636	684
Towns	218	677	311
Total	311	1313	422

Source: Zhiromskaia, *Polveka pod grifom "sekretno"*, 82.

of Civil War veterans in the localities as well as those radiating from his inner circle outwards are concerned, this was initially a successful venture.[49] Yet because the conditions continued to exist which made personal connections essential, networks soon reappeared—they were simply a systemic feature of living in an economy of scarcity and an underdeveloped government structure.[50] Indeed, the very functioning of the system depended on them. 'The weakness of the formal rules designed to structure political life,' writes one specialist, 'meant that the most important channels of political intercourse were personal. Bonds of friendship, political alliance or support became the main currency of political life.' It was personal relationships which served as 'the major sinews binding the system together'.[51]

Local cliques also created another persistent problem: a chronic knowledge deficit in the central state. Practically all information moving through the official hierarchy was 'heavily censored and distorted by officials too frightened to tell the truth'.[52] What one official from a local planning commission noted for the economic sphere was true for the Soviet system as a whole: 'We knew that enterprises rarely do not lie'.[53] Simply put, the central administration never really knew what happened on lower levels. Under Stalin's dictatorship, the Soviet state was basically blind, despite the attempts to overcome this disability by a variety of means—sending plenipotantiaries into the regions to find out the true state of affairs, creating ever growing networks of informers to encourage information flow outside the corrupted official hierarchies, and encouraging letters of complaints and denunciations to obtain 'signals from below'.[54] Research in Soviet archives can give historians a very good sense of this information deficit—the researcher can spend days reading ever similar sounding, completely formulaic reports, until suddenly some scandal, a letter of complaint, or an investigation from the centre opens up vistas onto a world otherwise hidden.

IV

We cannot understand the spread of terror outwards from the Party in 1937 and 1938 without admitting this normalized 'blindness' of the Soviet state, connected as it was with sudden, fleeting moments of vision. The mass operations under order No. 00447 were a reaction to a moment when much of the tenacious histories continuing under the surface of standardized reports became suddenly starkly apparent. The strength of two groups in particular was unnerving to Stalin and his entourage—religious believers and former 'kulaks'. Both became visible as a result of the public discussion and subsequent institutionalization of the Stalin Constitution.

The new constitution, adopted after a five-month public discussion on 5 December 1936, could rightly be celebrated as 'the most democratic in the world' (alas, as more than one historian has pointed out, its words had only little relation to actuality). Rather than disenfranchising the old 'exploiting classes' and weighing the vote in favour of the urban working class, as the Constitution of the Russian Republic of 1918 had done, the new constitution gave equal rights to all citizens. The logic behind this shift was the perception that the revolution from above had been successful, capitalism, the bourgeoisie, and the kulaks had been liquidated and socialism reached.[55] A second major change concerned religion. Article 124 promised freedom of conscience and religious practice, article 125 the freedom of expression, the press, and assembly, and article 135 gave all citizens the right to vote, independent of their religious affiliation.[56] How, then, did kulaks and religious believers become targets of the terror only half a year after the proclamation that they were now full citizens free to express themselves?

One way to read this sequence of events is that the Stalinist leadership had assumed, optimistically, that the revolution from above had rooted out religious organization along with the exploiting classes.[57] Religiosity and religious organization, bereft of their 'objective base' in the 'means of production', were assumed to have been defeated, which made active repression unnecessary. In internal discussions about the constitution, Stalin claimed that the 'situation and alignment of forces in our country at the moment is such that we can [only] win politically' by establishing secret ballots in future elections—a dangerous proposal if he did not believe that the majority of the population was now fully on his side.[58]

Popular reactions to the new basic law were thus unexpected. To the nervous hilarity of the Central Committee Plenum, several religious communities in Ukraine passed resolutions thanking Comrade Stalin for the constitution, while peasants citing the new freedom of religion had demanded permission from confused local authorities to organize processions (*krestnye khody*). In Kazakhstan, new mosques opened without authorization by the state and the 'agitation' of the 'mullahs' led to mass pilgrimages to old and famous religious sites. The 1937 census further revealed the dynamic and resilient world hidden under propaganda images of happy peasants in love with Bolshevism and statistical reports about the fulfilment and over-fulfilment of production norms. The destruction of religious institutions during the first revolution from above had not eliminated religiosity—the practices and beliefs, which continued to suffuse the lives of the majority of the population. As census takers slogged through the snow to reach even the most distant rustic, these city boys and girls were shocked to encounter 'simply savage people ... exceptionally hostile minded religious types, who harbor a horrible hatred towards Soviet power'.[59] The statistical results were disturbing, too. 57 per cent of the population (16 years and older) proclaimed themselves to be 'believers'.[60] No wonder Stalin had the census suppressed and the census takers executed.

The sudden visibility of religion as a result of the Stalin constitution and the 1937 census showed in stark colours that the anti-religious campaign during the first revolution from above had been a complete failure. The destruction of religious institutions had not eliminated religiosity and the 'agents of obscurantism' had merely been forced underground. In the context of the ongoing blood purges, where the political liquidation of enemies within the Party had been replaced by their physical extermination, and within an increasingly threatening international context, it only made sense to use similar methods on these hostile and apparently incorrigible 'savages'. According to official statistics, in 1937 and 1938 the NKVD arrested 50,769 church-followers and 'sectarians'. Maybe 80 per cent of the arrested clergy were shot. The physical annihilation of religious leaders was thus, on one level, a mere radicalization of means; it was an attempt to once and for all 'solve' the 'problem' of religion in Soviet society.[61]

One can trace a similar prehistory for another major category of victims of the 'mass operations' of 1937 and 1938: former kulaks.[62] Exiles (*trudposelentsy*) read the constitution as allowing them to leave their places of banishment and return home. Many did not wait for the expected passports, but simply ran away, trying to return home on their own steam. When they arrived in their places of origin, they demanded their former property back. As this property had been redistributed, and the houses had often been transformed into parts of the farm administration, such demands caused strain and instability in the countryside, particularly if they were successful.[63] Runaway exiles suddenly returned to pick up their expected passports or appeared at NKVD offices to demand these documents. Worse still, many 'special settlers' also planned retribution against the closest allies of Bolshevik rule in the village:

> The new Constitution gave all special settlers (*trudnoselentsy*) the exactly same rights as all citizens of the USSR. In a couple of days, we'll all go home. At home we'll make short work, first of all, of those activists who dekulakized and exiled us. And then we'll go to such [far away] places, where they cannot find us. We have suffered at their hands, now [it's time] for them to have a taste of us.[64]

It became increasingly clear that it was hard to keep former kulaks in their places of exile and that hundreds of thousands were on the run, hiding under assumed identities throughout the Soviet Union.[65] As in the case of religious leaders, the publication of the draft constitution released the hidden energies and aspirations of this group. Many were deeply hostile to Soviet power. During a meeting to discuss the projected basic law, to cite a particularly glaring example, one peasant proposed to add the right 'of the existence of fascist parties'.[66] From the perspective of the political leadership, the sudden reappearance of defeated 'enemies' must have been unnerving, as it showed how tenuous the victory in the revolution from above had been. The plan to hold contested, multi-candidate elections (a plan made public in July 1937 and only abandoned quietly in October) now seemed particularly dangerous. The tenaciousness of the group of 'runaway kulaks' (*beglye kulaki*) and the littering of the population with 'anti-Soviet elements' seemed to call for more final solutions to this 'problem'. Under Stalin's leadership, they were soon found, producing the largest number of corpses of the Great Terror.[67]

If the sudden insight into the reality on the ground thus helps explain why the terror spread from a small group of Stalin's personal enemies to the population at large, the increased visibility of local cliques does the same for its spread throughout the political system. Once the police started investigating local situations, they invariably found very strong 'family circles' who had lied to the centre for years and often engaged in all kinds of illegal practices necessary to fulfil the plan either in reality or, more often than not, on paper. These looked like conspiracies, because they were, in a sense, just that: not in the sinister meaning of enemies of the people having wormed their way into the Soviet state (as Stalin would have it) but in the sense of corruption, nepotism, and arbitrary rule of by necessity closely knit groups suspicious towards outsiders.[68]

Much of the Great Terror, thus, was an extreme reaction to several moments of clear vision about how life really was in the land of Socialism—for the leadership a shocking insight into its own isolation and lack of popular support. After the Terror, it seems that the Stalinists again settled down into wishful thinking, which explains why the considerable privatization of Soviet agriculture remained a secret. Stalin, like many an executive in large corporations, trusted the aggregate statistics on agricultural labour more than reports of lower-level officials with intimate local knowledge. When, in May 1939, on the Central Committee plenum he was confronted with reports about the real state of affairs, he refused to believe them, quoting his tabulations instead.[69] The dictator, who according to Khrushchev took movies about the happy life in the countryside as accurate representation of Soviet agriculture, was quite literally 'seeing like a state'.[70]

The tool of his vision, however, became, if not more accurate, then increasingly focused. The professionalization of the apparatus of coercion in particular made outright terror less and less of a necessity. After some relapses during the first, chaotic phase of the war with Germany, a 'normalization' of repressive practice thus became an option. These much less spectacular techniques relied on policing and the judicial system rather than extra-legal and lethal violence. The effects were, however, significant, in particular of the post-war theft laws as well as the incredibly punitive workplace regulations from 1940 onwards, which victimized many more people than the more spectacular repressions of the pre-war years.[71]

V

The Soviet state under Stalin, then, was a limping Behemoth—a frightening monster, strong enough to destroy, uproot, displace, but too weak to build, nurture, or develop.[72] It was this very weakness, so ill-connected to the grandiose claims at total reconstruction of humanity and society, which enhanced the brutality of the regime. A strong state does not require exemplary violence—the very definition of 'power' is the ability to make people do what you will.[73] Where such a chance of cooperation is evenly distributed throughout the population, overt coercion is unnecessary. Where it is not, naked violence takes its place. 'Repression signifies that the mechanisms powerful states use to make citizens do what they do not want to do (such as work sixty-hour weeks, live exiled from their families, say things they do not believe) are not properly functioning,' writes a student of the colonization of the western borderlands, wittingly comparing them to her own society, the United States. 'Stalinist violence in the thirties exposes an ineffectual state desperately trying to maintain power by last-ditch efforts—threats, coercion, and violence.'[74] A lesser leader would have balked at the task and tried to reach more realistic goals, maybe by more consensual means. It required a man of the brutality, callousness, and paranoia of Stalin to force along the social transformation that actually happened in the Soviet Union. In this sense only, Stalin was 'really necessary'—not in order to prepare the Soviet Union for war, but in order to prepare it in the bloody and inhumane manner which took place in reality.[75] 'Stalinism' is thus an accurate term for the rampage of the limping Behemoth in the 1930s in particular. While getting less lethal and shifting from extermination to detention in the 1940s and early 1950s, this state was still 'Stalinist', as the dictator prevented further normalization, and continued to keep his associates on the edge of their seats by arresting some of them—or their family members—once in a while. The outrage of the beginning pogrom against Jewish doctors at the end of Stalin's life also required the dictator's helping hand.[76]

Stalin, of course, did not rule on his own. Even the most despotic dictator requires more than violence to stay in power. At the very least, he needs to keep the loyalty of his closest allies. After all, he needs somebody to administer the repression on which a tyrant's power seems to be based. In order to do so, he needs to establish that his rule is legitimate. In theory, he can do this in three ways—by appeal to the legality of his dominance (rational rule); by pointing towards that which has always been the case (traditional rule); or by claiming the status of an outstanding personality, a saint or hero (charismatic rule). Stalin's domination of the political system started as the final kind but soon transformed into a new type, which Hannah Arendt has called 'totalitarian'. At first, Stalin's position within the ruling circle was indeed based on persuasion and charm. During the years 1928 to approximately 1934, his henchmen frequently threatened to resign if Stalin bullied them. Stalin then had to apologize and persuade them to keep working. It seems that he was quite good at playing people, getting them to do what he wanted—the very definition of a powerful man. In this early phase of Stalinism we thus see this mysterious phenomenon—charisma—in action. The common interest of the group in building its power against the older Bolsheviks also played its part, and was further enhanced by seniority. Stalin was a master in exploiting the services of the young and ambitious. They were loyal to him as clients to a powerful patron, but also as trusted junior partners promoted to clear up the mess of their incompetent seniors. They were also, partially as a result of all these processes, partially because of Stalin's personality and skilful manipulation, enthralled by his charisma: 'I was spellbound by the patience and sympathy for others that he showed at Politburo meetings in the mid thirties,' remembered the rising star Khurshchev, who was by no means singular with what his biographer diagnosed as a 'bad case of Stalin worship'.[77]

The Great Terror shifted the ground of Stalin's rule from charisma to fear. From the late 1930s onwards, the dictator's closest allies trembled in horror, as he was able to decide a person's fate in the whim of a moment. It became increasingly hard to counteract his power, because it was Stalin who controlled the security organs and who made sure to replace any police boss who seemed to become too self-reliant. The war brought a temporary and partial relapse into an older system of rule, as the Marshals—in particularly the singularly fearless and tough Zhukov— were given some leeway, if they survived the first, catastrophic phase of the war. After 1945, Stalin retreated from micro-managing government, which freed him to terrorize his henchmen and prevent them from ganging up on him.[78]

There was more at play, however, than only fear fuelled by outrageous acts of unpredictable violence and the insecurity and fluidity of the positions of the retainers. In ensuring the continued loyalty of Stalin's men to their overlord, something else was at work as well—a psychological mechanism less readily graspable, which indeed was a metamorphosis of the old charismatic spell. By the post-war years, the Stalinists themselves had fallen prey to the cult of personality around Stalin, which they had constructed in the 1930s to legitimize their rule.[79] They held Stalin in awe, they surely feared him, maybe hated him at times. But they were also caught in something akin to the Stockholm syndrome—the odd phenomenon that victims of kidnappings start to identify with the hostage-taker. Stalin's henchmen—their wives in prison, their friends executed as enemies, themselves increasingly under threat to go down the same route—loved him. They loved him in the way a child loves a strict, choleric, and violent father, or a battered wife loves an abusive husband—it is impossible to live with the brute, but how could you ever leave? The real emotional dependence of the despot's closest comrades on their father figure became clearest in the moment of Stalin's greatest weakness—the aftermath of the German attack in 1941. With the army in full-scale retreat everywhere and Stalin holing himself up at his dacha, the generals could have staged a coup; the civilian leadership could have ousted him. But nobody took the obvious steps. Instead, the top soldiers continued to stand to attention, even if sometimes with tears in their eyes. The civilian leaders, in their turn, did what they could to get their dreaded and beloved leader back. They simply could not conceive life without him.[80] Only the dictator's death finally broke the spell. Paralyzed by a stroke, left alone on the floor for long hours before anybody dared to enter the room, in pyjamas soiled by his own urine, surrounded by trembling doctors too scared to do anything, and equally mortified courtiers torn between elation and fear, his last words, uttered when he was first found, were incomprehensible, but memorable: *dzhhh, dzhh.*[81] It was the sound of a new era.

CHAPTER 6
APOCALYPSE, DIALECTICS, AND THE WEATHER

❝ It was not necessary to wash our brains—there was nothing else in them than Soviet ideology. ❞

Grigorii Chukhrai[1]

❝ Hitler will get rid of you Communists: long live Hitlerism, down with Communism! ❞

**Citizen Fomichev, engineer at Stalin
Automobile Plant, 1941[2]**

❝ You can't prove to me that the new constitution is democratic. After all, we don't have a place for other parties, which means no full democracy, no freedom, but in other countries freedom and democracy exist in reality. ❞

**Citizen Naumov challenging a lecturer
in a public meeting, 1937[3]**

❝ weather still fine and sunny with a mild north wind it was down to 28 Below in the morning. today was the first day of manure hauling from the stable out to the cabbage patch up the bridge. ❞

**Diary of Collective Farmer Ignat
Danilovich Frolov, 11 January 1937[4]**

I

We cannot fully understand the rampage of the limping Behemoth without exploring the world-view of those in power. There can no longer be much doubt that Stalin and his entourage were committed Marxists and thought of themselves as Leninists. These were not counter-revolutionaries who spoke one language in public and another one in private. The opening of the archives has shown quite clearly that they conversed in the peculiar idiom of Bolshevism among themselves and many of their policies can only be understood within the tradition of Leninism, rather than as those of Thermidorian reactionaries.[5] When Stalin told the Central Committee Plenum in July 1928 that there were only three ways to accumulate capital: plunder colonies, take up loans, or extract a 'tribute' from the peasantry; when he argued further that only the latter, what he termed 'internal accumulation', was available to the Soviet Union; when he continued that 'extraordinary measures must be viewed dialectically, because everything depends on the conditions of time and place'—he did not argue like a reactionary or a statist modernizer, but like a Marxist.[6] When, in 1931, he wrote to his deputy, Kaganovich, that the leadership should not forget 'for a minute...the fundamental interests of the revolution and socialist construction'; when he railed against functionaries who were 'captives of their bureaucracies'; when he dismissed 'the jackasses among the petty bourgeoisie and the philistines', he presented himself to his closest comrade as what he thought he was: a revolutionary.[7]

Even during the most brutal episodes of Stalin's era, many top-level Bolsheviks showed a devotion to the cause and its leader, which sometimes borders on the incredible. When Julia Piatnitskaia's husband of seventeen years, a high-ranking Communist, was arrested in 1937 and accused of planning terrorist acts against the state, his wife struggled with her trust in him and eventually convinced herself that he, indeed, was an enemy. 'Obviously,' she wrote in her diary, 'Piatnitsa never was a professional revolutionary, but a professional scoundrel—a spy or provocateur.'[8] When in 1936 another high-ranking official, Georgii Piatakov, learned of the arrest of his wife, he was likewise ready to fully accept the official reading that all those detained were guilty of conspiracy against the revolution. 'I read the confessions and classified letter,' he wrote to his friend and comrade Ordzhonikidze. 'I am outraged beyond belief. I am unbearably ashamed that such despicable things took place right under my own nose…After all, this is a triple or quadruple betrayal of me [by my wife].' To demonstrate that he did, indeed, mean it, he also offered to personally execute the treasonous spouse. Others turned their handgun on themselves once they saw the writing of their own arrest on the wall, but, like Beso Lominadze in 1935, left suicide notes stressing the depth of their belief in the Communist gospel:

> **In spite of my mistakes, I have devoted my entire adult life to the Communist cause, to the affairs of our party. I only regret that I didn't live to see a decisive struggle in the international arena.…**
>
> **I die fully believing in the victory of our cause.[9]**

To insist on the leadership's revolutionary credentials does not necessarily blame Marx for what happened in the Soviet Union in the 1930s and 1940s. Stalinism was not, as one historian has written, simply the 'absolute institutionalization of Marxism as an instrument of power'.[10] It was not the only legitimate child springing from Marx's brain. Historically, many paths lead from old Karl, and most end up in political movements or analytic traditions far removed from the Soviet 1930s, 1940s, and 1950s. While there is a logical line moving from Marx to Lenin and on to Stalin, as both the official reading and anti-Marxist critics had it, there are equally valid alternatives leading, for example, to what the Stalinists despised as 'social fascism'—the mainstream, reformist, and democratic labour movement which left its marks on many, if not all, industrialized societies. Nevertheless, one of these lines *did* lead to Bolshevism and on to Stalinism. Stalin's men were, among other things, disciples of the bearded prophet.[11]

Talking, thinking, writing, and dying in 'Bolshevik' did not make the leaders into automatons remote-controlled by the iron logic of Marx's thought. Marxism has always been a multifaceted and complex ideology, which called not for rigid, timeless laws of human behaviour, or fixed moral imperatives, but for historically contextualized analysis. Political decisions had to conform to the 'historical moment' within the dialectical unfolding of history of which the actor-analyst was a part.

Leninism, and following it Stalinism, stood in this flexible tradition, and erred if anything on the side of tactical adjustability and thus action rather than on the side of dogma and reflection. There was 'dogmatic Marxism and creative Marxism', as Stalin admonished more theoretically consistent comrades already in 1917, when action mattered more than scholarship. 'I stand by the latter,' he clarified.[12] Rather than a blueprint for decision making, then, we might view Stalinist ideology as a style of thought, a tendency to see things in a peculiar light, a set of core assumptions making certain decisions more likely than others, a style deeply indebted to Bolshevism, or, more specifically, the Leninism of the Civil War years.

One aspect of this style was mistrust of spontaneity, decentralization, and market relations. This attitude again goes back to Marx, although it does not follow logically from his analysis of capitalism as a system. The bourgeois mode of production, as the great theorist called it in his magnus opus *Das Kapital*, depended on the exploitation of labour and the alienation of its products. It was work, real exertion of necessary energy to transform natural products into useful items, which added value. The trick of the capitalist owner of the means of production was to pay the labourer less than he (or indeed she) added, and thus to 'appropriate surplus value'. Nothing in this scheme logically condemns the market, the 'sphere of distribution', in Marx's terms, or those labouring in it. In fact, one could easily conceive of the work of traders as adding value to the product, as gathering information about what consumers want or need and organizing distribution does require exertion, thus labour, and thus adds value. However, the bohemian analyst, enthralled as he was with the romance of the lower classes, did not conceive of the market in this way, but inconsistently but not inconsequentially argued that nothing in the sphere of distribution added value save the efforts of transportation workers. Shopkeepers, forwarding and shipping agents, and other 'bourgeois' and 'petty bourgeois' types only further appropriated surplus value produced elsewhere.[13]

The alternative to the 'anarchy of the market' was rational distribution. A utopian novel, written by a Bolshevik after the failed revolution of 1905, described the future world of Communism as something of a space opera. A revolutionary is whisked away from Petersburg to Mars, where Communism already exists, and finds an 'Institute of Statistics' in charge of channeling the distribution of labour and goods. Detailed computations and accurate tracking of stockpiles and work hours allow each Martian to choose rationally where to work. As a result of such total knowledge and individual responsibility (not coercion or self-interest) 'equilibrium' is established 'by a stream of volunteers'. While the author, Alexander Bogdanov, fell into disfavour because he challenged Lenin for the leadership, his novel was wildly popular among rank and file Bolsheviks during the Revolution of 1917, was reprinted several times to circulate in hundreds of thousands of copies in the 1920s, and saw another renaissance during the first revolution from above, reportedly even influencing Stalin himself.[14] Technocratic fantasies such as these were reinforced during the First World War, when most warring nations, including Russia, did in fact experiment with central planning of production and distribution. Germany and Britain had introduced much more stringent economic controls than Russia, and many read this discrepancy as the reason for Russia's collapse. Such experiences and practical examples dovetailed well with Lenin's vaguely held ideas about a Marxist organization of society and led, during the period of the Civil War, to a first experiment with regimented distribution. When Stalin and his team looked for ways to cut through the Gordian knot of exchange relations between the city and the countryside in order to finance their revolution from above, they reached quite logically for these experiences and imaginaries.[15]

Market relations were not the only 'irrational' forces Bolsheviks were suspicious of. Their mistrust of spontaneity also extended to religion, or what Marx had famously called the 'opium of the people'.[16] Originally, this was not an unsympathetic position towards believers, as spirituality was 'the *expression* of real suffering and a protest against real suffering'. Taking religion as a sedative was 'the sigh of the oppressed creature'; it laid bare 'the heart of a heartless world and the soul of soulless conditions'.[17] Once conditions improved, i.e. once capitalism was abolished, religion was to wither away, the argument went. Not that any of this followed logically from the analysis of capitalism laid out in Marx's magnus opus. Why should non-alienated labour and socialism not go hand in hand with religion? In fact, the Russian experience suggested that they would. The most successful communal experiments after the Revolution were religious communes, run by a variety of non-orthodox groups.[18]

But Marxism was not a philosophy rationally deduced from first principles, let alone empirical realities. It was part of the radical tradition emanating from the French Revolution. In this original upheaval of the modern world, two conditions conspired to make religion into one of the major enemies of the revolutionaries. There was the general mistrust towards 'irrationality' these children of the Enlightenment brought with them and which predisposed them to deify rationality and abstraction rather than gods created in humanity's image. Secondly, the Catholic Church was one of the largest landowners and a secure part of the French establishment and thus quite naturally came under attack by those seeking radical change. Established religions responded in kind throughout the nineteenth century, usually taking side against the 'godless socialists'. By the time Russia descended into revolutionary upheaval by the early twentieth century, militant atheism was part of the repertoire of the revolutionaries and invested with emotionally entrenched meaning far beyond anything ideologically necessary or rationally expedient. Given their zeal, however, it was not illogical either. Marxism–Leninism aspired to 'the total explanation of the past, the total knowledge of the present, and the reliable prediction of the future'.[19] As such, it could not tolerate alternative cosmologies with similarly wide-ranging ambition. The belief in Marxist eschatology was supposed to be absolute for Party members and Komsomols in particular. A Communist, quite simply, could only be an atheist. Anything else was a sign of backwardness.[20]

Another central part of Marxist cosmology was the belief that society was made up of classes, and that political allegiance could be deduced from an individual's position within this system of stratification. Class, while quite marginal in the systemic analysis presented in *Kapital*, was at the centre of Marx's thought when polemicizing and calling for action. As the lines of the *Communist Manifesto* had it: 'The history of all hitherto existing society is the history of class struggles'.[21] Bolsheviks acted accordingly, mistrusting and often discriminating against 'former people' who had done well under the previous regime and promoting 'proletarians' and 'poor peasants' in their stead. The onslaught on 'bourgeois specialists' and the training of new, 'red' cadres from the working classes during Stalin's first revolution from above stood as much in this tradition as the brutal war against 'kulaks' in the same period or the execution of 'former kulaks' or religious leaders during the Great Terror. Such assumptions were not mere fantasy, either, but made some sense historically: during the revolutionary year of 1917, political allegiance, indeed, had been strongly structured by class position and it was also true that people who had been victimized by the new regime tended to hold grudges. The problem with this way of thinking was, on the one hand, that it tended to become a self-fulfilling prophecy (the assumption of enmity led to discrimination which bred resentment); on the other hand, given the highly fluid nature of Tsarist society at the end of its existence, it was only in exceptional cases that a person could be neatly classified in class terms. Too many had moved up, down, and sideways before 1917, and the upheaval of war, revolution, and civil war enhanced the irregularity, unevenness and complexity of individual as well as family biographies. Nor could Stalin's regime be much more confident than Lenin's in 1920 that workers were indeed loyal to it.[22]

As time went on, class became less pertinent as a tool to understand what was going on in Stalin's Soviet Union, and nationality instead rose in prominence. The period saw the revival of Great Russian nationalism as Soviet patriotism, which started to replace the internationalism of the interwar years. This shift could be dated back to Stalin's notion of 'Socialism in one country' of 1924, and it started to come to the fore in the mid-1930s, and was reinforced by victory in the Second World War, which was quickly dubbed 'the Great Patriotic War of the Soviet Union'. The history of nationalism is one of the intriguing stories of the rise of a category the original revolutionaries were quite hostile to, but which they inadvertently fostered. Originally, Bolsheviks—like most Marxists—were internationalists. Nationalism was yet another ruse invented by the capitalists to cloud the minds of the oppressed and veil their class rule behind the pretty words of love of country and tribe. Rather than confronting this enemy head on (as in the case of religion) a more tactical approach was chosen. Nationalisms were the great competitors for the loyalty of 'the masses' in the multiethnic empire that was Tsarist Russia. By fostering a 'socialist' kind of national consciousness, which was appropriate for the current state of unfolding historical forces, the patriotism of the not-yet conscious masses could be harnessed for the best of the revolution and snapped away from the forces of reaction. Such a tactic was made even more appropriate by the notion that nationalism might well be a necessary step in the dialectical unfolding of history—in order to get to socialism, one needed to pass through the national stage. The result was, of course, that a sense of national belonging was prescribed even to populations who did not possess it to begin with. Ascribed categories mattered, as they gave or prevented access to goods and services; consequently most Soviet citizens learned quickly that not only did they have a nationality, but this was also a good thing. In the 1930s, this generally benevolent approach to ethnic particularism showed its dark underbelly when affirmative action for non-Russian groups flipped over into ethnic cleansing of suspect nations, in particular from the borderlands, in preparation for war. At the same time, and for the same reason, the propaganda apparatus took on what the rulers considered more likely to mobilize the majority of the population behind the regime: Great Russian nationalism became a central aspect of official mobilization from the mid-1930s onwards, coming into its own during the Great Patriotic War never to leave the stage again.[23]

The reverse of pride in one's own nation is the hatred of others. The most virulent tradition of ethnic animosity was anti-Semitism, a feeling with a long and involved history. Some of the most dreadful pogroms of the nineteenth century had happened in the Russian Empire between 1881 and 1884. Anti-Jewish violence was as much part of worker behaviour at the turn of the century as were militant strikes, and frequently one spilled over into the other. The emancipation of Jews, as everywhere else, did nothing to soften such sentiment, and indeed the often visible success of the assimilated stoked the animosity of those who struggled to adjust to the modern world—'the assessor, the fraternity student, the petty bureaucrat, the pedantic schoolmaster, and the thick-skulled peasant', as one historian typified. In 1903–1906 these resentments exploded in a second wave of vicious Jew-bashing, and during the First World War pogroms returned and almost became the norm during the Civil War, when the Whites as well as peasant anarchists staged more violence against Jews and their property. Although Red Army units at times engaged in pogroms as well, the victorious Bolsheviks were the one major party of the Civil War which was expressly anti-anti-Semitic, a legacy which, for Jews, made the choice on which side to fight relatively straightforward.[24] The victory of Lenin's Party, however, only further confirmed anti-Semitic sentiment—the stereotype of the 'Jewish Bolshevik', which would become so influential in the Nazi view of the world, was circulating widely among the Soviet population. In the early 1920s Old Believers (one of the homegrown Christian sects) thought that Communism served 'Jewish interests' and routinely referred to regime supporters as Jews. The anti-Semitic pamphlet *Protocols of the Elders of Zion* (1905) circulated throughout the Soviet Union and among several religious groups, and by the end of the decade it was still read publicly in some Novgorod area villages. Anti-religious songs of Komsomols were countered with shouts of 'beat the *zhidy* [yids]', the Jewish background of high-profile Bolsheviks was a recurrent theme of popular conversation and church closures were commented upon with 'The yids are taking away the churches'.[25]

The onslaught on peasant society during Stalin's revolutions from above did nothing to soften such moods. A 1931 leaflet accused local officials of 'behaving like yids' before indulging in violent fantasies: 'Well we'll build a grave for you that'll fit so tight you can't turn round but first we'll burn the office down or blow it up[,] we'll give no quarter to the yids, we're not scared of you we'll cut your throats every one of you!'[26] Sectarians continued to believe that 'the "yids" were in power', which the NKVD construed as 'slanderous anti-Soviet sermons' worthy of execution in 1937.[27] The Great Terror thus might have exterminated anti-Semites, but it could not liquidate anti-Semitism, which resurfaced soon after the German attack. Already in 1941 the well-known racism of the Nazis—which before 1939 Soviet propaganda had stressed enough for widespread knowledge—was greeted with enthusiasm by some: 'Good, the war's begun—they'll kill the Jews'. Nor did those expressing these sentiments necessarily wait for the Germans to do the dirty work. Equating the elite with the Jews, Moscow mobs stopped cars attempting to flee the advancing *Wehrmacht*, pulled out the passengers and assaulted them with cries of 'beat the Jews'. The anger and resentment which broke forth in these incidents also found their expression in the wartime rumour of the 'Tashkent partisans', i.e. the proposition that Jews did not fight, but were hiding out far behind the front lines. This narrative gained currency swiftly after the German attack and would remain one of the staples of war and post-war popular misconceptions.[28] They were reinforced by the seepage of Nazi propaganda into Soviet society, the relative invisibility of Jewish heroism in Soviet media, and the visibility of evacuated Polish Shtetl-Jews, who had escaped the Holocaust to the east, in regions such as Western Siberia and Central Asia.[29] After the war, the anti-Cosmopolitanism campaign, which was not directed solely against Jews, but could easily be read that way, further stoked the fires of hatred.[30] Many who had moved into positions of authority since the 1920s brought their anti-Semitism with them, transforming the old party of anti-anti-Semites into one where anti-Jewish sentiment was widespread. From the war onward, opportunities for Jews rapidly decreased in the Party and in society as a whole.[31]

Nationalism and anti-Semitism are good examples for how ideology transformed to arrive at Stalinism from Bolshevik precedents. Such change was driven in part by necessary compromises with popular sentiment in an age of total war. In part, such attitudes also bubbled up from below, moving with the people who ascended from the peasantry and the working class into the elite under Stalin. Such variation has sometimes been seized upon by those who want to clearly separate the one from the other. However, such change was also completely consistent with a basic assumption of Leninism itself—that ideology had to be adjusted to real historical circumstance, a flexibility which true believers described as 'dialectics', and which had formed one of the reasons for Bolshevism's great success. It allowed the leadership to engage in the struggle, do what was necessary to win, and not worry too much about consistency, dogmatic purity, or even—peak of all 'petty-bourgeois' vices—morality. Already Lenin had assumed that the correct path was always the one which promised success: means and ends were not in harmony, but rather in a 'dialectical' relationship which meant that whatever helped the cause was 'historically necessary'. War would lead to peace, and Communism might be best reached by allowing private trade. The state would wither away once it was strengthened enough to enforce the dictatorship of the proletariat, and thus democracy. The delusion, or arrogance, that armed with the correct ideology, a superior intellect, and good organization, the revolutionary leader could see further than others and will the future into existence was also not foreign to the original leader of the Bolsheviks. Stalin was, in many ways, a faithful student of his migraine suffering mentor.

If dialectical elasticity with regards to means and policies was one central tenet of Stalinist style of thought, the tendency to see the world as riddled with enemy intrigue was another. Again, we can trace this attitude partially to Marxism more generally, which, in its popular variants, always found a cabal of capitalists intent on keeping the working class down behind anything from religion to war, from feminism to the welfare state. This attitude can be followed back to the great bearded prophet himself, when he was in one of his polemical moods, which established him as a politician, as opposed to his flights of highly abstract analysis, which built his reputation as a theorist. Organizing itself as a conspiracy already before the revolution and assuming that others functioned just as they did, the Bolsheviks, in turn, tended to see history not so much as 'the history of class struggle' but as a story of competing secret societies intent at grabbing world domination. This paranoia was only reinforced by the experience of the Civil War and was probably especially strong among Stalin's team, which had managed to get into power by conspiratorial means in the first place. But this world-view was also widespread among the Party faithful more generally, who lived, quite literally, in a universe of intrigue and, hence, anxiety.[32]

As in the case of class analysis, the assumption of hidden enemies everywhere was not merely fantastic, either—paranoiacs may have enemies, too. The Soviet Union was littered with people who had grudges against Bolshevism in general and Stalinism in particular; informal networks were a reality as well as necessity of everyday life on every level; and much of the outside world was bitterly hostile to the first socialist state. Ideology did not impose a completely inaccurate picture of society onto the brains of the Stalinist elite; what it did do was to flavour their analysis of the facts they encountered on the ground. The preponderance of conspiracy theory nudged those in power to read events around them as caused by malevolently organized groups rather than search for systemic reasons for their existence.

Internal and external threats were linked in the elite's view of the world. Commenting on the news that the Soviet diplomatic representative to Poland, P. L. Voikov, had been assassinated by a 'Russian monarchist', Stalin wrote to Molotov in 1927: 'One feels the hand of England [behind this murder].... They want to repeat Sarajevo [in 1914, which triggered the First World War].' Linking the domestic with the global, he ordered using imprisoned monarchists as 'hostages', immediately shoot 'five or ten' of them and declare that 'for every assassination attempt we will shoot new groups of monarchists'. Moreover, the OGPU should search, arrest and 'completely liquidate' groups of 'monarchists and all kinds of white-guards' who were, he claimed, hidden throughout the Soviet Union. 'Voikov's murder gives us a reason for the complete destruction of monarchist and white-guard cells in all parts of the Soviet Union. The task of strengthening our homefront demands this from us.'[33] A little later, on 17 July 1927, the leader returned to this theme. 'The course of terror taken by the agents of London changes the situation in its core. This is open preparation for war.' Therefore, the 'central task' for the leadership was now 'the cleansing and strengthening of the home-front'.[34]

That shortly after such repeated calls for mobilizing the rear Stalin launched his first revolution from above is more than just coincidence. The leader repeatedly stressed the connection with the threat of war. Defending 'extraordinary measures' in grain procurement in 1928, he argued that state grain reserves were central for defence, in order to avoid a two front war—'with the Poles at the front and the *muzhiks* [peasants] at the home-front'.[35] In a much quoted speech in 1931 he returned to the same theme, defending the frantic and destructive pace of his revolution by putting it into the context of the *longue durée* of Russian history, a story of 'continual beatings'. Russia, he said,

was beaten by the Mongol khans. She was beaten by the Turkish beys. She was beaten by the Swedish feudal lords. She was beaten by the Polish and Lithuanian gentry. She was beaten by the British and French capitalists. She was beaten by the Japanese barons. All beat her—because of her backwardness, because of her military backwardness, cultural backwardness, political backwardness, industrial backwardness, agricultural backwardness. They beat her because to do so was profitable and could be done with impunity....Such is the law of the exploiters—to beat the backward and the weak. It is the jungle law of capitalism.

Living in the wilderness, one had to sharpen the claws; surrounded by war mongering capitalists, the Soviet Union needed to prepare for total war, cost it what it may. The other option was annihilation by the imperialist enemy:

Do you want our socialist fatherland to be beaten and to lose its independence? If you do not want this, you must put an end to its backwardness in the shortest possible time and develop a genuine Bolshevik tempo in building up its socialist economy....

We are fifty or a hundred years behind the advanced countries. We must make good this distance in ten years. Either we do it, or we shall go under.[36]

Similarly, the Great Terror was quite literally understood as the purging of society from potential fifth columnists in preparation for the coming war. That there was little sign of organized resistance in 1937 did not matter, given the conviction that 'wreckers' (*vrediteli*) were hidden everywhere and were likely 'to do their spoiling work not in peace-time, but in the period immediately preceding war or during war itself', as Stalin told the Central Committee in 1937.[37] The shocking moments of clear vision in 1936 and 1937, discussed in Chapter 5, did their part in convincing the leadership that decisive measures were necessary. Looking back from the 1970s, Molotov, one of the great survivors, put it this way:

1937 was necessary. Bear in mind that after the Revolution we slashed right and left; we scored victories, but tattered enemies of various stripes survived, and as we were faced by the growing danger of fascist aggression, they might have united. Thanks to 1937 there was no fifth column in our country during the war.[38]

To the leaders, then, the apparently irrational blood-letting of 1937 and 1938 made perfect sense since they lived in a universe of conspiracy, total war, relentless competition, and millenarian expectation. The fight for utopia would be fierce, bloody, and tough. But Bolsheviks were hard men, and ready to do whatever it took to win the final battle.

II

That the leadership's actions were informed by its own ideology may not surprise. After all, many of these people had dedicated their lives to the Revolution often long before 1917 and in other instances during the Civil War, when it was far from clear who would eventually win. What about the rest of the population, however? We might return here to Grigorii Chukhrai, whose memoirs we explored in detail in the first chapter of this book. Ideology is at the very centre of this text. It is his commitment to, belief in, and devotion to the complex 'Socialism–Bolshevism–Stalinism', which forms the core message of Chukhrai's autobiography, his interpretation of his 'generation' and his polemic with the present. Stalinism, indeed, was more than just a terrorist police state ruling by fear alone. From the outset of their rule, the Bolsheviks invested considerable energy, intellect, and money into winning the hearts and minds, indeed the souls, of their subjects. They built an impressive propaganda apparatus, attempting to make their ideology inescapable and all-encompassing. Movies and festivals, posters and rituals, newspapers and music, novels and poetry attempted to saturate the universe of signs with Bolshevik iconography, symbolism, and ideas. The cultural, ideological, and discursive were central aspects of the reality of Stalinism.[39]

There is not one answer to the question of 'belief' in this rhetoric. What is clear is that most had to learn the language of Bolshevism, if only to get ahead in life. In particular in the cities, the factories and bureaucracies, this language was ubiquitous and was spoken increasingly fluently by more and more people.[40] Farmers started to name their cows 'Shock Worker', 'Steel', 'Freedom', or 'Construction Site', while mothers called their sons 'Atheist' and their daughters 'Stalina'.[41] But words were not enough and the learning process was considerably more involved than simply acquiring a new vocabulary. Stalinism was not graduate school, and just learning to converse in the latest jargon would not do. In order to speak properly, one needed to be able to perceive reality in a specific way, which was modelled by the best examples of literature and the arts. 'Socialist realism', the official doctrine for creative works since 1934, was more than just an aesthetic dogma. It was a way of seeing, of properly perceiving the world around oneself not as it was but as it would become beyond the horizon, once the 'final battle' the Internationale proclaimed was won and Communism built, or sometimes just over the next hill, at the end of the next plan period.

The trick was to describe the present 'through the prism of an imagined future', to see a Palace of Soviets where uninitiated only perceived a foundation pit filled with groundwater, where people, profanely, went skinny dipping and fishing for carp, which had mysteriously made the unplanned pond its habitat.[42]

Stalin himself saw and spoke in this vein when 'presenting his plans and his wishes as accomplished fact'. To talk back to the leader and point out the real state of affairs meant missing the point and demonstrating that one was not able to properly see Bolshevik, as such announcements were not meant to truthfully represent empirical fact but 'to encourage Party organizations and the other sectors of the administration to come into line with the "actual situation" as it allegedly existed "everywhere else"'.[43] Chukhrai looked at reality that way when he explained away all troubling phenomena as remnants of the seventeenth century which had nothing to do with his society's essence, its 'avant garde', which had already arrived in the future of the twenty-first.[44] Lev Kopelev, another true believer, also made sense in this manner of the Great Purges: 'Chasing away the depressing, frightening or disheartening doubts, I convinced myself and others that the main line was healthy, that all crimes and lies were inevitable, passing illesses of a society which was healthy overall.'[45] As one respondent of the Harvard Interview Project summarized this approach to reality: 'I thought, that all the difficulties were connected with the sacrifices which were necessary for the building of socialism and that after a socialist society was constructed, life would be better. That is what Stalin kept telling us.'[46]

The further one moved into the inner circles of the regime, the more important such fluency of speech and such clarity of vision became, an interaction between social position and ideological commitment that was further reinforced by true believers finding it easier to conform in the first place.[47] Ideological conformity was further smoothed by the social exclusivity of the elite's sphere. As citizens moved from the outer layers of the regime to its inner core, they tended to interact less and less with the regime's victims and, if they did so, the latter would be inclined to speak Bolshevik back to them. The enormous gap between the world the majority lived in and the discursive universe the decision makers, specialists, and intellectuals spun around their privileged lives in their apartments in Moscow, Leningrad, or Kiev was stabilized by this exclusivity. In the inner circles of power, beneficiaries spoke to each other in the vocabulary of official discourse, inadvertently convincing each other of the truth of their fantasies.

The extent of the gulf separating the top of Party and Government from ordinary folks can be gauged by the simple fact that the 1937 census was, after several delays, scheduled for 5 and 6 January. Nobody in this deeply atheist milieu seemed to remember that this date was the Orthodox Christmas, which meant, in the words of one historian, 'that the data collection coincided with a religious festival as well as the end of the customary drunken New Year celebrations'.[48] Those counted on these days responded with their own conspiracy theory. Tapping into a rather long memory of mass killings, such rumours warned that this timing was 'not accidental. Obviously, there will be a St. Bartholomew's Day massacre (*Varfolomeevskaia noch*)'.[49]

The corollary of the nested rings of radicalism, where members of one layer only spoke to similarly radical members surrounding them, was that the regime's many victims, excluded as they were from the discursive world of the movement's core, often reacted to their fate by bitterly embracing critical stances towards socialism, or at least *this* socialism. Leaflets posted during the night of 27 September 1937 in a village near Kiev, for example, proclaimed:

> **Long Live Trotsky!**
> **Long Live Hitler!**
> **Down with Communism—Give Us War!**
> **Peasants, demand Hitler in power—under him life will become better.**

The sheets were signed, 'in German' (as the NKVD put it), by 'Hitler'.[50] Hailing the enemy did not necessarily mean that those in opposition held clear views about alternatives to the Soviet system. Many in fact embraced 'the system' while rejecting 'the regime' (i.e. the particular persons in power).[51]

Others, however, did imagine alternatives. One Ukrainian war veteran, born in 1893, was sentenced to ten years imprisonment in 1952 because he had expressed a quite distinctly liberal world-view—he was hostile to collective farms, believed in the freedom of the word and the positive influence of self-interest and private property. He also knew that all of these existed in a country called 'Amerika'.[52] Similar ideas, which fashioned a counter utopia to Soviet reality drawing on an imaginary country somewhere beyond the borders, in a golden past of Tsarism, or during the 1920s New Economic Policy, were shared by other demobilized soldiers of younger generations, born in 1909 in one case and 1919 in another.[53] The trip abroad many citizens took during the war as well as new propaganda media of the Western powers available after its end made such views more common. However, they were not completely new either. Many people who were alive in the 1930s, after all, could remember a different order of things, be it late Tsarism or the NEP, and could and did tell their children about them. The consistent hostility of the majority of Soviet citizens towards the collective farm system in itself points to an alternative model of how society and the economy should be ordered—on the basis of peasant smallholding, private trade, and self-regulating family economies. Free speech and democratic elections were also mentioned as alternatives to a dictatorship cloaking itself in populist garb.[54] Not everybody was fooled by the official view of what was 'democratic', as citizen Naumov in one of the epigraphs to this chapter illustrates.

Most jarring to the authorities were those who seemed to embrace the official language to criticize not only individual policies, but also the regime itself. 'What right do these Bolsheviks have', wrote a schoolgirl in her diary in December 1934, 'to deal with the country and its people so cruelly and arbitrarily, to so brazenly proclaim outrageous laws in the name of the people, to lie and hide behind big words that have lost their meaning: "socialism" and "communism".'[55] Comparisons with Tsarism abounded in popular conversations, and often the new regime looked less than glorious as a result: Soviet power was 'worse than tsarism; it's wearing the workers out'; if the Bolsheviks wanted to govern 'then give us bread.... Otherwise, go to hell [and] give us the old "exploited" life!'; the Party was 'deceiving the workers' and was oppressing them 'worse than under capitalism'; life now was 'worse than serfdom' because the Party built 'socialism...on the workers' backs'.[56]

Partially, such outbursts were an appropriation of official discourse. Often enough, however, these were competing visions of what socialism meant, visions the regime tried to suppress but was unable to do so consistently. Stalinism was only one variant of Bolshevism, and Bolshevism not the only revolutionary patrimony. People did not forget this basic fact just because those in power pronounced themselves the only true heirs of that peculiar composite being, *Marx–Engels–Lenin*, and of socialism, and of revolt more generally. After all, 1917 had only happened a bit over a decade ago when Stalin launched his own revolution, and many had personal histories entangled with it, while many more had members of their families who had been involved in one way or another.[57] When people 'spoke Socialist' they did not necessarily converse in the language of power.[58]

Prior to the great blood-letting of 1937 and 1938 there were, thus, many in the Party, or just excluded from it, who were both Marxists and anti-Stalinists. It was entirely possible to mobilize the latter against the former, as in the following famous example, the 'Riutin Platform' of March 1932, which accused Stalin to have turned dialectics into sophistries, and ideology into unprincipled hocus-pocus. The authors even dared to call the great leader a pile of excrement:

> To place the name of Stalin next to the names of Marx, Engels, means to mock Marx, Engels, and Lenin, means to mock the proletariat, to lose all shame and to transgress all limits of baseness; to place Lenin's name next to the name of Stalin is like placing [Mount] Elbrus next to a dung-heap; to place the works of Marx, Engels and Lenin next to the 'works' of Stalin is like placing the music of great composers like Beethoven, Mozart, Wagner and others alongside the music of a street organ-grinder.[59]

Such views were not restricted to the old Bolshevik elite either. 'No one has a liking for Soviet authority, but consider you torturers of the Russian people', claimed an anonymous letter to Stalin and Kalinin in March

1930. 'We want Comrade Trotsky to be right and Comrade Bukharin and other comrades', the writers continued angrily, calling Komsomols 'dumbbells and sheep' and the leadership 'violators and not rulers of the Russian people'.[60]

What sounded like Bolshevik lingo were often alternative claims to a living tradition which the regime tried to commandeer for itself. As memory was not only personal, but also collective, embedded in shop floor lore, gossip, and family conversations, people could draw on events beyond their own, personal horizon. For this reason, the Revolution of 1905, when *soviets* were first invented and when the Bolsheviks were only one small faction in a colourful landscape of labour radicalism, could be invoked during the First Five-Year Plan by workers critical of the increasing exploitation they saw all around themselves: 'Remember how our fathers fell victim in 1905 because they didn't want to work on four looms?', asked one weaver to an upset crowd of textile workers. 'How many Cossack whips did we get? We struggled for socialism then. But what do we see now? Oppression. We won't accept four looms; we won't put our brother-workers out.'[61] Even the youngest cohorts could partake in this tradition, as they were, as a rule, not raised by 'Bolshevism' but in their families. It was because mothers and fathers continued to speak to their children that even schoolgirls like Nina Lugovskaia could be steeped in the lore of the old Russian intelligentsia from where their parents hailed. This tradition allowed her to hate Stalin and his regime (*I decided that I had to kill the bastards*) while wavering between adoration and pity, both from afar, for 'the Russian people' (*I have to agree with Turgenev when he says, 'the Russian people need freedom least of all'. They don't need freedom because they can't hold onto it.*).[62]

Moreover, the traditions of radicalism themselves, the writings of Marx and Lenin, which the regime claimed as its heritage, were full of highly subversive ideas, anti-establishment impulses and romantic calls to arms. They could easily be 'misunderstood', particularly by the young. As if to show that interpretations of history stressing the force and independent stubbornness of ideas have a point, the post-war years abound in examples of student groups who fashioned themselves in this romantic tradition while drawing on the works of Marx and Lenin to criticize the Stalinist regime as counter-revolutionary.[63] They stood in a long line of student radicalism in Russia, a phenomenon going back to the nineteenth century, which also left traces in the 1930s. The murder of Kirov in 1934 was greeted by many romantically inclined youth as a sign that a revolutionary underground existed, that an uprising and revolution would soon occur and pull them out of their prosaic everyday lives.[64] The regime tried to instrumentalize such feelings during its mobilizational campaigns in the First Five-Year Plan, but the policies to be implemented by young enthusiasts were too obviously directed against those who were meant to be the backbone of any true revolution (workers and peasants) and had contradictory results. Collectivization, in particular, presented the perpetrators with such an ambiguous role that doubts were unavoidable.[65]

In the countryside, far away from the inner circles of power, one could get along with relatively little of the official vocabulary, at least in everyday life. The intriguing 1937 diary of the collective farmer Ignat Danilovich Frolov, for example, is concerned with the hauling of manure, the changing agricultural work, the price of goods on the market, onions, potatoes and wheat, birth, deaths, and accidents, religious holidays, and—above all—the weather. The momentous events unfolding all around him during this year of heightened state terror were obviously far beyond his horizon. The most Bolshevik moment in the diary is when 'the chairman of the Collective Farm left…for Moscow for talks on illuminating the village with Electricity'.[66] That Bolshevik cosmology was relatively unimportant for how daily life made sense to the peasantry does not mean that they could not speak Bolshevik when required. When in 1937 ordinary people were encouraged to identify 'enemies of the people', peasants knew exactly who they were: those who had forced them in the collectives and then run the devilish things, squeezing 'the people' dry. They responded enthusiastically to this chance to get even with these 'ogres' and 'swine', writing denunciations and serving as willing witnesses during regional show trials.[67]

While villagers might choose to speak in the regime's idiom, more often than not they were deeply hostile to a regime which had brought them nothing but grief. 'The prevailing opinion,' writes one historian, 'was that Stalin, as the organizer of collectivization, was the peasants' inveterate enemy: they wished him dead, his regime overthrown, and collectivization undone, even at the cost of war and foreign occupation.'[68] Collectivization and dekulakization ensured that even much of youth—often seen as logical allies of Bolshevism—became severely disgruntled. Simply put, victimization as children of kulaks, priests, and other disenfranchised 'former people' bred resentment and hostility, as the authorities knew well. In their top-secret reports, the security organs fashioned such groups of disgruntled villagers into 'counterrevolutionary organizations', which in most cases was a severe overstatement bred by the propensity to see conspiracy everywhere. Nevertheless, the secret police captured the reasons for hostility to the regime well, when it reported that these 'kulak organizations and groups' could draw on the large (and growing) pool of former members who had been excluded from the Communist Party for their inability or unwillingness to tow the central party line—former Red Partisans, too independent and able to point to their exploits during the Civil War; the village intelligentsia, including teachers and doctors, who saw and understood the destructiveness of the Party line first hand.[69] For similar reasons, working-class revolutionaries of long standing quite openly attacked the policies of the Party, and in many instances insisted on their right to speak their mind even when arrested.[70]

III

If much of the engagement with the official world in the village was in negative terms, peasants (and peasants-turned-workers) were not, on the whole, without an alternative cosmology of their own. Rather than Bolshevik, they spoke and thought in the language of religion. As one anti-Bolshevik leaflet, confiscated in 1930, put it: 'Soviet power is the enemy—religion is your friend'.[71] At the beginning of Stalin's first revolution from above, there were five times more churches in the countryside than reading huts, which could have spread the secular gospel instead.[72] In the rural Ukraine in 1927, church *membership* ran as high as 85 per cent in some regions and as low as 38 per cent in others. Even among urban workers, 4 per cent were attached to parishes, while the urban population as a whole included between 14 and 22 per cent.[73] In the western borderlands over half of schoolchildren, when asked about their belief in God, replied affirmatively,[74] and surveys in other regions of the empire in the 1920s and 1930s show that as many as half of all schoolchildren were under the spell of 'religious obscurantism'.[75] No wonder that dekulakization was accompanied by a massive anti-religious drive—an assault not only on the clergy but on the parish and parishioners.[76] This campaign had some success as far as organized observance was concerned. If in 1926 there had been 79,000 officially counted ministers of religion in the Soviet Union, by 1937 their number had collapsed to only 31,000.[77] The number of religious buildings declined from 73,963 before 1917 to 20,665 actively used houses of worship, most of them in the Russian Republic.[78] By 1936 the authorities believed that only 28 per cent of religious communities were still operating.[79]

As far as popular religiosity was concerned, however, the same campaign was of dubious success as the 1937 census showed (Table 5). The percentage of believers among the population was most likely underreported in these data, as many did not respond to the question about religion at all, because there were rumours about potential reprisals against believers. Of those who did respond, 57 per cent identified themselves as believers. Predictably, the more educated were less likely to be believers than the illiterates; there was a positive correlation between age and religiosity; and women affirmed their belief more often than men. These are patterns which hold true in many populations in twentieth century societies. More worrisome from the official point of view, and highly indicative for the failure of the Bolshevik gospel to take over the hearts and minds of those who had no personal memory of Tsarism, was the third of literate sixteen to nineteen year olds, and 71 per cent of illiterates of the same cohort, who declared their addiction to the 'people's opium'. And while religion was more prevalent in the countryside than the city, even in Leningrad—birthplace of the revolution—33 per cent of the population declared themselves believers.[80] Such numbers confirmed earlier fears that peasant-workers refused to deposit their worldview before crossing the city limits.[81]

The Stalinist leadership took these data quite seriously and answered not only with the suppression of the census but also with a savage onslaught on religious cadres and believers during the mass operations of the Great Terror.[82] This attempt to finally solve the religious question

Table 5 Percentage of religious believers according to the 1937 census

Age group	Literates who answered question about religion	Illiterates who answered question about religion	All respondents who answered question about religion	Women (literates and illiterates)
16–19	32.5	71.0	35.2	45.1
20–29	38.7	74.8	44.7	55.4
30–39	44.1	78.9	52.4	63.6
40–49	52.0	83.6	63.7	74.6
50–59	64.8	88.7	77.9	85.4
60–69	78.8	92.5	88.2	91.7
70 and older	87.1	94.5	92.9	94.5
unknown	41.2	23.5	30.6	88.6
Total	44.5	84.4	56.7	66.8

Source: V. B. Zhiromskaia, I. N. Kiselev, and Iu. A. Poliakov. *Polveka pod grifom "sekretno": Vsesoiuznaia perepis' naseleniia 1937 goda* (Moscow: Nauka, 1996), 98 (adjusted for computation errors); V. B. Zhiromskaia and Iu. A. Poliakov (eds.), *Vsesoiuznaia perepis' naseleniia 1937 goda: Obshchie itogi. Sbornik dokumentov i materialov* (Moscow: Rosspen, 2007), 122–123.

failed as earlier attacks had. By the time the war started, popular 'obscurantism' was alive and well. There were 'many religious people in the Red Army,' observed one memoirist, recalling 'how village lads, before going into battle, would whisper the Lord's Prayer and cross themselves repeatedly.' When confronting death, many soldiers grasped at the straw a supernatural presence offered the drowning—*Gospodi pomilui* (Lord, have mercy!).[83] The war, this world of incomprehensible violence and destruction, often activated dormant needs for spirituality. 'It began in war time,' recalled one son of religious parents his reconversion from '100 per cent atheist' to '100 per cent religious': 'As to explain supernatural and cosmic events, I began to feel that there must be some force, some God that created all and commanded all.'[84] At the frontline, in particular, the political commissars might offer love of the motherland or hatred for the enemy, maybe even socialism and comrade Stalin, 'but they could do little to fulfil the spiritual needs of the Red Army soldiers coming mostly from peasant families with strong religious traditions'.[85]

Despite the absence of an overall policy of religious services in the Red Army, there were local initiatives to provide ministers of faith. One officer reported, when interviewed in the West some years later, that 'during the war, they asked the soldiers whether a chaplain should be sent in if they wanted to'.[86] Lectures of Metropolitan Nikolai to 'large gatherings of officers' are also documented.[87] Controversy continues about the level of the wartime religious revival, but it is clear that some did find the supernatural, while many others came out of the underground once anti-religious policies were eased.[88] Moving through an apocalyptic landscape, soldiers encountered a lost God, quite literally, under the rubble of war. Others simply held on to the beliefs they had acquired from their parents and grandparents. Whether recent convert or longstanding believer, the wartime relaxation of admission standards at the front allowed the religious world which existed outside the Stalinist core to spread its tentacles from the village into the very heart of the Soviet regime—the Communist Party. After the war, the latter's purity had to be restored by removing believers.[89] This purge of the backward and the superstitious from the ranks of the enlightened and the rational made religious misconduct a quickly rising category for exclusion from the Party. While the statistics presented in Table 6 unhelpfully lump together religious behaviour with other unenlightened matters, the category of people excluded for 'feudal view of women, polygamy, [and] religious rituals' grew to a high point of 4,065 cases in 1948, the year demobilization ended—sixty-seven times the size of this category at war's end.

It is thus clear that religious sentiment other than Bolshevism was alive and well in the Soviet Union throughout the period we call Stalinism. Such cosmologies were one of the force fields which pulled some Soviet citizens together, while alienating them from those with other world-views and ritual everyday practices; they served both to hold groups together and fracture society into a kaleidoscope of subcultures, each with its own history and historical memory and thus developmental path. What is less easy to establish is the crossover, interaction, and mixing of these milieus. How deeply held were these beliefs, and to what extent were they perceived by the individual involved as opposed to the official world-view?[90]

Table 6 Exclusions from the Communist Party for 'Feudal View of Women, polygamy, religious rituals'

year	total cases	Index of growth (multiples of the 1945 number)	percent of total exclusions	Index of growth (multiples of the 1945 percentage)
1945	61	1.0	0.1	1
1946	292	4.8	0.3	3
1947	852	14.0	0.7	7
1948	2,551	41.8	1.5	15
1949	4,065	66.6	2.9	29
1950	2,667	43.7	2.3	23
1951	1,003	16.4	1.2	12
1952	863	14.1	0.9	9
1953	596	9.8	0.4	4

Source: Edward D. Cohn, 'Disciplining the Party: The Expulsion and Censure of Communists in the Post-War Soviet Union, 1945–1961.' PhD diss., The University of Chicago, 2007, 540–551.

There was nothing inherently anti-Soviet in religious adherence as loyal service of many religious believers in the war showed. As Metropolitan Sergii put it in a declaration of 1927, one had to show 'not in words but in deeds' that even the most enthusiastic members of orthodoxy, 'and not only its traitors' could be 'devoted citizens of the Soviet Union'.[91] Two decades later, believers of all generations agreed, seeing no contradiction between religiosity and sovietness.[92] Such attempts to find a third way between religious adherence and Soviet loyalty—to 'hedge cosmological bets'—always chafed, however, against the deeply ingrained anti-religious feelings of communist purists and the totalitarian intolerance towards competing world-views and independent organization. At best, temporary, tactical toleration could be accepted.[93]

Most scholars agree that there was an overall weakening of religious affiliation between the generations.[94] It is not easy to find good documentation for this claim, beyond the impressions of individual witnesses, which is contradicted by other impressionistic data such as the observation that about 40 per cent of the 8,000 or so worshippers who flocked to Pascal services in St Pimen's Church in Moscow in 1945 were 'young people'.[95] Systematic data which would allow comparing the number of believers over time are lacking. Only the 1937 census asked Soviets to declare if they were believers or not. Often, the generational differences in these data are read as supporting the thesis of a weakening of religion among the younger cohorts, but these numbers might as well reflect differences in life cycle stage rather than generation: churches fill with the aged rather than the young in many societies.

Whatever the long-term trends, the fact of the matter is that religions other than Bolshevism were far from 'overcome' in Stalin's time.[96] Part of this durability can be explained by the continuing need for metaphysical guidance in a world of upheaval, violence, and despair. Belief in larger forces of good and evil which lead humans from the outside (including magical belief in a variety of spirits and sprites, devils and demons) might have been the only rational way to make sense of a situation where life was shaped by forces completely beyond the control of the individuals, their families, and their immediate communities, powers which frequently acted erratically and at times completely incomprehensibly.[97] 'The world of sinners, which surrounds us,' a young Baptist woman put it in the 1940s, 'is a corrupted world that produces all kinds of sinful barbarities and crimes.'[98] As real suffering continued in a heartless world the oppressed creature continued to sigh. Marxism–Leninism–Stalinism could fill the void only partially, particularly for victims of the regime or those confronted with death, grief, and loss.[99]

Part of the explanation also lies in the resilience of the family as a unit of social organization and its centrality in the raising of the young generation. 'At home religion was obligatory,' goes one typical memory. 'Father and mother both were religious, and so was I. Mother taught me religion and at least inwardly I have always kept something of it.'[100] Children would be exposed to atheist propaganda in school, and sometimes that was the end of it. Frequently, however, these ideas were queried in the intimacy of the household and the authority of parents turned out to be firmer than that of teachers. 'I thought about it, and then I would come home from school and ask my father. I used to listen to him more than to the teachers. He said that the teachers are all simply phonograph records.'[101] Strong families with religious ties could keep the child from joining anti-religious organizations in school: 'Were I to join such an organization and were my father to find out this, it would have been bad,' remembers another displaced Soviet interviewed after the war.[102] A war veteran, born into a working-class family in 1919, remembers that she was 'of course' baptized. She received an icon as a present from her grandmother and kept it all her life. Lest she lapse, her mother later enforced the baptism of the grandchild. 'Mama said: "If you don't baptize him, I won't have anything to do with him." ' The official anti-religious campaigns ('*Whoever is for Easter is against Socialism*') had little impact on the family's observance of holidays: 'They forbade this, they forbade that, but it made no difference: We celebrated all the holidays, including Easter. I've celebrated Easter all my life.'[103]

Things were not always so clear cut. Many youth were torn between the religion of their parents and the religion of the state. 'I was very confused. I would hear one thing at school and then when I would go home, I would find my mother praying.... I was always thinking about religion and trying to decide who was right, the school or my parents. I finally decided that my parents were right.' Reality helped with this decision: 'the more I learned, the more I saw life, the more I became convinced that my parents were right, and I have been a religious man ever since.'[104] The onslaught on religion sometimes had the unintended effect of turning young Soviets of religious background, who had become atheists as children, back to their parents' view of the world: 'when the Soviets attacked religion very much, something in me woke up, and I returned to the orthodox church.'[105]

Moreover, this is not only a story where tradition stubbornly refuses to wither away. Religions were dynamic, not static. Some denominations, such as the Baptists, who had come to Russia in the late 1860s, grew rapidly after the revolution of 1917. While numbers are hard to pin down with accuracy, an official study of 1912 had counted 114,652 Baptists and Evangelical Christians (a splinter group of the former); in 1928, the Baptists alone estimated their strength at 200,000 baptized participants and an additional 800,000 family members and other regular attendees.[106] The growth of such non-orthodox adherents might have been aided by the until 1927 relatively lenient official policy towards 'sects', as the new rulers, employing the vocabulary of their predecessors, labelled non-orthodox groups.[107] But the religious dynamism was not restricted to these believers. The regime's pressure on the clergy and church resources unintentionally shifted authority downwards into the hands of parishioners, reinvigorating the parish and democratizing the clergy. Together, these effects explain the religious revival of the 1920s, which in particular benefited the most conservative wing of Orthodoxy, but went far beyond the borders of the established church.[108] As recent research has demonstrated, Russian popular culture throughout the revolutionary period was 'animated' by 'a genuine spiritual quest' encompassing a wide variety of religious seeking.[109]

Research on non-orthodox Christianity under Stalin is still in its infancy, but it is quite clear that a range of groups managed to survive and gained converts. Baptists, for one, did not cease proselytizing their neighbours after the anti-religious onslaught of Stalin's first revolution from above, and such efforts continued into the post-war years.[110] Consider, for example, the former Komsomol, a factory worker, who stated after the war that the Communist Youth League 'never gave me any support, but in the sect of the Baptists I am surrounded by caring attention and even receive some material help.' Or consider the statistic that in 1948 as many as 40 per cent of new converts to Baptism were youth.[111] Consider, finally, the highly decorated war veteran who, upon return to his factory after victory, 'fell under the influence of the sect of evangelical Christians [one wing of the Russian Baptists] and actively participated in it, started to preach and become the sect's spiritual leader,' as a *Pravda* correspondent reported in a secret report from Voroshilovgrad in the early 1950s.[112] In the long run, the 'Western-oriented sects' which had arrived in Russia in the nineteenth century—such as Baptists or Seventh Day Adventists—tended to absorb believers from Russian non-orthodox groups like the Klysts, Molokans, Dukhobors, Skoptsy, or Subbotniki.[113]

The religious landscape of Stalinism, thus, was far from simple. The 1937 census allows a glimpse at its diversity and the relative weight of different groups at one point in time. The vast majority (75 per cent) of those who claimed to be believers identified themselves as Russian Orthodox and 15 per cent as Muslim. Jewish believers accounted for 0.5 per cent of the sample, Buddhists and Lamaists for 0.2, and 'Shamanists' for 0.1 per cent. A large group, amounting to 6.4 per cent of believers were lumped together as 'others', while the largest identified groups were Christian: Protestants (0.8 per cent), Catholics (0.8 per cent), Armenian Orthodox (0.3 per cent) and 'other Christians' (0.7 per cent).[114]

Among the latter were individuals like Grigorii Ivanovich Putilin, born in 1893 and a member of the 'Ioannites' since the 1920s. This nativist apocalyptic sect of self-declared followers of the charismatic St John of Kronstadt (1829–1908) had emerged at the turn of the century. The hard core was deeply anti-Semitic, pro-Tsarist and anti-revolutionary and made logical bedfellows for the Whites during the Civil War. Identifying the Bolsheviks with the Antichrist made them less than popular with the new regime, which often lumped in orthodox Christians' veneration of the saint with this millenarian heresy. Despite their outright hostility to the regime and continuous repression, they managed to survive, recruit new members and thus annoy the atheist Party-State. We know of a Ioannite group in Kalinin, which was arrested in 1938, and in December 1951 fourteen people were sentenced by the Rostov province court to camp sentences of between ten and thirty-five years for their activities, secret meetings, and successful recruitment (i.e. conversion) of new members. The sect's literature was still circulating in the 1960s.[115]

As time went on, the religious landscape became, if anything, more complex. The westward expansion from 1939 brought more Catholics, Uniates, Lutherans, Jehovah's Witnesses, and practicing Jews, but also Orthodox believers into the Soviet orbit and the wartime relaxation of anti-religious policies encouraged the revival of religious practice everywhere. Orthodox Christianity thrived. After Metropolitan Sergii had, on the day of the German invasion, called on all faithful to defend the country, he proceeded to ignore Soviet law and began collecting funds for the war effort. The government, under mortal threat from the Nazi invaders, reciprocated with a more lenient religious policy, which soon became even more pronounced from 1943 onwards, when the Soviet state tried to use the Orthodox Church as an agent in its pacification and Russification of the reconquered western borderlands. Orthodox believers and the regime were suddenly on the same side, a tactical retreat by Stalin which was also motivated by the hope that religious toleration could be exploited internationally. Now, the regime attempted to control Orthodoxy rather than eliminate it, a shift which was symbolized by a meeting between Stalin and the Church leadership in 1943, followed by the creation of the Council for the Affairs of the Orthodox Church. From here to the end of Stalin's life, the church was left in peace so long as it remained loyal, cooperated in ruling the western border and otherwise focused on spiritual concerns only—a Soviet concordat.[116]

Many now thought that God was on the Soviets' side, and the victorious war seemed to confirm this assumption. The desperate years 1941 to 1947, years of war, extreme destruction, and post-war famine, but also of relatively lenient religious policies of the regime, saw an upsurge in overtly religious behaviour of large sectors of the population. Holy springs and sacred lakes and other spiritual places attracted hundreds and thousands. Mass processions and ritual bathing in frozen rivers annoyed the authorities as much as did students praying the Lord may help them 'pass the exam'. From 1947, a half-hearted anti-religious campaign revived, focusing largely on youth. Nevertheless, church attendance remained high, particularly during religious holidays. Church weddings and baptisms continued to punctuate the life path and mark important passages from one stage to the next, and young people continued to be seen among the crowds, sometimes in numbers.[117] Overall, however, as far as orthodoxy was concerned, the wartime policies of 'regulating' church activities continued into the post-war years. Meanwhile, non-orthodox Christian denominations continued to suffer from the regime's attempt to 'liquidate' them, forcing practitioners underground.[118]

IV

Popular hopes, fears, and aspirations found expression also in millenial rumours, which showed remarkable similarities over time. One such tale held that a foreign intervention was imminent, that it would succeed 'without fail' (*obiazatel'no*) and that after the violent end of the Soviet order the kolkhozes would be disbanded. Such wish-fulfilling fantasies already emerged during the 1927 war scare when peasants had declared

that they would not fight for a regime which exploited them economically.[119] Apocalyptic hopes resurfaced during collectivization and
remained 'one of the most persistent' rumours of the 1930s.[120] Deported
kulaks ('special settlers') indulged each other with stories of imminent
war triggering a coup d'etat.[121] Peasants fantasized that soon 'there will
be war... and the Soviet power will fall'. The 'troops of the Roman Pope'
were said to be 'marching in Moscow to the sound of drumbeats' and
'the Christ-loving military forces will attack from America'.[122] Migration
to the cities and the harrowing living and working conditions in the
ramshackle industries ensured that such ideas travelled well beyond the
village. 'Stop work! You want to starve us!' yelled striking workers in a
Rybinsk porcelain factory. 'It's you devil communists who have brought
us to this. Let there be war.'[123]

These desperate longings were remarkably stable, exchanging only the
enemy who would bring deliverance from the Bolshevik menace according to the latest international situation. During the collectivization and
dekulakization drive in early 1930, the British, Poles, Chinese, or Japanese
were hoped-for invaders, flanked by 'bands' of apocalyptic 'horsemen'
who would slaughter peasants who had joined the collectives;[124] during
the famine of 1932–33 the Poles and the Japanese were expected to go to
war, which would lead to the collapse of the kolkhozes;[125] and during the
Great Terror, Belorussian Commissar of Interior V. D. Berman reported
that 'anti-soviet agitation of hostile elements in the village' was focusing
on 'the threat of war of the Poles and the Germans against the USSR',
which would lead 'necessarily' to a victory of the anti-Soviet forces, who
would shoot anybody attempting to stay in the collective farms.[126] With
the rise of Nazism, Hitler became the hope in some of the rumours,
which predicted that he would invade, destroy Soviet power 'and make
short work of the communists'.[127] A Cossack, who was arrested in 1937
as the presumed leader of an 'anti-Soviet organization', was waiting
impatiently for the inevitable war, which would allow Cossack youth to
take up arms against the Soviets, while the older generations would
destabilize the Soviet home front. The resulting Soviet defeat would lead
to the return 'of the old free life, the old rights, and most importantly
would liquidate all collective farms'.[128] On 7 November 1938, a group of
family members of repression victims, armed with daggers, violently

broke up a meeting of collective farmers in the village of Stepanovka in Novosibirsk region, yelling 'Down with Soviet Power!' and 'Soon the Japanese will come!'[129]

In the end, the Japanese were a disappointment, but the Germans performed to expectation, invading in 1941. Finally, it seemed to Ukrainian villagers and Moscow residents alike, that the apocalyptic visions had come true. 'Previously I wept,' uttered one wife of a victim of the Great Terror, 'now you will weep.' Other Muscovites repeated this refrain: 'they will take you apart and shoot the Bolsheviks;' 'We've got nothing to fear from the war...the Germans will come and put Communists on the left and us on the right. They'll shoot the Communists, and we'll be left to live again.'[130] The cruel experience of large sectors of the population with actual occupation from 1941 did not change the hope that somehow outside forces would liberate the country. All that victory in the Great Patriotic War changed was that in the post-war years the symbol of this hope—the German liberators (who had turned out to be worse than the Bolsheviks)—was replaced by the Americans (just as official propaganda replaced the man-eating Fascist with the equally blood-thirsty GI).[131] Even nuclear war could now become part of the liberating apocalypse: once the bomb was dropped, 'there will be changes and everything will be different'.[132]

Popular discourse had a deeply apocalyptic undercurrent throughout Stalin's time in power. One could read this persistence as a sign of popular appropriation of propaganda, as war hysteria was a constant feature of the official mindset as well, albeit with reverse value judgements. However, the point is not that ordinary people—peasants, workers, soldiers—read official newspapers or listened to agitators. Of course many did. But the particular way they understood them, how they filtered the information and reinterpreted it, cannot be explained by a binary interaction between individuals and official discourse. Rather, the latter was interpreted in the context of an ongoing 'conversation of rumours'—an expression of the continuing existence of not a uniform *vox populi* invariably resisting the state, but a variety of relatively independent, and widespread, 'popular opinions' about how society should be ordered.[133]

An informed citizen thus not only read the newspaper, listened to the radio, and went to the movies but also kept abreast of the latest rumours.[134] That official propaganda was not simply believed does not mean that it had no impact on the way people understood the world. The Soviet newspapers were, for example, full of reports about the plight of blacks in the United States, as proof of the cruelty of capitalist oppression. When footage of a Detroit riot reached the Soviet Union, this documentary material was widely shown in order to educate the public about the evils of capitalism. Audiences, however, mistrusted the footage. In one scene a black man was hurled through the air by a white mob. For a short second, one could see his shoes. These shoes were much better than anything the Soviet audiences wore. This little detail became crucial in deciphering this documentary: As everybody knew blacks were horribly exploited in the United States; consequently, they could not wear shoes that would be worn only by the big bosses within Stalinist society; ergo, this movie was a fake. Surely, it was produced by Soviet propaganda and the guy with the good shoes was a Soviet actor in blackface.[135]

Apocryphal or not, this story illustrates the state of affairs by the late 1930s, when information about the outside world was extremely scarce, while rumour and conjecture were rich sources of information. In 1939, the Soviet Union started to expand beyond its initial boundaries. The annexation of Eastern Poland was only the first of many forays abroad, which would have serious implications for the already patchy ideological integration of this society. While unable, despite its monopoly on the means of mass communication, to effectively control the circulation of ideas within the Soviet Union, the regime had been relatively successful in controlling information coming in from elsewhere.[136] During the 1930s, the Soviet Union was—more or less hermetically—sealed from the outside world, which served as a canvas to paint Soviet reality in somewhat brighter colours. The image of the capitalist abroad as one of utter exploitation and of horrors worse than anything Soviet citizens could imagine, was—together with the approach to reality through an imagined future—one of the major devices attempting to control popular opinions. Given the obvious brutality of Stalin's regime and the no less obvious poor performance of the economy in delivering consumer goods, the brainwashing had never completely succeeded. With the expansion west, this ideological control became even more unstable.

Soviet soldiers were confused about the abundance of goods available in eastern Poland (this shock would have been even worse if they had actually known that they had just invaded one of the poorest regions of Europe!). Some managed to make sense of it in the right way (*the Poles might have perfume and silk stockings, but the Red Army had tanks and guns, and see who won*), but others, after asking if it was really true that they could buy as many wristwatches and as much sausage as they liked, went on a mad consumption spree.[137] This problem would return once the Red Army marched into Germany, although here more were able to sublimate this shock into anger ('Why did these people who were living so well have to invade us?'[138]) Nevertheless, the Soviet Union was not the same after millions had seen that one of the basic premises of the official view of the world was patently incorrect.

There was not one single impact of the war on Soviet consciousness, because there had not been a uniform consciousness to begin with. In 1941, some reacted with indifference ('Hitler, Soviet power, they're all the same to me'. 'What concern of ours is it who wins?'), others with *Schadenfreude* ('You've got what you deserved. First you fed him, now he'll shoot you'). Some tried to evade conscription, others destroyed their party or Komsomol cards and wore crosses instead; some shot their commissars and went over to the enemy; others volunteered enthusiastically, signed up for wartime bonds, or readily worked longer hours for victory; and nearly everybody put their own household on a wartime footing by withdrawing savings from the bank and stockpiling essential supplies.[139] While many true believers eventually managed to keep their doubts under control, the catastrophe of the first months of the war had destabilizing effects: 'We had planned to fight on foreign soil, but we are fighting on our own, and on top of this we are surrendering our towns.'[140]

V

If it is thus true that it was hard to avoid official discourse, it is equally true that ideas, values, and beliefs of other origin were as inescapable for most Soviet citizens as the Stalinist view of the world. To use the words of two historians playing with those of another, Soviet citizens spoke

Bolshevik 'as well as other languages'.[141] Given the contradictory nature of the symbolic universe circulating by word of mouth, official propaganda, through books left over from pre-revolutionary times, through rituals both secular and religious, and sometimes by radio waves or even, from 1939 onwards, personal observation of life abroad, to remain faithful to the regime and its ideas required active participation of the believer, not just passive reception of official discourse. Would-be faithful had to actively subjugate their own selves to the demands of ideology.

There were a variety of reasons why Soviets should try to wash their own brains. One was what the regime, always suspicious but equally realistic, described as 'careerism'. Getting ahead in life required speaking Bolshevik fluently and it also meant, more often than not, implementing policies directed against the very milieu one came from. Psychologically speaking, for all but the most cynical individuals (who certainly existed as well) it was much easier to get on with the work at hand if one actually believed that careerism and the dubious actions required were, in fact, parts of a higher, sacred plan, 'historically necessary' steps, part of a 'dialectic', which would, in the end, turn what at the face of it were exploitation, repression, and self-advancement into the shining light of the Communist dawn.

Ideology also had its own attractions. Socialism and Communism, in all their forms, had won over some of the brightest and most humane minds all over the world. Anybody who had experienced the destructive potential of capitalism in the first half of the twentieth century was inclined to doubt that the unfettering of private gain was the path to prosperity, social justice, or even political stability. The major alternatives to unrestrained greed were either a conservative welfare state along the lines of Bismarck's Reich, some form of socialism, or, the new kid on the block since the First World War, fascism. That some historians find it worthy of explanation that many would chose, for idealistic reasons, 'socialism' only shows how far removed we are from the world of the 1920s, 1930s, 1940s, and 1950s.[142]

Others were less drawn by socialism than by what seemed like a reincarnation of the pre-revolutionary service state. Many in the creative intelligentsia re-enacted the ethos of their aristocratic or military parents. Konstantin Simonov, one of the central bards of Stalin's regime, was a case in point. As his biographer put it, he inherited from his parents 'the public-service values of the aristocracy and, in particular, its ethos of military duty and obedience which in his mind became assimilated to the Soviet virtues of public activism and patriotic sacrifice, enabling him to take his place in the Stalinist hierarchy of command.' To be a Stalinist (or, for that matter, a Bolshevik) meant, first of all, to completely subject oneself to the party line, to suppress personal qualms, objections, or judgements and to implement, instead, what the centre decreed, even if it went against friends, family, or the own social circle. Given this basic requirement, those who were, like Simonov, brought up in the tradition of the Tsarist service class were, indeed, well prepared to become 'ordinary Stalinists'. Elevating duty to the highest moral imperative, such individuals were 'left with few other means to judge or regulate' their own behaviour than in terms of submission to the demands of the Stalinist system.[143]

If Stalinism managed to tap into the old service class ethos, the Bolshevik impetus to submerge the self in the collective could mobilize a long standing desire of the intelligentsia to belong 'to the people' or, at the very least, to a collective. Such longings to submerge the alienated self in the presumed truth of the larger whole, at last to become a complete person by aligning one's own poor soul with the sacred forces of history, could fuel aggressive and at times self-destructive attempts at internal reforging, silencing of personal doubts and replacing them by the correct state of affairs as represented by official discourse. The old Party hand accepting his own destruction because he came to understand it as in the interest of the Party is only the most radical version of what was a fairly widespread and intense longing.[144]

To become a Stalinist was one thing. To remain one was another one altogether. When talking of 'ideology' in the context of the Soviet Union, we do not mean that people were necessarily well-read in political, social, or economic theory of Marx, or Lenin, or even Stalin, although a certain minimum of understanding was necessary in order to be able to use the official way of speaking, seeing, and thinking. More important than particular ideas was a willingness 'to accept whatever the supreme authority might proclaim today, tomorrow, or in a year's time'.[145] This imperative to concur mentally with sometimes quite radical turnarounds as parts of the inevitable 'dialectic of history' had destabilizing effects on the true believers. The frequent changes in the Party line on a variety of issues could easily lead to cynicism, if not counter-acted aggressively by the individual. As one independently minded old hand of the revolutionary struggle put it after his arrest, it was impossible, without an 'astrolabe or a solar chronometer', to know exactly what the right Party line was. Given that, he noted slyly, only comrade Stalin had such a 'mechanical apparatus installed in his head,' one had 'to be a sage of sages to guess exactly how to speak.'[146]

Kapiton Vasil'evich Klepnikov, the man uttering these phrases, had been born in 1880 and could thus be considered contaminated with the old, pre-Bolshevik, pre-Stalinist world.[147] Younger Soviets did not grow political astrolabes in their brains either. Although a large section of the population had received a completely Soviet education by the time the Second World War started (in 1937, 42 per cent of the population was younger than 20, i.e. born after 1917), it was not inoculated against the danger of impure thoughts. One defector described the destabilizing effects on true believers of his generation, who had to adjust themselves to 'absolute truths' of one year becoming 'gross deviations from the truth' the next.[148]

> Let us for a moment consider a young Russian, born in 1917, whose earliest memories would include the death of Lenin. The names of Trotsky, Zinoviev, and perhaps Stalin would have come to his ears in those years— names of men who had been the loyal comrades of Lenin and in all respects heroes of the great October Revolution. He would have heard much of this revolution, too, and of the happiness it was to bring to the whole world.
>
> Then, when he was 10 or 11, he would have discovered that Trotskyism was despicable, though Bukharin and Rykov were still names to cheer when heard. Somewhat later, when ready to orient himself in political matters, he would have found out that communism was the classless society in which oppression would be eliminated and where each would contribute according to his abilities and be rewarded according to his needs.

This only half-imaginary Russian would then witness—if old enough to be mobilized by the Komsomol, potentially as a perpetrator, otherwise likely as a bystander—the violent campaign to collectivize the peasantry and liquidate the kulaks as a class. He would live through a famine, which was quite obviously connected to the destruction of peasant society in the early 1930s, or at least he would experience severe food shortages if living outside of the immediate starvation zone. He would have been told—and likely had told others—that these were just unavoidable difficulties of the transition period when Socialism was still in the future and the young Soviet state surrounded by enemies. He would read in astonishment that all the leaders of the Revolution, save Stalin and some of his immediate entourage, were enemies of the people who had plotted unimaginable crimes against the Soviet state. At about the same time, in 1936, he would learn the disappointing news, announced by Stalin himself, that Socialism had already eventuated and that the life of hardship he saw all around him was the fulfilment of the old dream of liberation from exploitation and alienated labour. *This* was what they had been working, struggling, and suffering for? In 1937 and 1938, then, the young man was likely to have friends, family, and loved ones disappear as enemies of the people, if he was lucky enough to escape arrest himself. The war added new confusions: the invincible Red Army was shockingly unprepared for war, the Tsarist past and Russian nationalism rather than Socialism or comrade Stalin were motivating the troops to fight, the evil capitalists sent canned beef and trucks to aid the Soviet war effort, and the exploited workers and peasants of Capitalism turned out to not only live much better than anybody in Socialism, but were also disappointingly disinterested in solidarity with the Soviets.[149]

Such thoughts were dangerous, even if the Communist kept his worries to himself. Even secretly held doubts were, after all, treasonous; moreover, if one vacillated but continued to live like a Communist one became not more than a cynical self-seeker, a careerist, a petty-bourgeois individual. Nobody who had joined the Party out of conviction could accept such a self-image very easily. The only way to remain a Communist, to be part of the larger whole, participate in the Party's march to the bright horizon, was to overcome such doubts, to purge one's own soul, to excise one's thoughts from such heresies and thus to rejoin the collective. The Bolsheviks had a name for such work on the self—'self-criticism' (*samokritika*). It could be enhanced, helped along, and enforced by public confessionals called 'criticism and self-criticism' (*kritika i samokritika*). These rituals had originated as part of the techniques by which the conspiracy of revolutionary saints had kept the elect clean during revolutionary struggle and were frequently used to deal within the Party with personal infractions or to purge hidden enemies from the ranks. The accused would get up in front of the collective to endure *kritika* from the crowd: the comrade was rude, had slept with a co-worker's wife, or had uttered words displaying lack of vigilance or wrong dialectics. The accused then had to respond to such attacks, humbly accept the critique, and castigate himself, ending on a promise to not do it again.[150]

Self-criticism was hard work, and success was by no means guaranteed. Many who wanted to belong to the heroic collective on its march to a radiant future—and this longing went far beyond the institutional boundaries of the Party itself—used their diaries as tools to remake their own selves, to wipe their minds from 'anti-Soviet' thoughts, to cleanse their polluted souls from alien emotions. Sometimes they succeeded, but such one-time success in rejoining the blessed did not guard from new, devilish temptations. Heretical thoughts and—even harder to control—feelings were likely to creep back into the mind of the true believer. Remaining a loyal Soviet subject in mind and soul required true exertion, constant vigilance, and discipline. Conforming ideologically was not easy. Rather, non-conformity and cynicism formed the path of lesser resistance, even if it, too, came with dangers. Becoming and remaining a Communist, by contrast, was extremely hard work, which, moreover, constantly teetered at the brink of failure given the onslaught of destabilizing realities.[151]

Personal victimization, or the victimization of people near and dear, could push the doubting subject over the edge. One post-war refugee who was interviewed by American sociologists interested in the Soviet citizens' everyday lives, traced his own disaffection back to an encounter 'with the peasant poet Pavel Vassilyew...and with Professor C., who taught French revolution.' The doubts planted in the young man's head by these two critics of the regime were enhanced by a whole series of people around him falling victim: his nanny's family was dekulakized, which 'did disturb me a great deal', his sister died in prison in 1934; his father was executed; his mother was arrested; Pavel Vassilyew was shot in

1937. It was these 'personal experiences' he made responsible for his change of heart 'from the enthusiastic acceptive into sharply rejecting' the regime and its policies.[152] Given the personal work involved in maintaining a Stalinist soul, the mere social exclusivity of the elite thus could only aid, but not ensure ideological conformity. The onslaught of reality was often simply too much. When Colonel-General Vasilii Gordov was selected to stand as a Supreme Soviet delegate he had to travel all over his electoral district to speak to those who had the privilege to vote for him. 'When I saw everything, all this horror,' he confided to his wife and a close friend in a conversation secretly recorded by state security, 'I was completely reborn. I could not look at this. From there came the moods, thoughts. . . . I am now convinced that if they dissolve the collective farms today, then tomorrow there would be order, a market, there will be everything.' This train of thought, which started with the observed plight of the peasantry, soon centred on the political system as the unobservable root cause. Stalin, he reasoned, must know about the people's predicament; thus in order to change the situation, 'we would need to have genuine democracy.'[153] Such anti-Stalinist self-transformation could not be tolerated. Gordov was arrested in 1947 and shot in 1950.

CHAPTER 7
'THANK YOU, COMRADE STALIN!'

66 Thank you, Comrade Stalin, for a happy childhood! 99
Propaganda slogan[1]

66 In preparation for the Siberian job I had a lot of work to do in Moscow, where I was given a fine room at the Metropole Hotel, all expenses paid by the government, and plenty of money. I could have what I wanted. Oh, it's no small thing to be a favoured son of the Central Committee. The whole business of dictatorship, in fact, looks different, less grim, less tyrannical, when viewed from somewhere near the top. 99
Victor Kravchenko, 1947[2]

I

Stalinism was, to some, not only attractive because of its ideology—a combination of can-do attitude, hard-headed realism, and utopian outlook. Uncle Joe's regime was also appealing because it provided possibilities for the hard working, loyal, and ambitious to move up in the world. Many a man of humble origin made a dizzying career and had much he could thank Comrade Stalin for, and the revolution he embodied. As a result of such mobility, much of the upper and middle reaches of Party and government under Stalin were staffed by self-educated men of lower class origin, practical functionaries rather than theorists, often with 'impeccable civil war credentials'.[3]

A short sketch of this elite can identify several subgroups. The old hands of pre-revolutionary struggle were divided among themselves between intellectuals (who, like Bukharin, had often spent more time in exile before 1917) and the practitioners of the underground (who, like Stalin, often came from the lower classes). These 'old Bolsheviks' were born before the turn of the century and were veterans of war, revolution, and civil war. A second set had joined the Party during or after the Civil War, but were in generational and sociological terms not so different from their more established peers. Like the first contingent, they were ethnically diverse with a significant share of plebeians with rather limited education among them; like the first group, too, the Civil War had deeply shaped their world-view. Together, these categories are summarized as the 'first generation' in table 7. A younger cohort, the 'second

Table 7 Three Generations of Stalinists—Central Committee membership by cohort

	absolute numbers				
year	first	second	third	unknown	total
1917	29	0	0	0	29
1934	137	2	0	0	139
1939	66	64	0	9	139
1952	62	166	1	7	236
1971	10	281	105	0	396
	relative numbers (%)				
1917	100	0	0	0	100.0
1934	98.6	1.4	0.0	0.0	100.0
1939	47.5	46.0	0.0	6.5	100.0
1952	26.3	70.3	0.4	3.0	100.0
1971	2.5	71.0	26.5	0.0	100.0

Note: First generation: born in 1900 or before (Stalin's generation)

Second generation: born between 1901 and 1920 (the 'Brezhnev generation')

Third generation: born between 1921 and 1940.

Source: Evan Mawdsley and Stephen White, *The Soviet Elite from Lenin to Gorbachev. The Central Committee and Its Members, 1917–1991* (Oxford and New York: Oxford University Press, 2000), 279.

generation' in the tabulation above, was born between the turn of the century and the end of the Civil War. Their education had been disrupted by the violent upheavals from 1914 onwards, and they received training in improvised educational facilities during the 1920s and early 1930s. Notwithstanding such makeshift education, their preparation was often superior to what the plebeians of the old guard could muster. Their outlook was shaped by the main upheavals of Stalin's time in power: the first and second revolutions from above and the Great Patriotic War.[4]

The Great Purges removed many from the first generation and replaced them with Stalin's new men, a process which can be studied in the Central Committee, a relatively well documented case (see Table 7). As is easily discernable from Table 7, the blood-letting of 1937 and 1938 changed the composition of the elite dramatically, catapulting many of the second generation of leaders into power. At the same time, however, it was not a complete replacement of one cohort by the other. Rather, two generations of Stalinists 'coexisted at Central Committee level for a decade and a half after 1939'.[5]

This Stalinist elite was thoroughly entrenched after the Great Purges and the war made relatively little difference for its composition—note how few of the 1952 members were born after 1921. Even as late as 1971, this generation could command only a negligible share of the top elite, which instead was dominated by the Brezhnev generation (Table 7). A small minority of peasant soldiers who entered the Party at the front and moved into higher education after demobilization did join the elite in the late years of Stalinism. Others, who had been on the way up in the world before the war, continued this trajectory after war's end. But by and large wartime service was not connected with social mobility and the prominence of veterans in the elite after victory was a reflection of the extent to which the male population had been drafted between 1941 and 1945. Lacking further bloody cadres exchanges of the Great Purges type, the post-war years saw the confirmation and entrenchment of Stalin's new elite, making the generation of Brezhnev (the 'second generation' in Table 7), who had risen to the top in the 1930s, the movers and shakers of the Soviet state until the younger Gorbachev managed to displace the now old men in the 1980s.[6]

That social mobility was widespread does not mean that everybody moved into leadership positions. For one, the elite was just that: an elite. Most humbly, maybe 6 to 9 per cent of peasants were Stakhanovites—a position which came with moderate privileges.[7] Further up the hierarchy the ranks quickly thinned. Stalin defined the Party's leadership, in military terms, as a corps of officers of between 133,000 and 194,000 men. At the top were the 'generals' (*generatitet*), some 3,000 to 4,000; below them came the 'officers' (*ofitserstvo*) of middle leaders, maybe thirty to forty thousand strong, followed by the NCOs (*unter-ofitserstvo*) of maybe 100 to 150 thousand.[8] This approximately 0.1 per cent of the population was surrounded by a wider sector of administrators and technicians, which composed the broader privileged classes. The 1937 census counted 11.9 million employed in various white collar (*sluzhashchie*) jobs. These 7 per cent of the population included, however, everything from secretary and typist to Politburo members. Leading personnel, even including the lowly position of kolkhoz chair, constituted only 1.3 million. The elite proper also included higher technical personnel, scientists, professors, and academicians, journalists and authors, actors, ballerinas, artists and other 'art workers', and planning and controlling functionaries. Together, these elite office holders amounted to approximately 12 per cent of the employees and less than 1 per cent of the population at large. Even if we quadruple their number (to account for dependents) the Stalinist elite tallied less than 4 per cent of the population of 162 million.[9] It is thus obvious that not the entire pre-revolutionary labouring masses were transformed into Stalin's new class. Nevertheless, the reverse remains correct: About three-quarters of personnel in various specialist jobs 'came from working-class and peasant families'.[10]

The 'right' social background (poor or middle peasant or, better, proletarian) was only the necessary, but not a sufficient condition to become a member of this new class. Of the over 700,000 peasants who joined the Party during collectivization maybe half reached more or less responsible positions at one point in time—only to be sacked for 'incompetence' (i.e., lack of education or inability to deal with impossible demands), purged as scapegoats for the agricultural disasters of the 1930s, or removed from the ranks as 'aliens' after the regime's policies towards the peasantry had alienated these former allies. In the end, only about a quarter of the new peasant-communists of 1930–32 became part of Stalin's elite—as a rule after they left the countryside to be workers and, ultimately, functionaries.[11]

Stalinist affirmative action, thus, was not just a quota system without quality control. To rise in the world required talent, determination, and extremely hard work, both for the cause and on oneself, in order to continue conforming and thus performing. Ideological commitment, nearly boundless energy, extreme loyalty, and capacity to work to the brink of exhaustion were the attributes Stalin's men brought to the job. It was these qualities which the leader valued in his environment, and his entourage in turn tried to recruit men like themselves, all down the line to the people who were promoted from humble backgrounds into positions of local authority. This was a regime of 'can-do' managers, of problem solvers, of trouble shooters, not of debating intellectuals or careful specialists. No wonder that the former, once in power, were likely to be hostile to the latter, who would not stop blabbering, deciding to form commissions to further study rather than solve a problem at hand, drawing out meetings without finding resolutions, pointing towards the limits of willpower, the structural defects of a design, or the breaking point of humans and machines.[12]

Stalinist affirmative action was not the root cause of the widespread social mobility during the interwar years, but an instrumentalization of pre-existing pressures from below. Consider the Russian peasant boy who had foresworn his rustic background to become a skilled worker and—the poor man's version of an *intelligent*—a 'conscious proletarian' already before the revolution. After 1917, his will to better himself pushed him to open doors now accessible to men of his background. With only five years of formal schooling he became Rector of the Communist University in Petrograd in 1921, moved on to head the Central Committee's press bureau in 1924, and was appointed director of the CC's Department of Historical Research in 1925. Who knows where he could have gone, had he not associated with the left opposition? But even with this stain on his biography, Semen Ivanovich Kanachikov could serve as a TASS correspondent and as editor of important journals and survived the Great Purges, to die in 1940. His memoirs, published in 1929, 1932, and 1934, tell the story of his pre-revolutionary life as one of hard work on himself, his skills, and his intellect—an autobiography of a self-made man.[13] Or consider the peasant lad turned worker, one Nikita Khrushchev, who had dreamt of becoming an educated engineer before the revolution. He became one of Stalin's henchmen instead, once revolution and Civil War had thrown him off course. Once his life veered into politics, this field of activity turned out to be equally and even more instantly rewarding for the ambitious.[14] These were stories of liberation from backward and oppressive backgrounds and not so different from those of the sons and daughters of shtetl Jews who left their milieu to become, to the annoyance of thick-skulled anti-Semites, one of the most visible groups of the new Soviet elite.[15]

By the time we join the story, this first generation 'new class' had sent its children to newly created elite schools, which trained a generation devoted to the Cause by force of circumstance, conviction, and education—the generation of Chukhrai. In many cases social mobility, high status, and ideological conviction reinforced and mutually constituted each other. Stalin's men and their children never had the problem of capitalist *nouveaux riches*, who rely on endowing second rate intellectuals to make up an ideology explaining why their private wealth is in the public interest. Stalinists knew that they were in the elite because of ideological commitment and intellectual prowess; that they won in the various power struggles and ended up on top only confirmed that their ideology was correct and their commitment to the Revolution honest.

As we have seen in the previous chapter, however, the personal (which, to Bolsheviks, was political), the professional (which was deeply personal) and the political (which was a profession) did not always fit together so nicely. The practice to judge loyalty not by words (which could be insincere), or deeds (which could constitute a mask) but by 'objective' factors—which 'in the final instance' always determined everything else, even if a son did 'not answer for his father'—could destabilize even the most sincere attempt to believe in the Bolshevik gospel. Stepan Podlubnyi was a case in point. In many ways he looked and behaved like the older generation of peasant or working-class strivers, the Kanachikovs, Khrushchevs, or Ezhovs. Trying to leave the cockroaches as well as an unloved father behind, he fashioned himself as a city boy, chronicling his work on his Stalinist soul in his diary. All seemed well for a while, but soon 'objective factors' intervened. Podlubnyi was the 'son of a kulak' and this background would cause him continuous problems in his twin attempts to belong ideologically and to advance personally.[16]

Social mobility was by no means restricted to the top elite. During Stalin's first revolution from above, 150,000 new cadres of working-class origin—the Brezhnev generation—were trained, ready and eager to assume positions of responsibility. These jobs, however, were in the hands of people barely a decade older, but much less trained than the 'promotees' (*vydvizhentsy*). While not the main reason for the Great Terror, it was not an unhappy coincidence from the leader's point of view that the blood-letting among the old Bolsheviks made place for Stalin's new men. The dictator was certainly aware of the problem and its possible solution, when in a 1937 speech to the Central Committee Plenum he noted that the regime now had 'tens of thousands of capable, talented people. We only have to know who they are and promote them in time, so that they don't stand too long in one and the same place and start to rot.' The horrible events of the Great Terror, therefore, were also Stalin's second revolution, when the cadres trained during the first finally got positions to fill.[17]

The quick promotions from the workbench via crash education into management could be dizzying as well as rewarding. They certainly were connected to a lot of work, personal sacrifice, and exertion—circumstances which made the sense of self-worth of these careerists more than just the misrecognition of structural forces as personal will-power. Once in positions of authority, however, the lack of experience of the new cadres led to disorientation. Promotees frequently asked not only for advice on how to conduct their jobs, but also for guidelines on how to behave. How, in fact, was the proletarian manager to dress, live, and talk? Insecure in their new status and overwhelmed by their new responsibilities, they longed for symbols legitimizing their elevated position. Groping for a new code of behaviour, they reached for what was already there—the old code of respectability and self-perfection of pre-revolutionary origin, now relabelled 'communist morality'. Marxist critics were thus half right when they linked the retreat from revolutionary symbolism in the 1930s and the apparent return of 'petty bourgeois' behaviour to the rise of a 'new class'. Seen from within the group who drove it, however, this Great Retreat was not counter-revolution. Rather than a betrayal of the promise for a better life for the proletariat, for those who made their way into the new elite, this was 'revolution accomplished'. Paradoxically, of course, this revolution also meant that old intelligentsia notions of culturedness, respectability, and physical culture reaffirmed themselves and were propagated as behavioural norms to 'the masses'—from collective farmers in the Russian heartland to the nomads at the Arctic Circle.[18] While culturedness was thus supposed to apply to every citizen, no matter how humble or backward, there was also an increasing stratification of advice: the lower orders were admonished to wash their hands and faces, or change their underwear, while the new elite was told to teach its children (who presumably had already mastered the art of wielding a tooth brush) 'true politeness', which spoke of 'nobility of character'.[19]

The new elite thus distinguished itself from the lower classes (from where it had emerged) by applying rather old-fashioned conventions. Stalin's self-made men, moreover, also knew that given their hard work for the revolution, Soviet power, and comrade Stalin personally, they also deserved a good life, which, after all, had been one of the revolution's promises. With the victory of Socialism over the forces of the past, the old-fashioned revolutionary asceticism could go. Leatherjackets and boots were replaced by smart suits and ties for men, and make-up, heels and skirts for women. The communist household was no longer a Spartan place filled with books and papers only, but became increasingly cosy and its inhabitants 'cultured'. Rubber trees, embroidery, curtains, and white table cloth made their appearance. Sitting in their well-ventilated living rooms at their writing desks, in an upright manner, in moments of leisure after work and exercise ('physical culture'), the new class could, under the calming light of orange lamp shades, check its own progress up the ladder of civilization by completing surveys in popular magazines, which started to replace the self-help books and brochures of earlier decades. 'Are you a cultured person?', these asked, and answered affirmatively if the subject could recite 'at least' one Pushkin poem, name 'five plays by Shakespeare', and four or more African rivers.

A cultured person had 'a favourite composer' and could name 'his three major works', could list five Soviet made cars, give the decimal for 3/8, know about 'the three most significant sport tournaments of the last year and their results', had visited an arts exhibition in the previous year and was able to 'describe the three paintings which you liked most'. Additional points could be scored if the citizen had read Stendhal's *Red and Black* as well as Turgenev's *Fathers and Sons* and was able to explain 'why the Stakhanovite movement became possible in our country'. Otherwise, the journal shouted at the reader to WORK ON YOURSELF in order to become cultured in the future.[20]

All these efforts bore fruit. Already by 1934, Moscow's elite had become so sophisticated that when the Bavarian anarchist Oskar Maria Graf put on his lederhosen to have a first look at this socialism, he not only stopped conversations in the fashionable Metropole Hotel, but to his delight also put his fellow émigrés to flight. Better avoid being associated with somebody so disrespectfully dressed (like a rustic! in Moscow!!). And not only dressed. When Graf was accosted by an acquaintance with 'Man, you're not planning to run around Moscow in this get-up?' he played the naive peasant Socialist: 'Did you think I'll have a suit made, just for Moscow?'[21]

II

Bavarians like Graf (who eventually emigrated to New York, where his eccentricity raised fewer eyebrows) were, indeed, rather curious beings in Stalin's Moscow. Other minorities played a larger role, however. While usually referred to as 'Russia', the old Tsarist state had long been a multiethnic empire which accommodated non-Russians through co-optation of their elites. This accommodation was put under enormous stress by the spread of the fateful innovation of nationalism—the idea of French revolutionary origin that not only should every modern have one and only one nationality, but also that states should be organized on ethnic principles, inhabited and run by populations of homogenous ancestry. On the one hand, Russian nationalism at least at times took hold of the governing elites, transforming the multiethnic empire into a 'prison house of nations'. On the other hand, local elites saw the light, too, pushing the idea of their own 'nation' over which they, of course, would have a legitimate claim to rule. By the time the Bolsheviks came, somewhat, to power in 1917, nationalisms had emerged as a major alternative solution to the question of how society should be ordered in the modern world, and the new rulers had to address this competition in some way.[22]

They chose to do so in a manner not unlike the old imperial way of dealing with the multiple ethnicities, only that this time it was 'the masses' rather than 'the elites' who would be accommodated to the new regime. Rather than confronting nationalism head on—which they feared would be understood as Russian imperialism—they fostered a large array of national languages, territories, and cultures, sometimes inventing traditions which had not existed in the first place. Peasants in the western borderlands, who spoke a mixture of Ukrainian, Polish, and Russian dialects, with some Yiddish thrown in for good measure, learned with slight astonishment that they were, indeed, not 'locals' or 'Catholics' but Ukrainians, Poles, or Russians.[23] Such attempts to promote ethnic particularism has led one historian to quip that 'Soviet nationality policy was devised and carried out by nationalists'.[24] Only the Russians, it turned out, had no right to be proud of their nationality, as they had been the oppressor nation in the old regime and, therefore, had to tone down their self-affirmation. In the words of the Party Programme of 1919, the workers

of those nations which under capitalism were oppressor nations must take exceptional care not to hurt the national sentiments of the oppressed nations...and must not only promote the actual equality, but also the development of the language and literature of the working people of the formerly oppressed nations so as to remove all traces of distrust and alienation inherited from the epoch of capitalism.[25]

Stalin's first revolution from above stood in this tradition. While wreaking havoc among Ukrainian peasants, Kazakh nomads, and 'small peoples of the North' on the basis of (largely imagined) class difference, the Stalinists at the same time tried to promote cadres from minorities through specific affirmative action programmes. Even the reindeer herders and oceanic hunters of the far North, while bludgeoned into absurd 'collective farms' could at the same time apply to study at the 'Institute of the Peoples of the North'. While only a miniscule group actually did graduate—sixteen in 1931 and fifty in 1935, plus some 148 from various professional schools in 1934—those who did were likely to be pulled from the 'dark little village in the heart of the taiga' to the big city—a breathtaking experience. 'I never thought that I would some day live the way I live now. Life here [in Leningrad] is very strange to me, for I had never seen anything like it before, living as I did in complete ignorance and without any idea of culture and the successes of our socialist construction.'[26] Between 1930 and 1934, special quotas for minority students were in place in the elite universities of Moscow and Leningrad, and after the abolition of this 'mechanical' means of easing access, affirmative action in higher education continued in slightly revised form for what now no longer were 'culturally backward nationalities'. As backwardness had been eliminated during Stalin's first revolution from above, preferred admissions now went to the 'formerly culturally backward'.[27]

In fact, ethnic minorities entered the new elite in significant numbers. Communist Party membership is one indicator for this process. Uzbeks made up 37 per cent of the membership of the CP of Uzbekistan in 1927, a share which grew to 61 in 1933, then declined somewhat to remain at around half throughout the pre-war years. The organizations of Tadzhikistan and Kyrgyzstan had similar shares of their titular nationality.[28] Between 1926 and 1939 the rate of saturation of white collar positions in minority republics with people of the titular nation grew massively. In two republics—Armenia and Georgia—their share among the elite was even higher than their share among the population.[29] Despite the somewhat more muted support for promotion of nationalities after the end of the first revolution from above, then, Stalin's policies by 1939 effected the rise of a 'sizable indigenous white collar class' in both the eastern and western non-Russian republics of the empire. As a major authority on the subject concludes: 'In leadership positions and the cultural sector, titular nationals had on average achieved proportionate representation (in some cases, over-representation).' In the east, such successful mobility was partially hampered by the feeble success of minorities in penetrating technical specialties, in particular engineering, which dominated the leaders of the Brezhnev generation.[30] At the very top, too, this was a multiethnic elite with minorities like Georgians (Stalin, Ordzhonikidze, Beria), Jews (Kaganovich and Mekhlis), Poles (Kosior), Armenians (Mikoyan), or Latvians (Rudzutak) in senior positions. Over time, however, the elite was 'Russianized'. If the Central Committee of 1934 had included 54 per cent of Russians, after the Great Purges their share rose to 70 per cent. This not only meant that more Russians than others benefited from Stalin's second revolution from above at this level, but also that ethnic Russians moved from an under-representation in 1934 to an over-representation in 1939: their share in the Soviet Union's population was only 58 per cent. Ukrainians, too, moved from an under- to an over-representation.[31]

From the 1930s to the end of Stalinism, the obsession with national markers showed its ugly underbelly, when the increasingly panicked regime started ethnic cleansing operations, largely of diaspora nations—about 1.7 per cent of the total population—while affirmative action continued for the indigenous minorities.[32] It might seem paradoxical that these continued side-by-side, but the underlying logic was the same for both policies. Diaspora nations in the borderlands had been treated particularly well because it was assumed that this would convince their brothers and sisters beyond the border that life in Socialism was preferable to life under Capitalism. With the growing threat of war, however, ethnic minorities in the borderlands or even far behind the border, acquired an increasingly sinister meaning in the mind of the leadership. Would they not make common cause with the enemy in wartime? Were they not a fifth column? Looking closely at the composition of their empire, the leadership found disquietingly many self-assertive minorities with potential links to foreign states—a situation their own policies of assigning national categories, nurturing education and culture in the minority language, and promoting cadres on the basis of ethnicity had helped create in the first place. In the context of the increasing radicalization of social engineering in the 1930s, the result was ethnic cleansing operations in order to prepare the country for war.[33] This flip from benevolence to repression was accompanied by the growth of Russian nationalism as a legitimate part of official discourse. From the mid-1930s, the regime promoted the glorious Russian past as a new ideological glue for its fractured population.[34] The war itself, and the expansion to the

West, did its share to keep nationality as one of the most prominent markers of repression until the end of Stalin's life.[35] Now, even some of the indigenous minorities became 'enemy nations'.[36]

III

The Stalinist regime thus favoured, much of the time, ethnic minorities, making it possible for collective farmers from the Caucasus not only to excel in athletic pursuits, but also to brag about them in front of the leader:

MISOSTISHKHOVA: Now let me say a few words about myself. In my kolkhoz I am a record-holding worker of the kolkhoz fields. But in addition to that, I am also ready for labor and defense...

STALIN: How old are you?

MISOSTISHKHOVA: Seventeen. I am also a record-holding mountain climber. I was the first, together with Comrade Kalmykov, to climb the highest mountain in Europe, Elbrus....Now I'm preparing myself for parachute jumping. I haven't done it yet because I didn't have enough time after storming Mount Elbrus. But, Comrades, I give my word to Comrade Voroshilov that in parachute jumping I am also going to be ahead of the men. (*Tumultuous applause, turning into an ovation.*)[37]

This exchange between Stalin and a female over-achiever at a all-Union Stakhanovite meeting in the mid-1930s points to a sometimes neglected aspect of Stalinism: the promotion of women. The Soviet regime, to stress this point again, created not only oppression but also opportunities. And it directed these opportunities towards those who might be willing and able to break up Old Russia, Old Ukraine, Old Asia, or Old Siberia—in short, the old order, particularly in the countryside. Bolsheviks were, by and large, no feminists, but they saw the patriarchal family as an expression of underlying capitalist exploitation and crushing this institution was part of the class war in the village. Peasant women, thus, constituted a logical reservoir of allies in the countryside. In the Muslim societies of Central Asia and in the hunter-gatherer systems of the North, where other allies were hard to come by, women were even construed as a 'surrogate proletariat' in natural alliance with the regime. But in the Slavic heartlands, too, rural women were offered a coalition with the state, if they were ready to break up the patriarchal order. Not that this always worked. Peasants knew well that the authorities were less likely to punish rebelling women than protesting men; moreover, the confiscations of livestock during collectivization targeted a sector of the household economy which traditionally was under female control. Together, these factors combined to make 'women's riots' (*bab'y bunty*) into a widespread and characteristic form of peasant protest during the Stalin revolution.[38]

Nevertheless, some accepted the offer of a partnership with the regime to break the domination of their elders. Those who tried hardest were often youth, widows, orphans or other outsiders and marginals. 'I am not married', wrote the Stakhanovite livestock and dairy worker, K. F. Maksimovskaia, about herself in late 1935,

> I am still twenty-one years old and I live alone. I don't have anybody else, no kin. I lost my parents when I was one year and three months. I was brought up for five years at the Totemsky orphanage in the Northern Krai and then lived as a nanny at strangers' houses. It hurts even to remember now what I had to go through in my childhood living with strangers.

Many like her found a home in the Komsomol, the Party, the Cause: 'The sovkhoz took me in, raised me, educated me.' And: 'I can do any job even as well as a man.'[39] 'Soviet power, the party, and Comrade Stalin,' claimed Z. S. Budagian, an orphan-turned-Stakhanovite, 'took the place of my father; the kolkhoz became my home; and now I am in charge of a whole brigade.'[40] Most celebrated were the examples of Pasha Angelina and Maria Demchenko, who as tractor driver and combine operator, respectively, 'symbolized the new Soviet woman who owed her emancipation from the patriarchal family to collectivization and the wise leadership of Comrade Stalin'.[41]

Such escape from the power of men through guidance by the Father in the Kremlin could be exhilarating. 'How did I,' wrote Pasha Angelina in her 1948 autobiography, 'become an important state official and a Supreme Soviet delegate?' The daughter of a landless field labourer turned collective farmer she had become the only woman among the sixty thousand *traktoristy*, tractor drivers, who stood in the vanguard of

collectivization in 1930. As poor peasants, her family made natural allies
for the Bolshevik reconstructors of the countryside; her father and elder
brothers were Party members, one of them served as chairman of the
Committee of the Poor and later in the District Party Committee;
another of her brothers was the village Party cell's secretary; she herself
and her younger siblings were in the Komsomol; and together her family 'was in the forefront of kolkhoz construction, dekulakization, and
propaganda work'. Equally naturally, one of her brothers was put in
charge of the new collective's only tractor, and once he was promoted
away from the village—again not untypical for someone of his background and allegiance—Pasha took his place. Allowed she was, despite
snickers, but not trusted, 'even by my own friends.' She was a woman,
after all, who 'doesn't belong on a tractor.' Soon 'somebody kept spread-
ing vile rumours about me, and "God-fearing" old women, egged on by
the priest, would spit whenever they saw that "shameless Pasha" in her
overalls behind the wheel of a tractor.' Encouraged rather than beaten
down by such resistance, she soon organized an all-female tractor
brigade—after having secured support for this endeavour from the
political department of the Machine Tractor Station. In the Spring of
1933, the new brigade rolled out to the fields, only to be blocked by an
angry crowd of women, later joined by men as well. Only the intervention of the head of the political department allowed work to begin. 'The
same thing happened at the next kolkhoz: we almost got beaten up by
the local women, and two of my girls were locked up in a cellar.'
Eventually, 'we asserted our right to be tractor drivers'—and received
material rewards and fame to boot. She would meet Stalin ('Be brave,
Pasha, be brave,' the wise patriarch whispered, 'softly, so that only I
could hear'). Streets and ships were named after Pasha, the daughter of
a once landless peasant, for transgressing gender boundaries and working for the fulfilment of herself as well as the Five-Year Plan, which to
her seemed one and the same. Yet Pasha remained a tractor driver, while
many men of similar background and ability quickly fell up the steps.[42]

There was, then, something of a glass ceiling for ambitious young
women, who allied themselves with the regime: the higher in the official
hierarchy, the fewer women encountered on the corridors.[43] And there
was more than that. Men did fight back, and often aggressively. Angelina

was threatened repeatedly and eventually run over by 'kulak sons' and severely injured.[44] Women who participated in the 1927 unveiling campaign in Central Asia were subjected to beatings, rape, and murder. A decade later, and despite a concerted effort of the Soviet penal system to deal with the problem, little seems to have changed.[45] On 11 June 1938, in the town of Bakharden in Turkmenistan, 'for reasons of class hatred a Komsomol member, who had arrived from the village Karagan to participate in a course for propagandists, was severely wounded by her husband'.[46] Not long after this incident, on 2 June, in a different village, another agitator, Ak Bibi Kerim, who was also a Komsomol member and Village Councillor, 'was murdered by her husband in revenge for her active work in society (*aktivnaia obshchestvennaia rabota*)'. Other activists were beaten severely by their husbands to be brought back into line.[47] Such violence was not confined to Muslim regions, although as a consequence of the greater cultural gulf between the Bolsheviks and the rest of the population it appears to have been stronger here than elsewhere.[48]

Nor were the perpetrators necessarily men. Female shock-workers were frequently subjected to ridicule, threats, and actual deeds of violence, performed by opponents of the movement of both sexes.[49] Nor did it necessarily require violence to convince women that they should follow the obviously reasonable mores of their surrounding milieu rather than the crazy ideas of the city folks and infidels who came to bring them progress and civilization. In Central Asia, groups of women petitioned to be excluded from the unveiling campaign of 1927, a symbolic policy, which only closed the ranks of the indigenous population. It was 'a secret to no one,' a police report summed up the situation, 'that in Uzbekistan 95 percent of the population is against the unveiling of women.'[50]

Stalinism thus generated fierce contests over the gendered order of society, which were entangled with the onslaught on backwardness, religion, and rural ways of life.[51] Overall, the sign of the times seemed to point towards radical transformation of relations between the sexes. The simple fact that in the village after collectivization agricultural work was accounted for, led to challenges to the patriarchal order in the household:

178

> Mother won her card as a member of the collective farm, and on the card
> her work days were entered. She had as many work days as Father had.
> She used to take her membership card and wave it in Father's face.
>
> 'You always said you supported me. Now you see I am earning as
> much as you,' she declared. 'So I have as much to say as you have, don't
> I? You had better not say anything more to me.' The Father had nothing to
> say. He would mumble and keep the peace for the time being.[52]

A female Stakhanovite made a similar point in a mid-1930s speech: 'How
can your husband exploit you when you make more money than he
does,' she asked rhetorically. And added: 'That usually shuts him up.'[53]
During the First Five-Year Plan women entered the industrial workforce in unprecedented numbers, increasing their share in industrial
employment from 29 per cent in 1928 to 37 in 1934.[54] By the late 1930s,
71 per-cent of working age women—i.e. those between the ages of sixteen and fifty-nine—were engaged in wage labour. Many, particularly
the young, entered the elite, became 'managers, professionals, or government bureaucrats' or the wives of Party leaders.[55] Even the daughter of
deported 'kulaks' could move up in the world, first working as a nanny
for a family of Party functionaries, then marrying an officer, who after
the war became a general. In a reversal of fortunes not untypical for the
times, she could even offer, after the arrest of her old employees in the
Great Purges, to adopt their son.[56] Those women, who against all odds
managed to move into and hold on to some of the better paid positions
in the countryside, not infrequently profited from the Great Terror
clearing away the men who had hindered their further advancement. As
a result, collective-farm chairwomen could become heads of the regional
agricultural department, milkmaids were catapulted into the director-
seats of their milk-farms, and tractor drivers turned into directors of
machine-tractor stations.[57]
During the 1930s women's share in non-kolkhoz workforce had risen
from 27 in 1929 to 30 in 1933 and on to 38 per cent in 1940. The war
further boosted this trend, pushing the share up to 55 per cent in 1945.
With the disappearance of men, first to the front, and then into mass
graves, women had to step up to take over their positions. Throughout
late Stalinism, this percentage then fell somewhat, hovering between 47

and 48 per cent; but this decline was due to the return of men, not the disappearance of women from the workforce, whose absolute numbers continued to grow. In the countryside, this overall trend was even more extreme. From 1941 onwards, men were extremely scarce and their jobs, from tractor driver to kolkhoz chair, were increasingly performed by women. Both world wars opened up possibilities for women in all belligerent societies, but in most of the warring nations, the wartime liberalization of gender norms was undone after the guns fell silent. Not so in the Soviet Union. True, men replaced women as they returned from the front; but the continuing labour shortages and the extreme losses of men during the war meant that women remained, if they liked it or not, in the workforce.[58]

Systematic data is hard to find, which would allow to examine the extent to which women were pushed out of the positions they had acquired during the war. Figure 3 summarizes one such rare set of numbers. It charts two lines over time. On the top is the absolute number of women secretaries of primary organizations—the lowest level of administration within the Communist Party. The lower line shows these

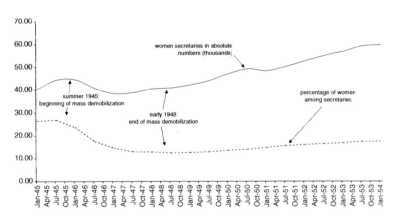

Figure 3 Women as secretaries of primary Party organizations, 1945–1954

Sources: Russian State Archive of Contemporary History (RGANI) f. 77, op. 1, d. 4, ll. 79, 176, 177; d. 5, ll. 81, 82, 174, 175; d. 6, ll. 81, 182, 183; d. 7, ll. 82, 83, 178, 179; d. 8, ll. 83, 84, 89, 90. For a reconstruction of the demobilization waves see Edele, *Soviet Veterans of the Second World War*, 23, table 1.1.

women again, only this time as a percentage of all secretaries of this level. The approximate start and end points of mass demobilization are indicated with double arrows. Both lines show that women lost the secretary's chair in large numbers once soldiers returned from the war. Their tally fell from a high point of 44,580 by 1 January 1946 to a low point of 38,555 one year later; the relative figure decreased even more dramatically, from 27 per cent in early July 1945 to 13 per cent a year later. This difference was caused by a dramatic and continuous expansion of the number of primary organizations, and thus the number of secretaries. Women were not, however, completely excluded from benefiting from this growth of the Party. In fact, as the two lines in the chart show, the number of positions held by women increased already from July 1947 and even the relative numbers recovered somewhat from January 1949 onwards.

Stalinist society, thus, continued to offer women the chance of self-advancement, including the gendered conflicts such social mobility fuelled. The apparent retreat from revolutionary values in the mid-1930s, moreover, did not displace the earlier discourse on gender equality. In Central Asia, women remained the surrogate proletariat throughout the pre-war years.[59] In the Slavic regions, too, historians have concluded that 'no "Great Retreat" from emancipatory goals can be discerned in the Soviet government's policies'. Peasant women continued to enjoy 'more opportunities to engage in non-traditional activities than ever before'.[60] Throughout the 1930s, moreover, the state ran a campaign against absconding husbands, trying to track them down, force them to pay child support, or shame them in the press. In this campaign, 'the weights of central instructions and propaganda was on the side of the deserted wives, not the husbands'.[61] This campaign continued during and after the war, despite new legislation encouraging male promiscuity in order to replace the dead. As before, the results of such efforts were rather mixed.[62]

Despite the conservative turn in the mid-1930s, many in the younger generation were raised in the spirit of quite radical gender norms. Hundreds of thousands of Komsomol girls were brought up to expect to fight 'like men', should this become necessary. The enthusiasm with which these 'violent women' volunteered for service in 1941 is proof that they did not know that the proper place for a woman at war was behind the frontline.[63] Their further experience, however, also indicates that such a radical view of gender equality was far from consensual in Stalinist society. Both in the army and in their later life, these women were frequently confronted with what today would be called 'sexism'—they were treated as if they were frontline whores, who had joined the army merely to snatch the men from honourable women-folk back home. As compelling as the story of these women warriors is, moreover, they formed only a small minority of the female contribution to the war effort. For the majority, the experience was one of a further spurt in employment, replacing the men who had gone to the front to fight and die.[64]

The most striking aspect of gender relations in the Soviet Union, then, is how despite the large share of female employment, despite the general upheaval within society, despite the possibilities opened up for women, and despite the discourse of gender equality—the 1936 constitution guaranteed 'equal rights with men in all spheres of economic, state, cultural, social and political life'[65]—patriarchal values reasserted themselves. In Central Asia 'startlingly little changed' in the general pattern of relations between the sexes and Bolshevik authorities displayed 'deep despair' about 'their continuing failure to have much of an impact—at least not the kind of impact they sought—on patterns of Uzbek family life'. In the villages of Ukraine, Belorussia, and Russia, too, central policy did not have the intended results. The promotion of women into positions of authority often led to the proliferation of 'representative' positions, rather than the displacement of men.[66] Despite some 'freeing' of positions during the Great Terror, it was only during the war that women did replace men in the countryside—often only as long as hostilities continued. Such poor results of the official policy to promote women were not just caused by the male chauvinism of lower officialdom, but equally by 'resistance on the part of the peasant women themselves'. That it was indeed possible to 'throw off the yoke of patriarchal peasant culture' was demonstrated by the minority of young peasant women who did take the opportunity offered by official policy. The majority, however, did not try.[67] This was partially caused by deeply engrained conservatism, but also by the fact that the deal the 'new Soviet women' got was far from advantageous upon closer inspection. Female employment did not equal liberation but the rise of the double shift of wage labour followed by domestic chores. In the case of peasant women, who not only had to work the kolkhoz fields while running the household and raising the children, but also look after the household's private plot and animals, this load often grew to a triple burden. The difference of these results to the social mobility of men is telling. The latter was so successful because it instrumentalized widespread popular aspirations; the transformation of gender roles, by contrast, was so contradictory because it was diametrically opposed to popular understandings of what was proper and what was not.[68]

IV

There are two ways to interpret employment data of women after the war. Optimists would stress, like the preceding paragraphs, that while there were some losses for employment in leading positions during and after demobilization, there was also recovery of such positions. The negative interpretation, by contrast, emphasizes the economic compulsion involved. A careful study of household budget surveys can demonstrate that urban households after the war attempted to reduce the number of adults employed, in order to use some of their labour capacity to run the household and raise the children. Those who stayed at home tended to be women, as childcare was, by and large, considered women's business. Nevertheless, an initial decline of household members in gainful employment was soon reversed by a continuing trend towards full employment. Moreover, the share of adults employed never reverted to the pre-war situation, but remained on a significantly higher level. As a result of the horrendous wartime losses, many households after 1945 were, in fact, headed by women, and such families showed a higher than average participation of adult members in the workforce in order to make ends meet. Even for families with a father, life remained extremely hard, and often one income was not enough to feed the family.[69]

This basic point needs to be kept in mind in any discussion of social dynamics under Stalin: the advancement of significant numbers of people took place in front of the backdrop of misery for most. As spectacular as social mobility was for proletarians-turned-managers; as remarkable as the affirmative action programmes on the basis of class, gender, and ethnicity were—in the final analysis, the majority of the population did not better its lot. While millions of peasants became proletarians, such technically 'social mobility' went hand in hand with a severe decline in living standards for the new proletarians.[70] 'Real wages for non-agricultural wage earners and salaried employees,' states one classic study, 'dropped by from 22 to 43 per cent between 1928 and 1940, and—largely as a result of the Second World War—were approximately 50 per cent of the 1928 level In the year 1948. They did not begin to approach the 1928 level until around 1952.'[71] Moreover, not only the standard of living but also the quality of life nose-dived throughout the Stalin years. The quickly built cities as a rule under-invested in such essential public health infrastructure as sewage systems or public baths (not to speak of indoor toilets and running water in the new workers' settlements). Many lived in the most squalid conditions in places euphemistically named 'Shanghai'—slum settlements of sheds and dugouts outside of public oversight or police surveillance. Many more dwelled in barracks, dormitories, or the improvisation-turned-form-of-life of the 'communal apartment', with a family to a room and shared kitchens and bathrooms, where available.[72]

It is in this general context of misery and hardship that we need to place the Stalinist discourse and practice of welfare and civilian consumption. Needless to say, shortages, long lines, and recurrence of rationing were not ideological goals of the regime; neither were high infant mortality, diseases caused by under-nourishment, poor living conditions, and inadequate healthcare. These were perceived as short- or medium-term hardships, unavoidable on the way to Communism, but certainly not desired results of social engineering. Quite the opposite, the regime continued to promise a good life to the population and at least at times acted to provide welfare in various senses of the word— social security, consumption, common luxury, medical care, and education.[73]

There were, also, some real achievements with regards to the latter two, although these were by no means as spectacular as the Soviets wanted both domestic and international audiences to believe. The census of 1897 had counted only 27.7 per cent literacy, a share which had risen to 50 per cent by 1937. While the data are not easily comparable, as the definition of 'literacy' changed over time, these numbers still indicate respectable growth in the educational levels of the population. The largest successes were with the young generation, as Figure 4 below shows. Soviets born after the upheavals of war, revolution, and civil war tended not only to be more literate than their older compatriots; more spectacularly, as the lack of differentiation of the two lines in Figure 4 indicate, in the younger generation the literacy gap between the sexes was effectively eliminated. Nevertheless, such successes were well below the official claims that illiteracy had been, in the jargon of the times, 'liquidated'.[74]

Progress in healthcare—the other Soviet claim to fame in the field of welfare policies—occurred in fits and starts. During Stalin's first revolution from above, Soviet healthcare was—like everything else—enlisted in the industrialization effort. The earlier focus on prevention now shifted to

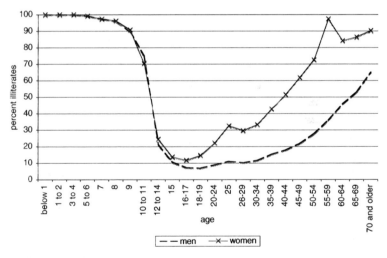

Figure 4 Percentage of illiterates by age group and sex according to 1937 census (% of age group)

Source for raw data: V. B. Zhiromskaia and Iu. A. Poliakov (eds.): *Vsesoiuznaia perepis' naseleniia 1937 goda: Obhchie itogi. Sbornik dokumentov i materialov* (Moscow: Rosspen, 2007), 112 (both sexes); 114 (men);116 (women).

a preoccupation with repairing labour capacity. Healthcare also became—like housing and consumption—part of the mobilization to work. By providing care in clinics attached to workplaces, healthcare became a privilege connected to employment rather than a social right of each citizen. The result was a rigidly stratified system of health provision according to the service provided to the state. At the top of this pyramid stood the excellent Kremlin hospital, at the bottom the sick bays of the labour camps. In the countryside, little healthcare was available and traditional medicine and grandmother's cures remained more important than modern medical practice. By the late 1930s this focus on productionism, and the connected stratification of healthcare, started to weaken. The Third Five-Year Plan of 1938 marked the beginning of a shift towards more expenditure for welfare, a trend which gathered force after the war. As one specialist of Soviet socialized medicine concludes, 'welfare state building was a significant feature of the Late Stalinist years.' Within the confined space of the final eight years of Stalin's life, the number of medical doctors working in the land of the Soviets nearly doubled, while healthcare started to shift from the 'production principle' (which provided healthcare at the point of employment) to a universalized system.[75]

Because they had implications for industrial capacity and defence, education and healthcare were relatively high on the list of priorities of the Stalinist regime. The same cannot be said for social security, which had once been declared a major goal of the Revolution. Given the dire fiscal straits the new regime found itself in, pensions and unemployment benefits remained developed only on the level of principled statements. Welfare legislation under Stalin became a privilege granted in exchange for service to the regime. It thus served, like much of healthcare, to mobilize to labour and defence.[76] Consumption was used in similarly hierarchical ways as a means to control the population. Official discourse set great store in images of abundance, advertising such exotic condiments as ketchup (produced by the Chief Canned Goods Trust) and promising caviar with champagne as the fare of everyday Soviets. For the time being, however, such common luxury was reserved to the elite, who had access to 'closed' stores as well as internal distribution networks of their workplaces. As in the case of healthcare, access to food, consumer goods, and housing was rigidly stratified according to region (with Moscow at the top) and job (the more important a position, the better fed, shod, and housed the official). The pinnacle was occupied by central government and Party functionaries, writers, composers, and other cultural figures as well as the officer corps. Engineers, Stakhanovites, and shock-workers made up the elite in the factories, while regular workers, exploited though they were, had still better access than collective farmers who would have been at the utter bottom were it not for the inmates of the labour camps.[77]

There were, again and again, some brighter moments within the general misery of life under Stalin. After the starvation crisis of 1932–33, the regime sobered up somewhat from its 'plan-drunkenness', retreated from its utopian planning and shifted to more realistic goal setting. As a result, 'positive economic trends' emerged in late 1933 and gathered steam in 1934. A further moderation in economic policies towards the peasantry and an expansion of the decision making capacity of economic managers in industry during 1935 and 1936 led to a continuation of economic growth during these years. While the focus remained on heavy industry, a moderate rise of consumption levels was allowed as well, and greatly exaggerated in public discourse. In retrospect, this period of moderate recovery of living standards—although still well below the 1927 base line—became known as the 'three good years' of 1934–36. Such hopeful developments were short-lived, however. Already in 1936 new problems became visible. The economic set-back was partially caused by radically increasing military spending, which was exacerbated by domestic and international imbalances. The devastation of the Great Terror did its share to slow the economy to a 'snail like crawl'. From 1937 until the outbreak of war with Germany, the Soviet economy stagnated and consumption levels were hit disproportionably, as resources were transferred at an increasing rate from welfare to warfare.[78]

The war with Germany had devastating consequences. With maybe 27 million war related deaths, 6 million destroyed houses, more than 70 thousand flattened villages, and 17,010 ruined urban settlements of all sizes, the pre-war woes of labour shortage, housing crisis, and public health nightmare continued on an even higher level. The return of famine in 1946–47 only added to this social, economic, and human catastrophe.[79] The regime tried its utmost to somewhat increase consumption levels, as the famine had shown that the breaking point had been reached. The basis for economic recovery was the demobilization of the army between 1945 and early 1948, which was accompanied by a cautious conversion to peacetime output. Soon, pre-war production levels for basic consumer goods—cloth, sugar, shoes—were attained again. Rationing was abolished in 1947 and prices on consumer goods were cut seven times between 1947 and 1955 (measures, which did not lose in popularity by being largely illusory in real terms). Such rays of hope, however, were soon covered over by the clouds of a new military confrontation. The Korean War of 1950–53 again convinced the leadership to transfer resources to military production and to replenish the army's ranks to well above pre-war strength. The result was, again, a depression of consumption levels and consumer goods production.[80]

V

For the majority of the population, those who did not have the privilege to see the dictatorship over needs from 'somewhere near the top', then, life under Stalin was extremely grim. Even in the darkest years, however, people continued to try and enjoy their lives as best as they could. There were those totally committed activists, who would live most of the day for the cause of building Communism. But even they did not stop to fall in love, play, or drink, in short—enjoy themselves. Many more tried to escape the cold and demanding world they were placed in.

Escapism included, of course, the traditional heavy drinking, including imbibing to absolute incapacitation. 'Vodka, it is clear, plays an important part in the lives of Soviet men', as a sociologist has stated the obvious with scholarly gravitas.[81] In the early years of Stalinism, the state discouraged drinking and even imposed dry laws in some settlements. Soon, however, state interest trumped revolutionary puritanism. Faced with what he thought was an imminent attack by 'the Poles', Stalin ordered to 'bring our current army reserves up from 640,000 to 700,000'. Such expansion of the armed forces would, of course, cost money. 'Where,' the leader asked rhetorically, 'can we find the money? I think vodka production should be expanded.... We need to get rid of a false sense of shame and directly and openly promote the greatest expansion of vodka production possible for the sake of a real and serious defence of our country.'[82] This strategy soon generated about a fifth of total state revenue; vodka became, in the words of one historian, 'the motor of the Soviet economy': other shortages notwithstanding 'even in the most remote corners of the Soviet Union, vodka supplies never ran low'.[83] During the war, the famous 'frontline 100 grams'—a waterglass full of vodka—became standard issue to the troops in order to increase morale before an attack.[84] After the war, boozing increased, if anything. Demobilization was a big party for many, and veterans did not stop hitting the bottle after return to civilian life. In Moscow, drinking establishments were everywhere. One foreign observer in the immediate post-war years reported that at every principal street corner there was 'a wooden kiosk where one may buy cigarettes, mineral water, sandwiches—and vodka.' He watched a truck driver jump out of his vehicle one morning at half past ten, run to one of these kiosks, gulp down 'ten and one half ounces of vodka' and drive off 'at high speed'.

> After him, other passers-by stopped at the same kiosk; and during the five minutes that I spent there...the vodka flowed freely, in glasses of three and one half, seven, or ten and one half ounces. I soon became accustomed to these bibulous scenes and paid no more attention to them, reflecting only that at the present price of vodka a very considerable part of the national income was being transformed into 'little sunshine'.[85]

It was only under Khrushchev that the state started a new campaign to sober up its population, even turning such alcohol-fuelled institutions as the Moscow *Kokteil Khall* into an ice-cream parlour.[86]

Intoxication was not the only escape from the harsh world of Stalinism. Many fled into the world of fantasy. For one, there were novels of pre-revolutionary vintage, which continued to circulate.[87] More easily available were works of socialist realism, the official dogma for literature, movies, and the arts—a fairy tale world in itself. Socialist realist novels and movies were full of larger-than-life heroes battling dark forces in the name of Communism. Part adventure tale, part mythology, they also allowed imaginary wish fulfilment, as the successful socialist dragon-slayers got material rewards such as motor bikes, suits, pretty shoes, or sewing machines, not to speak of love and happiness in return for their feats in the building of Communism. Following Stalin's explicit requests, movie makers turned away from experimental art and produced socialist realist epics and musical comedies instead. While not devoid of ideological messages, such light fare could be consumed, after a long workday, for the song and dance only. After the war, the regime managed to terrify its creative intelligentsia to such an extent that these highly privileged movie makers, like their composer colleagues, simply failed to produce much, in order to avoid getting into trouble for ideological mistakes and potentially lose their livelihood together with their apartments, dachas, and holidays. The result was a 'picture famine', which the leadership tried to counter by releasing movies taken as trophies from Germany. In a strange twist of fate, then, among the most popular actors in late Stalinism was the Nazi starlet, Marika Rökk, and the American swim champion, Johnny Weissmuller. To the shock of Soviet puritans, the latter strutted as Tarzan across Soviet screens in 1951, leading to ape-like howls filling the hallways of student dormitories.[88]

For men, soccer as a spectator sport was a major diversion. Soviet football culture resembled in many ways its European equivalent. It was largely homo-social, that is dominated by one sex: men. Fanship included spending time with one's pals in the stadium, drinking, and getting into fist-fights with fans from the other team.[89] Soccer and drinking point to the question of the gendered nature of leisure time activities. Women tended to have less time to spare than men. As in many other societies, the major burden of housework fell on women, who in addition also had to work. The one household-related chore men did fulfil was shopping, or rather, hunting and gathering goods in the economy of shortages.[90]

One leisure-time activity both men and women enjoyed was music and dance. During the first revolution from above popular dances were outlawed. The foxtrot was declared a 'dance of slaves', Western pop music 'the song and dance of the period of the catastrophe of capitalism', and the tango 'the music of impotents'. Even Viennese waltzes were declared 'counter-revolutionary'. In 1929, a ban on saxophones was contemplated, but not institutionalized—this happened in the renewed anti-jazz campaign after the Second World War. With the end of Stalin's first revolution, however, popular music resurfaced. The dance craze of the 'Red Jazz Age' (1933–36) was so pervasive that the commander of the Red Army, Kliment Voroshilov, made dance classes mandatory for his officer corps, while Viacheslav Molotov, then chairman of Sovnarkom, the Soviet government, learned to tango. Even small towns saw the emergence of dance halls, and dance places in public parks were filled with enthusiasts moving their bodies to the rhythms of the foxtrot, the rhumba, and the waltz. Despite periodic crackdowns throughout the Stalin years, jazz remained popular with large sectors of the public. Whenever the mobilizing pressure was eased—after the first and the second Stalin revolutions, or after the war—jazz re-emerged vigorously.[91] During a renewed repression of this 'Western decadence' in the late 1940s, an entire new subculture emerged: the 'stiliagi', or 'style-hunters'. This was a youth culture, originating with the sons of the elite, which found Stalinism deeply boring and fashioned themselves after what they thought America looked like. Their heroes were Tarzan and Benny Goodman, not Lenin and Stalin.[92]

The *stiliagi* embodied the intersection of two of the major force fields holding Stalinist society together—elite welfare and mass escapism. Sons (and some daughters) of Stalin's elite, they had the necessary means to focus on lifestyle and dress. In themselves, however, these were not pursuits frowned on by the guardians of socialist respectability. The problem was not attention on outer appearance, but making style into an end in itself rather than a means to acquiring culturedness. As M. I. Kalinin had preached to teachers in 1938, culture was 'a very broad conception, ranging from the washing of one's face to the latest heights of human thought'. It was necessary to acquire the gestures, habits, and discipline necessary for a cultured person, but one needed to avoid 'slipping into philistinism'.

Clean hands, neat dress, essential comforts in the home, etc.—all these are signs of a people's culture. Public meetings, dramatic circles, social evenings with dancing, etc. are signs of social culture. Communists take part in them, justly regarding them as factors of cultural development. But all this can also turn into a philistine pastime. Indeed, it requires a considerable level of culture and political insight to be able to draw the boundary line between philistinism and real cultural progress. The Marxist regards these achievements as a means, a new foothold for further advance. For the philistine, on the contrary, they are an end in themselves.

**He wants to rest on his achievements, he becomes a slave of his sur-
roundings, adapts his morals accordingly, and lulls his faculty for thought.
That sort of thing must be combated.**[93]

In the end, alas, 'philistinism' won the battle, with the *stiliagi* as its most
sophisticated avant garde. While there continued to be many earnest
fighters for Socialism in the post-war years, a growing number of youth
of all social strata focused on personal belongings and 'style', even though
groping for different models depending on their circumstances. The
sons of the privileged might crave for real American suits and listen to
foreign jazz on their own radio receivers in their own rooms; working
youth, by contrast, might spent their money 'quite irresponsibly', as the
Komsomol newspaper complained in 1948, on such luxuries as dough-
nuts, sunflower seeds, ice cream, and a 'signet ring—a large yellow ring
with a sparkling glass centre'. Such extravagant consumption meant that
poor Vasilii Shukhov could neither afford to buy 'good quality locknit
underwear' nor make ends meet until the next payday. Given such dire
straits, the imaginary West the *stiliagi* devoted much of their longing to
was thoroughly out of reach for most of urban youth, to say nothing of
the countryside. In their search for style advice and behavioural models,
then, most youngsters had, for the time being, to look elsewhere. The
most likely fashion they would emulate was the chic of the criminal
underworld, which already in the interwar years had attracted many
wannabees ('We beat them up mercilessly', remembered one of the
originals).[94]

In post-war Stalinism, the preoccupation with a narrowly defined
good life, which had taken hold not only of the general population, but
even the Communist vanguard, was still combated, half heartedly, in
didactic fiction. Eventually, however, as the soft Stalinists themselves
tried to settle down after the dictator's death and the exciting years of
Khrushchev's thermo-nuclear neo-Leninism, they would accommodate
these widespread desires in what is sometimes called the 'privatized',
'acquisitive', or 'dacha socialism' of the 1970s. It was then, decades after
Stalin's death, when the society he had inadvertently helped to mould
came into its own—a society of consumerism and escapism paradoxically lodged within an economy of scarcity.[95]

CHAPTER 8
ECONOMY OF SCARCITY, ECONOMY OF FAVOURS

> **&&** If you don't steal from the state, you're stealing from your own family. **77**
>
> **Soviet folk wisdom[1]**

> **&&** The lessons of this war make it clear that the Soviet order proved not only the best way to organize the economic and cultural development (*pod"em*) of our country during times of peaceful building, but also the best way to mobilize all the powers of the people to repulse the enemy during wartime. Put together 26 years ago, Soviet power has transformed our country in a short historical period into an unconquerable fortress. **77**
>
> **Comrade Stalin, 6 November 1943.[2]**

I

This book is about the system of social relations between Soviet people under the rule of Stalin, or, in the convenient abbreviation of its title, 'Stalinist society'. So far, the stress has been less on overall integration than on centrifugal forces and the splintering of the Soviet population into a dazzling array of groups and subgroups—families, nationalities, churches, classes and status groups, beneficiaries and victims of state policy, men and women, young and old, Communists and non-Party people, regional, local, and central administrators etc. Much of this society was found to be in flux, both geographically and socially, and the ways people dealt with this fluidity were structured by a wide variety of long, often contradictory and competing histories, not by one uniting history. Families were found to be central to most citizens' lives, but the interests of families and the interests of the overall social formation were neither in sync nor mutually constituting; the state was found to be the extremely weak and internally fractured institutionalization of the rulers' totalitarian aspirations rather than the all-knowing and all-controlling edifice of modernist imagination; ideologies, world-views, and religions turned out to fragment Soviet society rather than uniting it under the umbrella of state-generated discourse; and social mobility, affirmative action, and welfare were of benefit to only small minorities, while most had to find solace in escapist culture, religion, or the bottle. Fragmentation rather than unity, dislocation rather than integration, anomie rather than consensus were the central markers of this society in upheaval.

If this was so, however, the central event of the two and a half decades of Stalin's rule—the victory over Germany—remains somewhat of an enigma, Lend-Lease Aid notwithstanding. Given that the Stalinists had relatively limited control over their society and given that they did not command the loyalty of the majority of their subjects, how could they win a war against the advanced military machine of the Nazis, a machine, after all, nobody had been able to withstand until the Soviets showed that it could be done? The short answer is economic.[3] The Soviets, quite simply, managed to out-produce the Germans from the start, were able to field many more machines, guns, shells, and humans in the killing fields of what the aggressors, somewhat profanely, called the 'Eastern Front'.[4] Theirs was an economy geared, first and foremost, to wartime production and emergency mobilization, which suited it well to the demands of war; and despite the best efforts of the rulers to the contrary, the Soviet economy remained remarkably flexible and decentralized, which allowed it to adapt well to the catastrophe of wartime.

This final point is central. As we shall see in this chapter, there never was a planned economy in the Soviet Union. Rather, what we find is 'planlessness...euphemistically called a planned economy'.[5] There was planning, of course; there were planners, and plans; but the actual economy was far removed from the neat statistical tables set out not only to describe but to prescribe its operations. This lack of control was galling to the rulers, as their totalitarian aspirations were constantly subverted by reality; at the same time, the remarkable complexity, flexibility, and ability to self-organization, improvisation, and make-do which characterized this economy also ensured that these same rulers stayed in power despite the destruction they brought down on their own people in the 1930s and the even more catastrophic annihilation visited upon them by Nazi Germany between 1941 and 1945.

The organization of production and distribution was central not only to the war effort but also to the way the Soviet system worked more generally; the economy of scarcity was probably the most important factor pulling Soviet citizens together in a larger whole. At its centre was a rigidly stratified regime of access to goods and services, embedded into complex and spontaneous relations of exchange which redirected many resources. Together, these disparate processes created a system of economic coercion which left most people little choice but to comply with its overall demands, if they wanted to survive, let alone prosper. They could and did work it to their least disadvantage, thereby both altering and reproducing it; but they could not escape participation in it. This was not the economy the leadership had set out to construct, but the one they got as a result of their actions.[6]

II

The actually existing Stalinist economy was a complex interaction of a state-run command system, a large variety of 'informal adjustive mechanisms' of those trying to work within and around its shortcomings, elements of legal markets, small-time production and distribution of goods, the remnants of a peasant economy, households as central economic actors, and illegal relations of exchange, corruption, and informal wheeling and dealing holding these various aspects together.[7] It was an economy headed by 'a vicious dictator and violent central government', which focused on 'extracting key resources from local economic associations', which were otherwise left to their own devices to manage human and other resources under their jurisdiction. These local associations—regional governments, factories, collective and state farms—functioned as 'subcontractors under force' more than as part of an integrated socialist economy.[8]

The Soviets claimed to run a rational economy as an alternative to the 'anarchy of the market'. Ostensibly, the central government's planning agency, Gosplan, set the plans, Commissariats (later Ministries) refined them for their field of supervision, while their subordinate enterprises faithfully executed them. In real life, however, the abstract work of the planners had little relation to what happened on the ground. Engineers and production managers felt 'superior to government employees', resented the planning organs' inefficiency and delighted in 'the ease with which they pulled the wool over the eyes of planners'. Those who supposedly ran this economy on the basis of their statistical tables (computed, one must add, with the use of an abacus and tabulated by hand) noted in frustration that 'large factories refused to cooperate' with what was supposed to be 'the economic general staff. We should have been able,' the official added, 'to have influence, to check on production, to check on assortment. But the planning commission was limited to paper figures.'[9]

Such frustration was caused not only by the low level of technology involved in the planning process, the lack of training of many cadres at all levels, and the institutional under-development of the Soviet state. These were all real enough, but there were systemic reasons which went well beyond such shortcomings and could afflict any attempt to run an entire country as a corporation (and, one might add, afflicts large firms and bureaucracies anywhere). The basic problem is one of information about the real resources available, as in hierarchical organizations there are pronounced incentives for managers on all levels to understate revenues and overstate costs when reporting up the line.[10] These pressures were, if anything, exacerbated in the Soviet command economy. The cadres running production—the management of factories and farms—were under enormous pressure to fulfil plan quotas. The incentives were both negative and positive. On the positive side, managers were paid according to a bonus system rewarding output; on the negative side, they were subject to tough sanctions for failure, including imprisonment and at times death. They were thus likely to do whatever was necessary to fulfil the plan.[11]

The first problem was maintaining a workforce able to do the job. Despite increasingly brutal laws attempting to tie workers to their factory and collective farmers to the land, labour turnover was a continuous headache. The only way to keep workers was to attempt to provide marginally better living conditions than were available elsewhere, hence the investment into company housing, food catering facilities, factory shops, and canteens. For many workers, their workplace rather than the public system of distribution provided housing, healthcare, and food, which made the site of employment a central focus of everyday life. Even so, only very limited funds were available for such company paternalism, not only were catering, housing, and healthcare nearly always lagging behind what the management would have liked to have implemented; more importantly, the necessary funds needed to be siphoned off from production—one reason for cooking the books.[12]

Even if workers could be enticed to stay in the factory, which by and large they could not, the management's problems did not end. It now needed to secure the raw materials necessary to actually produce what the plan asked for. Acquisitions were never easy, given the crude planning system, departmental egotism, and the inability to properly monitor distribution. Supply was, in the words of two economists, 'the true weak point of the Soviet system'.[13] Enterprises resorted to the employment of special 'pushers' (*tolkachi*) able to contact other enterprises directly and negotiate deals, swaps of materials, or exchanges on the understanding that the favour would be returned in the future. That in real economic life wheeling and dealing did not disappear also ensured hoarding of anything and everything. Factory managers never knew what they would need to be able to make the necessary bargains with other enterprises to get the raw materials, spare parts, or machinery that they needed to fulfil the plan. Such stockpiling of goods increased their scarcity as it took them out of circulation for the time being. Micro-economic rationality thus led to macro-economic irrationality.[14]

A third reason to hoard and to cook the books was the constant danger of changing plans. Both the annual control figures and the five-year numbers were constantly renegotiated between the central Commissariats and the factories. Lobbying by some enterprises could increase the burden of others as did political expediency and government meddling with the process. Enterprise managers thus constantly had to be ready to shift production at relatively short notice, which compounded the problem of finding raw materials, labour, and spare parts. As a result, they kept hoarding all three, if at all possible, in order to be ready for the endemic 'storming' at the end of plan periods. Soviet managers thus lived, as a classic study put it, in 'a system of enormous uncertainty, in which hoarding is the only rational principle of survival'.[15]

Finally, the absence of the iron fist of hard budget constraints exacerbated the problem. Hoarding labour and supplies is costly—workers need to be paid, warehouses need to be kept heated, their roofs patched, etc., whether or not they produce something somebody wants to buy. In a capitalist economy, enterprises need to take these costs into account, as ignoring them will eat away at profit and, in the worst case, bankrupt the company. In the Soviet system, however, a factory could not go bust; and thus there was little incentive to do anything about costly hoarding, particularly as it seemed the only way to deal with the endemic shortfalls (which were partially reproduced by the practice). Scarcity, thus, was not just a product of economic under-development or the political decision to produce guns rather than butter. It was also an intrinsic part of this economic system, which one classic study has described fittingly as an 'economy of shortage'.[16]

There were thus great incentives to cook the books on each level of the production process. As knowledge of the true resources available would only lead to increasing plan figures, these needed to be kept secret from the next higher level of administration. This basic fact of economic life did not remain hidden from the higher echelons. The planners and higher level economic managers knew that the enterprises were constantly lying to them. As they had to assume that there were more resources available than they were told, the tendency would be to always ask for more than their subordinates told them was possible—further thwarting any rational planning.

III

This system was able to produce both quality and quantity as long as the 'consumers' of these goods were part of the state's power structure. The users of military equipment, for example, were. The high brass of army, air force, or navy, had access to the highest decision makers who could and would impose heavy sanctions on those deemed responsible for failure to deliver these essential goods. Not that this prevented substandard output, but it made it much less likely, which explains why the Soviets soon managed not only to construct more, but also often better tanks, planes, and guns than the Germans, while the Soviet economy was never able to produce enough and quality consumer goods—toilet paper, shoes—for the population at large. Moreover, in the military sphere, central target setting was beneficial, as it ensured a limited number of models, which made supply of spare parts much easier than in the German army, which had to contend with a vast array of different machinery, all in need of highly specialized replacement parts.[17]

As the majority of the population, in sharp contrast, was unable to consistently mobilize the central government on its behalf, the needs of ordinary citizens were only marginally integrated into the state's system of production. The economic demands of everyday Soviets were relevant only in so far as their satisfaction was required for the production of the goods that actually mattered. The regime quickly learned that it had to attend to workers' provisions, lest labour productivity fall too far to be tolerated. This was not just a matter of granting enough to eat to allow the labouring population to regenerate and reproduce, as Marx would have taught his students (and they learned rather simple facts the hard way—if you take too much grain from the peasants, they will starve). It was also a matter of providing what economists describe, with far too much technical sophistication, as a 'fair wage', in order to ensure that people not only go through the motions, but actually work sufficiently hard to make capital investment worthwhile in the first place. To calibrate the exact level of this moving target was a constant struggle for the policymakers, and capital investment cycles reflect their continuous attempt to find the optimal level of commitment to consumption to ensure maximum investment into heavy industry and armaments.[18] In the countryside the equivalent fight was over the amount of grain that could be extracted without the peasants either rebelling or starving. The ebbs and flow of agricultural policy reflect this attempt to determine, by trial and error, where the sweet spot would be.

Stratification of access to consumer goods and detailed calibration of material incentives were two other aspects of the attempt of the political leadership to coerce a reluctant population to do the regime's bidding, without wasting too many resources on human consumption rather than the means of production and destruction. This system found its purest form during times of rationing, when access to even basic goods was channelled to those workers and employees perceived to be the most essential and when remaining outside this distribution system threatened starvation. But even during the 'better' years, when rationing was not in place, a hierarchy of distribution of goods and services gave those deemed essential to the Stalinist state better access than others, instituting a finely grained hierarchy of status groups, which structured the life chances of Soviet citizens to a considerable degree. The interaction of scarcity with (sometimes minor) privileges created a matrix of economic incentives and economic coercion pushing Soviet citizens to participate in the system to an extent ideological indoctrination could never have achieved.[19] More than anything, then, this was a dictatorship not over hearts and minds, but 'over needs'.[20]

IV

Seen from the top, the dictatorship over needs was centred around the planning agencies and Commissariats (later Ministries) on the one hand, and enterprises (factories, farms, building trusts, etc.) on the other. From the perspective of the individual citizen the two main institutions were the place of employment (i.e. the enterprise or bureaucracy) and the household, often based on blood relations. Households and families were not only the prime institutions for raising children, and caring for the sick, injured and aged; they were also economic units in their own right. As we have seen in Chapter 4, lawmakers acknowledged this basic fact not least in inheritance, property, and divorce legislation, which made relatives responsible for each other.

Rural households possessed the highest degree of economic autonomy—paradoxically, given the exploitation of the kolkhoz peasantry. Collective farmers had a right to their private garden plot and to a small number of farm animals, and to the marketing of their produce on the legal kolkhoz markets. Despite crippling taxation, this ability to produce and distribute agricultural goods privately ensured that peasants continued to concentrate on their miniscule gardens while trying to avoid the basically unpaid work in the collectives as far as this was feasible. Moreover, households continuously encroached on collective lands, reprivatized tools and animals well beyond the legally permissible, and the regime waged a near constant struggle against these tendencies, a struggle which led to failed campaign after failed campaign.[21]

Urban households were less autonomous, because they often lacked independent means of production. As city dwellers needed to get access to goods and services either through the public distribution system or—more often—closed distribution through their place of employment, state and enterprise policy loomed larger in their world than the weather. However, it would be an exaggeration to view urbanites as completely dependent on relations with the state. After all, much of the urban housing stock was privately owned. In Soviet parlance, such houses were 'personal property', which according to legal scholastics was something essentially different from the wicked 'private property' of capitalists. Nevertheless, it could be bought and sold, rented out, and inherited, and even built with the aid of state loans.[22] In 1940, 37 per cent of urban residences were 'personally' owned, a share which fell to 34 per cent in 1950, presumably because of wartime destruction, but not for lack of effort of ordinary Soviets to reconstruct their shattered lives after victory. Given the extreme difficulties citizens faced in an economy of shortage, the share of housing built on their initiative and on their own responsibility is impressive (see figure 5).[23] Many town dwellers also had continuing family ties with the countryside, keeping a conduit for produce open; and during and after the war, gardening for food became a central occupation of city dwellers as well, and again the family and the household were the basic units of production as well as consumption.

Not all Soviet citizens, moreover, were employed in state enterprises. The 1937 census counted 3.5 million independent farmers (*edinolichniki*), 378,301 craftsmen working in cooperatives, plus an additional 530,955 working on their own, 11,716 'free professionals' (*liudi svobodnykh professii*) and 4,281 citizens who lived off rental income from rooms or houses. 3,306 Soviets were listed as 'non-labouring groups' and 223,424 as 'others'.[24] There continued to be a substantial 'private sector' of the economy, especially with regards to the production of basic consumer goods.[25] In

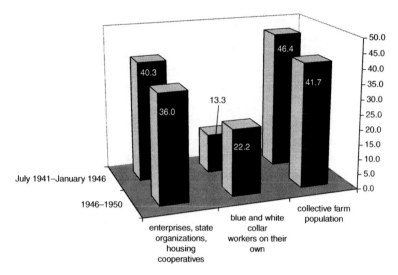

Figure 5 Housing construction, share of built housing space by builder (per cent)
Narodnoe khoziaistvo SSSR 1922–1972. Iubileinyi Statisticheskii Ezhegodnik (Moscow: Statistika, 1972), 365.

1939 just under 3 per cent of the urban population, or 1.1 million people, were artisans, labouring either on their own or as part of producers' cooperatives. Their role in the economy, however, hugely transcended their numbers, which seem to have grown subsequently as well. Private tailors and cobblers, for example, pocketed a large share of what citizens expended on acquisition and maintenance of clothes and footwear during and after the war.[26] Cottage industries, such as the weaving of cotton cloth, expanded massively throughout the 1940s, and much of artisanal production by 1948 was done privately (and often illegally).[27] The fruits of their labour were traded, by the producers themselves or by middlemen, at the open-air bazaars, which were the centres of consumer goods circulation during and after the war. These were also the natural habitat of other privateers—the professional trader (or 'speculator' in Bolshevik), buying up and reselling scarce goods for profit, and the beggar, two professions which demobilized soldiers often took up, particularly if injured.[28] Together, independent trades, trade collectives, bazaars, and kolkhoz markets constituted something of a middle ground linking the official with the unofficial economy. Legal in principle, they were always likely to slide into forbidden practices and were thus connected to that central realm of the Soviet sphere of distribution described by such monikers as 'second economy', 'counter economy', or 'black market'.[29]

A wide array of market and quasi-market relations thus governed the distribution of consumer goods. This relatively autonomous sphere of circulation was entangled with the state economy on the one hand, and informal relations of exchange, on the other. The latter are sometimes confused with corruption—the outright and illegal purchase of services from state functionaries. Such behaviour did exist, of course, but was less prevalent than another mechanism—mutual help.[30] The Russian word for this phenomenon is *blat*, which was, according to one proverb, 'higher than Stalin'. It denoted networks of exchange between ordinary citizens on the principle of mutual back-scratching. One person might have access to rare goods, say footwear, and give friends, family, and their friends and family priority access to it. The recipients would still, in most instances, pay for the goods received, but being able to acquire them in the first place was the crucial matter. The gatekeepers, who thus circumvented the officially instituted hierarchies of distribution, would usually not directly benefit (as in bribery), but provided this service 'for friends'. They could, of course, expect reciprocation from the network once they needed help in turn—and such circumstance would arise soon, given the systemic scarcity of everything. The principle of generalized reciprocity which governed these networks, and the related emotional ties between its members, also allowed participants to see what they did as an expression of friendship (a good thing), while if it occurred outside their own circle, it was *blat* (a morally reprehensible activity). The centrality of informal exchange within the Soviet economy under and ever since Stalin allows to describe this economy of scarcity also as an 'economy of favours'.[31]

Favours were solicited and granted not only horizontally, between friends or family members, but also vertically between patrons and clients. This phenomenon was more relevant to the higher strata of society, in particular those most privileged to begin with, as they had the best access to top-level decision makers who could help, say, a star author to obtain a better apartment, a dacha, or a travel pass to a holiday home. Those further down in the social hierarchy had less chance to consistently mobilize patrons in their favour, but not for lack of trying. For those least fortunate, supplication writing—to newspapers, the Supreme Soviet, famous comrades, or even Stalin personally—was the one avenue for getting high-level involvement in the resolution of life problems, lack of access, or supply bottlenecks. Such attempts were encouraged by the leadership, as letters from the population were one of the few sources of information not distorted by their own reporting system, and at times they would intervene to 'right' a perceived 'wrong'.[32]

The really existing Stalinist economy, then, was a far cry from the official picture of a rationally administered, planned system of allocation of resources for the greatest benefit of society. Much of the distribution of products in particular, but even a large share of the sphere of production as well, were far from controlled by the command centre in Moscow. Again and again, the leadership asserted its power by increasingly punitive labour laws, converting more and more of the workforce into quasi-indentured hands. The introduction, in late 1938, of workbooks marked the beginning of ever tightening regulations, which worsened during the war and continued well into the post-war years. These attempts to tie down workers to their plants, however, were constantly subverted in a situation of continuing labour shortage, poor policing, and ongoing upheaval, and material incentives continued to be offered as force alone turned out to be unproductive.[33]

V

The closest the regime came to actually running a command economy, where labour could be forced to work, consumption curbed to a minimum (or even, in many cases, a starvation diet), and all resources devoted to economic pursuits free hands could not be motivated to perform, was inside the GULAG.[34] Stalin's first revolution from above resulted in masses of exiles transported to remote regions and dumped in the middle of nowhere, with virtually no planning. Regional authorities were usually unprepared for dealing with what was both a human disaster and an administrative nightmare. For central policymakers, however, the constantly rising numbers of prisoners in camps, colonies, and special settlements could also appear as an opportunity. Already in the 1920s, some authorities had drawn on the long Russian tradition of forced labour and internal exile when thinking about using penal labour 'as a means for opening up the vast natural resources of the Soviet Union'. Such economic considerations, to be sure, did not cause the various deportations, arrests, and imprisonments in the first place, but once prisoners were available, they were put to what the Kremlin slave masters thought was a good use.[35]

As a result, maybe two out of every hundred Soviet workers were GULAG inmates.[36] Under usually harrowing conditions, prisoners built at the time highly celebrated projects, such as the White-Sea–Baltic Canal (*Belomorkanal*) or the Baikal–Amur Railroad (BAM), projects whose economic worth and engineering savvy are questioned by historians today. By 1940, the NKVD economy included twenty different sectors of the overall economic system, with a particular strength in non-ferrous metallurgy (32 per cent of GULAG output), forestry (16 per cent), and fuel production (5 per cent). Labour camp socialism was not a minor or isolated part of the overall economy, accounting for 11 per cent of all capital investment on the eve of the Second World War, and producing 47 per cent of nickel, 76 per cent of tin, 40 per cent of all cobalt, 41 per cent of chrome-iron ore, 60 per cent of gold, and 25 per cent of timber. After the war, it produced over 10 per cent of the gross industrial production of the Soviet Union as a whole, including all the platinum, mica, and diamonds, more than 90 per cent of gold, beyond 70 per cent of tin, 40 per cent of copper, 33 per cent of nickel, and 13 per cent of timber. Slave labour built some 10 per cent of postwar residences in Moscow.[37]

During the war, the GULAG population fell as prisoners were converted to cannon fodder at a time when mortality rates in the system rose. Nevertheless, prisoners' labour was essential to the war effort—8 per cent of the non-agricultural workforce was confined in 1942–45, a number including 'special settlers'. And most of them were engaged in war-related production, giving credence to Victor Kravchenko's claim that those 'who talk excitedly of the ultimate Russian victory as proof of "the success of the Soviet system" would be closer to the truth if they glorified the success of large-scale state peonage.' The NKVD economy produced between 10 and 15 per cent of ammunitions during the war, as well as essential wooden ammunition boxes, parts of field telephones, gas masks, mortar stands, and uniforms.[38]

Whatever its contribution to victory and to 'the construction of Socialism', slave labour had its disadvantages, too. By the post-war years, those running the sprawling archipelago of camps, special settlements, and colonies had started to realize that it cost more to administer, guard, house, and feed the GULAG population than their exploitation of resources in remote regions paid in return. Forced labour, it turned out, was extremely unproductive, which nudged administrators in the same direction the leadership had taken with respect to 'free' labour. They were forced to admit that material incentives were needed in order to raise productivity, eventually concluding that it would be best 'to abolish the existing system of forced labour due to its economic inefficiency and lack of potential', as a man who should have known, Stalin's enforcer Lavrenti Beria, wrote shortly after his master's death.[39] From a macro-economic and macro-social perspective, moreover, the GULAG proved disastrous, with long-term consequences unforeseen by the Stalinist leadership. The easy availability of forced labour lessened incentives to improve productivity, rationalize production, and enhance the level of mechanization. Moreover, GULAG mores—extreme cynicism, violence, a callous approach to the life and well-being of subordinates—seeped into society at large with which it was connected through a 'revolving door' of prisoner releases and re-arrests—a social consequence at least as far-reaching as the economic effects of slave labour.[40] Incidentally, this close link between the realm of confinement and the world outside of the barbed wire did nothing to diminish private initiative or social self-organization. In the camps as well, informal exchange, trade, and small-scale production of the necessities of everyday life were as ubiquitous as corruption, not to mention violence, theft, and extortion.[41] Much of the camps' internal life was indeed run not by prison guards, but by criminal gangs.[42]

VI

The varied units of the Stalinist economy—the central party-state, economic enterprises, collective farms, the GULAG archipelago, households—were in a dynamic and changing relationships with each other.

The state did not so much control or plan this economy, but managed it by crude levers of command and coercion and the slightly more subtle methods of taxation and material incentives.[43] Periods of firm centralization and brutal extraction of resources and labour alternated with times of lesser pressure. During Stalin's first revolution from above, planning 'disappeared in the plan', rationing, the threat as well as administration of violence, and ideological overdrive were used to club workers to produce and peasants to give up their grain.[44] The results were disorder, famine, plummeting living standards, and chaotic growth of heavy industry—enough to convince the leaders that they had overdone their centralizing push. There followed some three 'good years' of more realism, with the legalization of peasant trade (in May 1932) and the resulting opening of kolkhoz markets, the abolition of rationing (which had been in force, for many goods, from 1928–34 and was abolished piece by piece in 1935–36) and its replacement by 'socialist trade', more moderate target setting in the Second Five-Year Plan (1933–37), and greater investment in consumer goods production. All of this left greater leeway to enterprises, households, and families to run their own affairs until the centre again pushed for centralization as one aspect of Stalin's second revolution of the terror. Many local networks were wiped out in this attempt to harness everybody and everything to the commands of Moscow, but once the terror subsided they reappeared, since they were an economic as well as a political necessity. The country returned to the normal unplanned economy which had emerged in the early 1930s.[45]

The war with Germany encouraged contradictory tendencies. On the one hand the state was further centralized in the State Defense Committee (headed by Stalin), to coordinate the military effort and focus all economic energies on the war. On the other hand, whatever planning there had been was replaced by emergency management by plenipotentiaries, as the Five-Year-Plan was suspended for the duration of hostilities and all resources—including GULAG labour—were mobilized for war. The control over civilian consumption was all but abandoned, devolving to the level of the enterprise and the household, which now were in charge also of food production in the Soviet version of the 'victory garden', while black marketeers took over the distribution of all the scant necessities of wartime civilian life.[46]

It is in this Janus-faced centralization-decentralization of the wartime years that we can find the secret of Stalin's victory. The regime, simply put, focused on what it did best—producing military hardware by means of command planning, brutal coercion, callous rationing, and severe discipline; meanwhile it let the citizens do what they knew how to do best—to fend for themselves and their loved ones, by pulling strings, tending to their own gardens, pooling resources, and helping friends, family, and the friends and family of friends and family. Enterprises mediated between these two poles of the wartime economy, fulfilling the plan imposed on them as well as they could, while assisting their labour force in the struggle to survive the harsh wartime years. Factories, too, produced their own food and collective farms looked the other way when peasants reprivatized more and more of the land, tools, and cattle.

The post-war years saw the return to the pre-war normalcy of Stalinist economics, i.e. the reining in of the most radical of the wartime decentralizations, such as the flowering black market and the partial reprivatization of collective farms. This relapse was not due to an inability to imagine alternatives to pre-war Stalinism. There were some within the state who argued for the legalization of the black market, which could then be taxed, and the abolition of the collective farms was a daydream of many—from returning peasant soldiers to the generals who had commanded them. The political elite, however, and Stalin in particular, would have none of it. They continued to believe, against all evidence, that state command was good and social self-regulation bad. The Stalinist economy as it had developed in the 1930s remained, as the epigraph to this chapter has it, 'the best way to organize the economic and cultural development of our country'. At the same time, the policymakers again tried to appease the population by shifting resources to consumption—at least until this strategy ran aground on the reef of the Korean War, the sharpest outgrowth of that larger atoll of challenges called the Cold War. Despite this partial remilitarization, however, living standards slowly rose back to pre-war standards at least, and the post-war famine of 1947 proved to be the last of its kind. The Soviet economy finally grew out of its crisis mode and matured to a 'mundane shortage economy', which was progress in so far as nobody starved to death from now on. This economy, however, continued to function in the both complex and inefficient ways outlined in this chapter. It would remain basically unchanged until the radical reforms under Gorbachev and his successors at the end of the century.[47]

VII

What held the fractured population together, then, was the iron grip of economic necessity. It was possible to live under Stalin without adhering to official ideology; one could even get by participating marginally in political ritual, particularly if one lived outside of the cities; but it was impossible to not participate in economic activity if one did not want to starve to death. The extent to which an individual's acquisition of the necessities of life was dominated by formal or informal mechanisms depended on the extent of inclusion into the system of power. At the top, the inhabitants of the Kremlin were largely reliant on official channels of distribtion, which supplied them with housing, furniture, dachas, food, clothes, drink, education for the children, and healthcare for all. The further one moved from Red Square, the less central did the official network of distribution become, as the goods circulated throughout its pathways were never enough and were redirected by informal means. The further one got from the centre of power, the more important outright market mechanisms became—*blat* still relied on relative privilege since somebody in the network needed to be placed strategically enough to siphon off goods from the official network. Once such access dried up in the lower social groups, direct exchange for money in the collective farm markets, bazaars, and the illegal black market entangled with both became more important, as did the production of food for subsistence or the home-production of goods for sale.

To describe the economy under Stalin, then, as a planned economy is extremely misleading. It was an economy where the central government tried to appropriate as much wealth as possible to run a warfare state, while the majority of the population had to fend for itself and even the official units of production—enterprises and factories—were forced to act in entrepreneurial ways within quasi-markets. Why, then, were the market mechanisms in this economy misrecognized and often outlawed? It was not that the obvious was unthinkable to Soviets; the problem was not that the scales had not yet fallen from their eyes because they lacked outsiders lecturing them on the virtues of decentralized goods exchange or the role of self-interest in motivating people to work (as puffed-up consultants believed in the 1990s). The latter was recognized as important already in a celebrated speech by Stalin in 1931, became central after the abolition of rationing in the mid-1930s and again after 1947, and even in the GULAG, material incentives went hand in glove with coercion, even starting to replace it by the late Stalinist years.[48] Even more far reaching market reforms were pondered in 1932–33 and then again after the war.[49] The problem was that following such thoughts to their logical conclusion was unacceptable for a regime as hostile to social self-organization as Stalin's. For the dictator and his entourage, Marxism and Socialism had become defined by a lack of the market, and in a world where capitalism bred the welfare state and socialism was mostly good at organizing society for warfare, anti-market fundamentalism was indeed all that was left to distinguish socialists from liberals. The success in the war—which the leaders unsurprisingly attributed to their own actions rather than to social self-organization—became the 'proof' that the system worked. Victory effectively 'locked in' the basic institutional settlement of Stalinism, despite the availability of more potent alternatives.[50] Soviet society would suffer for decades to come from this elevation of the non-market to a central ideological fetish, even as market mechanisms had always been and continued to be central to the way this economy functioned in actuality.

PART III

CHAPTER 9
POLITICS OF HISTORY

❝ We have finished our discussion. ❞

Franz Neumann, 1944[1]

I

This book has argued two theses about life under Stalin: that Soviet people and their relations, behaviours, and ideas cannot be reduced to a single cause or origin; and that in so far as the many contradictory histories were held together in one common entity, it was the compulsions of making a living, embedded as they were in a complex system of producing, distributing, and consuming goods and services, which mattered most. Both theses have their own history.

The analysis presented in Chapter 8 is deeply indebted to what could be described as the Gerschenkron school of Soviet economics—a largely qualitative enterprise focusing on practices and a long-term historical perspective, rather than quantification, let alone model building. Such research flourished in the United States during the post-war years, only to decline for complex reasons from the early 1960s. As economists increasingly focused on mathematical modelling of idealized systems and historians drifted towards cultural studies this tradition is nearly extinct today.[2] The idea of multiplicity within one historical terrain— the second major thesis of this book—might be seen as of more recent origin. It could be beholden to postmodern sensibilities, where 'master narratives' were declared oppressive and 'multiculturalism' became the vaguely glimmering star guiding those who, not more precisely, defined themselves as 'progressives'.[3] But the stress on not only the existence, but the legitimacy of histories other than those of great men, great ideas, and great states can also be followed back to the 1960s and their academic offspring—history from below, women, gender, and subaltern studies— and their insistence that the powerless, too, have their histories.[4] In the Soviet field these trends were represented by a group loosely identified as 'revisionists'. That the title of one famous study—*Stalinist Simplifications and Soviet Complications*—resonates with parts of the argument of this book is a symptom for its indebtedness to this body of scholarship.[5] But, historians of ideas might point out, such interest in complexity was just the re-emergence of a considerably older sensibility. What one literary critic has described as the 'romantic' or 'anarchist' approach to the past can be followed back to the nineteenth century, when history as a modern discipline first took shape. Historians of this mindset see the past quite literally as a foreign country, but one they visit not in order to conquer and subject, but one they approach as tourists or maybe ethnologists, full of wonder about the colourful variety of human folly.[6]

To embrace such a genealogy means to break with a fundamental assumption of modern thought—that things necessarily get better through change; that the latest is the best; and that the newer the more brilliant. Such a turn from progressivism does not necessarily mean to adopt the conservative alternative—the older, the better—which has equally little to recommend itself. By constructing a golden age of 'serious research' before the fall into ideology it just inverts the narrative of progress rather than replace it. Neither a plot of rise and fall, nor a single success story, the history of at least the English-language scholarship on the Soviet Union under Stalin is one of successive dominance of particular research agendas, each marginalizing certain questions and privileging particular answers. Taken together, however, this rich patrimony adds up to a complex vision of Stalinist society.

II

The intellectual tradition this book stands in was not one of disinterested intellectual endeavour. Scholarly engagement with Stalinism was never devoid of anger and zealotry. Even rather technical questions, such as the one about the role of 'society' in its history, were rife with political fears, ideological hopes, and contemporary concerns. The emotions have passed somewhat, which might allow a return to nominal definitions, such as the one offered in the introduction to this book. Society, it said, was a shorthand for 'the system of formal and informal relations among people that existed ... on the territory of the Soviet Union'.

This definition has a distinguished pedigree. In the classics of social theory—from Emile Durkheim to Talcott Parsons—'society' denoted the social totality, the overall system of relations between people on a given territory. This approach tended to the imposition of an all-encompassing social system integrating everything and anything. At times, analysts enthralled with such abstract theories slipped into barefoot functionalism, always uncovering the uses of any phenomenon for the social body, as surely nothing would evolve without reason. The Marxist tradition with its sharp eye for contradictions and conflict, but also the conservative Max Weber's appreciation of the infinite complexity of the real world, have often served as antidotes to such thinking. The more recent obsession of academics, cultural critics, and pundits with multiplicity and ambiguity has done much the same, sometimes slipping into what one polemicist has called a 'postmodern terrorism', which frightens students away from 'making some interesting structural connection or comparative generalization. The only safe essentialism' this disgruntled professor continued, 'is that there is no order to culture.'[7] By stressing both fragmentation and social integration, dislocation, and unification, this book has tried to steer a middle ground between such extremes. This was neither a well-integrated 'Stalinist Civilization', nor a 'quicksand society.'[8] There certainly was order to this chaos, or rather, a variety of orders, a multiplicity of tenacious histories unified only tentatively by the state's actions. This book thus concurs with a recent history which declared that 'the regime had no control over the multiple societies of the empire and their ways of life'. It parts from this study, though, by denying that we can distil an 'essence' of this social formation. Rather than boiling Stalinism down to some foul smelling substance, this book attempted the opposite: to open up the many and contradictory histories which intermingled, clashed, and sometimes simply coexisted in Stalin's empire.[9]

By doing so I have profited from a rich literature, but also broken with what many historians mean when they talk of 'society'—the non-state. Whenever limits of state power could be documented, whenever something happened, which had not been initiated by the government, then 'society' was at work. If peasants slaughtered their cows before entering the kolkhoz, society was at work as much as when the same farmers got drunk and cursed Soviet power. Society beat wives, engaged in upward mobility, supported or resisted the regime, and engaged in mutual protection networks. The term was, in the words of one critic, a 'residual category' which suffered 'from being ill-defined as everything external to the state'. It did not conceptualize 'the totality of what exists'.[10]

Society had not always been conceptually separated from the state. One of the earliest attempts to conceptualize the Soviet social formation indeed drew on the classical sociological tradition of seeing the state as part and parcel of the wider society. The Harvard Project on the Soviet Social System was a generously funded team effort to understand this society through large-scale interviewing of defectors and displaced persons after the war. That the US Air Force provided the money, believing that successful strategic bombing operations required detailed knowledge of the enemy, should not detract from the intellectual rigor of this enterprise.[11] The Harvard scholars saw the Soviet Union as a 'totalitarian society' in which 'those who hold political power attempt to coordinate for the attainment of their goals all the material and human resources of their society, extending even to the private feelings and sentiments of the population'. Such attempts were bound to fail, however, as the totalitarian government was part of a complex structure. The result of the interaction between the state and its social environment was the 'Soviet system', which these scholars defined as 'that distinctive total complex of traditional and Bolshevik institutions, values, and patterns of behavior which are manifested within the territory of... the Union of Soviet Socialist Republics.'[12]

In order to understand how this complex sense of Soviet society was transformed into the binary opposition between 'state' and 'society', we need to look at the context of this debate, as history writing is always also about the present. For most of their existence, Soviet Union specialists laboured within the intellectual ecosystem of the Cold War, and what they recorded was read as an intervention into current politics, or as part of an ideological debate about the enemy. Sometimes historians consciously constructed their research and prose in that way, while in other instances they could not escape this logic, even if they tried. This environment nudged them to separate 'the state' from 'society'.

The central concept which encapsulated these Cold War debates was 'totalitarianism', a term the current study, following the Harvard Project, embraces. It implies a basic set of comparisons, in particular between Stalinism and Nazism (although it does not necessarily rule out a wider frame of reference, as for some theorists 'the enlightenment' itself 'is totalitarian').[13] In a world of thermonuclear weapons, the assimilation of the new enemy to the old foe had quite worrying implications. After all, 'appeasement' had failed with Hitler, so only an aggressive stance against the 'other totalitarian dictatorship' would do, with all the apocalyptic consequences it could imply. Many were rightfully frightened by such prospects and were groping for alternatives. There were also other things to dislike about the dominant approach to studying the Soviet Union. A classic about the Soviet family, to cite one example I have drawn on repeatedly above, is littered with what many would now call 'sexism' and 'racism'.[14] Today's reader might forgive the author as a man of a different era—an intellectual grandfather with slightly outdated prejudices. To campus radicals of the 1960s, many of his statements, however, must have been hard to swallow. Moreover, non-academic discourse appropriated totalitarianism and made it into a caricature even of the most simple-minded social science writing on the subject. In this popularized version, a hugely efficient superstate swallowed the rest of society, atomizing individuals, and leaving them brainwashed by ideology and terrorized by the police, unable to act on their own.[15]

No wonder, then, that when the campus radicals became graduate students and eventually history professors, they concentrated on debunking this 'totalitarianism' and even the best of them, and sometimes against their better judgement, cannot stop engaging in this pleasure to this day. Most of these 'revisionists' were historians and as social history was the vogue of the day, they set out to explore 'the social' in Soviet society, too. This disciplinary perspective gave additional reason to attack 'the totalitarian model', as the older approaches were quickly branded.[16] Part of the project of social history was to find social causes for political events, which Marxists and non-Marxists alike tended to treat as dependent variables. Politics was the 'superstructure' which built on a more fundamental 'base', or, in one memorable nested metaphor, the 'crests of foam that the tides of history carry on their strong backs'.[17] In a totalitarian polity, by contrast, the political realm is emancipated to a larger degree than elsewhere from control and even influence from other force fields. Indeed, the Russian Revolution has been used in polemics against such self-proclaimed 'materialism'—here the 'superstructure' (ideology and politics) played a huge role in creating and changing the socio-economic 'base'.[18] If this was so, however, social history as commonly understood, was pointless. What mattered was what the state did. Serving both political and disciplinary ends, the attack on the concept of 'totalitarianism' was, hence, also necessary to establish social history as the leading discipline in the study of Stalinism. This bid was basically successful: the story that a simple-minded totalitarian model was overcome by nuanced social history is accepted widely even by those who, in their turn, want to revise the revisionists. In the process, however, historians have quietly, and largely unknowingly to themselves, appropriated much of what was best in the earlier scholarship on 'totalitarianism'. In particular, the work of the Harvard Project entered the unknown knowledge of a whole generation while being constantly attacked as 'cold war scholarship'.[19]

Another example of the same process is Merle Fainsod, a history-writing political scientist who was based, like the Interview Project, at Harvard's Russian Research Center. He pioneered, in the 1950s, not only the study of Stalinism through archival records (of the Smolensk Party Archive, which the war had displaced to the US) but also formulated the basic notion this book has recreated in the image of the 'limping Behemoth'—of the Stalinist system as a weak state with totalitarian ambitions. For Fainsod, Stalinism was a society 'of infinite complexity', and 'the totalitarian facade concealed a host of inner contradictions'. Terror and repression, grief and fear, went hand in hand with 'the creation of a new class of beneficiaries' whose 'coalescence...around the regime' made 'totalitarian controls ultimately effective'.[20] Fainsod's totalitarianism was so close to their own image of Soviet reality that, once the now tenured radicals reread his book in the 1990s, some of them simply declared him an honourary member of their own school of thought.[21]

There is, thus, a direct line from the old literature on totalitarianism to revisionist preoccupation with Soviet complications to recent neototalitarian approaches, the current book among them, which depict Soviet society as 'multilayered and complex...featuring multiple and often inconsistent traditions, discourses, and mentalities'.[22] Such continuities, however, are often obscured as scholars feel compelled to distinguish themselves from those who came before by claiming absolute novelty.

III

Historical debate, like magic, is also about words. In debunking the totalitarian strawman, the revisionists had to mobilize another word-fetish this study embraces—'Stalinism'. Most of the tenured radicals who called themselves 'socialist historians' in private and 'social historians' in public, started out with reevaluating the Bolshevik Revolution in a more positive light. Only a few of these soft Leninists, however, were Bolsheviks enough to embrace Stalin's revolutions from above as 'really necessary'.[23] Caught between a romantic infatuation with Lenin's coup—which they called a Revolution—and their studied disgust with the plebeian brutality of the 1930s, they set out to carve up the continuity of Soviet history into two discontinuous parts: Bolshevism here, Stalinism there.[24] For many on the American campus left, first the Bolshevik revolution, then the 1920s were a time for revolutionary dreams before the Stalinist nightmare.[25] Alternatives to the Stalin revolution were found in Bukharin's programme to prolong the NEP and hope for an evolutionary path to Socialism, while others claimed that Trotsky would have been essentially different from his plagiarist Stalin.[26] Only few on the left broke out of this anti-Stalinist consensus, claiming that Stalin's regime was not so bad after all and that the Great Patriotic War proved it—but they were quickly marginalized.[27]

There are, of course, good empirical grounds to distinguish the regime of the 1930s and 1940s from what came before and after, but, as in the parallel case of continuity and discontinuity in German history, the choice for stressing the one or the other was, in most cases, determined by politics rather than evidence.[28] Comparatively speaking, the German case would have to qualify as the deeper rupture anyway, as in the Soviet instance the late 1920s saw not the empowerment of a completely new group of plebeian radicals by a long established elite looking for a mass base for reactionary politics, but the victory of the plebeian faction within the Bolshevik party over the intellectuals who had taken power in their name. The new radicals came from the very centre of the political system rather than from its fringes. Stalin and his entourage did not have to become *salonfähig*; they were part of the revolutionary establishment to begin with. Nevertheless, most 'revisionists' settled on stressing change over continuity when it came to the revolutions from above.

In the process, they reified Trotsky's polemical term for the regime of victors to such a degree that, by the 2000s, one of them did not even have to stop to define the word when setting out to describe 'Stalinism as a Way of Life'.[29] Even the first spokesman for the next generation of 'post-revisionists' felt obliged, in 1995, to use 'Stalinism' rather than 'Bolshevism' when referring to the 'civilization' of the 1930s. This is all the more striking as this self-proclaimed Foucaultian embraced the teachings of one of the revisionists' archenemies, his adviser Martin Malia, when describing Stalinism not only as Socialism achieved but even as a brain-child of 'the Enlightenment', a potentially totalitarian phenomenon, as we already know. While continuing to use the now naturalized word, then, Stephen Kotkin undermined the old barrier between Stalinism and Bolshevism. While originally, 'Stalinism' had been erected to shield revolutionary Marxism from the Great Terror, now this dam was broken, and the murky waters of Stalinism contaminated not only all of socialism but even 'modernity' more broadly, and in particular state-led projects of social change and 'the welfare state'.[30]

There were dissidents, of course, even if the American academic and publicistic right would paint all 'revisionists' with the same brush. One of these was Sheila Fitzpatrick, an interloper from Melbourne with a partially Australian, partially British education, who would—decades later—train the largest contemporary school of historians of the Soviet Union, myself among them.[31] Fitzpatrick, not a Marxist and beholden to a rather old-fashioned belief in the historian's craft, by her own admission initially did not understand the politics of American academia. Such ignorance, however, did not keep her from joining the tussle right away. This daughter of an Aussie radical was by temperament predestined to lead and irritate rather than follow the crowd, and she clearly understood enough to plant intellectual bombshells at precisely the right locations.[32] The first one came disguised as an article on 'Cultural Revolution in Russia', in 1974, soon followed by a conference at Columbia University in November of the same year; the next grenade was contained in her book *Education and Social Mobility in the Soviet Union* of 1979.[33] Both pointed to support for Stalinism among the Party faithful—either by stressing that the leadership could simply 'unleash' the destructive tendencies of lower-level Party activists, or by uncovering the history of the beneficiaries of Stalin's revolutions from above. Such arguments were guaranteed to cause controversy. They raised right-wingers' blood pressure by suggesting that the Stalinists had a constituency, and they annoyed many on the left because of the less than flattering image they projected of 'the young, proletarian and Communist'.[34]

Later, Fitzpatrick continued her campaign to irritate others with unwanted facts. She doggedly countered the emerging view that it was just the unfortunate event of the Civil War which turned the Bolsheviks from 'alert politicians with an acute sensitivity to popular moods and desires' into brutal totalitarians.[35] Lenin's men, she quipped, were 'not Mensheviks' and the Civil War was the 'formative experience' for which 'their past and thoughts had prepared them'.[36] In her influential textbook she affirmatively quoted Richard Pipes—*persona non grata* among the academic left and himself discombobulated by her 'unrevisionist' account—and assimilated first Stalin's revolution and, in the second edition, even the Great Terror into the great sweep of the unfolding Russian Revolution.[37] Her continued guerilla tactics in the fight against the tyranny of academic dogma irritated both the right (who wanted to have her firmly in the opponent's camp) and the left, leading to an outpouring of emotion disguised as scholarship in a 1986–87 scuffle in the journal *Russian Review*.[38] The next generation of scholars, anxiously trying to cement their position by declaring a 'paradigm shift' and their own work as radically discontinuous (and better) than anything which came before, was subjected to the same intellectual judo, leading to much sniping behind the scenes and at least one public loss of temper against her refusal to submit to the new leadership.[39]

Given what we can now know about Lenin's regime in revolution and civil war, and given that revolutionary socialism has, at best, become a matter for antiquarians, the neat distinction between Bolshevism and Stalinism has become less and less convincing. Hence, this book, like many others published in the last decade, has treated the latter as a radicalized form of earlier incarnations of Soviet society, neither completely continuous nor completely discontinuous with the rest of revolutionary history. Mass executions, mass deportations, and a militarized command economy, to quote just the most visible aspects of 'Stalinism', did not spring from Stalin's paranoid brain, but were all tried out during the 'dirty war' of 1918–21.[40] With the Cold War over, the Soviet Union yet another failed empire, and even the legacy of the glorious French Revolution more and more under siege, even those who felt compelled to answer the rise of neo-conservatism with seven-hundred-page tomes included Stalin and his terror into their sweeping if uneasy history of the Furies of Revolution.[41] For both reasons of context and of evidence, then, much recent writing has followed the 'totalitarians' like Pipes or Malia, or the renegade 'revisionist' Fitzpatrick in including 'Stalinism' in the longer sweep of 'Bolshevism'.

Nevertheless, the term 'Stalinism' is still useful, as it stresses the role of the dictator's personality in the path actually taken. Echoing E. H. Carr and Alec Nove, one of the leading 'new Russian' historians, Oleg Khlevniuk, has argued that the 'spectrum of possible options' at the end of the 1920s was limited 'by the existence of a rigid political regime, by the need to implement an industrialization long overdue, and by the social and cultural realities of a relatively backward country'. These factors made a continuation of the NEP rather unlikely. However, the extreme brutality with which 'Stalinism' went about its business cannot be explained without Stalin's personal leadership. Many in his entourage were indeed 'soft Stalinists' who after the dictator's death would significantly alter the system, in particular by abandoning terror (not repression) as a means of rule.[42] Or, in the words of a specialist on Soviet policing, neither before the 1930s nor after Stalin's death 'did the Soviet regime employ methods of mass police repression to try to restructure the social, ethnic, and territorial boundaries of the country'.[43] 'Stalinism', therefore, is the period of Soviet history where the comparison with Nazi Germany makes most sense. It was, in other words, the 'totalitarian' phase of the transformation of Soviet society in the twentieth century.

IV

The Cold War is over, but the concepts it bred live on. Moreover, both in academia and in popular consciousness, the conflict seems to continue as yet another tenacious history. Richard Pipes in 1993 and the late Martin Malia as late as 2002 admonished their 'revisionist' colleagues to recant, as they had, allegedly, lost the Cold War of History.[44] On the other side of the frontline, some continue to declare, despite all evidence to the contrary, a 'growing consensus' that the NEP and its 'budding civil society' were viable alternatives to the revolution from above,[45] while others persist, as a service to revolutionary socialism, to rescue Leninism from Stalinism.[46] Most of such recycling of old positions causes relatively little controversy since these discussions, while not resolved, have run their course and have barely any relevance to contemporary political debate. An exception might well become the reinvention of Stalinism as a successful industrializing regime for 'developing' nations, a position which could feed into debates about how to lessen the gap between rich and poor countries—by state-managed economic change or through 'the free market', by dictatorship or democracy, or by any of the possible combinations of these basic approaches to politics and economics.[47]

The war, meanwhile, remains rife with political passions. Anybody who as much as intimates that something less than utter heroism brought victory to the glorious Red Army risks the scorn not only of Russian nationalists but also of comfortable American professors enamoured by the Soviet wartime narrative and enchanted by the comforting feeling a story of true gallantry gives the armchair soldier.[48] Likewise, any investigation into Soviet war preparations or Soviet war conduct ('atrocities') cannot remain 'value neutral' as it will be immediately seized upon by the extreme German right intent on perpetuating the dual myth of the pre-emptive strike and the reactive nature of *Wehrmacht* barbarism.[49]

While the corpses of old polemics thus continue to be jolted by occasional tremors, a new generation of historians declared they had moved on. Pipes and Malia were their grandparents, the revisionists their settled (and boring) parents, and they now the new rebellious (grand-) children.[50] The flag around which they rallied in order to escape the guiding lights of both totalitarianism and revisionism was inscribed with the word 'modernity'. One of the reasons for the rise of this concept was the ideological fallout of the breakdown of the Soviet Union in 1991.[51] Revolutionary change, maybe even the idea of an alternative to capitalism, seemed dead to many, although it continues to live on in small circles of ineffectual campus radicals all over the world. The self-congratulation of 'the West' went so far that some optimists announced an 'end of history'. Two decades later—after a catastrophic War on Terror seriously undermined the banks of the moral high ground and after a second world economic crisis shocked many free-marketeers back into the welcoming arms of the state—such claims might seem incredible. In the mid-1990s they were widely influential. What older generations had studied as *The Soviet Experiment* or abhorred as *The Soviet Tragedy* was no longer an issue—a radical alternative to Capitalism, brought about by violent revolution.

In this context, *modernity* allowed researchers to continue mining the Soviet experience for historical lessons once the old ones had become stale, allowing this past to speak to an increasingly globalized present, where maybe Kazakhstan and Montana truly were 'nearly the same place'.[52] Given both the vagueness of the term and the wide semantic field surrounding it, using the concept also allowed historians to 'do theory'—a necessary claim to intellectual sophistication within an academia increasingly fascinated with continental philosophy. The new spectre the post-revisionists projected onto the Soviet Union (just as totalitarian theorist had projected their own nightmare)[53] was that the comfortable suburban existence of middle-class America was indeed, and unbeknownst to those living within it, a totalitarian nightmare of Orwellian proportions. The state had spread its tentacles into all the interstices of everyday life and even all the way into the subjectivity of individuals (to use terms dear to the debate). A variant was the literature about the 'gardening state', which warned that attempts to build a more aesthetically, morally, or politically pleasing society had the tendency to produce mountains of corpses.[54]

Although often voiced by self-described progressives, this view had frequently highly conservative implications. Many struggled against this logic by stressing that only '*certain* schemes to improve the human condition have failed'.[55] Preempting an obvious critique, one author wrote: 'My study of Stalinist culture is not directed against the impulse to rationalize and improve society'. Restating a distinguished anti-revolutionary position embodied by the likes of Edmund Burke (1729–1797) or Karl Popper (1902–1994), he noted that piecemeal social engineering does not in itself 'pose a hazard'. His intention was 'not to criticize progressive social programs but rather to provide a cautionary tale regarding the uncritical application of purportedly scientific social reform'. Again echoing the conservative Whig and the liberal, the lesson of Stalinism was now that 'social change must be gradual and consensual if it is to succeed'.[56] Despite such disclaimers, critics have noted that the most violent of Stalin's policies—the mass operations of the Great Terror—serve poorly to illustrate how modernist projects lead to mass death. Rather than carefully planned gardening measures, they were 'unplanned, ad hoc reactions to a perceived immediate political threat', which activated the behavioural patterns of Civil War days, enhanced by the ideological celebration of violence.[57] This study has followed a similar line of reasoning by describing the forces of destruction as akin to slashing and burning, chopping and felling, rather than careful weeding.

A second obsession of the turn of the twenty-first century was with nationhood and nationalism in the Soviet Union. Again, there were precursors to this literature among both 'revisionists' and 'totalitarians', but once its relevance was demonstrated by the breakup of the Soviet Union in 1991, it was a culturally turned exponent of the former, Ron Suny, who would take a leading role in this growing literature.[58] The basic puzzle was to explain how and why a Marxist, Socialist State 'promoted ethnic particularism' until it could no longer control the ghosts it had conjured itself.[59] Soon, archival studies abounded, and today the field is getting increasingly crowded. That Soviet nation(s) building was so successful is sometimes seen as confirmation of the awesome power of modern states, assisted by ethnographers and bureaucrats, to assign arbitrary categories to people who did not have them otherwise. This reading magnifies the differences between ethnic and national identity—the state never tried to convince Russians to think of themselves as Japanese, for example, but built on pre-existing markers.[60] The Soviet construction of nationalities was so successful, moreover, not merely because ethnographers constructed, bureaucrats tabulated, and passports assigned them, but also because real advantage could be derived from asserting one's nationality in a state which gave special rights and privileges to 'oppressed nations'. Nationality, in other words, was a status and the Soviet Union an 'affirmative action empire'—a perspective which informed my own treatment of the issue in chapters above.[61]

A third and related preoccupation of the 1990s was an increasingly sophisticated debate about 'ideology'. This research, which picked up an old interest of the 'totalitarians', was initially fuelled by the 'linguistic' or 'cultural turn'.[62] Itself a result of the crisis of both Marxism and its cousins in the establishment—modernization theory and social science history—this overall fashion made a 'new cultural history' the dominant approach in most US graduate schools.[63] As this research matured, it started to focus more and more on the internal contradictions and the multifaceted nature of the far from monolithic field of official utterances.[64] This growing refinement of the debate, incidentally, also robbed the 'culturalist' interpretation of some of its force: if the ideology was not monolithic, we can no longer simply explain the Soviet elite's (let alone 'ordinary' citizens') behaviour by simply gesturing towards 'Marxism', 'Modernity', or 'the Enlightenment'. Moreover, more and more researchers became dissatisfied with the overly cognitive model of human action implicit in much of this literature. Many now look for ways 'beyond culture'—by focusing on 'experience', by exploring 'emotions' or, like this study, by reappropriating 'society' and 'the economy' as terms of analysis.[65] Some continue to follow the established ('revisionist') line of studying culture through institutions and practices rather than disembodied discourses,[66] or revert to comparative history,[67] while others, inspired by the experience of globalization of their own times, moved more and more towards 'entangled', 'transnational', or 'global' histories—approaches hoping to work out empirically, how ideas, practices, and institutions travelled between societies.[68]

Historians, of course, do not live exclusively in a world of ideological discourse, political or theoretical considerations. Politics of a very different, more localized kind are equally important. Indeed, academic struggles about position and prestige are more overt today than during times when personal ambition could be presented as a principled political stance. As historians became more attuned to the way academic power games work, many became more subtle in the art of citations—referring only to their friends while polemicizing against unstated others, a rising cynicism, often misrecognized as 'self-reflexivity'.[69] It has become nearly standard practice for editors of important journals to insist on the inclusion of certain works in footnotes, or even to simply insert them during the copy-editing process, while toning down attacks against 'their own' without authorial consent. Authors are sometimes subjected to bullying emails by colleagues whose work they criticized and emergent scholars are taken aside at conferences and warned, friendly but firmly, not to oppose the party line. Such practices are aimed at enforcing conformity while shunting the light of the public on the assumption that any publicity is good publicity. The corollary of such politicking is the accusation of 'plagiarism' levelled against others who might have similar ideas to one's own. Surprisingly, such denunciations have not yet led to libel suits, maybe because such venomous allegations are often uttered only in the corridors of universities or conference hotels rather than in writing.[70] The law's Damocles sword did, however, play a major role in an affair which elevated academic discourse to yet greater qualitative heights. It all started when one leading scholar wrote anonymous reviews on a commercial website, praising himself ('I hope he writes for ever') while dismissing the work of others. In the unfolding affair, he first denied authorship, unleashing his lawyer with threats of litigation. Soon thereafter he offered (again through his lawyer) his wife as the alleged writer only to finally owe up to his 'foolish errors' and 'small-minded and ungenerous' reviews. After more legal professionals got busy for the opposing side, he eventually agreed to pay damages to those he had earlier threatened.[71] The scandal marked a high-point in the history of non-academic tactics attempting to control the direction of the field. Such attempts are no longer motivated by politics, or ideology, as the old angry polemics during the Cold War had been. Nothing, really, is at stake in these petty squabbles for rank, status, and prestige within the small world of the academy.

V

Even in this miniature universe, however, nobody can be in the position of Stalin, or even 'team Stalin', enforcing one consistent (if changing) party line on others. Academia remains decentralized, which allows more than one intellectual history to coexist. Even in what remains the metropole of Russian history, US academia, the history of Stalinism studies was also a history of the many brain drains, the forced or voluntary migrations of intellectuals, scholars, and their ideas. While the standard accounts of Soviet historiography pit successive generations against each other, the field had always been a playground of intersecting but mutually incomprehensible histories, which began with the displacement of scholars as a result of the Revolution. Michael Karpovich at Harvard and George Vernadsky at Yale brought the traditions of the Russian liberal intelligentsia to US campuses. Karpovich also became a great school builder, training most of the big names of the first generation of American Russianists—Martin Malia, Richard Pipes, and Leopold Haimson among them. Malia and Pipes went on to chairs at Berkeley and Harvard, while Haimson went to Columbia. The first of these three followed his mentor in his appreciation of Russian prerevolutionary culture and politics and the stress on 1917 as a deep discontinuity and a 'tragedy'. The more independently minded Pipes, by contrast, argued in nearly all points against his advisor, and Haimson did much the same, only from a perspective more sympathetic to the revolutionary movement. It was he, too, who would train the hard core of the revisionists—including Ron Suny and Roberta Manning, who in turn supervised Arch Getty. This group became locked in a continuous polemic with the other two famous pupils of Karpovich. Pipes and

Malia were less prolific as graduate mentors, and the former's influence on his students seems to have been often negative—like William Rosenberg or Richard Stites, they tended to make common cause with the hated 'revisionists'. Malia would eventually train the inventor of 'post-revisionism', Stephen Kotkin, who, during a stint as a visiting professor in New York would deeply influence a group sometimes referred to as the Columbia school of the early twenty-first century—Peter Holquist, Jochen Hellbeck, Igal Halfin, and Amir Weiner.[72]

Such intellectual genealogies, however, were constantly complicated by interlopers from abroad. In the first post-war generation, Richard Pipes is a prominent example. A 'nonobservant Orthodox Jew' of Polish extraction, who managed to escape the Holocaust by the skin of his teeth, he made it his life's work to write theological history demonstrating 'what happens when people renounce faith in God'.[73] Alexander Gerschenkron, an Odessa-born, Austrian-educated polymath who was as much at home in economic theory as in literary criticism, is another instance of displaced central-European brilliance. He would train Joseph Berliner and Franklin Holzman, authors of path-breaking studies of the Soviet economy, which I drew on in Chapter 8.[74] The Marxist wing of the revisionists would be strongly influenced by Moshe Lewin, a Vilnius-born Jew who had escaped the Holocaust to the Soviet Union, worked as collective farmer, a miner, and a metal worker, joined the Red Army (but saw no action), moved to Poland in 1946, but soon left for France and in 1951 moved on to Israel, where he got his first degree. After disenchantment with Zionism when Israel helped attack Egypt in 1956, he returned to Europe, received a doctorate from the Sorbonne and was appointed to academic positions in Paris, then New York, Birmingham and Philadelphia.[75]

The shock troops of the academic right, meanwhile, were also replenished by East European émigrés. There was, for example, Victor Kravchenko, author of a famous memoir about life in the 1930s, on which I drew again and again in this study. This *vydvizhenets* turned celebrated defector would wage a veritable one-man war on Stalin once he had escaped his sphere of power, before striking it rich, losing it all, and shooting himself dead.[76] More famous still was the former Soviet officer, GULAG inmate, celebrated Soviet author turned outlaw, and leading representative of chauvinism-as-dissidence, Alexander Solzhenitsyn, who like many a Russian in American exile could never decide what to despise more—totalitarianism or consumerism.[77] The Polish philosopher Leszek Kolakowski is another, but very different, example of a displaced Eastern European familiar to the reader from the pages of this book. His experience of Nazi occupation and subsequent Communist takeover of his native Poland had taught him to take the role of the Devil in history 'extremely seriously' and his (re-)conversion from Marxism back to some kind of Catholicism made him the leading scholar of the former as an *Ersatz*-Religion.[78] Nor were displaced histories a merely Eastern affair. From London's bohemia came the brilliant poet, one-time diplomat, bon-vivant and long time freelance cold warrior Robert Conquest, a British ex-Communist atoning for his youthful sins by writing landmark studies of Stalin's terror.[79]

Nor were Eastern-Europeans and ex-Communists predestined to become Cold Warriors, as the example of Moshe Lewin shows. An earlier instance was Isaac Deutscher, a failed Polish revolutionary who had once turned down teaching positions in the Soviet Union before being excluded from the Party for his independent views. Remembering Karl Marx and the British Museum, Deutscher moved to England in 1939, thus escaping both what the Stalinists could have done to a 'renegade' and what the Nazis would have to a 'non-Jewish Jew' (and did to his parents, who were murdered at Auschwitz). Sublimating his frustrated revolutionary pretensions into celebrated tomes on Stalin and Trotsky, he refused to recant his Marxism even if it meant trouble with US visa authorities ('Why should I do in Washington what I refused to do in Moscow?'). His books (which he effectively co-authored with his wife, Tamara, although her name never appeared on the covers) brought him some fame and a modest living, but never an academic post. They continue to be in print and are read, largely outside of academia, as their literary qualities transcend their now outdated politics. They also made him one of the few acceptable old men for a New Left otherwise intent to not trust anybody beyond thirty and Deutscher was flown in to give authoritative lectures to anti-authoritarian crowds on 1960s campuses. The young neo-Marxist historians who emerged from the stormy sixties followed him in the separation of 'Leninist democracy' from 'Stalinist totalitarianism' and his term 'revolution from above' would become a standard phrase, even if its authorship is now often forgotten.[80] The current study, indeed, took the term from Robert C. Tucker, and relabelled his 'first and second phase' into the 'first' and 'second revolution from above'.[81]

Displacement has not ended, although now mostly for less bloody reasons. Among younger English-writing scholars, Russians, Israelis, exiled Soviet-Russian-Portugese-British-American Jews[82], Japanese unsuccessfully fleeing the fatherland, and self-hating Germans would bring their own histories with them, complicating interactions again, but also invigorating the discussion through different perspectives, socializations and modes of discourse.

The American scene was flanked, followed, or subverted by the British tradition, always less prone to intellectual fads and fashions, which also absorbed American Marxists or Germans fleeing a dysfunctional academic system. British scholarship, indeed, always stood as something of a stumbling block to the self-presentation of American academics. While in the US political history was connected to 'totalitarianism' and social history to revisionism, in Britain, both explicitly socialist historians like Deutscher and fellow travellers like E. H. Carr wrote political history, while Geoffrey Hosking wrote a social history of the Soviet Union which was deeply, and explicitly, indebted to the notion of 'totalitarianism'.[83] In the UK, indeed, the roles between those who thought the Soviet experiment had something to teach either 'the West' or 'the Third World' and those who construed it as a totalitarian evil empire were initially reversed. In the conflict between Carr and Leonard Schapiro, the 'nuanced' establishment initially won out against the younger 'totalitarian'.[84]

Carr's *oeuvre*, incidentally, also puts into doubt Fitzpatrick's only half ironic claim that 'in the 1970s I was a one-woman crusade to establish the discipline of history in the study of the Soviet past'.[85] This might well have been subjectively how she felt, but what in essence she did was carry Carr's project of a dispassionate study of the Soviet Union from Britain to the US. Carr, whom Fitzpatrick had met as a graduate student in the UK, is yet another of the many colourful intellectuals who shaped the study of the Russian Revolution and Stalinism. He could be, and was, faulted on many fronts, but surely he could not be accused of being either a Cold Warrior or not writing history. A book-ish intellectual with a bad heart who admired the powerful and the violent, a recovering liberal who searched for substitutes first in a some-what domesticated Nazism, then in a 'balanced' view of Soviet 'achieve-ments', Carr was an unwavering believer in human progress who came to see the state, and with it the Bolsheviks, as agents of this upward movement. A prodigious worker, he sacrificed three marriages to a fourteen volume history of Soviet Russia from October to Stalin's revo-lution. These controversial titles have stood the test of time in many respects and are still used to scare advanced students come exam time. The detailed empiricism of these weighty tomes stands in crass contrast to the studied relativism he exhibited in his maybe most influential book—*What Is History?*. Towards the end of his life, Carr teamed up with the younger R. W. Davies to complete *The Foundations of a Planned Economy*, which brought his history to the eve of Stalin's revolution.[86] Davies, a Marxist and Communist Party member until 1956, continued the work in *The Industrialisation of Russia*, another deeply empirical, step-by-step account of Soviet policies and their effects. By volume five, which brings the story to 1933, Davies, who also built an important centre for Soviet studies at the University of Birmingham and with it the 'Birmingham school' of Soviet studies, in turn had teamed up with a younger scholar, Stephen Wheatcroft. It remains to be seen if such 'needlework' (as Carr called his attention to detail) will be continued in decades to come.[87] The dispassionate empiricism and state-centredness of this tradition has lost nothing of its quality as an irritant, as the reception of Wheatcroft and Davies' book shows.[88]

Nor is Russian history restricted to the US and the UK. With the Birmingham trained Wheatcroft, the empire of dispassionate, empirical study of Soviet history spread its tentacles to its reluctant dominion, Australia, while the once young 'totalitarian', whose career Carr had tried to sabotage early on, supervised Graeme Gill, who would contrib-ute an important study of the origins of the Stalinist political order from down under.[89] The author of the current lines, too, a Bavarian with US graduate education, was washed up on these shores, and writes now from under the blue skies of the most remote capital in the world. And there were, of course, the German, Italian, or French traditions, which would often go unnoticed with the Americans (Malia and the Paris-trained Lewin were exceptions, and so is the newly founded journal *Kritika*), but produce a continuously growing library of both monographic and synthetic studies on Stalinism, some of which this book had drawn on repeatedly.[90]

VI

Until Perestroika, the interactions with the Soviet Union itself were largely one way—with foreign scholars reading Soviet research, often mining it for unintended or hidden information, while the Soviet side remained utterly insular.[91] Khrushchev's not-so-secret speech of 1956 on what he termed the 'cult of personality'—which laid all blame for only some of the brutality of Stalinism at the dictator's feet alone—was read all over the world, and added some new detail to what defectors had long claimed.[92] Such cautious de-Stalinization encouraged historians like Viktor Danilov to reassess the painful history of collectivization, or even, like Viktor Nekrich, to debunk the myth that the Soviet Union had been well-prepared for war. Neither of these, however, could be published in the increasingly stifling intellectual atmosphere once Brezhnev took over. Such work continued to circulate in samizdat, not least among the younger generation of *apparatchiki* who would become Gorbachev's men. The blockages to question what actually happened were removed, however, with Perestroika. From the mid-1980s until well into the Putin years, nearly every myth about Stalinism was exposed, though sometimes replaced by equally misguided counter-myths. The flood of historical writings and source publications was indeed such, that few historians could keep up with the mass of new material. Within Russia, pioneers like Danilov could finally pick up where he was forced to leave his investigation of the tragedy of the Soviet countryside, leading the charge in multi-volume source collections, which this book has relied on again and again.[93]

These older scholars were now joined by younger historians, often with some foreign training, who increasingly read Western works, which became available also, bit by bit, in Russian translations. Thus emerged a literature which was integrated into the worldwide discussion, but steeped in the sources and the culture in a way outsiders can rarely achieve.[94] This book has relied again and again on the fruits of their labour. Some fields are nearly entirely in Russian hands, as they have fallen out of fashion elsewhere. Such is the case, for example, with historical demography, on which this book has relied extensively.[95]

Integration into a global network of historical debate, however, is the exception in Russia today, as many historians continue to only read their native language. What, after all, could foreigners with their lack of *kul'tura* and their grammatically tortured, mispronounced Russian have to add to the history of the Fatherland? Much of what passes as history writing has little to do with disciplined exploration of evidence and a lot with finding a useful past under the rubble of the last decades. This quest also animated Grigorii Chukhrai, the memoirist whose work formed the topic of Chapter 1. Since he wrote, though, a distinct shift in the public discussion took place in Russia—a change, no doubt, he would have cheered, had he lived to see it. Under Putin and Medvedev, apologists for Stalin and his regime could feel that the state again supported their views, although those in power speak differently to different audiences.[96] Still, in a context where the offices of a not-for-profit organization trying to keep the memory of Stalin's victim alive can be raided by masked police forces; where Stalin's name is restored to the wall of *Kurskaia* metro station in Moscow under the pretext of authenticity; where a law is drafted to gag any critical appreciation of the Red Army's Second World War; where a Presidential Commission to Counter Attempts to Falsify History to the Detriment of Russia's Interests is set up to fight 'distortion of the truth about the war'; where an historian gets arrested for breaking 'privacy laws'—in such a context, nationalists irritated by the besmirching of the past by hostile foreigners and internal traitors alike can hope that their call on the state will be heard, to take side in the history wars over Stalin's grave.[97]

Meanwhile, other successor states to the Soviet Empire write their own histories, which have little in common with the Great Russian Past reconstructed in Moscow. In Uzbekistan a Victims of Repression Memorial Museum opened in 2002, an intriguing institution given the authoritarian Karimov regime. It displays archival documents, photographs, and statistics, inscribing Stalinist mass death into a long history of colonial victimization by Russia.[98] The Baltic States, whose troubled history had been conserved by exiles in Germany and elsewhere,[99] now experience a renaissance of interest by foreigners and locals alike—an emerging literature which is watched carefully by the Putin–Medvedev regime unhappy about reminders of anything not called 'liberation'.[100] The international Ukrainian national movement, meanwhile, attempts vigorously to follow the post-war trend of substituting past victimization for heroism as the foundational glue binding together the nation.[101]

The mythical moment here is the 1932–33 famine, which in the official interpretation became *Holodomor*—genocide by famine. This interpretation has its own history in exile. In English language scholarship the issue was first broached in a 1934 article in *Foreign Affairs*, written by the journalist William Henry Chamberlin, who had witnessed some of it while working in Russia.[102] His analysis of the causes and extent of this 'man-made disaster' was expanded three decades later in an essay in the journal *Soviet Studies*,[103] only to find its most famous expression in Robert Conquest's *Harvest of Sorrow* (1986).[104] The more recent notion that this was a 'genocide'—the premeditated attempt to destroy an ethnic group—is now enshrined in legislation in nineteen countries, including, of course, Ukraine itself. Those carefully weighing the available evidence usually conclude that while the famine was man-made and starvation was a risk the leadership was willing to take, the resulting mass death neither exclusively affected Ukrainians nor was it planned in advance or at this scale as a means of racial or class warfare. In the words of Conquest, who surely cannot be accused of being soft on Stalin, the dictator did not 'purposely inflict' the famine, but did not prevent the imminent catastrophe because he 'put "Soviet interests" other than feeding the starving first—thus consciously abetting it'.[105] Even those sympathetic with the 'Ukrainian' view thus note that 'there is no "smoking gun"...and one should not anticipate finding definite proof that Stalin had a clearly defined goal to destroy the Ukrainians as a nation'.[106] Such tentative consensus remains academic, however, as exile groups from Canada to the UK distribute educational materials for high school teachers meant to tell their students that there is 'no question that the famine was engineered by a government which specifically planned to destroy the Ukrainian nation and its people as a political and social force'.[107] Others up the ante by declaring 'the Ukrainian Famine of 1921–1923' a 'genocide' too.[108]

VII

Writing the history of Stalinism, then, has been a multinational as well as multidisciplinary enterprise from the start and continues to be of a complexity only few other historiographies exhibit. The result was one of the most exciting and expansive historical literatures university libraries have to offer. By the 1990s, the times had truly passed when a young scholar could have read everything written about Soviet history. Stalinism is a field which had been ploughed over for many decades by the brightest and most productive minds of the social sciences and humanities, along with scores of lesser scholars. Even the most disciplined and hard working graduate student today has little chance to truly 'read up on the historiography', i.e. the huge and ever expanding library of literature produced since the 1950s by historians, political scientists, psychologists, literary scholars, economists, anthropologists, and sociologists writing in French, Italian, German, Polish, Dutch, Russian, Ukrainian, English, Japanese, and doubtlessly other languages. With the opening of the archives, the outpouring of personal recollections, and the ability to conduct oral history interviews with surviving witnesses, the problem of too much information only became worse. This situation, of course, could have been conceived of as a chance, a huge opportunity for large groups of scholars to carve out their own niches and, together, further the knowledge about the past. However, in the humanities reputations are often made by personalities rather than teams, demonstrated nicely by the few recent examples of extremely well-funded multischolar projects, which nevertheless still produced single-authored books in the time-honoured tradition of the historian-artisan.[109] Moreover, the dominant story the Anglophone field of Soviet history told itself about its own past revolved around not cumulative accumulation of knowledge, but sharp discontinuities between generations of scholars: 'totalitarians' followed by 'revisionists'. If a new generation entered the game, as happened increasingly from the 1990s, when those trained by the baby-boomers began academic work, it obviously had to make its mark, and make it with a splash. Just furthering knowledge would not do. It had to be a 'paradigm shift'.

Paradigm shifts, however, are tricky to produce. Most of the truly revolutionary changes in the natural sciences came about, not by a genial mind rethinking everything but by chance mishaps in the laboratory, which upon closer examination produced results questioning the perceived wisdom in such a fundamental way that a new style of doing science, and with it new theories, were required.[110] Some hoped the opening of the archives would lead to such discoveries, explosions in the historical laboratory that would completely change our view of Soviet history. One such find were personal diaries of more or less ordinary Soviets, which could tell the historian something about how Stalinism felt from the inside. Some of the most celebrated recent work has focused on exactly this line of inquiry.[111] There were, however, two problems with this approach. First, to explore Stalinism from a personal perspective hardly amounted to a 'paradigm shift'. Dissident memoirs had followed similar lines decades earlier, and simply looking at the social totality from the perspective of the individual is surely an important approach to history, but could easily be seen as just adding to the fundamental work done by earlier generations.

This is where the work of philosopher Michel Foucault came to the aid, at the face of it a rather odd choice, as, to this luminary, a central institution of this society—the GULAG—'remained a paradox'.[112] Foucault's work on power and subjectivity implied that the social totality was constitutive of the psyche; it contended that reading personal documents did more than just explore the variegated world of individuals, but showed how the personal was indeed the political, how 'the state' was not external to, but deeply internal to 'the Stalinist subject'.[113] The leading scholars in this new subfield saw themselves in a line with Stephen Kotkin's Foucaultian masterpiece, *Magnetic Mountain*, but radicalized his notion of the inevitability of 'speaking Bolshevik' into the proposition that Stalin's subjects could not think outside official discourse.[114] The manifesto writers conveniently forgot that they had precursors both among the 'totalitarians' and the 'revisionists', but such willful amnesia strengthened their case for originality, thus leadership and hence the right to demand others to follow.[115] And many did heed the call, particularly within the parochial world of the metropole, but by the end of the first decade of the new millennium the approach has gathered acolytes throughout Europe as well. Predictably, too, by the time the once-radical thesis—that 'there were no coherent, explicitly formulated alternatives to the cognitive (and affective) framework offered by the Party state'—became a new orthodoxy, it also became an old hat. In fact, some of the original inventors had already subtly moved away from such empirically unsustainable if theoretically sophisticated ideas once 'Stalinist subjectivity' became an established field of study in itself.[116]

Alas, not everybody in the post-baby-boomer cohort was willing to follow the lead of the Foucaultians. Like every generation, this one, too, was internally incoherent, ideologically varied, and of extremely dissimilar personal backgrounds. Some even thought that the scholars of older generations actually had something to offer to their younger peers struggling to work their way through mountains of primary and secondary evidence. Starting from a different theoretical vantage point, indebted to the old totalitarianism, the slightly less ancient revisionism, or both, they seized upon other evidence coming from the archives. Some of the former revisionists did much the same and both groups of scholars presented data which contradicted the claims that Stalinism was deeply rooted in the individual. In particular, they were able to document, by drawing on secret internal police and party reports, that there was considerable opposition to Stalinism and that many Soviet citizens were severely disgruntled with the regime they lived under.[117]

It was at this juncture that the loudest polemic of the turn of the century emerged, the discussion about 'resistance' and 'belief', staged in part to launch (and promote) the new journal *Kritika*.[118] Three time-honoured tactics were employed in an attempt to dam the theory of the immersion of the subject into official discourse against the flood of falsifying evidence emerging from the archives. First, the facts themselves were questioned. Reports on the mood of the population had been assembled from evidence submitted by Party informants, lecturers and agitators, as well as by police agents, and had served as a major source of information for the leadership about the impact of its policies. These documents, which had already been used by Merle Fainsod in his classical study of Smolensk under Soviet rule, were now declared to be 'all produced by ideological agents with a revolutionary mission, which politicized their perception of "unhealthy" moods'.[119] Thus, they could not be trusted. This line of argument stood in a long tradition of ruling out certain genres of evidence as untrustworthy, as if there existed any historical sources which are clearly polished windows to the past. Such dismissals can affect memoirs (which are 'about as trustworthy as a bus station hustler'[120]), official pronouncements ('Foreigners who try to understand Stalin's policies…by studying the Soviet press…usually come up with a truckload of gibberish'[121]), or numbers ('lies, damned lies, and statistics'). The classical historian's response to such critique (a stance the current book embraces) is that a careful, contextualized reading of a wide variety of evidence is the most pragmatic and the most prudent course of action.[122] Such appeals initially went unheard, although close to a decade later they found expression in carefully researched monographs, released just in time to commemorate the 70th anniversary of the Great Terror.[123]

The second tactic was to hit the player rather than the ball, that is, to attack the historians instead of their evidence, a favourite weapon ever since the Cold War, although now opponents were no longer criticized for their presumed ideological errors, but for their naivety. A celebrated genealogy of 'the liberal subject in Soviet Studies' traced what the author called 'the Cold War view of human agency' and the 'academic conceptualizations of Stalinist man' from the 1950s to the 1990s, implying, though not stating, that historians projected the attitudes of their own society on a completely different terrain.[124] This clarification was left to another Young Turk, who declared that 'scholars tend to inadvertently project their own values on historical actors, endowing them with a liberal self-understanding and a striving for autonomy from the surrounding political environment'.[125] Predictably, such diagnosis, which was met with some protest from those subjected to it,[126] only egged on others to search for more evidence against the emerging dogma,[127] while a third group elegantly side-stepped the debate by demonstrating that resistance was indeed possible on the basis of official discourse itself.[128]

Most successful was the third prong of attack, the deconstruction and criticism of the term 'resistance' as too clumsy, too broad, and potentially misleading.[129] Many agreed, as words are easier discarded than facts, only to replace the category by alternatives such as 'recalcitrance' and 'disorderliness,'[130] 'self-protection' and 'disobedience', or by simply pluralizing the term into 'resistances'.[131] Chapter 6 of the current book stands as much in this tradition as my overall avoidance of the term 'resistance' (unless the participants were armed), and the parallel emphasis of 'tenacious histories' relatively independent of the limping Behemoth, its practices and discourses.

As so often, then, nobody really won this debate, but many on both sides slightly adapted their positions in the process. The result may have been progress in understanding the past, but it was far from a paradigm shift. This absence of a radical discontinuity is illustrated by those proclaiming its existence frequently resorting to the writing of angry book reviews, attacking those who do not submit to their intellectual leadership. A classic of the genre is Stephen Kotkin's review of Sarah Davies's book on popular opinion. Davies had mobilized striking archival evidence against some of the central assumptions in Kotkin's well-theorized tome on 'Stalinism as a civilization', a book researched largely before the archives opened.[132] Kotkin was not amused. In a review as angry as it was patronizing, he lectured his colleague on how she should have approached her sources and chided her for an 'insufficiently analytical' approach to historiography ('e.g. as Sheila Fitzpatrick has shown, Soviet flags were red, etc.').[133] This counter-attack was flanked by a pincer-movement on 'archival fetishism' (something wrong, apparently, with the sexuality of those working in archives), the proposition that ideas, not sources mattered, and the assertion that, anyway, archival research 'has consumed a good portion of my adult life'.[134] As if to show that such posturing is not a male prerogative, Kate Brown followed suit, in 2009, with an attack on Orlando Figes, who had also failed to submit to the dominance of the modernity school, instead dropping 'the whole dusty anvil of totalitarianism on the reader's toes'.[135] Such anger at non-recognition of the own presumed leading role only proves the point. Instead of a new paradigm, indeed, we have today the pluralization of approaches, methods, and styles, which might be better understood as

rival schools, although this metaphor is also too limiting, as hardly anybody willingly declares fellowship.[136]

Such fragmentation might well be a good thing. As one of the found-
ers of the field put it in a famous little book on what the profession is
all about, history is not only a conversation between the historian and
the sources, but also with other historians and the general public—a
never ending debate about past, present, and future.[137] We would thus
expect, in a global world, in societies which are both democratic and
diverse and thus ridden with many histories, that more than one discourse, more than a single idea, more than one paradigm exists and
coexists. If diversity is thus unavoidable, it is also intellectually desirable. This book, indeed, could not have been written without the many,
varied, and contradictory passions, which had fuelled the work of that
large group of quarrelling giants on whose shoulders the author has
tried to balance somewhat haphazardly. Their politics and caprices,
their enthusiasms and resentments, their ambitions and their fears
made them search for, and thus find, different aspects of that multifaceted society that was Stalinism, in the process creating a rich and
nuanced literature, which continues to be of relevance long after the
object of study has disappeared.

VII

The relevance of this historical experience to scholars and audiences outside the former Soviet Union is due to change in accordance with the
circumstances of their present. The social formation of Stalinism and the
society that grew out of it after the dictator's death offer such rich potential that I can only speculate here as to where the field might move in the
early twenty-first century. Three trends seem likely. First, the reappro-
priation of the concept of 'totalitarianism' is probably here to stay, as it
can serve polemical ends on both sides of the political spectrum. For
those advocating the national security state, the term can help to assimi-
late the new enemy—militant Islamic fundamentalism—to the long
line of evil the free world has fought in the last century. That the leaders
are now bearded rather than mustachioed matters less in this scheme
than the conviction that only tough-minded and pragmatic militancy

has a chance to succeed against such men and their movements. But 'totalitarianism' has its use for the Left as well in a world where history has returned with fingerprint machines at immigration, secret prisons and rendition, collateral damage and targeted assassinations. With public figures everywhere proclaiming the need to abolish civil liberties, roll out the barbed wire, and reintroduce torture to rescue the open society from its enemies, Stalinism might well teach some old lessons again, many of which the Cold Warriors of old would have embraced half a century earlier: about the dangers of the warfare state; about the results of gearing means single-mindedly to ends without discussing the morality of the former; about the resilience of plurality and difference even under the seeming monolith of dictatorial regimes, but also about how outside aggression can paper over such fissures and unite an otherwise disunited society.[138]

Secondly, the literature assimilating Stalinism to the modern gardening state will probably also continue in a world where the role and even the basic legitimacy of the welfare state continues to be politically contentious. It is likely (and desirable) that the debate will move now from grand theoretical designs to the study of particular policies, institutions, and practices. Moreover, the focus on the negative aspects—social engineering leading to mass death—will eventually be supplemented by studies focusing on the more positive aspects of modern statecraft. While the attachment of many Soviet citizens to free education, public healthcare, and a state pension system is well known in the field today, we still do not have a detailed history of the Soviet welfare state which would take advantage of the archival revolution.[139]

Finally, and closest to the mission of this book, a reinvigoration of economic history and the political economy of Stalinism (and post-Stalinism) is overdue after decades of neglect. This history is more than just a pastime for academics. Stalin and his 'team' tried to run an entire society like a company town, and failed.[140] The history of their failure contains more than one lesson for life in our corporate world, but is largely ignored by academic historians. During a period of massive economic upheaval and the most dramatic transformation of the world's economic systems, there is little sustained thought about economic matters outside of business schools and economics departments. Among

historians, only those ghettoized in what remains of the subfield of economic history still engage in the study of what matters most to the largest number of people today. In their attempts to be taken seriously by
economists, however, they frequently limit their audience by modelling
their arguments in abstract charts and littering their texts with highly
technical terms and equations. While the Gerschenkron school half a
century earlier was able to communicate complex economic matters in
plain English, most recent writing on the subject has trouble reaching
even other Stalinism scholars, let alone undergraduate students in the
humanities.

Again, this inability to speak to wider audiences is not entirely an
academic matter. An appreciation of the realities of the Soviet political
economy might open up the way to a more realistic understanding of
so-called 'capitalist' societies, where the relationship between ideology
and practice in many ways inverts the Soviet equivalent. Here, official
rhetoric claimed rational economic planning, while indeed this economy might have been even more anarchic than market centered alternatives; there, dominant discourse in most cases assumed that private
enterprise and the market either were, or at least should be, the principle drivers of economic action, while in reality the state always framed
this activity through legislation and re-distributed resources through
taxation and the provision of services of various kinds. Moreover, non-
economic organizations, such as families, churches, or other non-gov-
ernmental associations play an equally central role in the ways goods
and services are produced, distributed, and consumed in these societies, and few commentators would want them replaced by outright
market mechanisms. Once simplistic notions of what 'Soviet socialism'
actually was are removed from this debate, we can start to see modern
industrial societies as moving on many, complex, and varied continua
of social organization, rather than on one where 'state' and 'market' are
in an absolute, morally laden opposition.

NOTES

Introduction

1. Emile Durkheim, *The Division of Labor in Society*, trans. George Simpson (London: The Free Press of Glencoe, 1964), 28.

2. R. J. B. Bosworth, *Mussolini's Italy. Life under the Fascist Dictatorship, 1915–1945* (New York: Penguin Press, 2006), p. xxii.

3. On 'society' see also the discussion in Mark Edele, 'Soviet Society, Social Structure, and Everyday Life. Major Frameworks Reconsidered'. *Kritika: Explorations in Russian and Eurasian History* 8, no. 2 (2007): 349–73.

4. Katerina Clark, *Petersburg, Crucible of Cultural Revolution* (Cambridge and London: Harvard University Press, 1995).

5. For reappropriations of the concept of totalitarianism see *inter alia* Amir Weiner, *Making Sense of War. The Second World War and the Fate of the Bolshevik Revolution* (Princeton and Oxford: Princeton University Press, 2000); Orlando Figes, *The Whisperers. Private Life in Stalin's Russia* (New York: Metropolitan Books, 2007); and Michael Geyer and Sheila Fitzpatrick (eds.), *Beyond Totalitarianism. Stalinism and Nazism Compared* (Cambridge: Cambridge University Press, 2009).

6. Hannah Arendt, *The Origins of Totalitarianism*. New edn. with added prefaces (New York and London: Harvest Books, 1968).

7. Lynne Viola, *The Unknown Gulag. The Lost World of Stalin's Special Settlements* (Oxford and New York: Oxford University Press, 2007), 192.

8. Paul R. Gregory, *The Political Economy of Stalinism. Evidence from the Soviet Secret Archives.* (Cambridge, New York, Melbourne: Cambridge University Press, 2004).

9. Mark Edele and Michael Geyer, 'States of Exception: The Nazi-Soviet War as a System of Violence, 1939–1945', in *Beyond Totalitarianism. Stalinism and Nazism Compared*, eds. Michael Geyer and Sheila

Fitzpatrick (Cambridge and New York: Cambridge University Press, 2009), 345–95.

10. Mark Edele, *Soviet Veterans of the Second World War. A Popular Movement in an Authoritarian Society, 1941–1991* (Oxford: Oxford University Press, 2008).

11. For archival source collections, memoirs, and diaries, see the bibliography. The files of the Harvard Project are quoted below by schedule, volume, case, and page number. They are available at http://hcl.harvard.edu/collections/hpsss/index.html

12. A classical account of Stalin's rise is E. H. Carr, *The Russian Revolution from Lenin to Stalin (1917–1929)* (London: Macmillan, 1979). For more recent research see James Harris, 'Stalin as General Secretary: the appointments process and the nature of Stalin's power', in *Stalin. A New History*, eds. Sarah Davies and James Harris (Cambridge: Cambridge University Press, 2005), 63–82; and Robert Service, *Stalin. A Biography* (Cambridge, MA.: Harvard University Press, 2005), chs. 20 and 22.

13. This periodization is adapted from Robert C. Tucker, 'Stalinism as Revolution from Above', in *Stalinism. Essays in Historical Interpretation*, ed. Robert C. Tucker (New York: W. W. Norton & Company, 1977), 77–108. Tucker includes both the First Five-Year-Plan and the Great Terror in his concept of the Revolution from Above, while I distinguish between the two. On the Cultural Revolution see Sheila Fitzpatrick (ed.), *Cultural Revolution in Russia, 1928–1941* (Bloomington: Indiana University Press, 1978).

14. Matthew E. Lenoe, *The Kirov Murder and Soviet History* (New Haven: Yale University Press, 2010).

15. For an interpretation stressing the centrality of revolution and war in the thinking and behaviour of Stalin and the Stalinists see Kevin McDermott, *Stalin* (Houndsmills, Basingstoke: Palgrave Macmillan, 2006).

16. Jan T. Gross, *Revolution from Abroad. The Soviet Conquest of Poland's Western Ukraine and Western Belorussia*. expanded edn. (Princeton and Oxford: Princeton University Press, 2002); David Wolff and Gaël Moullec, *Le KGB et les pays Baltes 1939–1991* (Paris: Belin, 1999); and Elena Zubkova, *Pribaltika i Kreml'. 1940–1953* (Moscow: Rosspen, 2008).

17. See Sheila Fitzpatrick, 'Postwar Soviet Society: The "Return to Normalcy", 1945–1953', in *The Impact of World War II on the Soviet Union*, ed. Susan J. Linz (Totova, NJ: Rowman & Allanhead, 1985), 129–56. The best introduction to the post-war years remain Elena Zubkova, *Russia after the War. Hopes, Illusions, and Disappointments, 1945–1957*. Transl. Hugh

Ragsdale (Armonk and London: M. E. Sharpe, 1998); and id., *Poslevoennoe sovetskoe obshchestvo: politika i povsednevnost' 1945–1953* (Moscow: Rosspen, 2000). On anti-Semitism and the doctors' plot see Gennadii Kostyrchenko, *Out of the Red Shadows: Anti-Semitism in Stalin's Russia* (Amherst, NY: Prometheus Books, 1995).

Chapter 1

1. Grigorii Chukhrai, *Moia voina* (Moscow: Algoritm, 2001), 28.
2. Russian books mention, inside the cover, the date a book goes to the typesetter and the day it goes into print. In the case of *Moia voina*, the dates are 27 October and 30 November 2000, respectively. Chukhrai died on 28 October 2001, in Moscow.
3. Sheila Fitzpatrick, *Tear off the Masks! Identity and Imposture in Twentieth-Century Russia* (Princeton and Oxford: Princeton University Press, 2005).
4. S. A. Smith, 'The First Soviet Generation: Children and Religious Belief in Soviet Russia, 1917–41', in *Generations in Twentieth-Century Europe*, ed. Stephen Lovell (Houndsmills, Basingstokes: Palgrave Macmillan, 2007), 81.
5. Chukhrai, *Moia voina*, 5.
6. Abbott Gleason, *Totalitarianism. The Inner History of the Cold War* (New York, Oxford: Oxford University Press, 1995), 8, 211–16.
7. Quoted in Beate Fieseler, 'Die Invaliden des "Grossen Vaterländischen Krieges" der Sowjetunion—Eine politische Sozialgeschichte 1941–1991' (Habilitationsschrift, Ruhr-Universität Bochum, 2003), 481.
8. Chukhrai, *Moia voina*, 5.
9. Stephen Kotkin, *Magnetic Mountain. Stalinism as a Civilization* (Berkeley, Los Angeles, London: University of California Press, 1995).
10. See Ch. 4.
11. Chukhrai, *Moia voina*, 5–6. On the world of street children see Alan M. Ball, *And Now My Soul Is Hardened. Abandoned Children in Soviet Russia, 1918–1930* (Berkeley, Los Angeles, London: University of California Press, 1994).
12. Sheila Fitzpatrick, Alexander Rabinowitch, and Richard Stites (eds.), *Russia in the Era of NEP. Explorations in Soviet Society and Culture* (Bloomington and Indianapolis: Indiana University Press, 1991); Eric Naiman, *Sex in Public. The Incarnation of Early Soviet Ideology* (Princeton, NJ: Princeton University Press, 1997).
13. Chukhrai, *Moia voina*, 6–7.

14. On *kombedy* see Sheila Fitzpatrick, *Stalin's Peasants. Resistance and Survival in the Russian Village after Collectivization* (Oxford: Oxford University Press, 1994), 24 (quotation), 32; Lynne Viola, *Peasant Rebels Under Stalin. Collectivization and the Culture of Peasant Resistance* (Oxford: Oxford University Press, 1996), 16.

15. Chukhrai, *Moia voina*, 7.

16. See R. W. Davies and Stephen G. Wheatcroft, *The Industrialization of Soviet Russia 5. The Years of Hunger: Soviet Agriculture, 1931–1933* (Houndsmills and New York: Palgrave Macmillan, 2004), 412–15.

17. See the documents No. 258–61 in *Tragediia sovetskoi derevni. Kollektivizatsiia i raskulachivanie. Dokumenty i materialy v 5 tomakh 1927–1939. Tom 3: konets 1930–1933*, eds. V. Danilov, R. Manning, and L. Viola (Moscow: Rosspen, 2001), 634–8.

18. Michael Ellman estimates this number at circa 150,000. See his 'Stalin and the Soviet Famine of 1932–33 Revisited', *Europe-Asia Studies* 59, no. 4 (2007): 679, 684.

19. Chukhrai, *Moia voina*, 7.

20. Chukhrai, *Moia voina*, 8–9.

21. On the centrality of the state in everyday life see Sheila Fitzpatrick, *Everyday Stalinism. Ordinary Life in Extraordinary Times: Soviet Russia in the 1930s* (New York and Oxford: Oxford University Press, 1999).

22. Chukhrai, *Moia voina*, 9–11. The militia was united organizationally with the political police (the OGPU) in 1930 and reorganized into the NKVD in 1934. On the relationship between the two security organs see Paul M. Hagenloh, '"Chekist in Essence, Chekist in Spirit": Regular and Political Police in the 1930s', *Cahiers du Monde russe* 42, no. 2-3-4 (2001): 447–76.

23. Chukhrai, *Moia voina*, 11–12.

24. Eugenia Semyonovna Ginzburg, *Journey into the Whirlwind* (San Diego, New York, London: Harvest Books, 1995), 308–13.

25. Quoted in Andrea Graziosi, 'G. L. Piatakov (1890–1937): A Mirror of Soviet History', *Harvard Ukrainian Studies* 16 (1992): 105.

26. On living arrangements in the cities see Fitzpatrick, *Everyday Stalinism*, 46–50; on Magnitogorsk see Kotkin, *Magnetic mountain*, ch. 4.

27. Chukhrai, *Moia voina*, 13–16.

28. Ibid., 18.

29. Ibid., 20.

30. Ibid., 21, 23–4.

31. Ibid., 25–6.

32. See the directives regarding the role of Communists and Komsomols in battle (15 July 1941), and the role of Military Commissars (20 July 1941), reprinted in *Glavnye politicheskie organy Vooruzhennykh sil SSSR v Velikoi Otechestvennoi voine 1941–1945 gg. Dokumenty i materialy*, ed. V. A. Zolotarev et al. (= *Russkii arkhiv: Velikaia Otechestvennaia*, vol. 17-6 (1-2)) (Moscow: Terra, 1996), 40–4, 48–51.

33. Chukhrai, *Moia voina*, 35–41, 47–54; David M. Glantz, and Jonathan House, *When Titans Clashed. How the Red Army Stopped Hitler* (Lawrence, Kansas: University Press of Kansas, 1995), 9, 95; and David M. Glantz, *Colossus Reborn. The Red Army at War, 1941–1943* (Lawrence: University Press of Kansas, 2005), 618–19, 186–8.

34. Chukhrai, *Moia voina*, 55–62; Glantz, *Colossus Reborn*, 186–7.

35. G. F. Krivosheev, *Soviet Casualties and Combat Losses in the Twentieth Century* (London: Greenhill Books, 1997), 94 (table 67).

36. Glantz, *Colossus Reborn*, 187; Chukhrai, *Moia voina*, 82, 88, 106–75, 119, 136.

37. Chukhrai, *Moia voina*, 159–70, 170–2; for a similar incident, this time involving another member of the unit, see 174–5.

38. Chukhrai, *Moia voina*, 181, 184, 190–222, 230–8, 248, 251, 254–60. On the formations and reformations of the airborne forces see Glantz, *Colossus Reborn*, 186–8.

39. See Mark Edele, *Soviet Veterans of the Second World War. A Popular Movement in an Authoritarian Society, 1941–1991* (Oxford and New York: Oxford University Press, 2008), ch. 1.

40. Grigorii Chukhrai, *Moe kino* (Moscow: Algoritm, 2002), 5–12, 26–9. For an overview over the famine see Elena Zubkova, *Russia After the War. Hopes, Illusions, and Disappointments, 1945–1957*. Transl. Hugh Ragsdale (Armonk and London: M. E. Sharpe, 1998), 40–50. For a detailed study see V. F. Zima, *Golod v SSSR 1946–1947 godov: proiskhozhdenie i posledstviia* (Moscow: Institut Rossiiskoi istorii RAN, 1996).

41. Chukhrai, *Moe kino*, 29–54.

42. Peter Vail, and Aleksandr Genis, *60-e. Mir sovetskogo cheloveka* (Moscow: Novoe literaturnoe obozrenie, 2001), 88–96.

43. Amir Weiner, *Making Sense of War. The Second World War and the Fate of the Bolshevik Revolution* (Princeton and Oxford: Princeton University Press, 2000), 20–1; Mark Edele, 'Soviet Veterans as an Entitlement Group, 1945–1955', *Slavic Review* 65, no. 1 (2006): 113–16.

44. Chukhrai, *Moia voina*, 26–7, 47, 68–75, 83, 246–7, 271. On the centrality of war movies in Soviet culture see Denise J. Youngblood, *Russian War*

Films. On the Cinema Front, 1914–2005 (Lawrence: University Press of Kansas, 2007). On the easing of admissions procedures in August 1941 (and a further watering down of standards in December of that year) see T. H. Rigby, *Communist Party Membership in the USSR 1917–1967* (Princeton, New Jersey: Princeton University Press, 1968), 251–3. For the number of wartime admissions to the Party see Edele, *Soviet Veterans of the Second World War*, 136.

45. See Ch. 9.
46. Chukhrai, *Moia voina*, 236–7, quotation: 236.
47. On the public discussion about the Soviet past from the mid-1980s onwards see R. W. Davies, *Soviet History in the Gorbachev Revolution* (London: Macmillan, 1989); and id., *Soviet History in the Yeltsin Era*. (New York: St Martin's Press, 1997).
48. Chukhrai, *Moia voina*, 27.
49. Ibid., 28–9.
50. On this point see also Susan Morrissey, *Heralds of Revolution. Russian Students and the Mythologies of Radicalism* (New York and Oxford: Oxford University Press, 1998).
51. Chukhrai, *Moia voina*, 64, 16–18, 20–2, 24, 64.
52. On socialist realism as a literary practice and a mode of perception see Katerina Clark, *The Soviet Novel. History as Ritual.* 3rd edn. (Bloomington and Indianapolis: Indiana University Press, 2000); and Sheila Fitzpatrick, 'Becoming Cultured: Socialist Realism and the representation of Privilege and Taste', in *The Cultural Front. Power and Culture in Revolutionary Russia* (Ithaca and London: Cornell University Press, 1992), 216–37.
53. Chukhrai, *Moia voina*, 21–2.
54. Chukhrai, *Moe kino*, 142.
55. Juliane Fürst, 'Prisoners of the Soviet Self?—Political Youth Opposition in Late Stalinism', *Europe-Asia Studies* 54, no. 3 (2002): 353–75; Anna Krylova, 'Identity, Agency, and the "First Soviet Generation"', in *Generations in Twentieth-Century Europe*, ed. Stephen Lovell (Houndsmills, Basingstokes: Palgrave Macmillan, 2007), 101–21.
56. See Ch. 4.
57. Chukhrai, *Moia voina*, 101–2; 216.
58. Chukhrai, *Moe kino*, 201–3.
59. Chukhrai, *Moia voina*, 196.
60. On the recruiting base of Guards and mechanized formations see John Erickson, 'Red Army Battlefield Performance, 1941–45: the System and the

Soldier', in *Time to Kill. The Soldier's Experience of War in the West 1939–1945*, eds. Paul Addison and Angus Calder (London: Plimco, 1997), 234; on Party membership Rigby, *Communist Party Membership*, 253.

61. Chukhrai, *Moia voina*, 170–2, 284, 228–9.
62. Ibid., 195.
63. Chukhrai, *Moia voina*, 194–6.
64. Ibid., 186–7. On the role of the master narrative in making sense of this war see Weiner, *Making Sense of War*.
65. This was a widespread approach to Soviet reality. Raymond A. Bauer, Alex Inkeles, and Clyde Kluckhohn, *How The Soviet System Works. Cultural, Psychological, and Social Themes*. (Cambridge: Harvard University Press, 1956), 29–35, esp. 34; Alex Inkeles and Raymond Bauer, *The Soviet Citizen. Daily Life in a Totalitarian Society* (Cambridge, MA: Harvard University Press, 1961), 291–95.
66. On the fluidity of the border between perpetrators and victims see also Wendy Z. Goldman, *Terror and Democracy in the Age of Stalin. The Social Dynamics of Repression* (Cambridge and New York: Cambridge University Press, 2007), 163–201.
67. Chukhrai, *Moe kino*, 7, 27.
68. On Romm's role in Chukhrai's career see Chukhrai, *Moe kino*, 35–54, esp. 49; for a portrait of Romm as a patron see ibid., 33–54, 97–100.

Chapter 2

1. Quoted by A. A. Pechenkin, 'Byla li vozmozhnost' nastupat'?', *Otechestvennaia istoriia*, no. 3 (1995): 44–59, here: 46.
2. Peter Holquist, '"Information Is the Alpha and Omega of Our Work": Bolshevik Surveillance in Its Pan-European Context', *The Journal of Modern History* 69 (1997): 415–50; Amir Weiner, *Making Sense of War. The Second World War and the Fate of the Bolshevik Revolution* (Princeton and Oxford: Princeton University Press, 2001), esp. 27–31; and id. (ed.), *Landscaping the Human Garden. Twentieth-Century Population Management in a Comparative Framework* (Stanford, Calif.: Stanford University Press, 2003).
3. The case for incremental as opposed to utopian social planning has been made repeatedly, usually with reference to the Soviet experience as the type to be avoided. For two examples separated by half a century see Karl R. Popper, *The poverty of historicism* (London: Routledge & Kegan Paul, 1957); and James C. Scott, *Seeing Like a State. How Certain Schemes to*

Improve the Human Condition Have Failed (New Haven and London: Yale University Press, 1998).

4. Simon Sebag Montefiore, *Stalin. The Court of the Red Tsar* (New York: Vintage Books, 2003), 65, 522.

5. *Izvestiia* 29 December 1934, p. 1, as quoted in Lewis Siegelbaum, ' "Dear Comrade, You Ask What We Need": Socialist Paternalism and Soviet Rural "Notables" in the Mid-1930s', *Slavic Review* 57, no. 1 (1998): 107–32, here: 116.

6. *Les rubiat—shchepki letiat*. For an example see Montefiore, *Stalin*, 218.

7. Robert Service, *Stalin. A Biography* (Cambridge, MA: Harvard University Press, 2005), 297.

8. For a general overview see Sheila Fitzpatrick, *The Russian Revolution*. 3rd edn. (Oxford: Oxford University Press, 2008).

9. S. Frederick Starr, *Red and Hot. The Fate of Jazz in the Soviet Union 1917–1980* (New York and Oxford: Oxford University Press, 1983); Richard Stites, *Russian Popular Culture. Entertainment and Society since 1900* (Cambride, New York, Melbourne: Cambridge University Press, 1994); Eric Naiman, *Sex in Public. The Incarnation of Early Soviet Ideology* (Princeton, NJ: Princeton University Press, 1997); and Anne E. Gorsuch, *Youth in Revolutionary Russia: Enthusiasts, Bohemians, Delinquents* (Bloomington: Indiana University Press, 2000), on the availability of drugs: 152. On Nepmen see Julie Hessler, *A Social History of Soviet Trade. Trade Policy, Retail Practices, and Consumption, 1917–1953* (Princeton and Oxford: Princeton University Press, 2004), ch. 3.

10. See Kate Brown, *A Biography of No Place. From Ethnic Borderland to Soviet Heartland* (Cambridge, MA: Harvard University Press, 2003), ch. 1. The official referring to Kazakh nomads is quoted ibid., 177. On Catholicism as a language and a nationality see ibid. 39.

11. Andreas Kappeler, *Russland als Vielvölkerreich. Entstehung. Geschichte. Zerfall* (Munich: C. H. Beck, 1993); Terry Martin, 'The Origins of Soviet Ethnic Cleansing', *The Journal of Modern History* 70, no. 4 (1998): 813–61, here: 825, 829; id., *The Affirmative Action Empire. Nations and Nationalism in the Soviet Union, 1923–1939* (Ithaca and London: Cornell University Press, 2001). On the paratroops see *Sovetskie vozdushno-desantnye. Voenno-istoricheskii ocherk*. 2nd rev. edn. (Moscow: Voennoe izd-vo, 1986), 9–10.

12. Cf. Sheila Fitzpatrick, 'The Soft Line on Culture and Its Enemies', in her *The Cultural Front. Power and Culture in Revolutionary Russia* (Ithaca and London: Cornell University Press, 1992), 91–114.

13. See Ch. 9.

14. Alec Nove, 'The 'Logic' and Cost of Collectivization', *Problems of Communism* 25, no. 4 (1976): 55–9, here: 55.

15. Stalin, 'The tasks of business executives. Speech delivered at the First All-Union Converence of Leading Personnel of Socialist Industry' (4 February 1931), in *Works*, vol. 13 (Moscow: Foreign Languages Publishing House, 1955): 31–44; here: 43.

16. I have profited here from Stephen Wheatcroft's unpacking of the terms 'terror' and 'repression'. See his 'The Scale and Nature of German and Soviet Repression and Mass Killings, 1930–45', *Europe-Asia Studies* 48, no. 8 (1996): 1319–53, esp. 1320–21.

17. For the raw data see 'Information of first special section of MVD SSSR on the number of arrests and prosecutions in the period 1921–1953' (11 December 1953), reprinted in *GULAG 1917–1960: dokumenty* (Moscow, 2000), 431–34. Note that these numbers differ in many details from those discussed by J. Arch Getty, Gabor T. Rittersporn, and Viktor Zemskov 'Victims of the Soviet Penal System in the Pre-War Years: A First Approach on the Basis of Archival Evidence', *The American Historical Review* 98, no. 4 (1993): 1017–49. There are also some minor variations between the numbers used here and those reproduced by V. P. Popov, 'Gosudarstvennyi terror v sovetskoi Rossii. 1923–1953 gg. (istochniki i ikh interpretatsiia)', *Otechestvennye arkhivy* 2 (1992): 20–31, here: 28. The basic dynamics, however, are the same. On the waves of executions compare also the much lower estimates in S. G. Wheatcroft, 'Towards Explaining the Changing Levels of Stalinist Repression in the 1930s: Mass Killings', in *Challenging Traditional Views of Russian History*, ed. S. G. Wheatcroft (Houndsmills, Basingstoke: Palgrave Macmillan, 2002), 112–45.

18. S. G. Wheatcroft and R. W. Davies, 'Population'. In *The economic transformation of the Soviet Union, 1913–1945*, eds. R. W. Davies, Mark Harrison, and S. G. Wheatcroft (Cambridge and New York: Cambridge University Press, 1994), 57–80; and Michael Ellman and S. Maksudov, 'Soviet Deaths in the Great Patriotic War: A Note', *Europe-Asia Studies* 46, no. 4 (1994): 671–80.

19. V. F. Zima, *Golod v SSSR 1946–1947 godov: proiskhozhdenie i posledstviia* (Moscow: Institut Rossiiskoi istorii RAN, 1996); Zubkova, *Russia After the War*, 40–50; Michael Ellman, 'The 1947 Soviet Famine and the Entitlement Approach to Famines', *Cambridge Journal of Economics* 24, no. 5 (2000): 603–30.

20. Golfo Alexopoulos, 'Amnesty 1945: The Revolving Door of Stalin's Gulag', *Slavic Review* 64, no. 2 (2005): 274–306.

21. *1933 g. Nazinskaia tragediia. Dokumental'noe nauchnoe izdanie* (Tomsk: Nauka, 2002); Nicolas Werth, *Cannibal Island. Death in a Siberian Gulag* (Princeton and Oxford: Princeton University Press, 2007); and Lynne Viola, *The Unknown Gulag. The Lost World of Stalin's Special Settlements* (Oxford and New York: Oxford University Press, 2007).

22. V. P. Danilov, 'Sovetskaia derevnia v gody 'Bol'shogo terrora'', *Tragediia sovetskoi derevni*, vol. 5.1: 7–50, here: 8; N. L. Pobol' and P. M. Polian, 'Deportatsionnye kampanii i deportatsionnye operatsii v SSSR (1918–1952)', in *Stalinskie deportatsii 1928–1953*, eds. N. L. Pobol' and P. M. Polian (Moscow: Demokratiia, 2005), 789–98; here: 789–90.

23. 572,000 plus unknown quantities for which data are missing.

24. Pobol' and Polian, 'Deportatsionnye kampanii', 791–5.

25. Pobol' and Polian, 'Deportatsionnye kampanii', 795–8; on the deportation of 'idlers' and 'parasites' see Jean Lévesque, 'Exile and Discipline: The June 1948 Campaign Against Collective Farm Shirkers', *The Carl Beck Papers in Russian & East European Studies* 1708 (2006).

26. Pavel Polian, *Ne po svoei vole… Istoriia i geografiia prinuditel'nykh migratsii v SSSR* (Moscow: OGI, 2001). On the centrality of deportation see also Brown, *Biography of no place*. 'Cumulative radicalization' is Hans Mommsen's term for the dynamic of National Socialism. For a discussion see Ian Kershaw, *The Nazi Dictatorship. Problems and Perspectives of Interpretation* (London and New York: Arnold, 2000), 263–4.

27. Andrea Graziosi, *The Great Soviet Peasant War. Bolsheviks and Peasants, 1917–1933* (Cambridge, MA: Harvard University Press, 1996); Lynne Viola, V. P. Danilov, N. A. Ivnitskii, and Denis Kozlov (eds.), *The War against the Peasantry, 1927–130: The Tragedy of the Soviet Countryside* (New Haven, CT: Yale University Press, 2005).

28. Viola et. al, *War against the Peasantry*, ch. 4.

29. Israel Getzler, 'Lenin's Conception of Revolution as Civil War', *Slavonic and East European Review* 74, no. 3 (1996): 464–72. Viola et al. *War Against the Peasantry*, 171–8.

30. G. Iagoda to Evdokimov et al. (11 January 1930), in *Tragediia sovetskoi derevni*, vol. 2: 103–4.

31. Stalin to Sholokhov (6 May 1933), reproduced in *Voprosy istorii* no. 3 (1994), 22.

32. Lynne Viola, *The Best Sons of the Fatherland. Workers in the Vanguard of Soviet Collectivization* (New York and Oxford: Oxford University Press, 1987); id. *Peasant Rebels under Stalin. Collectivization and the Culture of Peasant Resistance* (New York and Oxford: Oxford University Press, 1996),

chs. 4 and 5. On worries about the Red Army see id., *The War against the Peasantry*, 215, 242. On the role of the OGPU see id., 'The Role of the OGPU in Dekulakization, Mass Deportations, and Special Resettlement in 1930', *The Carl Beck Papers in Russian & East European Studies* No. 1406 (2000).

33. The policy of 'liquidating the kulaks as a class' was first mentioned by Stalin in a speech to Marxist agronomists (27 December 1929), and became explicit policy with the Central Committee decree of 5 January 1930, which ushered in the dekulakization campaign. Sheila Fitzpatrick, *Stalin's Peasants. Resistance and Survival in the Russian Village after Collectivization* (New York and Oxford: Oxford University Press, 1994), 48, 58; Viola, *Peasant Rebels*, 26. The decree is reprinted in V. Danilov, R. Manning, and L. Viola (eds.), *Tragediia sovetskoi derevni. Kollektivizatsiia i raskulachivanie. Dokumenty i materialy v 5 tomakh 1927–1939. Tom 2: noiabr' 1929–dekabr' 1930* (Moscow: Rosspen, 2000), 85–6.

34. OGPU operational report (3 May 1930), reprinted in *Tragediia sovetskoi derevni*, vol. 2, 405–9, here: 406, 408.

35. Stalin, 'Dizzy with Success', originally published in *Pravda*, 2 March 1930, here quoted from Stalin, *Works*, vol. 12 (Moscow: Foreign Languages Publishing House, 1955), 197–205.

36. Fitzpatrick, *Stalin's Peasants*, 289.

37. Viola, *Peasant Rebels*, 134.

38. Table 5–1 in Viola, *Peasant Rebels*, 136.

39. Report by North Caucasian military region (6 May 1930), reprinted in *Tragediia sovetskoi derevni*, vol. 2: 430–2.

40. OGPU report (15 March 1931), reprinted in *Tragediia sovetskoi derevni*, vol. 2: 787–808, here: 804.

41. Fitzpatrick, *Stalin's Peasants*, 103; Viola et al, *War against the Peasantry*, 268.

42. Hans-Henning Schröder, 'Kollektivisierung', in *Historisches Lexikon der Sowjetunion 1917/22 bis 1991*, ed. Hans-Joachim Torke (Munich: Verlag C. H. Beck, 1993), 144–7, here: 146.

43. Moshe Lewin, 'Who Was the Soviet Kulak?' in his *The Making of the Soviet System. Essays in the Social History of Interwar Russia* (New York: The New Press, 1994), 121–41.

44. Cf. Brown, *Biography of no place*, 83.

45. Viola, *The Unknown Gulag*, 30–1.

46. On the discussion about the famine see Ch. 9.

47. Sheila Fitzpatrick (ed.), *Cultural Revolution in Russia, 1928–1931* (Bloomington: Indiana University Press, 1978).

48. Gregory L. Freeze, 'The Stalinist Assault on the Parish, 1929–1941', in *Stalinismus vor dem Zweiten Weltkrieg: Neue Wege der Forschung*, ed. Manfred Hildermeier (Munich: Oldenbourg, 1998), 209–32.

49. Rolf Binner and Marc Junge. 'Vernichtung der orthodoxen Geistlichen in der Sowjetunion in den Massenoperationen des Großen Terrors 1937–1938', *Jahrbücher für Geschichte Osteuropas* 52, no. 4 (2004): 515–33.

50. On the purges see Robert Conquest, *The Great Terror. A Reassessment* (New York and Oxford: Oxford University Press, 1990); J. Arch Getty and Oleg V. Naumov, *The Road to Terror. Stalin and the Self-Destruction of the Bolsheviks, 1932–1939* (New Haven and London: Yale University Press, 1999). On the social dynamics of terror see Sheila Fitzpatrick, *Everyday Stalinism. Ordinary Life in Extraordinary Times: Soviet Russia in the 1930s* (New York and Oxford: Oxford University Press, 1999), ch. 8; and Wendy Z. Goldman, *Terror and Democracy in the Age of Stalin. The Social Dynamics of Repression* (Cambridge and New York: Cambridge University Press, 2007).

51. Olev V. Khlevniuk, 'The Objectives of the Great Terror, 1937–1938', in *Soviet History, 1917–53. Essays in Honour of R. W. Davies*, eds. Julian Cooper, Maureen Perrie, and E. A. Rees (New York: St Martin's Press, 1995), 161–3.

52. Martin, 'The Origins of Soviet Ethnic Cleansing', 823.

53. Khlevniuk, 'The Objectives of the Great Terror', 163.

54. Martin, 'The Origins of Soviet Ethnic Cleansing', 822.

55. Richard Pipes, *The Russian Revolution 1899–1919* (London: Collins Harvill, 1990), 790.

56. Both quotation are Trotsky's recollection as quoted by W. Bruce Lincoln, *Red Victory. A History of the Russian Civil War* (New York and London: Simon and Schuster, 1989), 134–5.

57. Fitzpatrick, *The Russian Revolution*, 76.

58. Wheatcroft, 'Towards Explaining the Changing Levels of Stalinist Repression', 114–15, tables 6.1 and 6.2.

59. See also J. Arch Getty and William Chase, 'Patterns of repression among the Soviet elite in the late 1930s: a biographical approach', and Sheila Fitzpatrick, 'The impact of the Great Purges on Soviet elites: A case study from Moscow and Leningrad telephone directories of the 1930s', both in *Stalinist Terror. New Perspectives*, eds. J. Arch Getty and Roberta T. Manning (Cambridge and New York: Cambridge University Press, 1993).

60. V. B. Zhiromskaia, I. N. Kiselev, and Iu. A. Poliakov, *Polveka pod grifom 'sekretno': Vsesoiuznaia perepis' naseleniia 1937 goda* (Moscow: Nauka, 1996), 75.

61. Cf. also Conquest, *The Great Terror. A Reassessment*, 258; O. V. Khlevniuk, *The History of the Gulag. From Collectivization to the Great Terror* (New Haven and London: Yale University Press, 2004), 168.

62. Cf. also Viola, *Unknown Gulag*, ch. 8.

63. For example, see the cases discussed in a 1938 NKVD report, reprinted in *Tragediia sovetskoi derevni*, vol. 5.2: 176–8.

64. The year 1937 reaches, in the available data-set, from 1 October 1936 to 1 January 1938. See the NKVD report on work in 1935–1937, reprinted in *Tragediia Sovetskoi derevni*, vol. 5.2: 24–6.

65. Collective peasants and single farmers (*edinolichniki*) together constituted 51 per cent of the population, according to the 1937 census. See Zhiromskaia, *Polveka pod grifom 'sekretno'*, 75.

66. Stalin to the 18th Party Congress, as quoted Yoram Gorlizki, and Oleg V. Khlevniuk, 'Stalin and His Circle', in: *The Cambridge History of Russia. Vol III: The Twentieth Century*, ed. Ronald G. Suny (Cambridge and New York: Cambridge University Press, 2006), 243–67, here: 266.

67. Yoram Gorlizki and Oleg Khlevniuk, *Cold Peace. Stalin and the Soviet Ruling Circle, 1945–1953* (Oxford and New York: Oxford University Press, 2004), 5.

68. Peter H. Solomon, *Soviet Criminal Justice under Stalin* (Cambridge, New York, Melbourne: Cambridge University Press, 1996).

69. Jan T. Gross, *Revolution from Abroad. The Soviet Conquest of Poland's Western Ukraine and Western Belorussia*. expanded ed. (Princeton and Oxford: Princeton University Press, 2002); Anna M. Cienciala, Natalia S. Lebedeva, and Wojciech Materski (eds.), *Katyn. A Crime Without Punishment* (New Haven and London: Yale University Press, 2007). For the numbers involved see Shelepin to Khrushchev, 3 March 1959, in ibid. 332–3: here 332. On Katyn and its afterlife see also Inessa Iazhborovskaia, Anatolii Iablokov, and Valentina Parsadanova, *Katynskii sindrom v sovetsko-pol'skikh i rossiisko-pol'skikh otnosheniiakh* (Moscow: Rosspen, 2009).

70. Karel C. Berkhoff, *Harvest of Despair. Life and Death in Ukraine under Nazi Rule* (Cambridge and London: The Belknap Press of Harvard University Press, 2004), 14–17. A study of these incidents, which is as gruesomely detailed as it is controversial is Bogdan Musial, *'Konterrevolutionäre Elemente sind zu erschießen'. Die Brutalisierung des deutsch-sowjetischen Krieges im Sommer 1941*. 2nd edn. (Berlin and Munich: Propyläen, 2001).

71. See Evan Mawdsley, *Thunder in the East. The Nazi-Soviet War 1941–1945* (London: Hodder Arnold, 2005), 65, 132, 168; and Michael Parrish, *The Lesser Terror. Soviet State Security, 1939–1953* (Westport, Connecticut and London: Praeger, 1996), ch. 3.

72. On the numbers: V. P. Naumov, 'Sud'ba voennoplennykh i deportirovannykh grazhdan SSSR. Materialy Komissii po reabilitatsii zhertv politicheskikh repressii', *Novaia i noveishaia istoriia*, no. 2 (1996): 91–112: here; 101; *GULAG 1918–1960*, 434. The NKVD numbers include all of 1941 and 1945.

73. R. G. Pikhoia, *Sovetskii soiuz: istoriia vlasti 1945–1991* (Novosibirsk: Sibirskii khoronograf, 2000), 35–43, 50–4, 56–8. Gorlizki and Khlevniuk, 'Stalin and his Circle', 261–3; Parrish, *Lesser Terror*, chs. 7 and 9; and V. N. Khaustov, V. P. Naumov, and N. S. Plotnikova (eds.), *Lubianka. Stalin in MGB SSSR. Mart 1946—mart 1953* (Moscow: Demokratiia, 2007).

74. Martin, 'The Origins of Soviet Ethnic Cleansing', 820, 823.

75. Amir Weiner, 'Something to Die for, a Lot to Kill For: The Soviet System and the Barbarisation of Warfare, 1939–1945', in *The Barbarization of Warfare* ed. George Kassimeris (New York: New York University Press, 2006), 101–25, here: 122.

76. David R. Shearer, *Policing Stalin's Socialism. Repression and Social Order in the Soviet Union, 1924–1953* (New Haven and London: Yale University Press, 2009), ch. 12.

77. Katrin Boeckh, *Stalinismus in der Ukraine. Die Rekonstruktion des sowjetischen Systems nach dem Zweiten Weltkrieg* (Wiesbaden: Harrassowitz Verlag, 2007), ch. 3.1.1; and Mark Edele, *Soviet Veterans of the Second World War. A Popular Movement in an Authoritarian Society, 1941–1991* (Oxford: Oxford University Press, 2008), 118, table 5.2 as well as ch. 5 passim.

78. The term 'national security state' is borrowed from Patrick Major and Rana Mitter, 'East is East and West is West? Towards a Comparative Socio-Cultural History of the Cold War', *Cold War History* 4, no. 1 (2003): 1–22.

79. L. P. Beriia to G. M. Malenkov, 26 March 1953, reprinted in *Lavrentii Beriia. 1953. Stenogramma iiul'skogo plenuma TsK KPSS i drugie dokumenty*, eds. V. Naumov and Iu. Sigachev (Moscow: Demokratiia, 1999), 19–21; here: 19.

80. Golfo Alexopoulos, 'Amnesty 1945: The Revolving Door of Stalin's Gulag', *Slavic Review* 64, no. 2 (2005): 274–306.

81. Raul Hilberg, Raul. *The Destruction of the European Jews* (New York: New Viewpoints, 1973).

82. Zygmunt Bauman, *Modernity and the Holocaust* (Ithaca, New York: Cornell University Press, 2000); Norman Naimark, *Fires of Hatred. Ethnic Cleansing In Twentieth-Century Europe* (Cambridge and London: Harvard University Press, 2001).

83. For the GULAG as a non-exterminationist institution see Steven A. Barnes, 'Soviet Society Confined: The Gulag in the Karaganda Region of Kazakhstan, 1930s–1950s'. PhD diss. (Stanford University, 2003).

Chapter 3

1. Gennady Andreev-Khomiakov, *Bitter Waters. Life and Work in Stalin's Russia* (Boulder: Westview Press, 1997), 100.

2. David Moon, *The Russian Peasantry 1600–1930. The World the Peasants Made* (London and New York: Longman, 1999), 49–63; B. N. Mironov, *Sotsial'naia istoriia Rossii perioda imperii (XVIII – nachalo XX v.). Genezis lichnosti, demokraticheskoi sem'i, grazhdanskogo obshchestva i pravovogo gosudarstva*. 2 vols. (St Petersburg: Dmitrii Bulanin, 2000), vol. 1: 315–18; Peter Gatrell, *A Whole Empire Walking. Refugees in Russia During World War I* (Bloomington, Indianapolis: Indiana Unversity Press, 2005).

3. Alfred J. Rieber, 'The Sedimentary Society', in *Between Tsar and People. Educated Society and the Quest for Public Identity in Late Imperial Russsia*, eds. Edith W. Clowes, Samuel D. Kassow, and James L. West (Princeton, NJ: Princeton University Press, 1991), 343–66; Elise Kimerling Wirtschafter, *Social Identity in Imperial Russia* (DeKalb: Northern Illinois University Press, 1997); Sheila Fitzpatrick, *Tear off the Masks! Identity and Imposture in Twentieth-Century Russia* (Princeton and Oxford: Princeton University Press, 2005).

4. Sheila Fitzpatrick, 'The Great Departure: Rural-Urban Migration, 1929–33', in *Social Dimensions of Soviet Industrialization*, eds. William G. Rosenberg and Lewis Siegelbaum (Bloomington, Ind.: Indiana University Press, 1993), 22.

5. Victor Kravchenko, *I Chose Freedom. The Personal and Political Life of a Soviet Official* (Bedfors Square: Robert Hale, 1947), 306, 311–12; Sheila Fitzpatrick, 'Postwar Soviet Society: The "Return to Normalcy," 1945–1953', in *The Impact of World War II on the Soviet Union*, ed. Susan J. Linz (Totova, NJ: Rowman & Allanhead, 1985), 149; id., 'War and Society in Soviet Context: Soviet Labor before, during, and after World War II', *International Labor and Working-Class History* 35, Spring (1989): 40–1; Donald Filtzer, *Soviet workers and Stalinist industrialization. The formation of modern Soviet production relations, 1928–1941* (Armonk, New York:

M. E. Sharpe, 1986), 111–12, 133–4, 233–53; R. W. Davies, Mark Harrison, and S. G. Wheatcroft (eds.), *The Economic Transformation of the Soviet Union, 1913–1945*. (Cambridge: Cambridge University Press, 1994), 65; V. B. Zhiromskaia, I. N. Kiselev, and Iu. A. Poliakov, *Polveka pod grifom 'sekretno': Vsesoiuznaia perepis' naseleniia 1937 goda* (Moscow: Nauka, 1996), 49–50; David Shearer, 'Elements near and Alien: Passportization, Policing, and Identity in the Stalinist State, 1932–1952,' *The Journal of Modern History* 76, no. 4 (2004): 835–81.

6. Moshe Lewin, *The Making of the Soviet System. Essays in the Social History of Interwar Russia* (New York: New Press, 1985); David L. Hoffmann, *Peasant Metropolis. Social Identities in Moscow, 1929–1941* (Ithaca and London: Cornell University Press, 1994); Stephen Kotkin, *Magnetic Mountain. Stalinism as a Civilization* (Berkeley, Los Angeles, London: University of California Press, 1995).

7. Siegelbaum and Sokolov (eds.), *Stalinism as a Way of Life*, http://www.yale.edu/annals/siegelbaum/English_docs/Siegelbaum_do_7.htm (accessed 31 March 2005).

8. Wendy Z. Goldman, *Terror and Democracy in the Age of Stalin. The Social Dynamics of Repression* (Cambridge and New York: Cambridge University Press, 2007), 75.

9. Kotkin, *Magnetic Mountain*, 137.

10. A. V. Mitrofanova (red.), *Rabochii klass SSSR nakanune i v gody Velikoi Otechestvennoi voiny 1938–1945 gg.* vol. 3 (Moscow: Nauka, 1984), 132.

11. William Moskoff, *The Bread of Affliction. The Food Supply in the USSR During World War II* (Cambridge: Cambridge University Press, 1990); Stephen Lovell, *Summerfolk. A History of the Dacha, 1719–2000* (Ithaca and London: Cornell University Press, 2003); P. Charles Hachten, 'Separate Yet Governed: The Representation of Soviet Property Relations in Civil Law and Public Discourse', in: *Borders of Socialism. Private Spheres of Soviet Russia*, ed. Lewis Siegelbaum (New York and Houndsmills: Palgrave Macmillan, 2006), 65–82.

12. R. W. Davies, *Crisis and progress in the Soviet economy 1931–1933*. vol. 4, 'The industrialisation of Soviet Russia' (London, Basingstoke: Macmillan, 1996), 240–1.

13. Nathalie Moine, 'Le miroir de statistiques. Inegalites et spheres privée au cours du second stalinisme', *Cahiers du monde russe* 44, no. 2–3 (2003): 481–518.

14. Robert Eugene Johnson, *Peasant and proletarian: the working class of Moscow in the late nineteenth century* (Leicester: Leicester University Press,

1979); James H. Bater, 'Transience, Residential Persistence, and Mobility in Moscow and St. Petersburg, 1900–1914', *Slavic Review* 39, no. 2 (1980): 239–54; James von Geldern. 'Life in-Betweeen: Migration and Popular Culture in Late Imperial Russia', *Russian Review* 55, no. 3 (1996): 365–83; Sheila Fitzpatrick, *Stalin's Peasants. Resistance and Survival in the Russian Village after Collectivization* (New York and Oxford: Oxford University Press, 1994), 97; Lewin, *The Making of the Soviet System*, 219–20; Jean Lévesque, '"Into the grey zone": sham peasants and the limits of the kolkhoz order in the post-war Russian village, 1945–1953', in *Late Stalinist Russia. Society between reconstruction and reinvention*, ed. Juliane Fürst (London and New York: Routledge, 2006), 103–19, esp. 112–16.

15. For a detailed investigation of the Soviet village in the 1930s, see Fitzpatrick, *Stalin's Peasants*; for the post-war years see O. M. Verbitskaia, *Rossiiskoe krest'ianstvo: ot Stalina k Khrushchevu* (Moscow: Nauka, 1992).

16. NKVD report on 'moods in the village before the harvest', (4 Aug 1938), reprinted in *Tragediia sovetskoi derevni. Kollektivizatsiia i raskulachivanie. Dokumenty i materialy v 5 tomakh 1927–1939. Tom 5, kn. 2: 1938–1939*, eds. V. Danilov, R. Manning, and L. Viola (Moscow: Rosspen, 2006), 183–6, here: 184.

17. Catherine Merridale, *Ivan's War. Life and Death in the Red Army, 1939–1945* (New York: Metropolitan Books, 2006), 362.

18. Mark Edele, 'Veterans and the Village: Red Army Demobilization and Postwar Demography', *Russian history/Histoire russe* 36, no. 2 (2009): 159–82.

19. Review file of case of 'anti-Soviet agitation', State Archive of the Russian Federation (GARF) f. A-461, op. 1, d. 1128, l. 7, 9.

20. Davies, *Crisis and Progress*, 241.

21. NKVD report on 'moods in the village before the harvest' (4 Aug 1938), 184.

22. For example, see the letter to Kalinin, 29 August 1938, reprinted in *Tragediia sovetskoi derevni*, vol. 5.2: 220–222, esp. 220; and Lévesque, 'Into the grey zone', 108–12.

23. For statistics see Filtzer, *Soviet workers and Stalinist industrialisation*, 52–3; on the post-war years see id., *Soviet Workers and Late Stalinism. Labour and the Restoration of the Stalinist System after World War II* (Cambridge, New York, Melbourne: Cambridge University Press, 2002).

24. Lewin, *The Making of the Soviet System*, 221.

25. Elena Zubkova, *Russia After the War. Hopes, Illusions, and Disappointments, 1945–1957* (Armonk and London: M. E. Sharpe, 1998); Pavel Polian, *Ne po*

svoei vole… istoriia i geografiia prinuditel'nykh migratsii v SSSR (Moscow: OGI, 2001); Rebecca Manley, *To the Tashkent Station. Evacuation and Survival in the Soviet Union at War* (Ithaca and London: Cornell University Press, 2009); Mark Edele, *Soviet Veterans of the Second World War. A Popular Movement in an Authoritarian Society, 1941–1991* (Oxford: Oxford University Press, 2008).

26. Andrew Gentes, 'Katorga: Penal Labour and Tsarist Siberia', *Australian Slavonic and East European Studies* 18, no. 1–2 (2004): 50, 52. See also id., 'Vagabondage and Siberia. Disciplinary Modernism in Tsarist Russia', in: *Cast Out. Vagrancy and Homelessness in Global and Historical Perspective*, eds. A. L. Beier and Paul Ocobock (Athens: Ohio University Press, 2008), 184–208.

27. O. V. Khlevniuk, *The History of the Gulag. From Collectivization to the Great Terror* (New Haven and London: Yale University Press, 2004), 18, 22, 55, 120, 180.

28. Nicolas Werth, *Cannibal Island. Death in a Siberian Gulag* (Princeton and Oxford: Princeton University Press, 2007), 35–42.

29. Reproduced in *1933 g. Nazinskaia tragediia. Dokumental'noe nauchnoe izdanie* (Tomsk: Nauka, 2002), 23–6, here: 25.

30. Ibid., 26.

31. Khlevniuk, *History of the Gulag*, 304.

32. OGPU report on deportation of kulaks (6 May 1930), reprinted in *Tragediia sovetskoi derevni. Kollektivizatsiia i raskulachivanie. Dokumenty i materialy v 5 tomakh 1927–1939. Tom 2: noiabr' 1929–dekabr' 1930*, eds. V. Danilov, R. Manning, and L. Viola (Moscow: Rosspen, 2000), 409–30; here: 420.

33. 'Diary of Stepan Filippovich Podlubny', in *Intimacy and Terror. Soviet Diaries of the 1930s*, eds. Véronique Garros, Natalia Korenevskaya, and Thomas Lahusen (New York: The New Press, 1995), 308–13 (20 December 1937); 304 (6 December 1937); and Nina Lugovskaya, *The Diary of a Soviet Schoolgirl. 1932–1937*. Trans. Joanne Turnbull (Moscow: Glas Publishers, 2003), 79 (17 January 1934).

34. Lugovskaya, *The Diary of a Soviet Schoolgirl*. 5–6, 41, 119.

35. Robert Conquest, *The Great Terror. A Reassessment* (New York and Oxford: Oxford University Press, 1990), 259.

36. Harvard Project on the Soviet Social System. Schedule A, vol. 25, case 492, male, 50, Ukrainian, mechanic.

37. Hannah Arendt, *The Origins of Totalitarianism. New Edition with added prefaces* (New York and London: Harvest Books, 1968), p. vii.

38. Senior sergeant Sergeev, letter to A. A. Zhdanov, 23 July 1947, reprinted in *Sovetskaia zhizn' 1945–1953*, eds. Zubkova et al, (Moscow: Rosspen, 2003), 36.

39. Beate Fieseler, 'The bitter legacy of the "Great Patriotic war". Red Army disabled soldiers under late Stalinism', in *Late Stalinist Russia*, 46–61.

40. Zubkova, *Russia after the war*, 25.

41. Khlevniuk, *History of the Gulag*, 126–7; Sheila Fitzpatrick, *Everyday Stalinism. Ordinary Life in Extraordinary Times: Soviet Russia in the 1930s* (New York and Oxford: Oxford University Press, 1999), 151–2; Paul Hagenloh, *Stalin's Police. Public Order and Mass Repression in the USSR, 1926–1941* (Baltimore: The Johns Hopkins University Press, 2009), 107–13, 182–94; David R. Shearer, *Policing Stalin's Socialism. Repression and Social Order in the Soviet Union, 1924–1953* (New Haven and London: Yale University Press, 2009), ch. 7.

42. Rachel Green, ' "There will not be orphans among us": Soviet orphanages, foster care, and adoption, 1941–1956'. PhD diss. (The University of Chicago, 2006), 29–63.

43. See the remarkable *Outlaw. The Autobiography of a Soviet Waif. By Voinov* (London: Harvill Press, 1955). For a thick description of this milieu see also Wendy Goldman, *Women, the State, and Revolution: Soviet Family Policy and Social Life, 1917–1936* (Cambridge: Cambridge University Press, 1993), 77. For a useful contemporary analysis of this milieu see also V. S. Krasuskii and A. M. Khaletskii, 'Sreda besprizornykh, ee traditsii i navyki', in *Nishchenstvo i besprizornost'*, eds. E. K. Krasnushkina, G. M. Segala, and Ts. M. Feinberg (Moscow: Izd-vo Moszdravotdela, 1929), 227–39.

44. Fitzpatrick, *Everyday Stalinism*, 171.

45. Harvard Project on the Soviet Social System. Schedule A, vol. 3, case 27, male, 26, Great Russian, Kolkhoznik. p. 49.

46. Joan Neuberger, *Hooliganism. Crime, Culture, and Power in St. Petersburg, 1900–1914* (Berkeley, Los Angeles, London: University of California Press, 1993); Alan M. Ball, *And Now My Soul Is Hardened. Abandoned Children in Soviet Russia, 1918–1930* (Berkeley, Los Angeles, London: University of California Press, 1994); Juliane Fürst, 'Between Salvation and Liquidation: Homeless and Vagrant Children and the Reconstruction of Soviet Society', *Slavonic and East European Review* 86, no. 2 (2008): 232–58, esp. 246–9; Fitzpatrick, *Tear off the Masks!* chs. 13 and 14; Federico Varese, 'The Society of the vory-v-zakone, 1930s–1950s,' *Cahiers du Monde Russe*, vol. 39, no. 4 (1998): 515–38; *Slovar' tiurmeno-lagerno-blatnogo zhargona*.

Rechevoi i graficheskii portret sovetskoi tiur'my (Moscow: Kraia Moskvy, 1992); Elena Zubkova, *Poslevoennoe sovetskoe obshchestvo: politika i povsednevnost' 1945–1953* (Moscow: Rosspen, 2000), 89–94; Edele, *Soviet Veterans of the Second World War*, 55, 61–4, 69–70, 92–5; Hubertus Jahn, *Armes Russland, Bettler und Notleidende in der russichen Geschichte vom Mittelalter bis in die Gegenwort* (Paderborn and Munich: Ferdinand Schöningh, 2010). Kravchenko, *I Chose Freedom*, 381.

47. Peter H. Solomon, *Soviet Criminal Justice under Stalin* (Cambridge, Cambridge University Press, 1996), 224.

48. Golfo Alexopoulos, 'Portrait of a Con Artist as a Soviet Man', *Slavic Review* 57, no. 4 (1998): 774–90; Sheila Fitzpatrick, 'The World of Ostap Bender: Soviet Confidence Men in the Stalin Period', *Slavic Review* 61, no. 3 (2002): 535–57.

49. Golfo Alexopoulos, 'Amnesty 1945: The Revolving Door of Stalin's Gulag', *Slavic Review* 64, no. 2 (2005): 275.

50. Juliane Fürst, 'The importance of being stylish: youth, culture and identity in late Stalinism', in *Late Stalinist Russia*, 216–17; Mark Edele, 'Strange Young Men in Stalin's Moscow: The Birth and Life of the Stiliagi, 1945–1953', *Jahrbücher für Geschichte Osteuropas* 50, no. 1 (2002): 37–61; Zubkova, *Poslevoennoe sovetskoe obshchestvo*, 94.

51. Khlevniuk, *History of the Gulag*, 344.

52. Katrin Boeckh, *Stalinismus in der Ukraine. Die Rekonstruktion des sowjetischen Systems nach dem Zweiten Weltkrieg* (Wiesbaden: Harrassowitz Verlag, 2007), 543.

53. See the report by Minister of Interior S. Kruglov and Militia boss W. Stakhanov on struggle to liquidate begging (20 February 1954), available at http://www.alexanderyak.org/almanah/inside/almanah-doc/10074(accessed_July-2010): Edele, *Soviet Veterans*, 93–4.

54. Boeckh, *Stalinismus in der Ukraine*, 454–75; Green, 'There will be no orphans', 23; Beate Fieseler, 'Die Invaliden des "Grossen Vaterlandischen Krieges" der Sowjetunion—Eine politische Sozialgeschichte 1941–1991'. Habilitationsschrift, Ruhr-Universitat Bochum, 2003.

55. Leon Trotsky, *The Revolution Betrayed. What is the Soviet Union and Where is it Going?* (New York and London: Pathfinder, 1972 [orig.: 1937]); M. S. Voslenskii, *Nomenklatura: the Soviet ruling class* (Garden City, NY: Doubleday, 1984); Jean-Paul Depretto, 'Stratification without Class', *Kritika: Explorations in Russian and Eurasian History* 8, no. 2 (2007): 375–88.

56. Sheila Fitzpatrick, *Education and Social Mobility in the Soviet Union 1921–1934* (Cambridge: Cambridge University Press, 1979).

57. Kravchenko, *I chose freedom*, 62.

58. Mark Edele, 'The Impact of War and the Costs of Superpower Status', *The Oxford Handbook of Modern Russian History*, ed. Simon Dixon, (Oxford: Oxford University Press, forthcoming).

59. Milovan Djilas, *The New Class: An Analysis of the Communist System* (New York: Praeger, 1957); Fitzpatrick, *Everyday Stalinism*, 103–5.

60. Kravchenko, *I Chose Freedom*, 308.

61. Vera S. Dunham, *In Stalin's Time. Middleclass Values in Soviet Fiction.* Enlarged and updated edn. (Durham and London: Duke University Press, 1990); Eric Duskin, *Stalinist Reconstruction and the Confirmation of a New Elite, 1945–1953* (New York: Palgrave, 2001).

62. Reginald Zelnik, ed. *A Radical Worker in Tsarist Russia. The Autobiography of Semen Ivanovich Kanatchikov* (Stanford: Stanford University Press, 1986).

63. William Taubman, *Khrushchev. The Man and his Era* (New York and London: W. W. Norton & Co., 2003).

64. Sheila Fitzpatrick, 'Stalin and the Making of a New Elite', in her *The Cultural Front. Power and Culture in Revolutionary Russia* (Ithaca and London: Cornell University Press, 1992), 149–82.

65. V. Kochetov, 'Choosing a career', *Literaturnaia gazeta*, September 7, 1954, reprinted in *Soviet youth: some achievements and problems*, ed. Dorothea L. Meek (London: Routledge & Kegan Paul, 1957), 97–103, citations: 98.

66. Fitzpatrick, *Everyday Stalinism*, 192–3; J. Arch Getty and Oleg V. Naumov, *The Road to Terror. Stalin and the Self-Destruction of the Bolsheviks, 1932–1939* (New Haven and London: Yale University Press, 1999), 198; Oleg V. Khlevniuk, 'The Objectives of the Great Terror, 1937–1938', in *Soviet History, 1917–53. Essays in Honour of R. W. Davies*, eds. Julian Cooper, Maureen Perrie, and E. A. Rees (New York: St Martin's Press, 1995), 159–60; *Tragediia sovetskoi derevni*, vol. 5.2: 53; Oleg V. Khlevniuk, *Master of the House. Stalin and His Inner Circle* (New Haven and London: Yale University Press, 2009), 49.

67. For victim numbers of the Great Terror see Ch. 3. For the post-war purge see Amir Weiner, *Making Sense of War. The Second World War and the Fate of the Bolshevik Revolution* (Princeton and Oxford: Princeton University Press, 2000), 82–126, numbers on p. 122.

68. Kravchenko, *I chose freedom*, 135, 137–8; 140–2.

69. Catherine Merridale, 'The 1937 Census and the Limits of Stalinist Rule', *The Historical Journal* 39, no. 1 (1996): 238.

Chapter 4

1. Golfo Alexopoulos, 'Stalin and the Politics of Kinship: Practices of Collective Punishment, 1920s–1940s', *Comparative Studies in Society and History* 50, no. 1 (2008): 91–117, here: 111.
2. Harvard Interview Project. Schedule A, vol. 36, case 142/(NY) 1664. Male, 37, Belorussian, High school teacher, p. 24.
3. Harvard Project. Schedule B, vol. 24, case 296, p. 15.
4. For an early history in documents see Rudolf Schlesinger (ed.), *The Family in the USSR. Documents and Readings* (London: Routledge & Kegan Paul, 1949). For overviews over revolutionary gender policies see Ronald G. Suny, *The Soviet Experiment. Russia, the USSR, and the Successor States* (New York and Oxford: Oxford University Press, 1998), 184–8; and Wendy Z. Goldman, *Women, the State and Revolution. Soviet Family Policy and Social Life, 1917–1936* (Cambridge and New York: Cambridge University Press, 1993), 103–9, esp. 106–7.
5. Goldman, *Women, the state, and revolution*, 49–50; B. N. Mironov, *Sotsial'naia istoriia Rossii perioda Imperii (xviii – nachalo xx v.). Genezis lichnosti, demokraticheskoi sem'i, grazhdanskogo obshchestva i pravovogo gosudarstva.* 2 vols. (St Petersburg: Dmitrii Bulanin, 2000), vol. 1: 174–7.
6. Goldman, *Women, the state, and revolution*, 49, 51–2.
7. Goldman, *Women, the state and revolution*, 211–12, 248–9, 331. On the controversy: ibid.: 214–53. On the Great Retreat see Nicholas Timasheff, *The Great Retreat: The Growth and Decline of Communism in Russia, 1886–1970* (New York: E. P. Dutton, 1946).
8. Mie Nakachi, 'Replacing the Dead: The Politics of Reproduction in the Postwar Soviet Union, 1944–1955', PhD diss., The University of Chicago, 2008; id. 'N. S. Khrushchev and the 1944 Soviet Family Law: Politics, Reproduction, and Language', *East European Politics and Societies* 20, no. 1 (2006): 40–68; and id., 'Population, Politics and Reproduction: Late Stalinism and Its Legacy', in *Late Stalinist Russia. Society between Reconstruction and Reinvention*, ed. Juliane Fürst (London and New York: Routledge, 2006), 167–91.
9. Catriona Kelly, *Children's World. Growing up in Russia 1890–1991* (New Haven and London: Yale University Press, 2007), 78–80, 103; id. *Comrade Pavlik. The Rise and Fall of a Soviet Boy Hero* (London: Granta Books, 2005), on the monument saga see esp. 2, 144–5, 150–1, 166, 187–9.
10. Alexopoulos, 'Stalin and the Politics of Kinship'.

11. Nina Lugovskaya, *The Diary of a Soviet Schoolgirl. 1932–1937* (Moscow: Glas Publishers, 2003), 41.

12. Corinna Kuhr, 'Children of "Enemies of the People" as Victims of the Great Purges', *Cahiers du monde russe* 39, no. 1–2 (1998): 211–12.

13. G. M. Dimitrov, diary entry (7 November 1937), reprinted in *Zastol'nye rechi Stalina. Dokumenty i materialy* (Moscow and St Petersburg: ARIO-XX, 2003), 147–50, here: 148.

14. H. Kent Geiger, *The Family in Soviet Russia* (Cambridge, MA: Harvard University Press, 1968), 123.

15. Mark Edele, *Soviet Veterans of the Second World War. A Popular Movement in an Authoritarian Society, 1941–1991* (Oxford: Oxford University Press, 2008), 115–16.

16. Alexopoulos, 'Stalin and the politics of kinship', 95, 108–9; Simon Sebag Montefiore, *Stalin. The Court of the Red Tsar* (New York: Vintage Books, 2003), 239–40, 317–19; Robert Service, *Stalin. A Biography* (Cambridge, MA: Harvard University Press, 2005), 523–4; V. A. Torchinov, and A. M. Leontiuk, (eds.), *Vokrug Stalina. Istoriko-biograficheskii spravochnik.* (St Petersburg: Filologicheskii fakul'tet Sankt-Peterburgskogo gosudarstvennogo universiteta, 2000), 57.

17. Kuhr, 'Children of "Enemies of the People"'. For examples see Jelena Bonner, *Mütter und Töchter. Erinnerungen an meine Jugend 1923 bis 1945* (Munich: Piper, 1992), 273; Sheila Fitzpatrick, and Yuri Slezkine (eds.), *In the Shadow of Revolution. Life Stories of Russian Women. From 1917 to the Second World War* (Princeton, NJ: Princeton University Press, 2000), 330. On the technicalities of adoption in these cases and the resulting close police surveillance see Alexopoulos, 'Stalin and the Politics of Kinship', 107.

18. Jean Lévesque, 'Exile and Discipline: The June 1948 Campaign against Collective Farm Shirkers', *The Carl Beck Papers in Russian & East European Studies* 1708 (2006), 36.

19. *Tragediia sovetskoi derevni*, vol. 3: 828.

20. NKVD report (7 April 1937), in: *Tragediia sovetskoi derevni*, vol. 5.1: 210–12, here: 212.

21. Inquiry of a Ukrainian raiispolkom chairman (13 August 1937), *Tragediia sovetskoi derevni*, vol. 5.1: 99.

22. NKVD report (14 January 1937), in: *Tragediia sovetskoi derevni*, vol. 5.1: 114–16, here: 114.

23. Alexopoulos, 'Stalin and the Politics of Kinship', 110.

24. Great Bucher, *Women, the Bureaucracy and Daily Life in Postwar Moscow, 1945–1953* (Boulder: East European Monographs, 2006), 118.

25. Nakachi, 'Population, politics, and reproduction', 34–5, tables 1.2, 1.3, 1.4.

26. E. V. Gutnova, *Perezhitoe* (Moscow: Rosspen, 2001), 244.

27. Harvard Project on the Soviet Social System. Schedule A, vol. 36, case 1705 (NY). Male, 49, Great Russian, Instructor-inspector in fishing kolkhozes, p. 39–40. For more on old age see Stephen Lovell, 'Soviet Russia's Older Generations', in *Generations in Twentieth-Century Europe*, ed. Stephen Lovell (Houndsmills, Basingstokes: Palgrave Macmillan, 2007), 205–26.

28. Geiger, *The Family in Soviet Russia*, 201, 205.

29. See Bonner, *Mütter und Töchter*, 26–7.

30. See Marc Bloch, *The Historian's Craft. Reflections on the Nature and Uses of History and the Techniques and Methods of Those Who Write It* (New York: Vintage Books, 1953), 40.

31. Liudmilla Alexeyeva and Paul Goldberg, *The Thaw Generation. Coming of Age in the Post-Stalin Era* (Boston, Toronto, London: Little, Brown, and Co., 1990). 11.

32. Alexeyeva, *Thaw Generation*, 12.

33. J. V. Stalin, 'The Fifth Anniversary of the First Congress of Working Women and Peasant Women' (10 November 1923), *Works*. vol. 5: 1921–1923 (Moscow: Foreign Languages Publishing House, 1953), 356–9, here: 358.

34. For a memoir showing the centrality of the nanny in child-rearing see Bonner, *Mütter und Töchter*, passim. On domestic servants in the 1930s see Sheila Fitzpatrick, *Everyday Stalinism. Ordinary Life in Extraordinary Times: Soviet Russia in the 1930s.* (New York and Oxford: Oxford University Press, 1999), 99–100. For a skeptical view on the availability of nannies after the war see Bucher, *Women, the Bureaucracy and Daily Life*, 33, 102, 135.

35. Inna Shikheeva-Gaister, *Semeinaia khronika vremen kul'ta lichnosti 1925–1953* (Moscow: N'iudiamed-AO, 1998), 5–6.

36. Victor Kravchenko, *I Chose Freedom. The Personal and Political Life of a Soviet Official* (Bedfors Square: Robert Hale, 1947), 55, 319–21 and *passim*.

37. Lev Kopelev, *I sotvoril sebe kumira* (Ann Arbor: Ardis, 1978), 139. On the techniques of working on the self see Ch. 6 below. On Jewish history as part of Soviet history see Yuri Slezkine, *The Jewish Century* (Princeton, NJ: Princeton University Press, 2004).

38. Geiger, *The Family in Soviet Russia* 43–116, esp. 88–9, 97.

39. S. Ia. Vol'vson, quoted in Goldman, *Women, the state, and revolution*, 1. On the paraphrase see ibid. 2.
40. Zinaida Tettenborn in 1918, quoted by Goldman, *Women, the state, and revolution*, 53.
41. Goldman, *Women, the state and revolution*, 59–100, esp. 97–8; Rachel Green, '"There Will Not Be Orphans among Us": Soviet Orphanages, Foster Care, and Adoption, 1941–1956' PhD. diss., The University of Chicago, 2006.
42. Geiger, *The Family in Soviet Russia*, 49–50.
43. Fitzpatrick, *Everyday Stalinism*, 142; see also Charles Hachten, 'Property Relations and the Economic Organization of Soviet Russia, 1941–1948'. PhD diss. The University of Chicago, 2005.
44. Alexopoulos, 'Stalin and the politics of kinship', 96.
45. See Ch. 8 below; Bucher, *Women, the Bureaucracy and Daily Life*; and Edele, *Soviet Veterans of the Second World War*, chs. 3 and 4.
46. Fitzpatrick, *Everyday Stalinism*, 140.
47. William Taubman, *Khrushchev. The Man and His Era* (New York and London: W. W. Norton & Co., 2003), 25.
48. Alexopoulos, 'Stalin and the politics of kinship', 97.
49. Goldman, *Women, the state and, revolution*, 102, 106–7, 296–336, 341, 331; Mark D. Steinberg, 'Worker-authors and the Cult of the Person', in *Cultures in Flux. Lower-Class Values, Practices, and Resistance in Late Imperial Russia*, eds. Stephen P. Frank and Mark D. Steinberg (Princeton, NJ: Princeton University Press, 1994), 168–84, here: 179–80; id., *Proletarian Imagination. Self, Modernity, and the Sacred in Russia, 1910–1925* (Ithaca and London: Cornell University Press, 2002); Laura Engelstein, *The Keys to Happiness. Sex and the Search for Modernity in Fin-De-Siecle Russia* (Ithaca and London: Cornell University Press, 1992); Joan Neuberger, *Hooliganism. Crime, Culture, and Power in St. Petersburg, 1900–1914* (Berkeley, Los Angeles, London: University of California Press, 1993). On the 1920s see Fitzpatrick, 'Sex and Revolution', in *The Cultural Front*; and Eric Naiman, *Sex in Public. The Incarnation of Early Soviet Ideology* (Princeton, NJ: Princeton University Press, 1997). For the support of the 1936 legislation among DPs see Geiger, *The Family in Soviet Russia*, 99.
50. Dan Healy, 'Sexual and Gender Dissent. Homosexuality as Resistance in Stalin's Russia', in *Contending with Stalinism. Soviet Power & Popular Resistance in the 1930s*, ed. Lynne Viola (Ithaca and London: Cornell University Press, 2002), 130–69, esp. 153–4, 157–8.

51. Cf. Geiger, *the Family in Soviet Russia*, 93–4. On the passportization and cleansing campaign see Nicolas Werth, *Cannibal Island. Death in a Siberian Gulag* (Princeton and Oxford: Princeton University Press, 2007), 14–15, 18–22.

52. *Naselenie Rossii v XX veke. Istoricheskie Ocherki.* 3 vols. (Moscow: Rosspen, 2000–2005), vol. 1: 187.

53. All comparisons for 1940. *Naselenie Rossii v XX veke*, vol. 2: 235. Outside of the cities, divorces were considerably lower. Cf. ibid., 351.

54. Fitzpatrick, *Everyday Stalinism*, 140.

55. *Naselenie Rossii v XX veke*, vol. 2: 252.

56. Hachten, 'Property Relations and the Economic Organization of Soviet Russia', 141.

57. Kravchenko, *I chose Freedom*, 67–8; Fitzpatrick, *Everyday Stalinism*, 133; Jochen Hellbeck, *Revolution on My Mind. Writing a Diary under Stalin* (Cambridge, MA and London: Harvard University Press, 2006), 115–64; Golfo Alexopoulos, *Stalin's Outcasts: Aliens, Citizens, and the Soviet State, 1926–1936* (Ithaca: Cornell University Press, 2003), 39.

58. Adele Lindenmeyr, *Poverty Is Not a Vice. Charity, Society, and the State in Imperial Russia* (Princeton, NJ: Princeton University Press, 1996), 203–12.

59. Rebecca Neary, 'Domestic Life and the Activist Wife in the 1930s Soviet Union', in *Borders of Socialism. Private Spheres of Soviet Russia*, ed. Lewis Siegelbaum (New York: Palgrave Macmillan, 2006), 107–22; Fitzpatrick and Slezkine, *In the Shadow of Revolution*, 31–366; Stephen Kotkin, *Magnetic Mountain. Stalinism as a Civilization* (Berkeley, Los Angeles, and London: University of California Press, 1995), 218–20; Vadim Volkov, 'The Concept of Kul'turnost': Notes on the Stalinist Civilizing Process', in *Stalinism. New Directions*, ed. Sheila Fitzpatrick (London and New York: Routledge, 2000), 219–22; Julie Hessler, 'Cultured Trade. The Stalinist Turn Towards Consumerism', in ibid., 200–1; Lewis H. Siegelbaum, *Stakhanovism and the Politics of Productivity in the USSR, 1935–1941* (Cambridge: Cambridge University Press, 1988), 213, 238–42; Fitzpatrick, *Everyday Stalinism*, 156–62; id. 'Becoming Cultured', in *Cultural Front*, 232–3; Schlesinger, *The Family*, 235–50; Mary Buckley, *Mobilizing Soviet Peasants. Heroines and Heroes of Stalin's Fields* (Lanham: Rowman & Littlefield Publishers, 2006), 273–9.

60. Douglas Northrop, *Veiled Empire. Gender & Power in Stalinist Central Asia* (Ithaca and London: Cornell University Press, 2004).

61. *Naselenie Rossii v XX veke*, vol. 1: 14, 154; vol. 2: 131, 366; V. B. Zhiromskaia, I. N. Kiselev, and Iu. A. Poliakov, *Polveka pod grifom*

'sekretno': Vsesoiuznaia perepis' naseleniia 1937 goda (Moscow: Nauka, 1996), 63; Geiger, The Family in Soviet Russia, 175.

62. Naselenie Rossii v XX veke, vol. 1: 185.
63. On Central Asia see Northrop, Veiled Empire, 271–2.
64. Cf. Fitzpatrick, Everyday Stalinism, 142. The data can be found in V. B. Zhiromskaia and Iu. A. Poliakov, Vsesoiuznaia perepis' naseleniia 1937 goda: obshchie itogi. Sbornik dokumentov i materialov (Moscow: Rosspen, 2007), 85.
65. Fitzpatrick, Everyday Stalinism, 145–6.
66. Geiger, The Family in Soviet Russia, 230–1.
67. Sula Bennet (trans. & ed.), The Village of Viriatino. An Ethnographic Study of a Russian Village from before the Revolution to the Present (Garden City, New York: Anchor Books, 1970), 245.
68. Naselenie Rossii v XX veke, vol. 2: 237 (data for RSFSR).
69. Cf. Fitzpatrick, Everyday Stalinism, 140, 141.
70. Harvard Project on the Soviet Social System. Schedule B, vol. 24, case 279, pp. 1, 8, 9.
71. Naselenie Rossii v XX veke, vol. 1: 71, 212; vol. 2: 265 (table 66). For more on the impact of demobilization see Mark Edele, 'Veterans and the Village: The Impact of Red Army Demobilization on Soviet Urbanization, 1945–1955'. Russian History 36, no. 2 (2009): 159–82.
72. Bennet, Viriatino, 247.
73. Naselenie Rossii v XX veke, vol. 2: 238–9 (data for RSFSR).
74. Naselenie Rossii v XX veke, vol. 2: 236.

Chapter 5

1. Franz Neumann, Behemoth. The Structure and Practice of National Socialism 1933–1944 (New York: Harper Torchbooks, 1966), p. xii.
2. Orlando Figes, The Whisperers. Private Life in Stalin's Russia (New York: Metropolitan Books, 2007), 32.
3. Stephen F. Cohen, 'Bolshevism and Stalinism', in Stalinism. Essays in Historical Interpretation, ed. Robert C. Tucker (New York: W. W. Norton, 1977), 3–29; Andrea Graziosi, 'G. L. Piatakov (1890–1937): A Mirror of Soviet History', Harvard Ukrainian Studies 16 (1992): 102–66.
4. For more on the impact of internal and external warfare on the emerging polity see Roger Pethybridge, 'The Impact of War', in his The Social Prelude to Stalinism (London and Basingstoke: Macmillan, 1974), 73–131; Peter Holquist, Making War, Forging Revolution. Russia's

Continuum of Crisis, 1914–1921 (Cambridge and London: Harvard University Press, 2002); and Joshua A. Sanborn, *Drafting the Russian Nation. Military Conscription, Total War, and Mass Politics, 1905–1925* (DeKalb, Illinois: Northern Illinois University Press, 2003).

5. Stephen G. Wheatcroft, 'From Team-Stalin to Degenerate Tyranny', in *The Nature of Stalin's Dictatorship. The Politburo, 1924–1953*, ed. E. A. Rees (Houndmills: Palgrave Macmillan, 2004), 79–107.

6. Oskar Anweiler, *The Soviets: The Russian Workers, Peasants, and Soldiers Councils, 1905–1921* (New York: Pantheon Books, 1974).

7. Don K. Rowney, *Transition to Technocracy. The Structural Origins of the Soviet Administrative State* (Ithaca and London: Cornell University Press, 1989). On the fate of the Soviets see Anweiler, *The Soviets*, 227–53. On the fate of the non-Bolshevik parties see Robert V. Daniels, *The Conscience of the Revolution: Communist Opposition in Soviet Russia* (New York: Simon and Schuster, 1969). On the takeover of ministries see T. H. Rigby, *Lenin's Government: Sovnarkom 1917–1922* (Cambridge and New York: Cambridge University Press, 1979), ch. 4. For an archive-based case study of a Commissariat see Heinzen, James. *Inventing a Soviet Countryside. State Power and the Transformation of Rural Russia, 1917–1929* (Pittburgh, PA: University of Pittsburgh Press, 2004).

8. Graeme Gill, *The Origins of the Stalinist Political System* (Cambridge and New York: Cambridge University Press, 1990), 52–5; Rigby, *Lenin's Government*, ch. 12.

9. Lewis H. Siegelbaum, *Soviet State and Society between Revolutions, 1918–1929* (Cambridge, New York, Melbourne: Cambridge University Press, 1994), 12–25; Helmut Altrichter, 'Sowjet(s)', *Historisches Lexikon der Sowjetunion*, 301–4; id., 'Ministerrat', *Historisches Lexikon der Sowjetunion*, 205.

10. Altrichter, 'Parteitag(e)', *Historisches Lexikon der Sowjetunion*, 236–8; Gill, *Origins*, 56–75 (quotation: 68).

11. Mark von Hagen, *Soldiers in the Proletarian Dictatorship. The Red Army and the Soviet Socialist State, 1917–1930* (Ithaca and London: Cornell University Press, 1990); Paul M. Hagenloh, ' "Chekist in Essence, Chekist in Spirit": Regular and Political Police in the 1930s'. *Cahiers du Monde russe* 42, no. 2-3-4 (2001): 447–76.

12. V. I. Lenin, 'The Question of Nationalities or "Autonomisation" (30 December 1922)', in *Collected Works*, vol. 36 (Moscow: Progress Publishers, 1966), 605–7, here: 605.

13. Vladimir Il'ich Lenin, 'What Is To Be Done? Burning Questions of Our Movement' (1902), in *Collected Works*, vol. 5 (Moscow: Foreign Languages Publishing House, 1961), 347–530.

14. T. H. Rigby, 'Early Provincial Cliques and the Rise of Stalin', *Soviet Studies* 33, no. 1 (1981): 3–28; Gill, *Origins*; Gerald M. Easter, *Reconstructing the State. Personal Networks and Elite Identity in Soviet Russia* (Cambridge and New York: Cambridge University Press, 2000).

15. This view goes back, ultimately, to Leon Trotsky, *The Revolution Betrayed. What Is the Soviet Union and Where Is It Going?* (New York, London, Montreal, Sydney: Pathfinder, 1972).

16. J. Arch Getty, 'Afraid of Their Shadows: The Bolshevik Recourse to Terror, 1932–1938', in *Stalinismus vor dem Zweiten Weltkrieg. Neue Wege der Forschung*, ed. Manfred Hildermeier (Munich: R. Oldenbourg Verlag, 1998), 169–91; Gabor T. Rittersporn, 'The Omnipresent Conspiracy: On Soviet Imagery of Politics and Social Relations in the 1930s', in *Stalinist Terror. New Perspectives*, eds. J. Arch Getty and Roberta T. Manning (Cambridge and New York: Cambridge University Press, 1993), 99–115; Sheila Fitzpatrick, 'The Legacy of the Civil War', in *Party, State, and Society in the Russian Civil War. Explorations in Social History*, eds. William Rosenberg, Diane P. Koenker, Ronald G. Suny (Bloomington and Indianapolis: Indiana University Press, 1989), 385–98, esp. 387; Robert C. Tucker, *Stalin in Power. The Revolution from above 1928–1941* (New York and London: W. W. Norton & Company, 1992); Service, *Stalin*, ch. 30.

17. T. H. Rigby, 'Was Stalin a Disloyal Patron?', *Soviet Studies* 38, no. 3 (1986): 311–24, here: 312.

18. Lynne Viola et al. (eds.), *The War Against the Peasantry, 1927–1930: The Tragedy of the Soviet Countryside* (New Haven: Yale University Press, 2005), ch. 4.

19. This had been the position of Robert Conquest, which in its broad outlines (if not always in detail) has been confirmed by archival research. See Robert Conquest, *The Great Terror. A Reassessment* (New York and Oxford: Oxford University Press, 1990). For archive-based support see Oleg Khlevniuk's work (quoted in footnote 21 below), succinctly summarized in his 'The Objectives of the Great Terror, 1937–1938', in *Soviet History, 1917–53. Essays in Honour of R. W. Davies*, eds. Julian Cooper, Maureen Perrie and E. A. Rees (New York: St Martin's Press, 1995).

20. Alec Nove, 'Stalin and Stalinism—Some Introductory Thoughts', in his *The Stalin Phenomenon* (London: Weidenfeld & Nicolson, 1993), 28; id., 'Stalin and Stalinism—Some Afterthoughts', in ibid., 201. On Stalin's

childhood see Robert C. Tucker, *Stalin as Revolutionary, 1879–1929: a study in history and personality* (New York: Norton, 1973).

21. For an effective overview see Yoram Gorlizki and Oleg V. Khlevniuk, 'Stalin and His Circle', in *The Cambridge History of Russia. Vol III: The Twentieth Century*, ed. Ronald G. Suny (Cambridge and New York: Cambridge University Press, 2006), 243–67. The already classical study for the 1930s is Oleg Khlevniuk, *Politbiuro. Mekhanizmy politicheskoi vlasti v 1930-e gody* (Moscow: Rosspen, 1996), now available in a revised edition as *Master of the House. Stalin and His Inner Circle* (New Haven and London: Yale University Press, 2009). For a recent collection of archival studies see E. A. Rees (ed.), *The Nature of Stalin's Dictatorship. The Politburo, 1924–1953* (Houndmills: Palgrave Macmillan, 2004). For a review essay on the state of research early in the new millenium see James R. Harris, 'Was Stalin a Weak Dictator?', *The Journal of Modern History* 75 (2003): 375–86.

22. Wheatcroft, 'From Team-Stalin to Degenerate Tyranny', 79–107; Khlevniuk, *In Stalin's Shadow*; id., *Master*, chs. 1–3; on Stalin's changing relationship with his retainers see also Service, *Stalin*; Simon S. Montefiore, *Stalin. The Court of the Red Tsar* (New York: Vintage Books, 2003). On the Great Peasant War see Graziosi, *The Great Soviet Peasant War*; 'Authoritative "older brother"', is, likewise, Graziosi's formulation. See his 'Piatakov: A Mirror of Soviet History', 133. For the comparison with Thatcher see J. Arch Getty, 'Stalin as Prime Minister: Power and the Politburo', in *Stalin. A New History*, eds. Sarah Davies and James R. Harris (Cambridge and New York: Cambridge University Press, 2005), 83–107.

23. Hannah Arendt, *The Origins of Totalitarianism. New edition with added prefaces* (New York and London: Harvest Books, 1968); Robert C. Tucker, *Stalin in Power. The Revolution from above 1928–1941* (New York and London: W. W. Norton & Company, 1992); Khlevniuk, *Master of the House*, chs. 5–6.

24. Constantine Pleshakov, *Stalin's Folly. The Tragic First Ten Days of World War II on the Eastern Front* (Boston and New York: Houton Mifflin Co., 2005), 216.

25. Evan Mawdsley, *Thunder in the East. The Nazi-Soviet War 1941–1945* (London: Hodder Arnold, 2005), 172–3, 206–9; Easter, *Reconstructing the State*, 101–3; P. Charles Hachten, 'Property Relations and the Economic Organization of Soviet Russia, 1941–1948'. PhD diss. (The University of Chicago, 2005); id., 'Separate yet Governed: The Representation of Soviet Property Relations in Civil Law and Public Discourse', in *Borders of*

Socialism. Private Spheres of Soviet Russia, ed. Lewis Siegelbaum (New York and Houndsmills: Palgrave Macmillan, 2006), 65–82; William Moskoff, *The Bread of Affliction; the Food Supply in the USSR During World War II* (Cambridge: Cambridge University Press, 1990); Yoram Gorlitzki, 'Ordinary Stalinism: The Council of Ministers and the Soviet Neopatrimonial State, 1946–1953', *The Journal of Modern History* 74, no. 4 (2002): 699–736; id. and Oleg Khlevniuk, *Cold Peace. Stalin and the Soviet Ruling Circle, 1945–1953* (Oxford and New York: Oxford University Press, 2004); E. A. Rees, 'Stalin as Leader, 1937–1953: From Dictator to Despot', in *The Nature of Stalin's Dictatorship*, 200–40.

26. Easter, *Reconstructing the State*, passim; Joseph S. Berliner, *Factory and Manager in the USSR* (Cambridge: Harvard University Press, 1957), 9, 261.

27. Khlevniuk, *Master*, 214, 255; Service, *Stalin*, 374; Rigby, 'Was Stalin a disloyal patron?', 320.

28. See Ch. 8 below.

29. Nicolas Werth, *Cannibal Island. Death in a Siberian Gulag* (Princeton and Oxford: Princeton University Press, 2007), 164.

30. Hachten, 'Property Relations', 282–3. On the development of the justice system see Peter H. Solomon, *Soviet Criminal Justice under Stalin* (Cambridge, New York, Melbourne: Cambridge University Press, 1996).

31. Stuart Finkel, 'An Intensification of Vigilance. Recent Perspectives on the Institutional History of the Soviet Security Apparatus in the 1920s', *Kritika: Explorations in Russian and Eurasian History* 5, no. 2 (2004): 299–320, here: 310.

32. R. W. Davies, *The Socialist Offensive. The Collectivisation of Soviet Agriculture 1929–1930* (London: Macmillan, 1980), 11.

33. David R. Shearer, 'Social Disorder, Mass Repression, and the NKVD During the 1930s', *Cahiers du Monde russe* 42, no. 2-3-4 (2001): 505–34, here: 509.

34. Catriona Kelly, *Comrade Pavlik. The Rise and Fall of a Soviet Boy Hero* (London: Granta Books, 2005), 64.

35. Werth, *Cannibal Island*, 35, 39–42; quotation: 40; 75–6.

36. For in-depth studies of policing see David R. Shearer, *Policing Stalin's Socialism. Repression and Social Order in the Soviet Union, 1924–1953* (New Haven and London: Yale University Press, 2009); Paul Hagenloh, *Stalin's Police. Public Order and Mass Repression in the USSR, 1926–1941* (Baltimore: The Johns Hopkins University Press, 2009).

37. See Chs. 1 and 3 above.

38. Easter, *Reconstructing the State*, 145 (quotation). See also Hagenloh, 'Chekist in Essence', 469–72, and *passim*; id., *Stalin's Police*, ch. 5; and Khlevniuk, *Master*, 92–3, 117–24.

39. Hagenloh, 'Chekist in Essence', 473; Shearer, 'Social Disorder', 513, 518–19.

40. Sheila Fitzpatrick, *Everyday Stalinism. Ordinary Life in Extraordinary Times: Soviet Russia in the 1930s* (New York and Oxford: Oxford University Press, 1999), 132–6, 193; id., *Tear Off the Masks! Identity and Imposture in Twentieth-Century Russia* (Princeton and Oxford: Princeton University Press, 2005); NKVD report (20 April 1937), in *Tragediia sovetskoi derevni. Kollektivizatsiia i raskulachivanie. Dokumenty i materialy v 5 tomakh 1927–1939. Tom 5, Kn. 1: 1937*, eds. V. Danilov et al. (Moscow: Rosspen, 2004), 239. For more examples see ibid. 247; Khlevniuk, *Master*, 198–9.

41. Sheila Fitzpatrick, 'The World of Ostap Bender: Soviet Confidence Men in the Stalin Period', *Slavic Review* 61, no. 3 (2002): 535–57; Mark Edele, *Soviet Veterans of the Second World War. A Popular Movement in an Authoritarian Society, 1941–1991* (Oxford: Oxford University Press, 2008), 44–5, 51–2, 71–2, 113–14, quotation: 51. On living underground in the post war years see also ibid., ch. 5; Golfo Alexopoulos, 'Portrait of a Con Artist as a Soviet Man', *Slavic Review* 57, no. 4 (1998): 774–90, here: 775. On the cleansing of cities in the 1930s see Werth, *Cannibal Island*; Hagenloh, 'Chekist in Essence' (citation: 469); David Shearer, 'Elements near and Alien: Passportization, Policing, and Identity in the Stalinist State, 1932–1952', *The Journal of Modern History* 76, no. 4 (2004): 835–81. On the clean up of cities from beggars after the war see Edele, *Soviet veterans*, 93–4; Sheila Fitzpatrick, 'Social Parasites. How Tramps, Idle Youth, and Busy Entrepreneurs Impeded the Soviet March to Communism', *Cahier du Monde russe* 47, no. 1–2 (2006): 377–408.

42. Davies, *The Socialist Offensive*, 52; Easter, *Reconstructing the State*, 85 (quotation), 118; Sheila Fitzpatrick, *Stalin's Peasants. Resistance and Survival in the Russian Village after Collectivization* (New York and Oxford: Oxford University Press, 1994), 175.

43. Draft order of NKVD SSSR 'O nedochetakh podgotovki i provedeniia massovykh poeratsii na Ukraine', February 1938, *Tragediia Sovetskoi derevni*, vol. 5.2: 50–6, here: 52; G. Kozlov to Andreev, Zhdanov, Malenkov (October 1938), *Tragediia sovetskoi derevni*, 5.2: 299–301.

44. Lewis Siegelbaum, and Andrei Sokolov (eds.) *Stalinism as a Way of Life. Abridged Edition* (New Haven and London: Yale University Press, 2004), 103–5; also available as document 45 on http://www.yale.edu/annals/siegelbaum/

45. Berliner, *Factory and Manager*, 281; Wendy Z. Goldman, *Terror and Democracy in the Age of Stalin. The Social Dynamics of Repression* (Cambridge and New York: Cambridge University Press, 2007), 87.

46. T. H. Rigby, *Communist Party Membership in the USSR 1917–1967* (Princeton, NJ: Princeton University Press, 1968), 52; V. B. Zhiromskaia, I. N. Kiselev, and Iu. A. Poliakov, *Polveka pod grifom 'sekretno': Vsesoiuznaia perepis' naseleniia 1937 goda* (Moscow: Nauka, 1996), 41; and Mark Edele, 'The Impact of War and the Costs of Superpower Status', *Oxford Hanbook of Russian History*, ed. Simon Dixon. (forthcoming).

47. Victor Kravchenko, *I Chose Freedom. The Personal and Political Life of a Soviet Official* (Bedfors Square: Robert Hale, 1947), 398–402. For more on work in the Soviet administrative 'madhouse' see David R. Shearer, *Industry, State, and Society in Stalin's Russia 1926–1934* (Ithaca and London: Cornell University Press, 1996), chs. 6–8.

48. *Pravda* 1 April 1937, quoted in Easter, *Reconstructing the State*, 104.

49. Easter, *Reconstructing the State*; James R. Harris, 'The Purging of Local Cliques in the Urals Region, 1936–7', *Stalinism. New Directions*, ed. Sheila Fitzpatrick (London: Routledge, 2000), 262–85; id., *The Great Urals: Regionalism and the Evolution of the Soviet System* (Ithaca, NY: Cornell University Press, 1996), ch. 6; Khlevniuk, *Master in the House*, chs. 5–6.

50. Raymond A. Bauer, Alex Inkeles, and Clyde Kluckhohn. *How the Soviet System Works. Cultural, Psychological, and Social Themes* (Cambridge: Harvard University Press, 1956); Alex Inkeles, and Raymond Bauer, *The Soviet Citizen. Daily Life in a Totalitarian Society* (Cambridge, MA: Harvard University Press, 1961); Alena V. Ledeneva, *Russia's Economy of Favours. Blat, Networking and Informal Exchange* (New York and Cambridge: Cambridge University Press, 1998); Stephen Lovell, Alena Ledeneva, and Andrei Rogachevskii (eds.), *Bribery and Blat in Russia. Negotiating Reciprocity from the Middle Ages to the 1990s* (New York: St Martin's Press, 2000).

51. Gill, *Origins*, 6.

52. Catherine Merridale, 'The 1937 Census and the Limits of Stalinist Rule', *The Historical Journal* 39, no. 1 (1996): 225–40, here: 236. On the role of cliques in creating this situation see Harris, 'The Purging of Local Cliques', 263.

53. Berliner, *Factory and Manager*, 279.

54. Alex Inkeles, *Public Opinion in Soviet Russia. A Study in Mass Persuasion* (Cambridge, MA: Harvard University Press, 1967); Sheila Fitzpatrick.

'Supplicants and Citizens: Public Letter-Writing in Soviet Russia in the 1930s', *Slavic Review* 55, no. 1 (1996): 78–105; James Heinzen, 'Informers and the State under Late Stalinism. Informant Networks and Crimes against "Socialist Property," 1940–53', *Kritika: Explorations in Russian and Eurasian History* 8, no. 4 (2007): 789–815.

55. Sheila Fitzpatrick, *The Russian Revolution*. 2nd edn. (Oxford and New York: Oxford University Press, 1994), 154–5; Siegelbaum, *Stalinism as a Way of Life*, 122–3. For the public debate see ibid., ch. 3; and J. Arch Getty, 'State and Society under Stalin: Constitutions and Elections in the 1930s', *Slavic Review* 50, no. 1 (1991): 18–35, esp. 23–8.

56. Siegelbaum, *Stalinism as a Way of Life*, 145.

57. The following interpretation is strongly indebted to Rolf Binner and Marc Junge. 'Vernichtung der orthodoxen Geistlichen in der Sowjetunion in den Massenoperationen des Großen Terrors 1937–1938' *Jahrbücher für Geschichte Osteuropas* 52, no. 4 (2004): 515–33. See also Shearer, *Policing*, ch. 9.

58. Khlevniuk, *Master*, 137. This perception might have been aided by rather optimistic reporting about police work. See Shearer, 'Social Disorder', 518.

59. Stenogramm of CC plenum meeting, 27 Feb. 1937, in: *Tragediia sovetskoi derevni*, vol. 5.1: 157–64.

60. Zhiromskaia, *Polveka pod grifom*, 98, table 17; 103. See also below, Ch. 6.

61. Binner and Junge, 'Vernichtung der orthodoxen Geistlichen', 523–4. On the international context see Oleg Khevniuk, 'The Reasons for the "Great Terror": the foreign-political aspect', in *Russia in the age of wars, 1914–1945*, eds. Silvio Pons and Andrea Romano (Milano: Geltrinelli, 2000).

62. Cf. J. Arch Getty and Oleg V. Naumov, *The Road to Terror. Stalin and the Self-Destruction of the Bolsheviks, 1932–1939* (New Haven and London: Yale University Press, 1999), 468–81; *Tragediia sovetskoi derevni*, vol. 5.1, 319–99; and J. Arch Getty, '"Excesses Are Not Permitted": Mass Terror and Stalinist Governance in the Late 1930s', *The Russian Review* 61, no. 1 (2002): 113–38; Viola, *Unknown Gulag*.

63. For examples, see *Tragediia sovetskoi derevni*, vol. 5.1: 239, 247.

64. NKVD report (11 Jan. 1937), in: *Tragediia sovetskoi derevni*, vol. 5.1: 84–6, quotation: 85.

65. Between 1932 and 1940, 629,042 people escaped 'special settlement'. Only 235,120 were caught and returned. V. P. Danilov, 'Sovetskaia derevnia v gody "Bol'shogo terrora"' in *Tragediia sovetskoi derevni*, vol. 5.1: 7–50, here: 15.

66. Spetssoobshchenie UNKVD Zapadnoi obl. 'O kontrrevoliutsionnnykh proiavleniiakh sredi edinolichnikov', (14 January 1937), *Tragediia sovetskoi derevni*, vol. 5.1: 114–16, here: 115. For more reactions see Sarah Davies, *Popular Opinion in Stalin's Russia. Terror, Propaganda, and Dissent, 1934–1941* (Cambridge, New York, Melbourne: Cambridge University Press, 1997), ch. 6.

67. Cf. Getty and Naumov, *The Road to Terror*, 468–9; Getty, 'Excesses', 122–6; id., 'State and Society', 28–32; Fitzpatrick, *Stalin's Peasants*, 280–5; Khlevniuk, *Master*, 173–9.

68. Harris, *Great Urals*, ch. 6; Fitzpatrick, *Everyday Stalinism*, ch. 8.

69. *Tragediia sovetskoi derevni*, vol. 5.2: 416–24.

70. N. S. Khrushchev, 'On the Cult of Personality and Its Consequences', in *The Stalin Dictatorship. Khrushchev's 'Secret Speech' and Other Documents*, ed. T. H. Rigby (Sydney: Sydney University Press, 1968), 23–89, here: 76; James C. Scott, *Seeing Like a State. How Certain Schemes to Improve the Human Condition Have Failed* (New Haven and London: Yale University Press, 1998).

71. See Ch. 2.

72. Kate Brown, *A Biography of No Place. From Ethnic Borderland to Soviet Heartland* (Cambridge, MA: Harvard University Press, 2003), 182, 183.

73. Max Weber, *Wirtschaft und Gesellschaft. Grundriss der verstehenden Soziologie. Studienausgabe.* 5th, rev. edn. (Tübingen: J. C. B. Mohr [Paul Siebeck] 1990), 28.

74. Brown, *Biography of no place*, 53. Compare also to Getty, 'Afraid of their Shadows'.

75. Cf. James R. Millar and Alec Nove, 'A Debate on Collectivization: Was Stalin really necessary?', *Problems of Communism* 25.4 (1976), 49–62.

76. For the post-war years see Gorlizki and Khlevniuk, *Cold Peace*; and G. V. Kostyrchenko, *Tainaia politika Stalina. Vlast' i antisemitism* (Moscow: Mezhdunarodnye otnosheniia, 2003).

77. William Taubman, *Khrushchev. The Man and His Era* (New York and London: W. W. Norton & Co., 2003), 105.

78. Service, *Stalin*, 520–30.

79. Balazs Apor, Jan C. Behrends, Polly Jones, and E. A. Rees (eds.), *The Leader Cult in Communist Dictatorships. Stalin and the Eastern Bloc* (New York: Palgrave Macmillan, 2004); Klaus Heller and Jan Plamper (eds.), *Personality Cults in Stalinism—Personenkulte im Stalinismus* (Göttingen: V&R unipress, 2004).

80. Pleshakov, *Stalin's Folly*, 218–20; Service, *Stalin*, 410–19.

81. For a colourful description of Stalin's last hours see Simon Sebag Montefiore, *Stalin. The Court of the Red Tsar* (New York: Vintage Books, 2003), 638–50; for his last words: 638.

Chapter 6

1. Grigorii Chukhrai, *Moia Voina* (Moscow: Algoritm, 2001), 21–2.
2. John Barber, 'Popular Reactions in Moscow to the German Invasion of June 22, 1941', *Soviet Union/Union Soviétique* 18, no. 1–3 (1991): 5–18, here: 13.
3. Secret police report, Stalingrad region, (27 January 1937), in: *Tragediia sovetskoi derevni*, vol. 5.1: 90–1, here: 91.
4. Veronique Garros, Natalia Korenevskaya, and Thomas Lahusen (eds.), *Intimacy and Terror. Soviet Diaries of the 1930s* (New York: The New Press, 1995), 13.
5. For a now classical, pre-archival treatment of Stalinism in the context of Marxist thought see Leszek Kolakowski, *Main Currents of Marxism. Its Origin, Growth, and Dissolution. Vol. III: The Breakdown* (Oxford: Clarendon Press, 1978), 1–182. For a recent, in-depth study of the ideological context of Stalinist politics see David Priestland, *Stalinism and the Politics of Mobilization. Ideas, Power, and Terror in Inter-war Russia* (Oxford: Oxford University Press, 2007).
6. Stalin's speech is reproduced in *The War against the Peasantry, 1927–1930: The Tragedy of the Soviet Countryside*, eds. Lynne Viola et al. (New Haven, CT: Yale University Press, 2005), 97–102. The quotations in question are on p. 98, 99, and 101.
7. R. W. Davies, Oleg V. Khlevniuk, and E. A. Rees (eds.), *The Stalin-Kaganovich Correspondence 1931–36* (New Haven and London: Yale University Press, 2003), 68–9.
8. Jochen Hellbeck, *Revolution on My Mind. Writing a Diary under Stalin* (Cambridge, Mass, and London: Harvard University Press, 2006), 1.
9. Oleg V. Khlevniuk, *In Stalin's Shadow. The Career of 'Sergo' Ordzhonikidze* (Armonk and London: M. E. Sharpe, 1995), 94–5, 76.
10. Kolakowski, *Main Currents*, vol. 3: 3.
11. Eric van Ree, *The Political Thought of Joseph Stalin. A Study in Twentieth-Century Revolutionary Patriotism* (London and New York: Routledge Curzon, 2002).
12. Reply to Preobrazhensky at Sixth Congress of Bolshevik Party, 3 August 1917, in *Works. Vol. 3: 1917 March–October* (Moscow: Foreign Languages Publishing House, 1954), 199–200, here: 200.

13. Karl Marx, *Das Kapital. Kritik der politischen Ökonomie* (Stuttgart: Kroener, 1957), esp.138–203 (on the production of surplus value), 119–27 (on the lack of production of value through exchange), 417 (on the production of value by transportation workers).

14. Alexander Bogdanov, *The Red Star. The First Bolshevik Utopia*, eds. Loren R. Graham and Richard Stites (Bloomington: Indiana University Press, 1984), esp. 65–8, here: 66 (quotation); on the influence among Bolsheviks see 12–16, 253 fn. 4.

15. Craig Paul Roberts, '"War Communism": A Re-Examination', *Slavic Review* 29, no. 2 (1970): 238–61; Diane Koenker, William G. Rosenberg, and Ronald G. Suny (eds.), *Party, State, and Society in the Russian Civil War. Explorations in Social History* (Bloomington and Indianapolis: Indiana University Press, 1989); Francis King, 'The Russian Revolution and the Idea of a Single Economic Plan 1917–28'. *Revolutionary Russia* 12, no. 1 (1999): 69–83; Peter Holquist, *Making War, Forging Revolution. Russia's Continuum of Crisis, 1914–1921* (Cambridge and London: Harvard University Press, 2002).

16. For a good introduction to the changing policies towards religion see Felix Corley, *Religion in the Soviet Union: An Archival Reader* (Houndmills, Basingstoke: Macmillan, 1996).

17. Karl Marx, 'Critique of Hegel's Philosophy of Right', (1844), in *Marx on Religion*, ed. John Raines (Philadelphia: Temple University Press, 2002), 170–82, here: 171.

18. Richard Stites, *Revolutionary Dreams. Utopian Vision and Experimental Life in the Russian Revolution* (New York and Oxford: Oxford University Press, 1989), 212; William Edgerton (ed.), *Memoirs of Peasant Tolstoyans in Soviet Russia* (Bloomington and Indianapolis: Indiana University Press, 1993).

19. Hannah Arendt, *The Origins of Totalitarianism*. New edition with added prefaces (New York and London: Harvest Books, 1968), 470.

20. On the centrality of conversion from Christianity to the life histories of revolutionaries see, e.g. Reginald Zelnik (ed.), *A Radical Worker in Tsarist Russia. The Autobiography of Semen Ivanovich Kanatchikov* (Stanford: Stanford University Press, 1986), ch. 5. On Marxist eschatology see Igal Halfin, *From Darkness to Light. Class, Consciousness, and Salvation in Revolutionary Russia.* (Pittsburgh, PA: University of Pittsburgh Press, 2000).

21. Karl Marx, and Friedrich Engels, *The Communist Manifesto*. With an Introduction and Notes by Gareth Stedman Jones (New York: Penguin, 1967), 219. For an interpretation of Marx attempting to rescue the theorist

from the polemicist see Moishe Postone, *Time, Labor, and Social Domination. A Reinterpretation of Marx's Critical Theory* (Cambridge and New York: Cambridge University Press, 1996).

22. Sheila Fitzpatrick, *Tear Off the Masks! Identity and Imposture in Twentieth-Century Russia* (Princeton and Oxford: Princeton University Press, 2005); Jeffrey J. Rossman, *Worker Resistance under Stalin. Class and Revolution on the Shop Floor* (Cambridge and London: Harvard University Press, 2005).

23. Richard Pipes, *The Formation of the Soviet Union: Communism and Nationalism, 1917–1923*, rev. edn. (Cambridge and London: Harvard University Press, 1964); Ronald G. Suny, *The Revenge of the Past. Nationalism, Revolution, and the Collapse of the Soviet Union* (Stanford: Stanford University Press, 1993); Yuri Slezkine, 'The Soviet Union as a Communal Apartment, or How a Socialist State Promoted Ethnic Particularism', *Slavic Review* 53, no. 2 (1994): 415–52; Terry Martin, *The Affirmative Action Empire. Nations and Nationalism in the Soviet Union, 1923–1939* (Ithaca and London: Cornell University Press, 2001); David Brandenberger, *National Bolshevism: Stalinist Mass Culture and the Formation of Modern Russian National Identity, 1931–1956* (Cambridge and London: Harvard University Press, 2002).

24. I. Michael Aronson, *Troubled Waters. The Origins of the 1881 Anti-Jewish Pogroms in Russia* (Pittsburgh, PA: University of Pittsburgh Press, 1990); John Klier and Shlomo Lambroza (eds.), *Pogroms. Anti-Jewish Violence in Modern Russian History* (Cambridge and New York: Cambridge University Press, 1992); Charters Wynn, *Workers, Strikes, and Pogroms. The Donbass-Dnepr Bend in Late Imperial Russia, 1870–1905* (Princeton, NJ: Princeton University Press, 1992); Yuri Slezkine, *The Jewish Century* (Princeton, NJ: Princeton University Press, 2004), 70, 165–80. On pogroms committed by the Red Army see Richard Pipes (ed.), *The Unknown Lenin. From the Secret Archive* (New Haven and London: Yale University Press, 1996), 5, 10.

25. Lynne Viola, *Peasant Rebels under Stalin. Collectivization and the Culture of Peasant Resistance* (New York and Oxford: Oxford University Press, 1996), 52–3; Corley, *Religion in the Soviet Union*, 64–6.

26. Catriona Kelly, *Comrade Pavlik. The Rise and Fall of a Soviet Boy Hero* (London: Granta Books, 2005), 65.

27. Corley, *Religion in the Soviet Union*, 112–15.

28. Barber, 'Popular Reactions', 13–14; Rebecca Manley, *To the Tashkent Station. Evacuation and Survival in the Soviet Union at War* (Ithaca and London: Cornell University Press, 2009), 111–15.

29. G. V. Kostyrchenko, *Tainaia politika Stalina. Vlast' i antisemitizm* (Moscow: Mezhdunarodnye otnosheniia, 2003), 242–9; Amir Weiner, *Making Sense of War. The Second World War and the Fate of the Bolshevik Revolution* (Princeton and Oxford: Princeton University Press, 2001), 219–22, 293–4.

30. Kiril Tomoff, *Creative Union: The Professional Organization of Soviet Composers, 1939–1953* (Ithaca, NY: Cornell University Press, 2006), ch. 6; Mark Edele, 'More Than Just Stalinists: The Political Sentiments of Victors 1945–1953', in *Late Stalinist Russia. Society between Reconstruction and Reinvention*, ed. Juliane Fürst (London and New York: Routledge, 2006), 172–3;

31. Slezkine, *Jewish Century*, ch. 4.

32. On the centrality of conspiracy see Gabor, T. Rittersporn, 'The Omnipresent Conspiracy: On Soviet Imagery of Politics and Social Relations in the 1930s', in *Stalinist Terror. New Perspectives*, eds. J. Arch Getty and Roberta T. Manning (Cambridge and New York: Cambridge University Press, 1993), 99–115; and J. Arch Getty, 'Afraid of Their Shadows: The Bolshevik Recourse to Terror, 1932–1938', in *Stalinismus vor dem Zweiten Weltkrieg. Neue Wege der Forschung*, ed. Manfred Hildermeier (Munich: R. Oldenbourg Verlag, 1998), 169–91.

33. Quoted in V. P. Danilov, 'Vvedenie. (Istoki i nachalo derevenskoi tragedii)', *Tragediia sovetskoi derevni*, vol. 1: 12–67, here: 23. See also the interpretation of this episode (which differs from the one offered here) in Viola et al., *The War Against the Peasantry*, 15–17.

34. Quoted in V. P. Danilov, 'Sovetskaia derevnia v gody 'Bol'shogo terrora', *Tragediia sovetskoi derevni*. vol. 5.1: 7–50; here: 11.

35. Stalin's speech at the July Plenum of the Central Committee, evening of 9 July 1928, in: *Tragediia sovetskoi derevni*, vol. 1: 319–31, here 326–7.

36. Stalin, 'The Tasks of the Business Executives. Speech Delivered at the First All-Union Conference of Leading Personnel of Socialist Industry, February 4, 1931', in: J. V. Stalin, *Works*, vol. 13: July 1930–January 1934 (Moscow: Foreign Languages Publishing House, 1955), 31–44, here: 40–1.

37. 'Materialy fevral'sko-martovskogo plenuma TsK VKP(b) 1937 goda', *Voprosy istorii*, no. 3 (1995): 3–15, here: 12.

38. *Molotov Remembers. Inside Kremlin Politics. Conversations with Felix Chuev*, ed. Albert Resis (Chicago: Ivan R. Dee, 1993), 254.

39. Katerina Clark, *The Soviet Novel: History as Ritual* (Chicago: University of Chicago Press, 1981); Peter Kenez, *The Birth of the Propaganda State: Soviet Methods of Mass Mobilization, 1917–1929* (Cambridge and New York:

Cambridge University Press, 1985); James von Geldern, *Bolshevik Festivals, 1917–1920* (Berkeley: University of California Press, 1993); Victoria E. Bonnell, *Iconography of Power. Soviet Political Posters under Lenin and Stalin* (Berkeley, Los Angeles, and London: University of California Press, 1997); Karen Petrone, *Life Has Become More Joyous, Comrades: Celebrations in the Time of Stalin* (Bloomington, Ind.: Indiana University Press, 2000); Jeffrey Brooks, *Thank You, Comrade Stalin! Soviet Public Culture from Revolution to Cold War* (Princeton, NJ: Princeton University Press, 2000); Matthew E. Lenoe, *Closer to the Masses: Stalinist Culture, Social Revolution, and Soviet Newspapers* (Cambridge, MA: Harvard University Press, 2004); Denise J. Youngblood, *Russian War Films. On the Cinema Front, 1914–2005* (Lawrence: University Press of Kansas, 2007). On the Soviet soul see: Jochen Hellbeck, 'Fashioning the Stalinist Soul: The Diary of Stepan Podlubnyi (1931–1939)', *Jahrbücher für Geschichte Osteuropas* 44 (1996): 344–75.

40. Stephen Kotkin, *Magnetic Mountain. Stalinism as a Civilization* (Berkeley, Los Angeles, London: University of California Press, 1995), ch. 5.

41. For the cow names see Sheila Fitzpatrick and Yuri Slezkine (eds.), *In the Shadow of Revolution. Life Stories of Russian Women. From 1917 to the Second World War* (Princeton, NJ: Princeton University Press, 2000), 338–9; for the children's names Richard Stites, *Revolutionary Dreams. Utopian Vision and Experimental Life in the Russian Revolution* (New York and Oxford: Oxford University Press, 1989), 111–12.

42. Sheila Fitzpatrick, 'Becoming Cultured: Socialist Realism and the Representation of Privilege and Taste', in her *The Cultural Front. Power and Culture in Revolutionary Russia* (Ithaca and London: Cornell University Press, 1992), 216–37, quotation: 217. On the foundation pit's uses see Timothy J. Colton, *Moscow. Governing the Socialist Metropolis* (Cambridge and London: Belknap Press, 1995), 334.

43. Moshe Lewin, *Russian Peasants and Soviet Power. A Study of Collectivization* (New York, London: W. W. Norton & Co., 1975), 457.

44. Chukhrai, *Moia voina*, 280.

45. Lew Kopelew, *Und schuf mir einen Götzen. Lehrjahre eines Kommunisten* (Göttingen: Steidl, 1996), 154. This section is neither included in the original Russian edition of 1978, nor in the English translation of 1981. Kopelev must have included it for the new German edition in reaction to questions about the impact of the Great Terror on his belief.

46. Harvard Project on the Soviet Social System. Schedule A, vol. 8, case 110 male, 33, Great Russian, military politruk, 107.

47. Raymond A. Bauer, Alex Inkeles, and Clyde Kluckhohn, *How the Soviet System Works. Cultural, Psychological, and Social Themes* (Cambridge: Harvard University Press, 1956), 29–35, 153–73.

48. Catherine Merridale, 'The 1937 Census and the Limits of Stalinist Rule', *The Historical Journal* 39, no. 1 (1996): 225–40, here: 228.

49. NKVD report, 5 January 1937, *Tragediia sovetskoi derevni*, vol 5.1: 86–7, here: 87.

50. NKVD report, before November 1937, *Tragediia sovetskoi derevni*, vol. 5.1: 519–21, here: 521.

51. Bauer, Inkeles, and Kluckhohn, *How The Soviet System Works*, 29–35, esp. 34; Alex Inkeles and Raymond Bauer, *The Soviet Citizen. Daily Life in a Totalitarian Society* (Cambridge, MA: Harvard University Press, 1961), 291–5.

52. Review file on anti-Soviet agitation, GARF f. A–461, op. 1, d. 1887.

53. Ibid., f. A–461, op. 1, d. 110; d. 114.

54. Inkeles and Bauer, *The Soviet Citizen*, 244–5; Edele, 'More Than Just Stalinists'.

55. Nina Lugovskaya, *The Diary of a Soviet Schoolgirl. 1932–1937*. Trans. Joanne Turnbull (Moscow: Glas Publishers, 2003), 141.

56. Rossman, *Worker Resistance*, 30, 51, 52, 33.

57. A famous example from émigré memoirs is Victor Kravchenko's father. *I Chose Freedom. The Personal and Political Life of a Soviet Official* (Bedfors Square: Robert Hale, 1947).

58. Examples abound in Rossman, *Worker Resistance*.

59. 'Platforma "Soiuza marksistov-lenintsev" ('gruppa Riutina')', *Izvestiia TsK KPSS*, no. 8 (1990): 165–207, quotation: 172.

60. Available at www.yale.edu/annals/siegelbaum/English_docs_/Siegelbaum_doc_9.htm (accessed 31 March 2005).

61. Rossman, *Worker Resistance*, 46.

62. Lugovskaya, *Diary, passim*; quotations: 41, 48.

63. Anatolii Zhigulin, 'Chernye kamni: Avtobiograficheskaia povest', *Znamia* 1988, no. 7: 10–75; no. 8: 48–119; Elena Zubkova, *Poslevoennoe sovetskoe obshchestvo: politika i povsednevnost' 1945–1953* (Moscow: Rosspen, 2000), 136–54; Juliane Fürst, 'Prisoners of the Soviet Self? Political Youth Opposition in Late Stalinism'. *Europe-Asia Studies* 54, no. 3 (2002): 353–75.

64. Kravchenko, *Freedom*, 168, 169; Lugovskaya, *Diary*, 130. For the history of student radicalism see Susan K. Morrissey, *Heralds of Revolution. Russian Students and the Mythologies of Radicalism.* (New York and Oxford: Oxford University Press, 1998).

65. Kravchenko, *Freedom*, 86–7, 105, 107–8, 132.

66. Garros et al., *Intimacy and Terror*, 11–58, quotation: 56. Cf. also Hellbeck, *Revolution on my mind*, 62–3.

67. Sheila Fitzpatrick, *Stalin's Peasants. Resistance and Survival in the Russian Village after Collectivization* (New York and Oxford: Oxford University Press, 1994), ch. 11.

68. Fitzpatrick, *Stalin's Peasants*, 288. Similarly: Stephan Merl, *Sozialer Aufstieg im sowjetischen Kolchossystem der 30er Jahre? Über das Schicksal der bäuerlichen Parteimitglieder, Dorsowjetvorsitzenden, Posteninhaber in Kolchosen, Mechanisatoren und Stachanowleute* (Berlin, Duncker & Humblot, 1990), 100–3.

69. OGPU report, 15 March 1931, *Tragediia sovetskoi derevni* vol. 2: 287–801, here 794–6.

70. Rossman, *Worker Resistance, passim*.

71. "Dokladnaia zapiska Sekretno-politicheskogo otdela OGPU o formakh i dinamike klassovoi bor'by v derevnve v 1930g.," (15 March 1931), *Tragediia sovetskoi derevni* vol.2: 287–801; here: 790.

72. Data for end of 1929. R. W. Davies, *The Socialist Offensive. The Collectivisation of Soviet Agriculture 1929–1930* (London: Macmillan, 1980), 54.

73. Gregory L. Freeze, 'The Stalinist Assault on the Parish, 1929–1941', in *Stalinismus vor dem Zweiten Weltkrieg: Neue Wege der Forschung*, ed. Manfred Hildermeier (Munich: Oldenbourg, 1998), 209–32, here: 212.

74. Data for 1929. Kate Brown, *A Biography of No Place. From Ethnic Borderland to Soviet Heartland* (Cambridge, MA.: Harvard University Press, 2003), 53, 252, fn. 2.

75. S. A. Smith, 'The First Soviet Generation: Children and Religious Belief in Soviet Russia, 1917–41', in *Generations in Twentieth-Century Europe*, ed. Stephen Lovell (Houndsmills, Basingstokes: Palgrave Macmillan, 2007), 79–100, here: 88.

76. Freeze, 'Stalinist Assault', *passim*.

77. Fitzpatrick, *Stalin's Peasants*, 204.

78. Edward E. Roslof, *Red Priests: Renovationism, Russian Orthodoxy, and Revolution, 1905–1946* (Bloomington: Indiana University Press, 2002), 185 (table 6.3).

79. Freeze, 'Stalinist Assault', 223.

80. N. B. Lebina, *Povsednevnaia zhizn' sovetskogo goroda: normy i anomalii 1920/1930 gody* (St Petersburg: Kikimora, 1999), 142.

81. Freeze, 'Assault', 213.

82. See Ch. 5.

83. Gabriel Temkin, *My Just War: The Memoir of a Jewish Red Army Soldier in World War II* (Navato: Presidio, 1998), 132.

84. Harvard Project on the Soviet Social System. Schedule A, vol. 23, case 470. Male, 37, Great Russian, engineer, p. 40.

85. Temkin, *My Just War*, 132.

86. Harvard Project on the Soviet Social System. Schedule A, vol. 5, case 56. Male, 36, Great Russian, Army officer, p. 36.

87. Memoirs of Archpriest A. Medvedskii, quoted in Tatiana A. Chumachenko, *Church and State in Soviet Russia. Russian Orthodoxy from World War II to the Khrushchev Years* (Armonk, New York, London: M. E. Sharpe, 2002), 195 fn. 4.

88. Chumachenko, *Church and State*; Zubkova, *Poslevoennoe sovetskoe obshchestvo*, 102–10; Daniel Peris, '"God Is Now on Our Side": The Religious Revival on Unoccupied Soviet Territory During World War II', *Kritika: Explorations in Russian and Eurasian History* 1, no. 1 (2000): 97–118; Karel C. Berkhoff, 'Was There a Religious Revival in Soviet Ukraine under the Nazi Regime?', *The Slavonic and East European Review* 78, no. 3 (2000): 536–67; Weiner, *Making Sense of War*, 309–13.

89. Mark Edele, *Soviet Veterans of the Second World War. A Popular Movement in an Authoritarian Society, 1941–1991* (Oxford: Oxford University Press, 2008), 64–70.

90. For a group which consciously tried to escape the dichotomy between 'religion' and 'Bolshevism' see Roslof, *Red Priests*.

91. Michail V. Skarovskij, 'Die russische Kirche unter Stalin in den 20er und 30 Jahren des 20. Jahrhunderts', in *Stalinismus vor dem Zweiten Weltkrieg: Neue Wege der Forschung*, ed. Manfred Hildermeier (Munich: Oldenbourg, 1998), 233–53, here: 241.

92. Peris, 'God is now on our side', 103; Juliane Fürst, 'Not a Question of Faith—Youth and Religion in the Post-War Years', *Jahrbücher für Geschichte Osteuropas* 52, no. 4 (2004): 557–70, here: 562–6, here: 569.

93. William B. Husband, *'Godless Communists'. Atheism and Society in Soviet Russia 1917–1932* (DeKalb: Northern Illinoi University Press, 2000). 'Hedging cosmological bets' is his term, cf. 118–24.

94. This view goes back, at the very least, to the Harvard Interview Project. See, e.g. H. Kent Geiger, *The Family in Soviet Russia* (Cambridge, MA.: Harvard University Press, 1968), 132; 310–11; Inkeles and Bauer, *The Soviet Citizen*, 380–1.

95. Roslof, *Red Priests*, 200.

96. Already the classics of Soviet social history knew this well: Merle Fainsod, *Smolensk under Soviet Rule* (New York: Vintage Books, 1958), 437–40.
97. Cf. Smith, 'The First Soviet Generation', esp. 96. For an introduction into the world of Russian demons, sprites, and other spirits see T. A. Novichkova, (ed.), *Russkii demonologicheskii slovar'* (St Petersburg: Peterburgskii pisatel', 1995).
98. Fürst, 'Not a question of Faith', 560.
99. On the state religion's deficiencies see Geoffrey Hosking, *A History of the Soviet Union 1917–1991*. Final edition (London: Fontana Press, 1992), 221. On the centrality of death and grief in the Soviet experience see Nina Tumarkin, *The Living & the Dead. The Rise and Fall of the Cult of World War II in Russia* (New York: BasicBooks, 1994); Catherine Merridale, *Night of Stone. Death and Memory in Russia* (London: Granta Books, 2000).
100. Harvard Project on the Soviet Social System. Schedule A, vol. 27, Case 522. Male, 38, Great Russian, radio technician, p. 13.
101. Ibid., vol. 15, Case 284. Male, 35, Ukrainian, movie operator, p. 30.
102. Ibid., vol. 11, Case 142. Male, 27, Belorussian, elementary school teacher, p. 22.
103. Vera Ivanovna Malakhova, 'Four Years as a Frontline Physician', in *A Revolution of Their Own. Voices of Women in Soviet History*, eds. Barbara Alpern Engel and Anastasia Posadskaya-Vanderbeck (Westview Press, 1998), 175–218, here: 182–3. The quotation in brackets is from Freeze, 'Stalinist Assault', 216.
104. Harvard Project on the Soviet Social System. Schedule A, vol. 16, Case 323. Male, 33, Ukrainian, doctor, pp. 18–19.
105. Ibid., vol. 11, Case 139. Female, 64, Great Russian, doctor, p. 16.
106. Heather J. Coleman, 'Becoming a Russian Baptist: Conversion Narratives and Social Experience', *Russian Review* 61, no. 1 (2002): 94–112, here: 95.
107. Ethel Dunn and Stephen D. Dunn, 'Religion as an Instrument of Culture Change: The Problem of the Sects in the Soviet Union', *Slavic Review* 23, no. 3 (1964): 459–78. For a detailed study of the Baptists before Stalin's first revolution from above see Heather J. Coleman, *Russian Baptists and spiritual revolution, 1905–1929* (Bloomington: Indiana University Press, 2005).
108. Freeze, 'Stalinist Assault', 210–12.
109. Coleman, 'Becoming a Russian Baptist', 95.
110. For an example from 1933 see Harvard Project on the Soviet Social System, schedule vol. 28, case 537. Male, 26, Ukrainian, chauffeur, p. 32; on the post-war years see Fürst, 'Not a question of faith', 567.

III. Fürst, 'Not a question of Faith', 560.

112. Edele, *Soviet Veterans*, 70, 245 fn. 93.

113. Dunn, 'Religion as an Instrument of Culture Change', 474–5.

114. Zhiromskaia, *Polveka pod grifom*, 99.

115. Edele, *Soviet Veterans*, 70; Walter Kolarz, *Religion in the Soviet Union* (New York: St Martin's Press, 1961), 363–5; Nadieszda Kizenko, *A Prodigal Saint. Father John of Kronstadt and the Russian People* (University Park: The Pennsylvania State University Press, 2000).

116. Roslof, *Red Priests*, 190–4; Corley, *Religion in the Soviet Union*, ch. 5. Steven Merritt Miner, *Stalin's Holy War. Religion, Nationalism, and Alliance Politics, 1941–1945* (Chapel Hill and London: The University of North Carolina Press, 2003). For a short history of the Witnesses, who were soon spread through of deportation all over the USSR, see Christel Lane, *Christian Religion in the Soviet Union. A Sociological Study* (London: Allen & Unwin, 1978), 185–7.

117. Fürst, 'Not a question of Faith', 559–62; Chumachenko, *Church and State*, ch. 2.

118. Katrin Boeckh, *Stalinismus in der Ukraine. Die Rekonstruktion des sowjetischen Systems nach dem Zweiten Weltkrieg* (Wiesbaden: Harrassowitz Verlag, 2007), 475–531; Corley, *Religion in the Soviet Union*, 152–3.

119. OGPU report, 4 August 1927, in: *Tragediia sovetskoi derevni*, vol. 1: 84–5.

120. Fitzpatrick, *Stalin's Peasants*, 6, 288.

121. Kelly, *Comrade Pavlik*, 67.

122. Fitzpatrick, *Stalin's Peasants*, 67–8.

123. Wendy Z. Goldman, *Terror and Democracy in the Age of Stalin. The Social Dynamics of Repression* (Cambridge and New York: Cambridge University Press, 2007), 27.

124. Viola, *Peasant Rebels*, 57–8.

125. Fitzpatrick, *Stalin's Peasants*, 289.

126. Report to Ezhov, 3 April 1938, in *Tragediia Sovetskoi derevni*, vol. 5.2, 87–9, here: 88. For more striking quotations from 1937 and 1938 see also Fitzpatrick, *Stalin's Peasants*, 293–4; and NKVD report to Ezhov, 7 August 1938, in *Tragediia Sovetskoi derevni*, vol. 5.2: 187.

127. *Tragediia sovetskoi derevni*, vol. 5.1: 115.

128. NKVD report, 8 January 1937, *Tragediia sovetskoi derevni*, vol. 5.1: 81–3, here: 82.

129. NKVD report, late 1938, *Tragediia sovetskoi derevni*, vol. 5.1: 252–6, here 256.

130. Barber, 'Popular Reactions', 13.
131. Review file on anti-Soviet agitation GARF f. A–461, op. 1, d. 1887, l. 9.
132. Ibid., 152, l. 8.
133. Viola, *Peasant Rebels*, 58; Fitzpatrick, *Stalin's Peasants*, 67; 287–96, esp. 293–4. Sarah Davies, *Popular Opinion in Stalin's Russia. Terror, Propaganda, and Dissent, 1934–1941* (Cambridge and New York: Cambridge University Press, 1997).
134. For a systematic analysis of the citizens' 'information system' see Inkeles and Bauer, *The Soviet Citizen*, ch. 7.
135. Inkeles and Bauer, *The Soviet Citizen*, 183.
136. Bauer, Inkeles, and Kluckhohn, *How the Soviet System Works*, 29–35; Inkeles and Bauer, *The Soviet Citizen*, 159–88.
137. Jan T. Gross, *Revolution from Abroad. The Soviet Conquest of Poland's Western Ukraine and Western Belorussia*, expanded edn. (Princeton and Oxford: Princeton University Press, 2002), 45–50.
138. Norman Naimark, *The Russians in Germany. A History of the Soviet Zone of Occupation, 1945–1949* (Cambridge, MA, and London: The Belknap Press of Harvard University Press, 1995), 78. For another example see Antony Beevor, *The Fall of Berlin 1945* (New York: Penguin, 2003), 34.
139. Barber, 'Popular Reactions', quotations 10, 12. On shooting commissars followed by desertion see Karel C. Berkhoff, *Harvest of Despair. Life and Death in Ukraine under Nazi Rule* (Cambridge and London: The Belknap Press of Harvard University Press, 2004), 12–13.
140. Barber, 'Popular Reactions', 12.
141. Lewis Siegelbaum and Andrei Sokolov (eds.), *Stalinism as a Way of Life. Abridged Edition* (New Haven and London: Yale University Press, 2004), 5.
142. For a suggestive reconstruction of the international space of experience and expectation of the interwar years see Stephen Kotkin, 'Modern Times: The Soviet Union and the Interwar Conjuncture', *Kritika: Explorations in Russian and Eurasian History* 2, no. 1 (2001): 111–64.
143. Orlando Figes, *The Whisperers. Private Life in Stalin's Russia* (New York: Metropolitan Books, 2007), p. xxxviii, 56–64, 503. See also Matthew Rendle, 'The Problems of "Becoming Soviet": Former Nobles in Soviet Society, 1917–41', *European History Quarterly* 38, no. 7 (2008): 7–33.
144. For a famous literary representation of this logic see Arthur Koestler, *Darkness at Noon* (New York, Toronto, London, Sydney, Auckland: Bantam Books, 1968). An in-depth study of this phenomenon is Hellbeck, *Revolution on my mind*.

145. Kolakowski, *Main Currents*, vol. 3: 4.
146. Rossman, *Worker Resistance*, 76–7.
147. Ibid., 63.
148. G. F. Achimov, 'The Second Soviet Generation', *Problems of Communism*, 1 (1952), 12. Percentage calculated from 1937 census data. Iu. A. Poliakov (ed.), *Vsesoiuznaia perepis' naseleniia 1937 g. Kratkie itogi* (Moscow: Akademiia nauk SSSR, 1991), 78, 81.
149. Achimov, 'The Second Soviet Generation', 13–14.
150. Klaus-Georg Riegel, *Konfessionsrituale im Marxismus-Leninismus* (Graz, Vienna, and Cologne: Styria, 1985); and Oleg Kharkhordin, *The Collective and the Individual in Russia. A Study of Practices* (Berkeley, Los Angeles, London: University of California Press, 1999), ch. 4.
151. Kharkhordin, *The Collective and the Individual*; Hellbeck, *Revolution on my mind.*
152. Harvard Project on the Soviet Social System. Schedule A, vol. 4, Case 31. Male, 35, Great Russian, author and journalist, p. 30.
153. Transcript of taped conversation, sent on 3 January 1947 by Abakumov to Stalin, reprinted in *Georgii Zhukov. Dokumenty*, 641–3, here: 642–3.

Chapter 7

1. For example: Poster by Nina Vatolina, 1950, reproduced as fig. 6.13 in Victoria Bonnell, *Iconography of Power. Soviet Political Posters under Lenin and Stalin* (Berkeley, Los Angeles, and London: University of California Press, 1997), 277. For an analysis of the regime's discourse of gift giving see Jeffrey Brooks, *Thank You Comrade Stalin! Soviet Public Culture from Revolution to Cold War* (Princeton, NJ: Princeton University Press, 2000).
2. Victor Kravchenko, *I Chose Freedom. The Personal and Political Life of a Soviet Official* (Bedfors Square: Robert Hale, 1947), 316.
3. Sheila Fitzpatrick, *Education and Social Mobility in the Soviet Union 1921–1934* (Cambridge, London, New York, and Melbourne: Cambridge University Press, 1979); id., 'Stalin and the Making of a New Elite', in her *The Cultural Front. Power and Culture in Revolutionary Russia* (Ithaca and London: Cornell University Press, 1992), 149–82; and R. W. Davies, Oleg V. Khlevniuk and E. A. Rees (eds.), *The Stalin-Kaganovich Correspondence 1931–36* (New Haven and London: Yale University Press, 2003), 31-2 (quotation).
4. Evan Mawdsley and Stephen White. *The Soviet Elite from Lenin to Gorbachev. The Central Committee and Its Members, 1917–1991* (Oxford and New York: Oxford University Press, 2000), esp. chs. 2, 3, 8.

5. Mawdsley and White, *The Soviet Elite*, 82.
6. John D. Nagle, 'A New Look at the Soviet Elite: A Generational Model of the Soviet System', *Journal of Political & Military Sociology* 3, no. 1 (1975); Eric Duskin, *Stalinist Reconstruction and the Confirmation of a New Elite, 1945–1953* (New York: Palgrave, 2001); Mark Edele, *Soviet Veterans of the Second World War. A Popular Movement in an Authoritarian Society, 1941–1991* (Oxford: Oxford University Press, 2008), ch. 6.
7. Mary Buckley, *Mobilizing Soviet Peasants. Heroines and Heroes of Stalin's Fields* (Lanham: Rowman & Littlefield Publishers, 2006), 299.
8. Stalin's speech to the Central Committee Plenum, 3 March 1937, reprinted in *Voprosy istorii* no. 3 (1995): 3–15, here: 14.
9. V. B. Zhiromskaia and Iu. A. Poliakov (eds.), *Vsesoiuznaia perepis' naseleniia 1937 goda: Obshchie itogi* (Moscow: Rosspen, 2007), 136–9; 47 for the total population.
10. Fitzpatrick, *Education and Social Mobility*, 241.
11. Stephan Merl, *Sozialer Aufstieg im sowjetischen Kolchossystem der 30er Jahre? Über das Schicksal bäuerlicher Parteimitglieder, Dorfsozjetvorsitzenden, Posteninhaber in Kolchosen, Mechanisatoren und Stachanowleute* (Berlin: Duncker & Humblot, 1990), 22, 68.
12. J. Arch Getty, Oleg V. Naumov, and Nadezhda V. Muraveva, *Yezhov. The Rise of Stalin's 'Iron Fist'* (New Haven and London: Yale University Press, 2008); Loren R. Graham, *The Ghost of the Executed Engineer. Technology and the Fall of the Soviet Union* (Cambridge and London: Harvard University Press, 1993); Kees Boterbloem, *The Life and Times of Andrei Zhdanov, 1896–1948* (Montreal: McGill-Queen's University Press, 2004).
13. Reginald Zelnik (ed.), *A Radical Worker in Tsarist Russia. The Autobiography of Semen Ivanovich Kanatchikov* (Stanford: Stanford University Press, 1986).
14. William Taubman, *Khrushchev. The Man and His Era* (New York and London: W. W. Norton & Co., 2003).
15. Yuri Slezkine, *The Jewish Century* (Princeton, NJ: Princeton University Press, 2004).
16. Jochen Hellbeck (ed.), *Tagebuch Aus Moskau 1931–1939* (Munich: dtv, 1996); see also the analysis in id., 'Fashioning the Stalinist Soul: The Diary of Stepan Podlubnyi (1931–1939)', *Jahrbücher für Geschichte Osteuropas* 44 (1996): 344–75; and id., *Revolution on My Mind. Writing a Diary under Stalin* (Cambridge, MA. and London: Harvard University Press, 2006), ch. 5.

17. Fitzpatrick, 'Stalin and the Making of a New Elite', 180 and *passim*; Fitzpatrick, *Education and Social Mobility*, passim (187–8 for the number of promotees); Stalin quotation: *Voprosy istorii* no. 3 (1995), 14. For a similar interpretation of Stalin's remarks see Oleg Khlevniuk, *Master of the House. Stalin and His Inner Circle* (New Haven and London: Yale University Press, 2009), 172. On the Great Terror as 'Russia's second elite revolution' see also Mawdsley and White, *The Soviet Elite*, 280–1.

18. The two most famous Marxist interpretations of this phenomenon are Nicholas Timasheff, *The Great Retreat: The Growth and Decline of Communism in Russia, 1886–1970* (New York: E. P. Dutton, 1946); and Leon Trotsky, *The Revolution Betrayed. What Is the Soviet Union and Where Is It Going?* (New York, London, Montreal, Sydney: Pathfinder, 1972). See also Milovan Djilas, *The New Class: An Analysis of the Communist System* (New York: Praeger, 1957). For the non-Marxist interpretations followed here see Fitzpatrick, *Education and Social Mobility*, ch. 11; id., *The Russian Revolution*. 3rd edn. (Oxford and New York: Oxford University Press, 2008), ch. 6 ('revolution accomplished'); Yuri Slezkine, *Arctic Mirrors. Russia and the Small Peoples of the North* (Ithaca and London: Cornell University Press, 1994), 219–46; and David L. Hoffmann, *Stalinist Values. The Cultural Norms of Soviet Modernity, 1917–1941* (Ithaca and London: Cornell University Press, 2003), ch. 2.

19. Catriona Kelly, *Refining Russia. Advice Literature, Polite Culture, & Gender from Catherine to Yeltsin* (Oxford and New York: Oxford University Press, 2001), 283–4.

20. Vadim Volkov, 'The Concept of Kul'turnost': Notes on the Stalinist Civilizing Process', in *Stalinism. New Directions*, ed. Sheila Fitzpatrick (London and New York: Routledge, 2000), 210–30, here: 224 for the quiz); Kelly, *Refining Russia*, ch. 4. The classical study of the new elite's culture is Vera S. Dunham, *In Stalin's Time. Middleclass Values in Soviet Fiction*, enlarged and updated edn. (Durham and London: Duke University Press, 1990). See also Sheila Fitzpatrick, 'Becoming Cultured: Socialist Realism and the Representation of Privilege and Taste', in *The Cultural Front*, 216–37.

21. Oskar Maria Graf, *Reise in die Sowjetunion 1934* (Hamburg: Luchterhand, 1992), 25–6, 28.

22. Andreas Kappeler, *Russland als Vielvölkerreich. Entstehung. Geschichte. Zerfall* (Munich: C. H. Beck, 1993). For a succinct summary of the history of nationalism see R. J. B. Bosworth, *Nationalism* (London: Pearson Longman, 2007). For more on nationalism see also Ch. 6.

23. Kate Brown, *A Biography of No Place. From Ethnic Borderland to Soviet Heartland* (Cambridge, Mass.: Harvard University Press, 2003).

24. Yuri Slezkine, 'The Soviet Union as a Communal Apartment, or How a Socialist State Promoted Ethnic Particularism'. *Slavic Review* 53, no. 2 (1994): 415–52, here: 415.

25. V. I. Lenin, *Collected Works vol. 29 (March–August 1919)* (London: Lawrence and Wishart, 1965), 127.

26. Slezkine, *Arctic Mirrors*, 221–5, quotation: 222.

27. Terry Martin, *The Affirmative Action Empire. Nations and Nationalism in the Soviet Union, 1923–1939* (Ithaca and London: Cornell University Press, 2001), 373–6.

28. T. H. Rigby, *Communist Party Membership in the USSR 1917–1967* (Princeton, NJ: Princeton University Press, 1968), 372.

29. Martin, *Affirmative Action Empire*, 381, table 33. See also tables 34, 35, 36.

30. Ibid., 383–7; quotation: 385.

31. Mawdsley and White, *The Soviet Elite*, 54, 108, 249–50, 245 table 7.1, 248 table 7.2.

32. Martin, *Affirmative Action Empire*, 344.

33. Terry Martin, 'The Origins of Soviet Ethnic Cleansing', *The Journal of Modern History* 70, no. 4 (1998): 813–61.

34. David Brandenberger, *National Bolshevism: Stalinist Mass Culture and the Formation of Modern Russian National Identity, 1931–1956* (Cambridge and London: Harvard University Press, 2002).

35. Amir Weiner, *Making Sense of War. The Second World War and the Fate of the Bolshevik Revolution* (Princeton and Oxford: Princeton University Press, 2001).

36. Martin, *Affirmative Action Empire*, ch. 9. See also N. L. Pobol' and P. M. Polian (eds.), *Stalinskie Deportatsii 1928–1953* (Moscow: Demokratiia, 2005).

37. Sheila Fitzpatrick and Yuri Slezkine (eds.), *In the Shadow of Revolution. Life Stories of Russian Women. From 1917 to the Second World War* (Princeton, NJ: Princeton University Press, 2000), 340–1.

38. Gregory J. Massell, *The Surrogate Proletariat: Moslem Women and Revolutionary Strategies in Soviet Central Asia, 1919–1929* (Princeton NJ: Princeton University Press, 1974); Douglas Northrop, *Veiled Empire. Gender & Power in Stalinist Central Asia* (Ithaca and London: Cornell University Press, 2004); Matt F. Oja, 'From *Krestianka* to *Udarnitsa*. Rural Women and the *Vydvizhenie* Campaign, 1933–1941'. *The Carl Beck Papers in Russian & East European Studies* 1203 (1996). On women's riots see Lynne Viola,

Peasant Rebels under Stalin. Collectivization and the Culture of Peasant Resistance (New York and Oxford: Oxford University Press, 1996), ch. 6. On women in the North see Slezkine, *Arctic Mirrors*, 231–6.

39. Lewis Siegelbaum and Andrei Sokolov (eds.), *Stalinism as a Way of Life. Abridged edition* (New Haven and London: Yale University Press, 2004), 250, 251, 252.

40. Fitzpatrick and Slezkine, *In the Shadow of Revolution*, 336.

41. Siegelbaum, *Stalinism as a Way of Life*, 18–19.

42. Pasha Angelina, 'The Most Important Thing', (1948), reprinted in *In the Shadow of Revolution*, 305–21.

43. Mawdsley and White, *The Soviet Elite*, 109.

44. Angelina, 'The Most Important Thing', 318.

45. Northrop, *Veiled Empire*, 95–6; 258–64; Shoshana Keller, 'Trapped between State and Society: Women's Liberation and Islam in Soviet Uzbekistan, 1926–1941', *Journal of Women's History* 10, no. 1 (1998): 20–44.

46. NKVD report on 'terrorist and other counter-revolutionary occurrences in the village' (10 July 1938), reprinted in *Tragediia sovetskoi derevni*, vol. 5.2: 166–8, here: 167.

47. NKVD report on 'terrorist and other counter-revolutionary occurrences in the village' (22 June 1938), reprinted in *Tragediia sovetskoi derevni*, vol. 5.2: 135–7, here: 135–6.

48. Roberta T. Manning, 'Women in the Soviet Countryside on the Eve of World War II, 1935–1940', in *Russian Peasant Women*, eds. Beatrice Farnsworth and Lynne Viola (Oxford: Oxford University Press, 1992), 206–35, here: 225; Merl, *Sozialer Aufstieg*, 221–3.

49. Mary Buckley, 'Why be a shock worker or a Stakhanovite?', in *Women in Russia and Ukraine*, ed. Rosalind Marsh (Cambridge: Cambridge University Press, 1996), 199–213, here: 201–5.

50. Northrop, *Veiled Empire*, 91.

51. Buckley, *Mobilizing*, ch. 10.

52. Manning, 'Women in the Soviet Countryside', 222.

53. Fitzpatrick and Slezkine, *In the Shadow of Revolution*, 336.

54. R. W. Davies, *Crisis and Progress in the Soviet Economy 1931–1933* (London, Basingstoke: Macmillan, 1996), 443.

55. Barbara Evans Clements, 'Later Developments: Trends in Soviet Women's History, 1930 to the Present', in: *Russia's Women. Accommodation, Resistance, Transformation* eds. Barbara Evans Clements, Barbara Alpern Engel, and Christine D. Worobec (Berkeley: University of California Press, 1991), 267–78, here: 270.

56. See the example of Niusia, Elena Bonner's nanny. Jelena Bonner, *Mütter und Töchter. Erinnerungen an meine Jugend 1923 bis 1945* (Munich: Piper, 1992), 1–149, for her life as an officer's wife: 146–9; on her family background: 129–30.

57. Manning, 'Women in the Soviet Countryside', 225–6.

58. Susanne Conze, 'Weder Emanzipation noch Tradition. Stalinistische Frauenpolitik in den vierziger Jahren', in: *Stalinismus. Neue Forschungen und Konzepte*, ed. Stefan Plaggenborg (Berlin: Arno Spitz, 1998), 293–320; id., *Sowjetische Industriearbeiterinnen in den vierziger Jahren. Die Auswirkungen des Zweiten Weltkrieges auf die Erwerbstätigkeit von Frauen in der UdSSR, 1941–1950* (Stuttgart: Franz Steiner Verlag, 2001); Wendy Z. Goldman, *Women at the Gates. Gender and Industry in Stalin's Russia* (Cambridge: Cambridge University Press, 2002). Statistics from: *Zhenshchiny i deti v SSSR. Statisticheskii sbornik*, 2nd edn. (Moscow: Gosstatizdat, 1963), 100.

59. Northrop, *Veiled Empire*.

60. Manning, 'Women in the Soviet Countryside', 226.

61. Sheila Fitzpatrick, *Everyday Stalinism. Ordinary Life in Extraordinary Times: Soviet Russia in the 1930s* (New York and Oxford: Oxford University Press, 1999), 145.

62. Cf. Edele, *Soviet Veterans*, 71–4; and Mie Nakachi, 'Population, Politics and Reproduction: Late Stalinism and Its Legacy', in *Late Stalinist Russia. Society between Reconstruction and Reinvention*, ed. Juliane Fürst (London and New York: Routledge, 2006), 167–91.

63. Anna Krylova, 'Stalinist Identity from the Viewpoint of Gender: Rearing a Generation of Professionally Violent Women-Fighters in 1930s Stalinist Russia', *Gender & History* 16, no. 3 (2004): 626–53.

64. There is a growing literature, largely in article form, on women in the Red Army and their return to post-war life. For a classic see K. J. Cottam, 'Soviet Women in Combat During World War II: The Rear Services, Partisans and Political Workers', *Soviet Armed Forces Review Annual* 5 (1981): 275–94. Most recently, see: Euridice Cardona and Roger D. Markwick, '"Our Brigade Will Not Be Sent to the Front": Soviet Women under Arms in the Great Fatherland War, 1941–45', *Russian Review* 68 (2009): 240–62. For book-length studies see Svetlana Aleksievich, *U voiny—ne zhenskoe litso* (Moscow: Sovetskii pisatel', 1987); Reina Pennington, *Wings, Women, and War. Soviet Airwomen in World War II Combat* (Lawrence: University Press of Kansas, 2001); and Anna Krylova, *Soviet Women in Combat. A History of Violence on the Eastern Front*

(Cambridge: Cambridge University Press, 2010). For a discussion of their post-war fate see also Edele, *Soviet Veterans*, 73–8, 143–7.

65. *Constitution (Fundamental Law) of the Union of Soviet Socialist Republics* (Moscow, 1938), 104, as quoted in *Russia's Women* ed. Clements, Engel, Worobec, 268.

66. Merl, *Sozialer Aufstieg*, 133–4. See also Sheila Fitzpatrick, *Stalin's Peasants. Resistance and Survival in the Russian Village after Collectivization* (New York and Oxford: Oxford University Press, 1994), 181–3.

67. Oja, 'From *krestianka* to *udarnitsa*,' 34–5.

68. Merl, *Sozialer Aufstieg*, 132–40; 182–8. 'Triple burden' is Esta Kingston-Mann's term. See her 'Transforming Peasants in the Twentieth Century: Dilemmas of Russian, Soviet and Post-Soviet Development', in *The Cambridge History of Russia. Vol. III: The Twentieth Century*, ed. Ronald G. Suny (Cambridge: Cambridge University Press, 2006), 411–39.

69. Andrei Markevich, 'Soviet Urban Households and the Road to Universal Employment, from the End of the 1930s to the End of the 1960s', *Continuity and Change* 20, no. 3 (2005): 443–73, esp. 452–5. See also Greta Bucher, 'Struggling to Survive: Soviet Women in the Postwar Years', *Journal of Women's History* 12, no. 1 (2000): 137–59; and id., *Women, the Bureaucracy and Daily Life in Postwar Moscow, 1945–1953* (Boulder: East European Monographs, 2006).

70. Davies, *Crisis and Progress*, 108–10.

71. H. Kent Geiger, *The Family in Soviet Russia* (Cambridge, MA: Harvard University Press, 1968), 151–2.

72. Donald Filtzer, 'Standard of living versus quality of life: struggling with the urban environment in Russia during the early years of post-war reconstruction', in *Late Stalinist Russia*, 81–102; Kotkin, *Magnetic Mountain*, ch. 4, exp. 176–7; Fitzpatrick, *Everyday Stalinism*, 50–3; Timothy J. Colton, *Moscow. Governing the Socialist Metropolis* (Cambridge and London: Belknap Press, 1995), 339–51.

73. Programmatic on the Soviet welfare state see Stephen Kotkin, 'Modern Times: The Soviet Union and the Interwar Conjuncture', *Kritika: Explorations in Russian and Eurasian History* 2, no. 1 (2001): 111–64.

74. L. S. Rogachevskaia, Ia. E. Vodarskii, V. M. Kabuzan, 'Naselenie rossii v nachale XX veka', in *Naselenie Rossii v XX veke. Istoricheskie ocherki*, ed. V. B. Zhiromskaia, vol. 1: 7–30, here: 23; V. B. Zhiromskaia and Iu. A. Poliakov (eds.), *Vsesoiuznaia perepis' naseleniia 1937 goda: obshchie itogi. Sbornik dokumentov i materialov* (Moscow: Rosspen, 2007), 112. On the

comparability of different censuses see Ronald D. Libowitz, 'Education and Literacy Data in Russian and Soviet Censuses', *Research Guide to the Russian and Soviet Censuses*, ed. Ralph S. Clem (Ithaca and London: Cornell University Press, 1986), 155–70, esp. 167. See also L. S. Rogachevskaia, 'Gramotnost' i obrazovatel'nyi uroven' naseleniia Rossii v 1940–1950-e gg'., in *Naselenie Rossii v XX veke. Istoricheskie ocherki*, vol. 2: 312–41.

75. Christopher Burton, 'Medical Welfare During Late Stalinism. A Study of Doctors and the Soviet Health System, 1945–53'. Ph.D. diss, The University of Chicago, 2000, esp. the historical overview of the health system in ch. 1; quotation: 1; Michael Z. David, 'The White Plague in the Red Capital: The Control of Tuberculosis in Russia, 1900–1941'. PhD diss. (University of Chicago, 2007). On pharmaceuticals and traditional medicine see Mary Schaffer Conroy, *Medicines for the Soviet Masses During World War II* (Lanham: University Press of America, 2008).

76. Bernice Q. Madison, *Social Welfare in the Soviet Union* (Stanford, CA: Stanford University Press, 1968); Dorena Caroli, 'Bolshevism, Stalinism, and Social Welfare (1917–1936)', *International Review of Social History* 48 (2003): 27–54; Beate Fieseler, 'The Bitter Legacy of the "Great Patriotic War." Red Army Disabled Soldiers under Late Stalinism', in: *Late Stalinist Russia*, 46–61; and Edele, *Soviet Veterans of the Second World War*, ch. 4.

77. Fitzpatrick, *Everyday Stalinism*, ch. 4; Elena Osokina, *Our Daily Bread. Socialist Distribution and the Art of Survival in Stalin's Russia, 1927–1941* (Armonk, New York, London: M. E. Sharpe, 2001); Jukka Gronow, *Caviar with Champagne. Common Luxury and the Ideals of the Good Life in Stalin's Russia* (Oxford, New York: Berg, 2003). On the hierarchy of distribution in the factories and the steep stratification within the factories see Goldman, *Terror and Democracy*, 31–3; Jeffrey Rossman, *Worker Resistance under Stalin. Class and Revolution on the Shop Floor* (Cambridge and London: Harvard University Press, 2005), 59; and Kravchenko, *I Chose Freedom*, 174. On the fine gradations of the elite's privileges see ibid. 393–4. On stakhanovite privileges see Robert Maier, *Die Stachanov-Bewegung 1935–1938. Der Stachanovismus als tragendes und verschärfendes Moment der Stalinisierung der sowjetischen Gesellschaft* (Stuttgart: Franz Steiner Verlag, 1990), 130–46.

78. Naum Jasny, *Soviet Industrialization, 1928–1952* (Chicago: University of Chicago Press, 1961), 119–76, quotations: 120, 177; Roberta Manning, 'The Soviet Economic Crisis of 1936–1940 and the Great Purges', in *Stalinist*

Terror. New Perspectives, eds. J. Arch Getty and Roberta T. Manning (Cambridge and New York: Cambridge University Press, 1993), 116–41; Khlevniuk, *Master in the House*, 136 (quotation); Hoffmann, *Stalinist Values*, ch. 4, esp. 145; Osokina, *Our Daily Bread*, ch. 9.

79. Elena Zubkova, *Russia After the War. Hopes, Illusions, and Disappointments, 1945–1957* (Armonk and London: M. E. Sharpe, 1998); Michael Ellman and S. Maksudov, 'Soviet Deaths in the Great Patriotic War: A Note', *Europe-Asia Studies* 46, no. 4 (1994): 671–80; A. I. Barsukov et al. (eds.), *Velikaia Otechestvennaia voina 1941–1945. Vol. 4: Narod i voina* (Moscow: Nauka, 1999), 289, 294; Fürst (ed.), *Late Stalinist Russia*, esp. essays by Donald Filtzer and Beate Fieseler.

80. Vladislav Zubok and Constantine Plashakov, *Inside the Kremlin's Cold War. From Stalin to Khrushchev* (Cambridge, MA: Harvard University Press, 1996), 46; Aleksandr V. Pyzhikov, 'Sovetskoe poslevoennoe obshchestvo i predposylki khrushchevskikh reform', *Voprosy istorii*, no. 2 (2002): 33–43, esp. 34; Alec Nove, *An Economic History of the USSR 1917–1991*, new and final edn. (London: Penguin, 1992), 300; P. Charles Hachten, 'Property Relations and the Economic Organization of Soviet Russia, 1941–1948'. PhD diss., The University of Chicago, 2005, 478; Elena Zubkova, 'The Soviet Regime and Soviet Society in the Postwar Years: Innovations and Conservatism, 1945–1953', *Journal of Modern European History* 2, no. 1 (2004): 144–5, esp. 147-8; A. A. Danilov and A. V. Pyzhikov, *Rozhdenie sverkhderzhavy. SSSR v pervye poslevoennye gody* (Moscow: Rosspen, 2001), 103; John Gaddis, *We Now Know. Rethinking Cold War History* (Oxford and New York: Oxford University Press, 1997), 55; Yoram Gorlizki and Oleg Khlevniuk, *Cold Peace. Stalin and the Soviet Ruling Circle, 1945–1953* (Oxford and New York: Oxford University Press, 2004), 97–9.

81. Geiger, *The Family in Soviet Russia*, 248.

82. Fitzpatrick, *Everyday Stalinism*, 44; Lars T. Lih, Oleg V. Naumov and Oleg V. Khlevniuk (eds.), *Stalin's Letters to Molotov 1925–1936* (New Haven and London: Yale University Press, 1995), 209.

83. Julie Hessler, *A Social History of Soviet Trade. Trade Policy, Retail Practices, and Consumption, 1917–1953* (Princeton and Oxford: Princeton University Press, 2004), 164–5.

84. The ration varied between 50 and 200 grams, depending on the period of the war, whether the unit was engaged in frontline operations or stationed behind the lines, and whether or not it had distinguished itself in battle. See David M. Glantz, *Colossus Reborn. The Red Army at War, 1941–1943* (Lawrence: University Press of Kansas, 2005), 557–60.

85. Michel Gordey, *Visa to Moscow* (New York: Alfred A. Knopf, 1952), 36–7.
86. Harrison E. Salisbury, 'Russia Re-Visited: Crime Wave Goes Unchecked. Violence, Drunkenness and Graft Plague Communist Ruled Country', *The New York Times* Oct. 1, 1954, 25.
87. For an example see Bonner, *Mütter und Töchter*, 91, 234–6.
88. Richard Stites, *Russian Popular Culture. Entertainment and Society since 1900* (Cambride: Cambridge University Press, 1994), 64–97, 124–6; Katerina Clark, *The Soviet Novel. History as Ritual.* 3rd edn. (Bloomington and Indianapolis: Indiana University Press, 2000); Sarah Davies, 'Stalin as patron of cinema: creating Soviet mass culture, 1932–1936', in *Stalin. A New History*, eds. Sarah Davies and James Harris (Cambridge: Cambridge University Press, 2005), 202–25; Peter Kenez, *Cinema and Soviet Society, 1917–1953* (Cambridge: Cambridge University Press, 1992); Kiril Tomoff, *Creative Union: The Professional Organization of Soviet Composers, 1939–1953* (Ithaca: Cornell University Press, 2006); Irina Kondakova (ed.), '"Tarzan—chelovek ne isporchennyi burzhuaznoi tsivilizatsiei"', *Istochnik* no. 4 (1999): 99.
89. Robert Edelman, 'A Small Way of Saying "No": Moscow Working Men, Spartak Soccer, and the Communist Party, 1900–1945', *The American Historical Review* 107, no. 5 (2002): 1441–74.
90. Fitzpatrick, *Everyday Stalinism*, 54–8, 162.
91. Stites, *Russian Popular Culture*, 72–6, 118–19; S. Frederick Starr, *Red and Hot. The Fate of Jazz in the Soviet Union*, 3rd edn. (New York: Limelight Editions, 1994), chs. 5–11.
92. Elena Zubkova, *Poslevoennoe sovetskoe obshchestvo: politika i povsednevnost' 1945–1953* (Moscow: Rosspen, 2000), 151–4; and Mark Edele, 'Strange Young Men in Stalin's Moscow: The Birth and Life of the Stiliagi, 1945–1953', *Jahrbücher für Geschichte Osteuropas* 50, no. 1 (2002): 37–61.
93. M. I. Kalinin, 'Speech at a Conference of Best Urban and Rural Schoolteachers Convened by the Editorial Board of the Newspaper *Uchitelskaia gazeta*', (28 December 1938), in: id. *On Communist Education. Selected Speeches and Articles* (Moscow: Foreign Languages Publishing House, 1953), 63–94, here: 85–6.
94. I. Pikarevich, 'Why must Shukhov have a signet ring?', *Komsomolskaia pravda*, 13 April 1948, translated in Dorothea L. Meek, *Soviet Youth: Some Achievements and Problems* (London: Routledge & Kegan Paul, 1957), 171–2. For a different view about the stiliagi's social position, and for a discussion of the widespread preoccupation with the good life see Juliane

Fürst, 'The importance of being stylish: youth, culture and identity in late Stalinism', in: *Late Stalinist Russia*, 209–30; on the influence of the criminal underworld see ibid. 216–17 and Elena Zubkova, *Poslevoennoe sovetskoe obshchestvo: politika i povsednevnost' 1945–1953* (Moscow: Rosspen, 2000), 94. For the interwar years see *Outlaw. The Autobiography of a Soviet Waif. By Voinov* (London: Harvill Press, 1955), 158.

95. Vladimir Shlapentokh, *Public and Private Life of the Soviet People. Changing Values in Post-Stalin Russia* (New York and Oxford: Oxford University Press, 1989); James R. Millar, 'The Little Deal: Brezhnev's Contribution to Acquisitive Socialism', *Slavic Review* 44, no. 4 (1985): 694–706; and Mark Edele, 'The Impact of War and the Costs of Superpower Status', in *Oxford Handbook for Russian History*, (Oxford University Press, forthcoming).

Chapter 8

1. James Heinzen, 'Informers and the State under Late Stalinism. Informant Networks and Crimes against "Socialist Property", 1940–53', *Kritika: Explorations in Russian and Eurasian History* 8, no. 4 (2007): 789–815, here: 812.

2. Speech celebrating the 26th anniversary of the Great Socialist October Revolution, Moscow, 6 November 1943, reprinted in I. Stalin, *O Velikoi Otechestvennoi voine Sovetskogo Soiuza* (Moscow: Kraft, 2002): 95–106, here: 101–2.

3. For longer answers see, for example, Evan Mawdsley, *Thunder in the East. The Nazi-Soviet War 1941–1945* (London: Hodder Arnold, 2005); or Catherine Merridale, *Ivan's War. Life and Death in the Red Army, 1939–1945* (New York: Metropolitan Books, 2006).

4. Mark Harrison, *Accounting for War: Soviet Production, Employment, and the Defence Burden, 1940–1945* (Cambridge: Cambridge University Press, 1996); id., 'The USSR and Total War. Why Didn't the Soviet Economy Collapse in 1942?' In *A World at Total War. Global Conflict and the Politics of Destruction, 1937–1945*, eds. Roger Chickering, Stig Förster and Bernd Greiner (Cambridge: Cambridge University Press, 2005), 137–56.

5. Victor Kravchenko, *I Chose Freedom. The Personal and Political Life of a Soviet Official* (Bedfors Square: Robert Hale, 1947), 328.

6. For a quick overview of the problems of an economy of the Soviet type see Alec Nove, *An Economic History of the USSR 1917–1991*, new and final edn. (London: Penguin, 1992), 364–9.

7. On the role of incentives, markets and quasi markets see R. W. Davies, *Crisis and Progress in the Soviet Economy 1931–1933* (London, Basingstoke: Macmillan, 1996), 457. For an introduction to the overall system see R. W. Davies, 'Economic Aspects of Stalinism', in *The Stalin Phenomenon*, ed. Alec Nove (London: Weidenfeld & Nicolson, 1993), 39–74. On 'informal adjustive mechanisms', see Raymond A. Bauer, Alex Inkeles, and Clyde Kluckhohn, *How the Soviet System Works. Cultural, Psychological, and Social Themes* (Cambridge, MA: Harvard University Press, 1956), 74–81.

8. P. Charles Hachten, 'Property Relations and the Economic Organization of Soviet Russia, 1941–1948'. PhD diss., The University of Chicago, 2005, 50.

9. Joseph S. Berliner, *Factory and Manager in the USSR* (Cambridge: Harvard University Press, 1957), 282. Cf. also Paul R. Gregory, *The Political Economy of Stalinism. Evidence from the Soviet Secret Archives* (Cambridge: Cambridge University Press, 2004), esp. chs. 5 and 6.

10. This is an old insight, which is all-too-frequently overlooked by technocrats. See for example Michael Schiff and Arie Y. Lewin, 'The Impact of People on Budgets,' *The Accounting Review* 45, no. 2 (April 1970): 259–68.

11. Paul R. Gregory and Andrei Markevich, 'Creating Soviet Industry: The House That Stalin Built', *Slavic Review* 61, no. 4 (2002): 787–814; Berliner, *Factory and Manager*, esp. chs. 3, 4, 5.

12. Matthew J. Payne, *Stalin's Railroad: Turksib and the Building of Socialism* (Pittsburgh, PA: University of Pittsburgh Press, 2001), ch. 10. For the sharp eyed view of a memoirist see Gennady Andreev-Khomiakov, *Bitter Waters. Life and Work in Stalin's Russia. A Memoir* (New York: Westview Press, 1997).

13. Gregory and Markevich, 'Creating Soviet Industry', 813.

14. Berliner, *Factory and Manager*, esp. chs. 10, 11, 12; David Granick, *Management of the Industrial Firm in the USSR. A Study in Soviet Economic Planning* (New York: Columbia University Press, 1954), esp. ch. 8.

15. Berliner, *Factory and Manager*, 104.

16. Janos Kornai, *The Economics of Shortage*. 2 vols. (Amsterdam: North-Holland Publishing Co., 1980).

17. For a comparison of the proliferation of models in the German army with the Red Army's smaller spread see James Curry, 'The German-Soviet War of 1941–45: Was German Defeat Inevitable?', unpublished honours thesis, The University of Western Australia, May 2009, 15–16. On the German situation see David M. Glantz and Jonathan House, *When Titans Clashed.*

How the Red Army Stopped Hitler (Lawrence, Kansas: University Press of Kansas, 1995), 30.

18. Gregory, *Political Economy*, ch. 4.

19. Elena Osokina, *Za fasadom 'stalinskogo izobiliia'. Raspredelenie i rynok v snabzhenii naseleniia v gody industrializatsii 1927–1941* (Moscow: Rosspen, 1999); id., *Our Daily Bread. Socialist Distribution and the Art of Survival in Stalin's Russia, 1927–1941* (Armonk, New York, London: M. E. Sharpe, 2001); Sheila Fitzpatrick, *Everyday Stalinism. Ordinary Life in Extraordinary Times: Soviet Russia in the 1930s* (New York and Oxford: Oxford University Press, 1999), chs. 3 and 4; Jean-Paul Depretto, 'Stratification without Class', *Kritika: Explorations in Russian and Eurasian History* 8, no. 2 (2007): 375–88; and Stephen Kotkin, *Magnetic Mountain. Stalinism as a Civilization* (Berkeley, Los Angeles, London: University of California Press, 1995), 246.

20. Ferenc Feher, Agnes Heller and György Markus, *Dictatorship over Needs* (Oxford: Basil Blackwell, 1983).

21. Stephan Merl, *Bauern unter Stalin: die Formierung des sowjetischen Kolkhossystems, 1930–1941* (Berlin: Duncker & Humblot, 1990); O. M. Verbitskaia, *Rossiiskoe krest'ianstvo: Ot Stalina k Khrushchevu* (Moscow: Nauka, 1992); Sheila Fitzpatrick, *Stalin's Peasants. Resistance & Survival in the Russian Village after Collectivization* (New York and Oxford: Oxford University Press, 1994). The continuous tendency to privatize kolkhoz property is well documented archivally. See, for the late 1930s, *Tragediia sovetskoi derevni*, vol. 5.1: 93–4; vol. 5.2: 91,118–9, 311–17, 319–21, 356–60, 512–15, 515–23. On the situation after the war see, for example, E. Iu. Zubkova, L. P. Kosheleva, G. A. Kuznetsova, A. I. Miniuk, and L. A. Rogovaia (eds.), *Sovetskaia Zhizn' 1945–1953* (Moscow: Rosspen, 2003), 215–16 and Jean Lévesque, '"Into the Grey Zone": Sham Peasants and the Limits of the Kolkhoz Order in the Post-War Russian Village, 1945–1953', in *Late Stalinist Russia. Society between Reconstruction and Reinvention*, ed. Juliane Fürst (London and New York: Routledge, 2006), 103–19.

22. Hachten, 'Property Relations and the Economic Organization of Soviet Russia'; and Mark B. Smith, 'Individual Forms of Ownership in the Urban Housing Fund of the USSR, 1944–64', *Slavonic and East European Review* 86, no. 2 (2008): 283–305.

23. *Narodnoe khoziaistvo SSSR 1922–1972. Iubileinyi statisticheskii ezhegodnik* (Moscow: Statistika, (1972), 367.

24. V. B. Zhiromskaia and Iu. A. Poliakov, *Vsesoiuznaia perepis' naseleniia 1937 goda: Obshchie itogi. Sbornik dokumentov i materialov* (Moscow: Rosspen, 2007), 124.

25. Lewis H. Siegelbaum, 'Mapping Private Spheres in the Soviet Context', in *Borders of Socialism. Private Spheres of Soviet Russia*, ed. Lewis Siegelbaum (New York: Palgrave Macmillan, 2006), 1–21, esp. 5–8.

26. Andrei Markevich, 'Soviet Urban Households and the Road to Universal Employment, from the End of the 1930s to the End of the 1960s', *Continuity and Change* 20, no. 3 (2005): 443–73, here: 448, 460.

27. Julie Hessler, *A Social History of Soviet Trade. Trade Policy, Retail Practices, and Consumption, 1917–1953* (Princeton and Oxford: Princeton University Press, 2004), 286–8.

28. Hessler, *A Social History of Soviet Trade*, ch. 6; Mark Edele, *Soviet Veterans of the Second World War. A Popular Movement in an Authoritarian Society, 1941–1991* (Oxford: Oxford University Press, 2008), 61–4, 90–5. On 'speculators' see Heinzen, 'Informers and the State under Late Stalinism', 796.

29. For a classical exploration see Gregory Grossman, 'The "Second Economy" of the USSR', *Problems of Communism* 25, no. 5 (1977): 25–40.

30. On corruption see Heinzen, 'Informers and the State under Late Stalinism'; and id., 'A "campaign spasm": graft and the limits of the "campaign" against bribery after the Great Patriotic War', in *Late Stalinist Russia*, 123–41.

31. Sheila Fitzpatrick, '*Blat* in Stalin's Time', in *Bribery and Blat in Russia. Negotiating Reciprocity from the Middle Ages to the 1990s*, eds. Stephen Lovell, Alena Ledeneva and Andrei Rogachevskii (New York: St Martin's Press, 2000), 166–82; Alena V. Ledeneva, Alena V. *Russia's Economy of Favours. Blat, Networking and Informal Exchange* (New York and Cambridge: Cambridge University Press, 1998).

32. Sheila Fitzpatrick, 'Intelligentsia and Power. Client-Patron Relations in Stalin's Russia', in *Stalinismus vor dem Zweiten Weltkrieg. Neue Wege der Forschung*, ed. Manfred Hildermeier (Munich: R. Oldenbourg Verlag, 1998), 35–53; id., 'Supplicants and Citizens: Public Letter-Writing in Soviet Russia in the 1930s', *Slavic Review* 55, no. 1 (1996): 78–105; and Lewis H. Siegelbaum, ' "Dear Comrade, You Ask What We Need": Socialist Paternalism and Soviet Rural "Notables" in the Mid-1930s', *Slavic Review* 57, no. 1 (1998): 107–32.

33. Andrei Sokolov, 'Forced Labor in Soviet Industry: The End of the 1930s to the Mid-1950s. An Overview', in *The Economics of Forced Labor: the Soviet Gulag*, eds. Paul R. Gregory and Valery Lazarev (Stanford: Hoover Institution Press, 2003), 23–42; Donald Filtzer, *Soviet Workers and Stalinist Industrialization. The Formation of Modern Soviet Production*

Relations, 1928–1941 (Armonk, New York: M. E. Sharpe, 1986); id., *Soviet Workers and Late Stalinism. Labour and the Restoration of the Stalinist System after World War II* (Cambridge, UK: Cambridge University Press, 2002).

34. Steven A. Barnes, 'Soviet Society Confined: The Gulag in the Karaganda Region of Kazakhstan, 1930s–1950s', PhD diss., (Stanford University, 2003); Oleg Khlevniuk, 'The Economy of the OGPU, NKVD, and MVD of the USSR, 1930–1953. The Scale, Structure, and Trends of Development', in *The Economics of Forced Labor*, 43–66.

35. Lynne Viola, *The Unknown Gulag. The Lost World of Stalin's Special Settlements* (Oxford and New York: Oxford University Press, 2007), 4, 58; cf. also 54–5, 58–9; Galina Ivanova, *Labor Camp Socialism. The Gulag in the Soviet Totalitarian System* (Armonk, New York, and London: M. E. Sharpe, 2000), 70–2. On the political origins of the GULAG see, e.g. O. V. Khlevniuk, *The History of the Gulag. From Collectivization to the Great Terror* (New Haven and London: Yale University Press, 2004), 24, 331–3.

36. Paul Gregory, 'An Introduction to the Economics of the GULAG', in *The Economics of Forced Labor*, 1–21, here: 19.

37. Ivanova, *Labor Camp Socialism*, 83, 84, 110, 116; Khlevniuk, *History of the GULAG*, 333–6.

38. Edwin Bacon, *The Gulag at War. Stalin's Forced Labour System in the Light of the Archives* (New York: New York University Press, 1994), ch. 7, esp. 125, 137. Quotation is from Kravchenko, *Freedom*, 404.

39. Ivanova, *Labor Camp Socialism*, 86–7; 107–10; 122–5 (Beria quotation: 124); Valery Lazarev, 'Conclusions', in *The Economics of Forced Labor*, 189–97, esp., 196–7; Viola, *Unknown GULAG*, 7; Leonid Borodkin, 'Trud v GULAGe: mezhdu prinuzhdeniem i stimulirovaniem', in *Gulag: Ekonomika prinuditel'nogo truda*, eds. L. Borodkin, P. Gregorin, and Oleg Khlevniuk (Moscow: Rosspen, 2005), 129–56; Leonid Borodkin and Simon Ertz, 'Forced Labour and the Need for Motivation: Wages and Bonuses in the Stalinist Camp System', *Comparative Economic Studies* 47 (2005): 418–36.

40. Khlevniuk, *History of the GULAG*, 328–44. Golfo Alexopoulos, 'Amnesty 1945: The Revolving Door of Stalin's Gulag' *Slavic Review* 64, no. 2 (2005): 274–306; Ivanova, *Labor Camp Socialism*, 125–6.

41. Alexander Ripper, 'Coming to Terms with the Archipelago: The Soviet Labour Camps in the Experience of Prisoners, 1939–1953', unpublished honours thesis (The University of Western Australia, 2007). On corrup-

tion: James Heinzen, 'Korruptsiia v GULAGe: dilemmy chinovnikov i uznikov', in *GULAG: ekonomika prinuditel'nogo truda*, 157–74.

42. Federico Varese, 'The Society of the vory-v-zakone, 1930s–1950s', *Cahiers du Monde russe* 39, no. 4 (1998): 515–38.

43. Eugene Zaleski, *Stalinist Planning for Economic Growth, 1933–1952* (London and Basingstoke: Macmillan, 1980); Franklyn D. Holzman, *Soviet Taxation: The Fiscal and Monetary Problems of a Planned Economy* (Cambridge: Harvard University Press, 1955).

44. Moshe Lewin, 'The Disappearance of Planning in the Plan', *Slavic Review* 32, no. 2 (1973), 271–87.

45. On local economies run by closely-knit cliques and the Terror as an attempt to break them see James R. Harris, *The Great Urals: Regionalism and the Evolution of the Soviet System* (Ithaca, NY: Cornell University Press, 1996). The re-emergence of this economy after the terror is documented well in Berliner, *Factory and Manager*, which describes the post-purge, prewar situation.

46. Gregory, *Political Economy*, 119, 121; William Moskoff, *The Bread of Affliction; the Food Supply in the USSR During World War II* (Cambridge: Cambridge University Press, 1990); John Barber, and Mark Harrison, *The Soviet Home Front, 1941–1945: A Social and Economic History of the USSR in World War II* (London and New York: Longman, 1991), 77–93, 194–205; Jeffrey W. Jones, '"People without a Definite Occupation". The Illegal Economy and "Speculators" in Rostov-on-the-Don, 1943–1948', in: *Provincial Landscapes. Local Dimensions of Soviet Power, 1917–1953*, ed. Donald J. Raleigh (Pittsburgh, PA: University of Pittsburgh Press, 2001), 236–54; Julie Hessler, *A Social History of Soviet Trade. Trade Policy, Retail Practices, and Consumption, 1917–1953* (Princeton and Oxford: Princeton University Press, 2004), ch. 6; Hachten, 'Property Relations and the Economic Organization of Soviet Russia'; id., 'Separate yet Governed: The Representation of Soviet Property Relations in Civil Law and Public Discourse', in *Borders of Socialism*, 65–82. For a longer-term perspective see also Stephen Lovell, *Summerfolk. A History of the Dacha, 1719–2000* (Ithaca and London: Cornell University Press, 2003).

47. Julie Hessler, 'Postwar Normalisation and Its Limits in the USSR: The Case of Trade', *Europe-Asia Studies* 53, no. 3 (2001): 445–71; Donald Filtzer, 'The Standard of Living of Soviet Industrial Workers in the Immediate Postwar Period, 1945–1948', *Europe-Asia Studies* 51, no. 6 (1999): 1013–38; Yoram Gorlizki, and Oleg Khlevniuk, *Cold Peace. Stalin and the Soviet Ruling Circle, 1945–1953* (Oxford and New York: Oxford

University Press, 2004), 97–9; Mark Edele, 'More Than Just Stalinists: The Political Sentiments of Victors 1945–1953', in *Late Stalinist Russia,* 167–91; and V. Naumov (ed.), *Georgii Zhukov. Stenogramma oktiabr'skogo (1957g.) plenuma TsK KPSS i drugie dokumenty* (Moscow: Demokratiia, 2001), 641–3.

48. I. Stalin, 'New Conditions—New Tasks in Economic Construction. Speech Delivered at a Conference of Business Executives, June 23, 1931', *Works*, vol. 13 (Moscow: Foreign Languages Publishing House, 1955), 53–82, esp. the section on wages; Abram Bergson, *The Structure of Soviet Wages: A Study in Socialist Economics* (Cambridge: Harvard University Press, 1944); on piece rates and other incentives see Gregory, *Political Economy*, 102–6; on the post-war years: Filtzer, *Soviet Workers and Late Stalinism*, 232–41. On incentives in the GULAG see above.

49. R. W. Davies, 'The Socialist Market: A Debate in Soviet Industry, 1932–33', *Slavic Review* 43, no. 2 (1984): 201–23; Julie Hessler, 'A Postwar Perestroika? Toward a History of Private Trade Enterprise in the USSR', *Slavic Review* 57, no. 3 (1998): 516–42.

50. W. Brian Arthur. 'Competing technologies, increasing returns, and lock-in by historical events', *The Economic Journal* 99 (March 1989), 116–31.

Chapter 9

1. Franz Neumann, *Behemoth. The Structure and Practice of National Socialism 1933–1944* (New York: Harper Torchbooks, 1966), 459.

2. David C. Engerman, *Know Your Enemy. The Rise and Fall of America's Soviet Experts* (Oxford: Oxford University Press, 2009), ch. 4 (on economics). Recent exceptions are quoted in Chapter 8. Also note Lewis H. Siegelbaum, *Cars for Comrades: the Life of the Soviet Automobile* (Ithaca: Cornell University Press, 2008) and R. W. Davies, 'Stalin as economic policy-maker: Soviet agriculture, 1932–1936, in *Stalin. A New History*, eds. Sarah Davies and James Harris (Cambridge: Cambridge University Press), 121–39.

3. Christoph Conrad and Martina Kesel (eds.), *Geschichte schreiben in der Postmoderne. Beiträge zur aktuellen Diskussion* (Stuttgart: Reclam, 1994).

4. For the reflections of participants several decades on see, for example, Geoff Eley, *A Crooked Line. From Cultural History to the History of Society* (Ann Arbor: The University of Michigan Press, 2005); and William H. Sewell, *Logics of History. Social Theory and Social Transformation* (Chicago: The University of Chicago Press, 2005).

5. Gabor T. Rittersporn, *Stalinist Simplifications and Soviet Complications. Social Tensions and Political Conflicts in the USSR 1933–1953* (Chur: Harwood Academic Publishers, 1991).

6. Hayden White, *Metahistory: the historical imagination in nineteenth-century Europe* (Baltimore: Johns Hopkins University Press, 1973).

7. Marshall Sahlins, *Waiting for Foucault and Other Aphorisms.* 3rd. rev. edn. (Charlottesville, VA: Prickly Pear Pamphlets, 1999), 46.

8. Stephen Kotkin, *Magnetic Mountain. Stalinism as a Civilization* (Berkeley: University of California Press, 1995); Moshe Lewin, *The Making of the Soviet System. Essays in the Social History of Interwar Russia* (New York: New Press, 1994).

9. Jörg Baberowski, *Der Rote Terror. Die Geschichte des Stalinismus* (Frankfurt a. M.: Fischer Taschenbuch Verlag, 2007), quotation: 9.

10. Michael Burawoy, 'From Sovietology to Comparative Political Economy' in, *Beyond Soviet Studies*, ed. Daniel Orlovsky (Washington: The Woodrow Wilson Center Press, 1995), 72–102, here: 76. See also Mark Edele, 'Soviet Society, Social Structure, and Everyday Life. Major Frameworks Reconsidered', *Kritika: Explorations in Russian and Eurasian History* 8, no. 2 (2007): 349–73.

11. David C. Engerman, *Know Your Enemy. The Rise and Fall of America's Soviet Experts* (Oxford: Oxford University Press, 2009), ch. 2. On the ideologies of strategic bombing see Tami Davis Biddle, *Rhetoric and Reality in Air Warfare. The Evolution of British and American Ideas About Strategic Bombing, 1914–1945* (Princeton and Oxford: Princeton University Press, 2002).

12. Raymon A. Bauer, Alex Inkeles Inkeles, and Clyde Kluckhohn, *How the Soviet System Works. Cultural, Psychological, and Social Themes* (Cambridge: Harvard University Press, 1956), 20.

13. 'Aufklärung ist totalitär'. Max Horkheimer, and Theodor W. Adorno, *Dialektik der Aufklärung. Philosophische Fragmente* (Frankfurt a. M.: Fischer, 1995), 12. Similarly: J. L. Talmon, *The Origins of Totalitarian Democracy* (London: Secker & Warburg, 1952).

14. H. Kent Geiger, *The Family in Soviet Russia* (Cambridge, MA: Harvard University Press, 1968), e.g. 238 for an example of the former; or 241 for an example of the latter.

15. Abbott Gleason, *Totalitarianism. The Inner History of the Cold War* (New York, Oxford: Oxford University Press, 1995).

16 On the revisionism debate as a disciplinary shift from political science to history see Sheila Fitzpatrick, 'Revisionism in Soviet History', *History and Theory* 46 (2007): 77–91.

17. On the assumptions of social history see William H. Sewell, 'Whatever Happened to the "Social" in Social History?' in *Schools of Thought. Twenty-Five Years of Interpretive Social Science*, eds. Joan W. Scott and Debra Keates (Princeton and Oxford: Princeton University Press, 2001), 209–26. The metaphor is from Fernand Braudel, *The Mediterranean and the Mediterranean World in the Age of Philip II*, vol. 1 (London: Collins, 1972), 21.

18. One locus classicus for this polemic is Karl Popper's 1945, *The Open Society and Its Enemies*, vol. 2 (London: Routledge, 2003), 118–20.

19. For an effective historical challenge to this myth See Engerman, *Know Your Enemy* and id., 'The Ironies of the Iron Curtain. The Cold War and the Rise of Russian Studies in the United States', *Cahiers du Monde russe* 45, no. 3–4 (2004): 465–96. On the critics of 'totalitarianism' absorbing the insights of those they critique see Abbott Gleason, ' "Totalitarianism" in 1984', *The Russian Review* 43, no. 2 (1984): 145–59.

20. Merle Fainsod, *Smolensk under Soviet Rule* (New York: Vintage Books, 1958), quotations: 447, 452, 454.

21. Lewis Siegelbaum, and Andrei Sokolov (eds.), *Stalinism as a Way of Life*, abridged edn. (New Haven and London: Yale University Press, 2004), 4 and 310 fn. 6.

22. The quotation is from Lynne Viola's review of Orlando Figes' neo-totalitarian epic *The Whisperers*, in *Slavic Review* 67, no. 2 (2008): 442.

23. Alec Nove, 'Was Stalin Really Necessary?', *Encounter*, vol.18, no.4 (1962): p,. 86–92; and A. Nove and J. A. Millar, 'Was Stalin Really Necessary? A Debate on Collectivization', *Problems of Communism*, vol. 25, no.4 (1976): 50–61.

24. Stephen F. Cohen, 'Bolshevism and Stalinism', in *Stalinism. Essays in Historical Interpretation*, ed. Robert C. Tucker (New York: W. W. Norton, 1977), 3–29.

25. Richard Stites, *Revolutionary Dreams. Utopian Vision and Experimental Life in the Russian Revolution* (New York and Oxford: Oxford University Press, 1989).

26. Stephen F. Cohen, *Bukharin and the Bolshevik Revolution: A political Biography, 1888–1938* (New York: A. A. Knopf, 1973); id., 'Bukharin, NEP, and the Idea of an Alternative to Stalinism', in his *Rethinking the Soviet Experience: Politics and History Since 1917* (New York, Oxford University Press, 1985), 71–92. This perspective was also embraced by some Russian dissidents. See Roy Medvedev, *Let History Judge: The Origins and Consequences of Stalinism* (London: Macmillan, 1972). On Trotsky as

alternative see Robert V. Daniels, 'The Left Opposition as an Alternative
to Stalinism', *Slavic Review*, 50, no. 2 (1991): 277–85.

27. Robert W. Thurston, *Life and Terror in Stalin's Russia 1934–1941* (New
Haven and London: Yale University Press, 1996).

28. For the German discussion see Fritz Fischer, *From Kaiserreich to Third
Reich: Elements of Continuity in German History, 1871–1945* (London: Allen
& Unwin, 1986); David Blackbourn and Geoff Eley, *The Peculiarities of
German History. Bourgeois Society and Politics in Nineteenth-Century
Germany* (Oxford: Oxford University Press, 1984).

29. Siegelbaum and Sokolov, *Stalinism as a Way of Life*.

30. Stephen Kotkin, *Magnetic Mountain. Stalinism as a Civilization* (Berkeley,
Los Angeles, London: University of California Press, 1995); Martin Malia,
The Soviet Tragedy. A History of Socialism in Russia, 1917–1991 (New York:
The Free Press, 1994).

31. Jonathan Bone, Mark Edele, Matthew Lenoe, and Ron Suny, 'Roundtable:
What Is a School? Is There a Fitzpatrick School of Soviet History?',
Acta Slavica Iaponica 24 (2007): 229–41; Kiril Tomoff, Julie Hessler, and
Golfo Alexopoulos (eds.), *Writing the Stalin Era: Sheila Fitzpatrick and
Soviet Historiography* (Houndsmills and New York: Palgrave Macmillan,
2011).

32. For her own reflections see Sheila Fitzpatrick, 'My Father's Daughter:
A Memoir by Sheila Fitzpatrick', in *Against the Grain. Brian Fitzpatrick
and Manning Clark in Australian History and Politics*, eds. Stuart
Macintyre and Sheila Fitzpatrick (Melbourne: Melbourne University
Press, 2007); and id., 'Revisionism in Retrospect: A Personal View', *Slavic
Review* 67, no. 3 (2008): 682–704.

33. Sheila Fitzpatrick, 'Cultural Revolution in Russia 1928–32', *Journal of
Contemporary History* 9, no. 1 (1974): 33–52; id., *My Father's Daughter.
Memories of an Australian Childhood* (Melbourne: Melbourne University
Press, 2010). id., *Education and Social Mobility in the Soviet Union
1921–1934* (Cambridge: Cambridge University Press, 1979). On the
conference and the controversy, see Engerman, *Know Your Enemy*,
296–300.

34. Quotations from Fitzpatrick, 'Cultural Revolution', 35, 34.

35. The quotation, referring to the Bolsheviks in 1917, is from Ronald G.
Suny, 'Toward a Social History of the October Revolution', *The American
Historical Review* 88, no. 1 (1983): 31-52, here 51.

36. Sheila Fitzpatrick, 'The Civil War as a Formative Experience', in *Bolshevik
Culture: Experience and Order in the Russian Revolution*, eds. Abbott

Gleason, Peter Kenez and Richard Stites (Bloomington: Indiana University Press, 1985), 57–76, quotation: 74; id., 'The Legacy of the Civil War', in *Party, State, and Society in the Russian Civil War. Explorations in Social History*, eds. William Rosenberg, Diane P. Koenker, Ronald G. Suny (Bloomington and Indianapolis: Indiana University Press, 1989), 385–98, quotation: 387.

37. Sheila Fitzpatrick, *The Russian Revolution* (Oxford: Oxford University Press, 1982); 2nd edn. 1994, 3rd edn. 2008. Richard Pipes, '1917 and the Revisionists', *The National Interest* (Spring 1993), 68–79, here: 78.

38. See the discussion following Sheila Fitzpatrick, 'New Perspectives on Stalinism', *Russian Review* 45, no. 4 (1986): 357–73, discussion: 375–413, continued in vol. 46, no. 4 (1987): 379–431.

39. Amir Weiner, 'Review of Sheila Fitzpatrick, Tear Off the Masks!', *The American Historical Review* 112, no. 3 (2007): 959–61.

40. Robert Argenbright, 'Red Tsaritsyn: Precursor of Stalinist Terror', *Revolutionary Russia* 4, no. 2 (1991): 157–83; Richard Pipes and David Brandenberger, *The Unknown Lenin. From the Secret Archive* (New Haven and London: Yale University Press, 1996); and Peter Holquist, *Making War, Forging Revolution. Russia's Continuum of Crisis, 1914–1921* (Cambridge and London: Harvard University Press, 2002). 'Dirty war' (*sale guerre*) is Nicolas Werth's term. See his 'Un état contre son peuple. Violence, répressions, terreurs en Union soviétique', *Le livre noir du communisme. Crimes, terreur, répression*, eds. Stéphane Courtois et al. (Paris: Robert Laffont, 1997), 43–295, esp. 94–122.

41. Arno J. Mayer, *The Furies. Violence and Terror in the French and Russian Revolutions* (Princeton, NJ: Princeton University Press, 2000). He calls Stalin 'the heir and executor of the Russian Revolution' (609).

42. Oleg V. Khlevniuk, *In Stalin's Shadow. The Career of 'Sergo' Ordzhonikidze* (Armonk and London: M. E. Sharpe, 1995), 176 and 175 ('soft Stalinists').

43. David R. Shearer, *Policing Stalin's Socialism. Repression and Social Order in the Soviet Union, 1924–1953* (New Haven and London: Yale University Press, 2009), 4.

44. Richard Pipes, '1917 and the Revisionists', *The National Interest* (Spring 1993), 68–79; Martin Malia, 'Revolution fulfilled. How the revisionists are still trying to take ideology out of Stalinism', *TLS* 15 June 2001, 3–4; id., 'To the editors', *Kritika* 3, no. 3 (2002): 569–71.

45. Ronald G. Suny, *The Soviet Experiment. Russia, the USSR, and the Successor States*, 2nd edn. (Oxford: Oxford University Press, 2011), 236.

46. Kevin Murphy, *Revolution and Counterrevolution. Class Struggle in a Moscow Metal Factory* (Chicago: Haymarket Books, 2007). On his allegiance with 'revolutionary socialists' see x.

47. Robert C. Allen, *Farm to Factory: A Reinterpretation of the Soviet Industrial Revolution* (Princeton, NJ: Princeton University Press, 2003). For the obvious response see Michael Ellman, 'Soviet Industrialization: A Remarkable Success?', *Slavic Review* 63, no. 4 (2004): 841–9.

48. Michael J. Carley, 'Years of War in the East, 1939–45: A Review Article', *Europe-Asia Studies* 59, no. 2 (2007): 331–52. On the Russian scene see Mark Edele, Review of *Protivniki Rossii v voinakh XX veka. Evoliutsiia 'obraza vraga' v soznanii armii i obshchestva*. By Elena Seniavskaia (Moscow: Rosspen, 2006). In *The Journal of Power Institutions in Post-Soviet Societies* 9 (2009). http://www.pipss.org/index1966.html

49. Wolfgang Strauss, *Unternehmen Barbarossa und der russische Historikerstreit* (Munich: Herbig, 1999); Joachim Hoffmann, *Stalins Vernichtungskrieg 1941–1945*. 2nd rev. edn. (Munich: Verlag für Wehrwissenschaften, 1996).

50. 'From the Editors: Really-Existing Revisionism?', *Kritika* 2, no. 4 (2001): 707–11.

51. Stephen Kotkin, '1991 and the Russian Revolution: Sources, Conceptual Categories, Analytical Frameworks', *The Journal of Modern History* 70, no. 2 (1998): 384–425.

52. Kate Brown, 'Gridded Lives: Why Kazakhstan and Montana Are Nearly the Same Place', *American Historical Review*, 106, no. 1 (2001).

53. Gleason, '"Totalitarianism" in 1984', esp. 158–9.

54. See Ch. 2 above.

55. James C. Scott, *Seeing Like a State. How Certain Schemes to Improve the Human Condition Have Failed* (New Haven and London: Yale University Press, 1998). Italics mine.

56. David L. Hoffmann, *Stalinist Values. The Cultural Norms of Soviet Modernity, 1917–1941* (Ithaca and London: Cornell University Press, 2003), 187–88; Karl Popper, *The Poverty of Historicism* (London: Routledge & Kegan Paul, 1957); Edmund Burke, *Reflections on the revolution in France, and on the proceedings in certain societies in London relative to that event in a letter intended to have been sent to a gentleman in Paris* (London: J. Dodsley, 1790).

57. J. Arch Getty, '"Excesses Are Not Permitted": Mass Terror and Stalinist Governance in the Late 1930s', *The Russian Review* 61, no. 1 (2002): 113–38, here: 135–6.

58. Richard Pipes, *The Formation of the Soviet Union, Communism and Nationalism, 1917–1923* (Cambridge: Harvard University Press, 1954); Ronald G. Suny, *The Baku Commune, 1917–1918: Class and Nationality in the Russian Revolution* (Princeton: Princeton University Press, 1972); id. *The Revenge of the Past. Nationalism, Revolution, and the Collapse of the Soviet Union* (Stanford: Stanford University Press, 1993).

59. Yuri Slezkine, 'The Soviet Union as a Communal Apartment, or How a Socialist State Promoted Ethnic Particularism', *Slavic Review* 53, no. 2 (1994): 415–52.

60. Anthony D. Smith, *The Ethnic Origins of Nations* (Oxford and Cambridge: Blackwell, 1986); Jörg Baberowski, *Der Feind is überall: Stalinismus im Kaukasus* (Munich: Deutsche Verlags-Anstalt, 2003).

61. Terry Martin, 'Modernization or Neo-Traditionalism? Ascribed Nationality and Soviet Primordialism', in: *Stalinism. New Directions*, ed. Sheila Fitzpatrick (London and New York: Routledge, 2000), 348–67; id., *The Affirmative Action Empire. Nations and Nationalism in the Soviet Union, 1923–1939* (Ithaca and London: Cornell University Press, 2001). For interpretations stressing the modern state's power in molding social reality see Kate Brown, *A Biography of No Place. From Ethnic Borderland to Soviet Heartland* (Cambridge, Mass.: Harvard University Press, 2003); and Francine Hirsch, *Empire of Nations: Ethnographic Knowledge and the Making of the Soviet Union* (Ithaca: Cornell University Press, 2005).

62. Two landmark studies are Victoria E. Bonnell, *Iconography of Power. Soviet Political Posters under Lenin and Stalin* (Berkeley, Los Angeles, and London: University of California Press, 1997); and Jeffrey Brooks, *Thank You, Comrade Stalin! Soviet Public Culture from Revolution to Cold War* (Princeton, NJ: Princeton University Press, 2000).

63. Lynn Hunt (ed.), *The New Cultural History* (Berkeley, Los Angeles, London: University of California Press, 1989).

64. Katerina Clark, *Petersburg, Crucible of Cultural Revolution* (Cambridge and London: Harvard University Press, 1995); Karen Petrone, *Life Has Become More Joyous, Comrades: Celebrations in the Time of Stalin* (Bloomington, Ind.: Indiana University Press, 2000); Juliane Fürst, 'Prisoners of the Soviet Self?—Political Youth Opposition in Late Stalinism', *Europe-Asia Studies* 54, no. 3 (2002): 353–75; and David Priestland, *Stalinism and the Politics of Mobilization. Ideas, Power, and Terror in Inter-War Russia* (Oxford: Oxford University Press, 2007).

65. For a book-length manifesto see Victoria E. Bonnell and Lynn Hunt (eds.) *Beyond the Cultural Turn. New Directions in the Study of Society and*

Culture (Berkeley, Los Angeles, London: University of California Press, 1999). One example focusing on experience is Orlando Figes, *The Whisperers. Private Life in Stalin's Russia* (New York: Metropolitan Books, 2007). Much of the 'emotions' literature focuses on pre-Stalinism. Exceptions to this rule are Getty, 'Excesses are not permitted'; Gabor T. Rittersporn, 'The Omnipresent Conspiracy: On Soviet Imagery of Politics and Social Relations in the 1930s', in *Stalinist Terror. New Perspectives*, eds. J. Arch Getty and Roberta T. Manning (Cambridge and New York: Cambridge University Press, 1993), 99–115 (both on fear); Argyrios K. Pisiotis, 'Images of Hate in the Art of War', in *Culture and Entertainment in Wartime Russia*, ed. Richard Stites (Bloomington and Indianapolis: Indiana University Press, 1995), 141–56 (on hate); Sheila Fitzpatrick, 'Happiness and Toska: An Essay in the History of Emotions in Pre-War Soviet Russia', *Australian Journal of Politics and History* 50, no. 3 (2004): 357–71 and Adi Kuntsman, ' "With a Shade of Disgust": Affective Politics of Sexuality and Class in Memoirs of the Stalinist Gulag', *Slavic Review* 68, no. 2 (2009): 308–28.

66. In Sheila Fitzpatrick's work this line leads from *Cultural Revolution in Russia, 1928–1931* (Bloomington: Indiana University Press, 1978) to *Tear Off the Masks! Identity and Imposture in Twentieth-Century Russia* (Princeton and Oxford: Princeton University Press, 2005). In the same tradition stand Jeffrey Veidlinger, *The Moscow State Yiddish Theater. Jewish Culture on the Soviet Stage* (Bloomington and Indianapolis: Indiana University Press, 2000); Matthew Lenoe, *Closer to the Masses. Stalinist Culture, Social Revolution, and Soviet Newspapers* (Cambridge and London: Harvard University Press, 2004); and Kiril Tomoff, *Creative Union: The Professional Organization of Soviet Composers, 1939–1953* (Ithaca, NY: Cornell University Press, 2006).

67. Stephen Kotkin, 'Modern Times: The Soviet Union and the Interwar Conjuncture', *Kritika: Explorations in Russian and Eurasian History* 2, no. 1 (2001): 111–64.

68. Michael David-Fox, 'Multiple Modernities vs. Neo-Traditionalism: On Recent Debates in Russian and Soviet History', *Jahrbücher für Geschichte Osteuropas* 54, no. 4 (2006): 535–55; Michael Geyer and Sheila Fitzpatrick (eds.), *Beyond Totalitarianism. Stalinism and Nazism Compared* (Cambridge and New York: Cambridge University Press, 2009); and 'Fascination and Enmity: Russia and Germany as Entangled Histories, 1914–45', special issue of *Kritika: Explorations in Russian and Eurasian History* 10, no. 3 (2009).

69. It would break the unwritten rules to actually cite somebody here. But see Anthony Grafton, *The Footnote: A Curious History* (London: Faber and Faber, 1997).

70. In a rare event where such unsubstantiated claims of having had an idea first were made in print, even critics of the accused came to his aid, noting that 'scholars should have no trouble ascertaining' that the two studies in question are 'as different as apples and oranges'. Michael David-Fox, review of Matthew Lenoe, *Closer to the Masses*, in *Journal of Cold War Studies* 9, no. 1 (2007): 162–4, here: 164 (where a guide to the rest of the discussion can be found, too).

71. Richard Lea, 'Poison pen reviews were mine, confesses historian Orlando Figes', guardian.co.uk, 23 April 2010; Laura Roberts, 'Orlando Figes: Historian admits to writing anonymous reviews on Amazon', telegraph.co.uk, 24 April 2010; Alexandra Topping, 'Historian Orlando Figes agrees to pay damages for fake reviews', guardian.co.uk, 16 July 2010; and 'Dispute between Polonsky, Service, Figes and Palmer settled', *History Today*, 21 July 2010 (www.historytodayeditor.blogspot.com).

72. Norman Pereira, 'The Thought and Teachings of Michael Karpovich', *Russian History* 36 (2009): 254–77; David C. Engerman, 'The Ironies of the Iron Curtain. The Cold War and the Rise of Russian Studies in the United States', *Cahiers du Monde russe* 45, no. 3–4 (2004): 465–96.

73. Richard Pipes, *Vixi. Memoirs of a Non-Belonger* (New Haven and London: Yale University Press, 2003), quotations: 23, 56.

74. Henry Rosovsky, 'Alexander Gerschenkron: A Personal and Fond Recollection', *The Journal of Economic History*, 39, no. 4 (1979): 1009–13; Engerman, *Ironies of the Iron Curtain*, 483.

75. Nick Lampert, 'Preface', in *Stalinism. Its Nature and Aftermath*, eds. Nick Lampert and Gabor Rittersporn (Houndsmills, Basingstoke: Macmillan, 1992), p.ix-xii, here: p.x-xi; and Jonathan Haslam, *The Vices of Integrity. E. H. Carr 1892–1982* (London and New York: Verso, 1999), 245.

76. Kern, *Kravchenko case*.

77. On Solzhenitsyn see Michael Scammell, *Solzhenitsyn. A Biography* (London: Hutchinson, 1984).

78. Tony Judt, 'Leszek Kolakowski', *The New York Review of Books* (September 24–October 7, 2009): 6–8.

79. Andrew Brown, 'Scourge and poet', *The Guardian*, 15 February 2003.

80. On Stalin's revolution from above see Isaac Deutscher, *Stalin, a political biography* (London and New York: Oxford University Press, 1949). On Deutscher's life and influence, see R. J. B. Bosworth, *Explaining Auschwitz*

and Hiroshima. History Writing and the Second World War 1945–1990
(London and New York: Routledge, 1993), 156–58; and David Horowitz
(ed.), *Isaac Deutscher. The Man and His Work* (London: Macdonald, 1971).
The quotation, remembered by his wife, is on p. 68.

81. Robert C. Tucker, *Stalin in Power. The Revolution from above 1928–1941*
(New York and London: W. W. Norton & Company, 1992).

82. Yuri Slezkine, 'How I Became Multicultural', in *Intellectuals and the
Articulation of the Nation*, eds. Ronald Suny and Michael Kennedy (Ann
Arbor: The University of Michigan Press, 1999), 257–8.

83. E. H. Carr, *The Bolshevik Revolution, 1917–1923*, 3 vols. (London:
Macmillan, 1950–53); *The Interregnum, 1923–1924* (London: Macmillan,
1954); *Socialism in One Country, 1924–1926*, 3 vols. (1958–1964);
Foundations of a Planned Economy, 1926–1929, 3 vols., with R. W. Davies
(London: Macmillan, 1969–1978). A summary of the narrative of these
volumes is *The Russian Revolution: from Lenin to Stalin (1917–1929)*
(London: Macmillan, 1979). Geoffrey Hosking, *A History of the Soviet
Union 1917–1991. Final Edition* (London: Fontana Press, 1992).

84. See Haslam, *Vices of Integrity*, 157–65.

85. Sheila Fitzpatrick, 'Cultural Revolution Revisited', *Russian Review*, 58,
no. 2 (1999): 202–9, here: 205.

86. E. H. Carr, *What Is History?* (New York: Vintage Books, 1961). For his
Soviet history titles see fn. 83 above. On Carr's life, see Haslam, *The Vices
of Integrity*. On Fitzpatrick's correspondence with Carr see ibid., 253.

87. R. W. Davies, *The Industrialisation of Soviet Russia*, 5 vols (vol. 5 with
Stephen Wheatcroft) (London: Macmillan, 1980–2004). On R. W. Davies
see E. A. Rees, 'Introduction: a Tribute to R. W. Davies', in *Soviet History,
1917–53. Essays in Honour of R. W. Davies* eds. Julian Cooper, Maureen
Perrie, E. A. Rees (New York: St Martin's Press, 1995), p. xii–xxiii.

88. For example, review by Andrea Graziosi in *Slavic Review* 67, no. 3 (2008):
774–5; and the discussion about *Holodomor* below.

89. On Gill's LSE background and link to Schapiro see his PhD book *Peasants
and Government in the Russian Revolution* (New York: Barnes & Noble
Books, 1979), x.

90. On the internationalism of the field outside of the US see Michael
Confino, 'The New Russian Historiography and the Old—Some
Considerations', *History and Memory* 21, no. 2 (2009): 8–33. On Malia's
French connection see Catherine Evtuhov, 'Martin Malia (1924-2004)',
Kritika 6, no. 2 (2005): 447–52. For a now slightly dated introduction to
the German scene see Stefan Plaggenborg and Jean-Paul Depretto, 'La

recherche sur le stalinisme en Allemagne', *Le Mouvement social*, 196 (2001): 155–70. For a miniature update on the work on war and post-war see my review in *Slavic Review* 67, no. 4 (Winter 2008): 1013–14.

91. An exception were scholars specialized in debunking 'bourgeois' historiography. See Stephen White, 'The Soviet Carr', in *E. H. Carr. A Critical Appraisal* ed. Michael Cox (London: Palgrave Macmillan, 2000), 109–24.

92. T. H. Rigby (ed.), *The Stalin Dictatorship: Khrushchev's 'Secret Speech' and Other Documents* (Sydney: Sydney University Press, 1968).

93. On Soviet history from Khrushchev to Yeltsin see Roger D. Markwick, *Rewriting History in Soviet Russia. The Politics of Revisionist Historiography, 1956–1974* (Houndsmills, Basingstoke: Palgrave, 2001); R. W. Davies, *Soviet History in the Gorbachev Revolution* (Houndsmills, Basingstoke: Macmillan, 1989); R. W. Davies, *Soviet History in the Yeltsin Era* (Houndsmills, Basingstoke: Macmillan, 1997).

94. Among them are Oleg Khlevniuk, Nikolai Mitrokhin, Elena Osokina, and Elena Zubkova.

95. Leading specialists here include Viktor Zemskov, Pavel Polian, Iu. A. Poliakov, or V. B. Zhiromskaia.

96. Nanci Adler, 'The Future of the Soviet Past Remains Unpredictable: The Resurrection of Stalinist Symbols Amidst the Exhumation of Mass Graves', *Europe-Asia Studies* 57, no. 8 (2005): 1093–119; Vladimir Shlapentokh and Vera Bondartsova, 'Stalin in Russian Ideology and Public Opinion: Caught in a Conflict Between Imperial and Liberal Elements', *Russian History* 36 (2009): 302–25.

97. Andrew Osborn, 'Josef Stalin "returns" to Moscow metro', telegraph. co.uk, 5 September 2009. On the raid of the NGO *Memorial* in St Petersburg and the ensuing legal battle, see Orlando Figes, 'A Victory for Russian History', Index on Censorship, 14 May 2009, http://www. indexoncensorship.org/2009/05/orlando-figes-a-victory-for-history/ (accessed 7 October 2009). On the campaign to police the history of the second World War, see 'Campaign Launched Against "Falsification" of History', *The Current Digest of the Post-Soviet Press* 61, no. 20 (18 May 2009), 1–4. The draft law was brought before the Russian Parliament on 6 May 2009. It was published a little later, on 20 April 2009, and is available here: http://www.regnum.ru/news/1153517.html. By the time this book went to press, the law had not yet been passed, and there seemed to be government resistance against it. See David Stone, 'Update: Criminalizing Historical Distortion', russian-front.com, 10 January 2010. On the arrest of Mikhail Suprun see Luke Harding,

'Russian historian arrested in clampdown on Stalin era', guardian. co.uk, Thursday 15 October 2009. For a historian calling on the state to take sides in the history wars see E. S. Seniavskaia, *Protivniki Rossii v voinakh xx veka. Evoliutsiia 'obraza vraga' v soznanii armii i obshchestva* (Moscow: Rosspen, 2006), 254. See also the discussion on *Kritika* 10, no. 4, (Fall 2009).

98. Jeff Sahadeo, ' "Without the Past There Is No Future". Archives, History, and Authority in Uzbekistan', *Archive Stories. Facts, Fictions, and the Writing of History*, ed. Antoinette Burnton (Durham and London: Duke University Press, 2005), 45–67, here: 47.

99. Georg von Rauch, *Geschichte der baltischen Staaten* (Stuttgart: Kohlhammer, 1970).

100. For landmarks see David Wolff, and Gaël Moullec, *Le KGB et les pays Baltes 1939–1991* (Paris: Belin, 1999); Elena Zubkova, *Pribaltika i Kreml'. 1940–1953* (Moscow: Rosspen, 2008). On the politics involved see also Karsten Brüggemann, 'Russia and the Baltic Countries. Recent Russian-Language Literature', *Kritika* 10, no. 4 (2009): 935–56.

101. Peter Novick, *The Holocaust in American Life* (Boston: Houghton Mifflin, 1999); and Omer Bartov, *Germany's War and the Holocaust. Disputed Histories* (Ithaca and London: Cornell University Press, 2003), 142–3.

102. William Henry Chamberlin, 'The Ordeal of the Russian Peasantry', *Foreign Affairs* 12, no. 3 (April 1934): 495–507.

103. Dana G. Dalrymple, 'The Soviet Famine of 1932–1934', *Soviet Studies* 15, no. 3 (1964): 250–84; quotation: 250.

104. Robert Conquest, *The Harvest of Sorrow: Soviet Collectivization and the Terror-Famine* (New York: Oxford University Press, 1986).

105. R. W. Davies and Stephen G. Wheatcroft, *The Years of Hunger: Soviet Agriculture, 1931–1933* (= *The Industrialisation of Soviet Russia*, vol. 5) (Basingstoke: Palgrave Macmillan, 2004), 441 n., 145. For Conquests earlier, more radical statements see ibid. 441.

106. Hiroaki Kuromiya, 'The Soviet Famine of 1932–1933 Reconsidered', *Europe-Asia Studies* 60, no. 4 (2008): 663–75. The quotation from the sympathetic observer is from David R. Marples, 'Ethnic Issues in the Famine of 1932–1933 in Ukraine', *Europe-Asia Studies* 61, no. 3 (2009): 505–18, which also includes a very useful overview over the discussion. These articles are part of a discussion sparked by Davies and Wheatcroft's *The Years of Hunger*, involving, besides the two authors, Michael Ellman and Mark Tauger. See *Europe-Asia Studies* 57, no. 6 (2005); 58, no. 4 (2006); 59, nos. 4 & 7 (2007).

107. 'Ukrainian Famine-Genocide: Holodomor 1932–33', http://www.spiritsd. ca/ukrainian/eng_high_holodomor.htm. For the UK see Association of Ukrainians in Great Britain, 'Holodomor 1932–33, the Campaign for recognition', http://www.augb.co.uk/holodomor-1932–33-the-campaign-for-recognition.php (both accessed 23 September 2009).

108. Wasyl Veryha, *A Case Study of Genocide in the Ukrainian Famine of 1921–1923. Famine as a Weapon* (Lewiston: The Edwin Mellen Press, 2007).

109. Catherine Merridale, *Ivan's War. Life and Death in the Red Army, 1939–1945* (New York: Metropolitan Books, 2006); Catriona Kelly, *Children's World. Growing up in Russia 1890–1991* (New Haven and London: Yale University Press, 2007); and Figes, *The Whisperers* (2007).

110. Thomas S. Kuhn, *The Structure of Scientific Revolutions*. 2nd enlarged edn. (Chicago and London: The University of Chicago Press, 1970).

111. Igal Halfin, *From Darkness to Light: Class, Consciousness, and Salvation in Revolutionary Russia* (Pittsburgh, PA: University of Pittsburgh Press, 2000); id., *Terror in My Soul: Communist Autobiographies on Trial* (Cambridge, MA: Harvard University Press, 2003); Jochen Hellbeck, *Revolution on My Mind. Writing a Diary under Stalin* (Cambridge, MA, and London: Harvard University Press, 2006); and Irina Paperno, *Stories of the Soviet Experience, Memories, Diaries, Dreams* (Ithaca: Cornell University Press, 2009).

112. Jan Plamper, 'Foucault's Gulag', *Kritika* 3, no. 2 (2002): 255–80, here: 256.

113. For a roadmap to the discussion about self, identity, and subjectivity see Choi Chatterjee and Karen Petrone, 'Models of Selfhood and Subjectivity: The Soviet Case in Historical Perspective', *Slavic Review* (Winter 2008): 967–86.

114. Igal Halfin, and Jochen Hellbeck, 'Rethinking the Stalinist Subject: Stephen Kotkin's "Magnetic Mountain" and the State of Soviet Historical Studies', *Jahrbücher für Geschichte Osteuropas* 44, no. 3 (1996): 456–63; and Hellbeck, 'Fashioning the Stalinist Soul: The Diary of Stepan Podlubnyi (1931–1939)', *Jahrbücher für Geschichte Osteuropas* 44 (1996): 344–75.

115. 'Totalitarian' precursors are discussed in Edele, 'Soviet Society, Social Structure, and Everyday Life', 355–6; for a 'revisionist' see Robert W. Thurston, 'Fear and Belief in the USSR's "Great Terror": Response to Arrest, 1935–1939', *Slavic Review* 45, no. 2 (1986): 213–34; and his *Life and Terror in Stalin's Russia*.

116. The quotation is from Brigitte Studer and Heiko Haumann, 'Introduction', in *Stalinistische Subjekte. Individuum und System in der Sowjetunion und der Komintern, 1929–1953* (Zurich: Chronos, 2006), 39–80, here: 57. Compare this statement with Hellbeck's subtle discussion in *Revolution on my mind.*

117. Sheila Fitzpatrick, *Stalin's Peasants. Resistance & Survival in the Russian Village after Collectivization* (New York and Oxford: Oxford University Press, 1994); Lynne Viola, *Peasant Rebels under Stalin. Collectivization and the Culture of Peasant Resistance* (Oxford and New York: Oxford University Press, 1996); Sarah Davies, *Popular Opinion in Stalin's Russia. Terror, Propaganda, and Dissent, 1934–1941* (Cambridge, New York, Melbourne: Cambridge University Press, 1997); Jeffrey J. Rossman, *Worker Resistance under Stalin. Class and Revolution on the Shop Floor* (Cambridge and London: Harvard University Press, 2005).

118. A good, although partisan, introduction to the debate is Rossman, *Worker Resistance*, 14–17. See also Michael David-Fox, Peter Holquist, and Marshall Poe (eds.), *The Resistance Debate in Russian and Soviet History* (Bloomington: Slavica Publishers, 2003).

119. Jochen Hellbeck, reply to Sarah Davies, *Kritika* 1, no. 2 (2000): 439.

120. Constantine Pleshakov, *Stalin's Folly. The Tragic First Ten Days of World War II on the Eastern Front* (Boston and New York: Houton Mifflin Co., 2005), 278.

121. Victor Kravchenko, *I Chose Freedom. The Personal and Political Life of a Soviet Official* (Bedfors Square: Robert Hale, 1947), 421.

122. Marc Bloch, *The Historian's Craft. Reflections on the Nature and Uses of History and the Techniques and Methods of Those Who Write It* (New York: Vintage Books, 1953).

123. Lesley A. Rimmel, '*Svodki* and Popular Opinion in Stalinist Leningrad', *Cahiers du Monde Russe* 40, no. 1–2 (1999): 217–34; Olga Velikanova, 'Berichte zur Stimmungslage. Zu den Quellen politischer Beobachtung der Bevölkerung', *Jahrbücher für Geschichte Osteuropas* 47, no. 2 (1999): 227–36; Lynne Viola, 'Popular Resistance in the Stalinist 1930s: Soliloquy of a Devil's Advocate', *Kritika* 1, no. 1 (2000): 45–69; Hiroaki Kuromiya, *The Voices of the Dead. Stalin's Great Terror in the 1930s* (New Haven and London: Yale University Press, 2007); Figes, *The Whisperers*; and Lynne Viola, *The Unknown Gulag. The Lost World of Stalin's Special Settlements* (Oxford and New York: Oxford University Press, 2007).

124. Anna Krylova, 'The Tenacious Liberal Subject in Soviet Studies', *Kritika. Explorations in Russian and Eurasian History* 1, no. 1 (2000): 119–46; quotations: 120.

125. Jochen Hellbeck, 'Speaking Out: Languages of Affirmation and Dissent in Stalinist Russia'. *Kritika: Explorations in Russian and Eurasian History* 1, no. 1 (2000): 71–96; here: 73–4.

126. Sarah Davies, 'To the Editors', *Kritika*, 1, no. 2 (2000): 437–9.

127. Mark Edele, 'A "Generation of Victors?" Soviet Second World War Veterans from Demobilization to Organization 1941–1956'. Ph.D. diss., The University of Chicago, 2004, ch. 6, later revised as 'More Than Just Stalinists: The Political Sentiments of Victors 1945–1953', in *Late Stalinist Russia. Society between Reconstruction and Reinvention*, ed. Juliane Fürst (London and New York: Routledge, 2006), 167–91.

128. Juliane Fürst, 'Re-Examining Opposition under Stalin: Evidence and Context—a Reply to Kuromiya', *Europe-Asia Studies* 55, no. 5 (2003): 789–802.

129. Michael David-Fox, 'Wither Resistance?', *Kritika* 1, no. 1 (2000): 161–5.

130. Siegelbaum, *Stalinism as a Way of Life*, 10.

131. Lynne Viola (ed.), *Contending with Stalinism. Soviet Power and Popular Resistance in the 1930s* (Ithaca and London: Cornell University Press, 2002), 2.

132. The original research was a doctoral thesis: Stephen Kotkin, 'Magnetic Mountain: City Building and City Life in the Soviet Union in the 1930s: A Study of Magnitogorsk', PhD diss., University of California, Berkeley, 1988.

133. Stephen Kotkin, review of Sarah Davies, *Popular Opinion in Stalin's Russia*, *Europe-Asia Studies* 50, no. 4 (1998): 739–42; quotation: 742.

134. On the role of archives in his life: Stephen Kotkin, 'The State—Is It Us? Memoirs, Archives, and Kremlinologists', *The Russian Review* 61, no. January (2002): 35–51, here: 38. Originally, 'archival fetishism' is Dominick LaCapra's term see his *History & Criticism* (Ithaca, NY: Cornell University Press, 1985), 92. On Kotkin's use see his '1991 and the Russian Revolution', 386.

135. Kate Brown, 'Total recall', *TLS* 8 February 2008, 8–9, here: 8; see also Figes's reaction and Brown's forced retreat: *TLS* 15 February 2009, 6; and 22 February 2008, 6.

136. For a similar point see Lynne Viola, 'The Cold War in American Soviet Historiography and the End of the Soviet Union', *The Russian Review* 61, no. 1 (2002): 25–34, esp. 34.

137. E. H. Carr, *What is History*.

138. To my knowledge, the first book drawing explicitly these conclusions is Gary Kern, *The Kravchenko Case. One Man's War on Stalin* (New York: Enigma Books, 2007).

139. For one beginning see Christopher Burton's work on medical welfare. For example his 'Vseokhvatnaia pomoshch' pri stalinizme? Sovetskoe zdravookhranenie i dukh gosudarstva blagodenstviia, 1945–1953', in *Sovetskaia sotsial'naia politika: stseny i deistvuiushchie litsa, 1940–1985*, eds. Elena Iarskaia-Smirnova and Pavel Romanov (Moscow: Variant, Center for Social Policy and Gender Studies, 2008), 174–93).

140. Alfred G. Meyer, 'USSR, Incorporated', *Slavic Review* 20, no. 3 (1961): 369–76.

BIBLIOGRAPHY

1. Primary Sources

1.1 Archival document collections

Cienciala, Anna M., Natalia S. Lebedeva, and Wojciech Materski (eds.), *Katyn. A Crime Without Punishment* (New Haven and London: Yale University Press, 2007).

Danilov, V., R. Manning, and L. Viola (eds.), *Tragediia sovetskoi derevni. Kollektivizatsiia i raskulachivanie. Dokumenty i materialy v 5 tomakh 1927–1939.* 5 vols. (Moscow: Rosspen, 2001).

Davies, R. W., Oleg V. Khlevniuk, and E. A. Rees (eds.), *The Stalin-Kaganovich Correspondence 1931–36* (New Haven and London: Yale University Press, 2003).

Khaustov, V. N., V. P. Naumov, and N. S. Plotnikova (eds.), *Lubianka. Stalin in MGB SSSR. Mart 1946 – mart 1953* (Moscow: Demokratiia, 2007).

Kokurin, A. I., N. V. Petrov (eds.), *GULAG (Glavnoe upravlenie lagerei) 1917–1960: dokumenty* (Moscow, 2000).

Kondakova, Irina (ed.), ' "Tarzan—chelovek ne isporchennyi burzhuaznoi tsivilizatsiei" ', *Istochnik* 4 (1999).

Lih, Lars T., Oleg V. Naumov and Oleg V. Khlevniuk (eds.), *Stalin's Letters to Molotov 1925–1936* (New Haven and London: Yale University Press, 1995).

Naumov, V. (ed.), *Georgii Zhukov. Stenogramma oktiabr'skogo (1957g.) plenuma TsK KPSS i drugie dokumenty* (Moscow: Demokratiia, 2001).

Pipes, Richard (ed.), *The Unknown Lenin. From the Secret Archive* (New Haven and London: Yale University Press, 1996).

Pobol', N. L. and P. M. Polian (eds.), *Stalinskie deportatsii 1928–1953* (Moscow: Demokratiia, 2005).

Siegelbaum, Lewis, and Andrei Sokolov (eds.), *Stalinism as a Way of Life*. Abridged ed. (New Haven and London: Yale University Press, 2004).

Trenin, B. P. (ed.), *1933 g. Nazinskaia tragediia. Dokumental'noe nauchnoe izdanie* (Tomsk: Nauka, 2002).

Zolotarev, V. A. et al. (eds.), *Glavnye politicheskie organy Vooruzhennykh sil SSSR v Velikoi Otechestvennoi voine 1941–1945 gg. Dokumenty i materialy* (= *Russkii arkhiv: Velikaia Otechestvennaia*, vol. 17–6 (1–2) (Moscow: Terra, 1996).

Zubkova, E. Iu., L. P. Kosheleva, G. A. Kuznetsova, A. I. Miniuk, and L. A. Rogovaia (eds.), *Sovetskaia zhizn' 1945–1953* (Moscow: Rosspen, 2003).

1.2 Diaries and Memoirs

Alexeyeva, Liudmilla and Paul Goldberg, *The Thaw Generation. Coming of Age in the Post-Stalin Era* (Boston, Toronto, London: Little, Brown, and Co., 1990).

Gennady Andreev-Khomiakov, *Bitter Waters. Life and Work in Stalin's Russia* (Boulder: Westview Press, 1997).

Bonner, Jelena, *Mütter und Töchter. Erinnerungen an meine Jugend 1923 bis 1945* (Munich: Piper, 1992).

Chukhrai, Grigorii, *Moia voina* (Moscow: Algoritm, 2001).

——*Moe kino* (Moscow: Algoritm, 2002).

Edgerton, William (ed.), *Memoirs of Peasant Tolstoyans in Soviet Russia* (Bloomington and Indianapolis: Indiana University Press, 1993).

Engel, Barbara Alpern and Anastasia Posadskaya-Vanderbeck (eds.), *A Revolution of Their Own. Voices of Women in Soviet History* (Boulder: Westview Press, 1998).

Fitzpatrick, Sheila, and Yuri Slezkine (eds.), *In the Shadow of Revolution. Life Stories of Russian Women. From 1917 to the Second World War* (Princeton, NJ: Princeton University Press, 2000).

Garros, Véronique, Natalia Korenevskaya, and Thomas Lahusen (eds.), *Intimacy and Terror. Soviet Diaries of the 1930s* (New York: The New Press, 1995).

Ginzburg, Eugenia Semyonovna, *Journey into the Whirlwind* (San Diego, New York, and London: Harvest Books, 1995).

Gordey, Michel, *Visa to Moscow* (New York: Alfred A. Knopf, 1952).

Graf, Oskar Maria, *Reise in die Sowjetunion 1934* (Hamburg: Luchterhand, 1992).

Gutnova, E. V., *Perezhitoe* (Moscow: Rosspen, 2001).

Hellbeck, Jochen (ed.), *Tagebuch aus Moskau 1931–1939* (Munich: dtv, 1996).

Kopelev, Lev, *I sotvoril sebe kumira* (Ann Arbor: Ardis, 1978).

Kravchenko, Victor, *I Chose Freedom. The Personal and Political Life of a Soviet Official* (Bedfors Square: Robert Hale, 1947).

Lugovskaya, Nina, *The Diary of a Soviet Schoolgirl. 1932–1937*. Transl. Joanne Turnbull (Moscow: Glas Publishers, 2003).

Nevezhin, V. A. (ed.) *Zastol'nye rechi Stalina. Dokumenty i materialy* (Moscow and St Petersburg: ARIO-XX, 2003).

Outlaw. The Autobiography of a Soviet Waif. By Voinov (London: Harvill Press, 1955).

Resis, Albert (ed.), *Molotov Remembers. Inside Kremlin Politics. Conversations with Felix Chuev* (Chicago: Ivan R. Dee, 1993).

Shikheeva-Gaister, Inna, *Semeinaia khronika vremen kul'ta lichnosti 1925–1953* (Moscow: N'iudiamed-AO, 1998).

Temkin, Gabriel, *My Just War: The Memoir of a Jewish Red Army Soldier in World War II* (Navato: Presidio, 1998).

Zelnik Reginald (ed.), *A Radical Worker in Tsarist Russia. The Autobiography of Semen Ivanovich Kanatchikov* (Stanford: Stanford University Press, 1986).

Zhigulin, Anatolii 'Chernye kamni: Avtobiograficheskaia povest'', *Znamia* 1988. 7: 10–75; 8: 48–119.

1.3 Dogma, ideology, and official statements

Bogdanov, Alexander, *The Red Star. The First Bolshevik Utopia*, eds. Loren R. Graham and Richard Stites (Bloomington: Indiana University Press, 1984).

Kalinin, M. I., 'Speech at a Conference of Best Urban and Rural Schoolteachers Convened by the Editorial Board of the Newspaper

Uchitelskaya gazeta', (28 December 1938), in: id. *On Communist Education. Selected Speeches and Articles* (Moscow: Foreign Languages Publishing House, 1953).

Lenin, V. I., *Collected Works*, 45 vols. (Moscow: Foreign Language Publishing House, 1960–69).

Meek, Dorothea L. (ed.), *Soviet youth: some achievements and problems* (London: Routledge & Kegan Paul, 1957).

'Platforma "Soiuza marksistov-lenintsev" ("gruppa Riutina")', *Izvestiia TsK KPSS*, no. 8 (1990).

Rigby, T. H. (ed.), *The Stalin Dictatorship. Khrushchev's 'Secret Speech' and Other Documents* (Sydney: Sydney University Press, 1968).

Schlesinger, Rudolf (ed.), *The Family in the USSR. Documents and Readings* (London: Routledge & Kegan Paul, 1949).

Stalin, I. V., *Collected Works*, 13 vols. (Moscow: Foreign Languages Publishing House, 1952).

—— [speech to the Central Committee Plenum, 3 March 1937], *Voprosy istorii* 3 (1995), 3–15.

—— *O Velikoi Otechestvennoi voine Sovetskogo Soiuza* (Moscow: Kraft, 2002).

Trotsky, Leon, *The Revolution Betrayed. What Is the Soviet Union and Where Is It Going?* (New York, London, Montreal, and Sydney: Pathfinder, 1972).

1.3 Statistics

Krivosheev, G. F., *Soviet Casualties and Combat Losses in the Twentieth Century* (London: Greenhill Books, 1997).

Narodnoe khoziaistvo SSSR 1922–1972. Iubileinyi statisticheskii ezhegodnik (Moscow: Statistika, 1972).

Poliakov, Iu. A. (ed.), *Vsesoiuznaia perepis' naseleniia 1937 g. Kratkie itogi* (Moscow: Akademiia nauk SSSR, 1991).

Zhenshchiny i deti v SSSR. Statisticheskii sbornik, 2nd edn. (Moscow: Gosstatizdat, 1963).

Zhiromskaia, V. B., I. N. Kiselev, and Iu. A. Poliakov, *Polveka pod grifom 'sekretno': Vsesoiuznaia perepis' naseleniia 1937 goda* (Moscow: Nauka, 1996).

Zhiromskaia, V. B. and Iu. A. Poliakov, *Vsesoiuznaia perepis' naseleniia 1937 goda: obshchie itogi. Sbornik dokumentov i materialov* (Moscow: Rosspen, 2007).

2. Secondary Sources

Achimov, G. F., 'The Second Soviet Generation', *Problems of Communism*, 1 (1952).

Aleksievich, Svetlana, *U voiny—ne zhenskoe litso* (Moscow: Sovetskii pisatel', 1987).

Alexopoulos, Golfo, 'Portrait of a Con Artist as a Soviet Man', *Slavic Review* 57: 4 (1998).

—— *Stalin's Outcasts: Aliens, Citizens, and the Soviet State, 1926–1936* (Ithaca: Cornell University Press, 2003).

—— 'Amnesty 1945: The Revolving Door of Stalin's Gulag', *Slavic Review* 64: 2 (2005).

—— 'Stalin and the Politics of Kinship: Practices of Collective Punishment, 1920s–1940s', *Comparative Studies in Society and History* 50: 1 (2008).

Allen, Robert C. *Farm to Factory: A Reinterpretation of the Soviet Industrial Revolution* (Princeton, NJ.: Princeton University Press, 2003).

Anweiler, Oskar, *The Soviets: The Russian Workers, Peasants, and Soldiers Councils, 1905–1921* (New York: Pantheon Books, 1974).

Apor, Balazs, Jan C. Behrends, Polly Jones, and E. A. Rees (eds.), *The Leader Cult in Communist Dictatorships. Stalin and the Eastern Bloc* (New York: Palgrave Macmillan, 2004).

Arendt, Hannah, *The Origins of Totalitarianism.* New edn. with added prefaces (New York and London: Harvest Books, 1968).

Argenbright, Robert, 'Red Tsaritsyn: Precursor of Stalinist Terror', *Revolutionary Russia* 4: 2 (1991).

Aronson, I. Michael, *Troubled Waters. The Origins of the 1881 Anti-Jewish Pogroms in Russia* (Pittsburgh: University of Pittsburgh Press, 1990).

Baberowski, Jörg, *Der Feind is überall: Stalinismus im Kaukasus* (Munich: Deutsche Verlags-Anstalt, 2003).

—— *Der Rote Terror. Die Geschichte des Stalinismus* (Frankfurt a. M.: Fischer Taschenbuch Verlag, 2007).

Bacon, Edwin, *The Gulag at War. Stalin's Forced Labour System in the Light of the Archives* (New York: New York University Press, 1994).

Ball, Alan M., *And Now My Soul Is Hardened. Abandoned Children in Soviet Russia, 1918–1930* (Berkeley, Los Angeles, and London: University of California Press, 1994).

Barber, John, 'Popular Reactions in Moscow to the German Invasion of June 22, 1941', *Soviet Union/Union Soviétique* 18: 1–3 (1991).

——and Mark Harrison, *The Soviet Home Front, 1941–1945: A Social and Economic History of the USSR in World War II* (London and New York: Longman, 1991).

Barnes, Steven A. 'Soviet Society Confined: The Gulag in the Karaganda Region of Kazakhstan, 1930s–1950s'. PhD diss., (Standford: Stanford University, 2003).

Barsukov, A. I. et al. (eds), *Velikaia Otechestvennaia voina 1941–1945. vol. 4: Narod i voina* (Moscow: Nauka, 1999).

Bater, James H. 'Transience, Residential Persistence, and Mobility in Moscow and St. Petersburg, 1900–1914', *Slavic Review* 39: 2 (1980).

Bauer, Raymond A., Alex Inkeles, and Clyde Kluckhohn, *How The Soviet System Works. Cultural, Psychological, and Social Themes.* (Cambridge, MA.: Harvard University Press, 1956).

Bennet, Sula (trans. & ed.), *The Village of Viriatino. An Ethnographic Study of a Russian Village from before the Revolution to the Present* (Garden City, New York: Anchor Books, 1970).

Bergson, Abram, *The Structure of Soviet Wages: A Study in Socialist Economics* (Cambridge, MA.: Harvard University Press, 1944).

Berkhoff, Karel C. 'Was There a Religious Revival in Soviet Ukraine under the Nazi Regime?', *The Slavonic and East European Review* 78: 3 (2000).

——*Harvest of Despair. Life and Death in Ukraine under Nazi Rule* (Cambridge and London: The Belknap Press of Harvard University Press, 2004).

Berliner, Joseph S., *Factory and Manager in the USSR* (Cambridge, MA.: Harvard University Press, 1957).

Binner, Rolf and Marc Junge, 'Vernichtung der orthodoxen Geistlichen in der Sowjetunion in den Massenoperationen des Großen Terrors 1937–1938', *Jahrbücher für Geschichte Osteuropas* 52: 4 (2004).

Boeckh, Katrin, *Stalinismus in der Ukraine. Die Rekonstruktion des sowjetischen Systems nach dem Zweiten Weltkrieg* (Wiesbaden: Harrassowitz Verlag, 2007).

Bone, Jonathan, Mark Edele, Matthew Lenoe, and Ron Suny, 'Roundtable: What Is a School? Is There a Fitzpatrick School of Soviet History?', *Acta Slavica Iaponica* 24 (2007).

Bonnell, Victoria E., *Iconography of Power. Soviet Political Posters under Lenin and Stalin* (Berkeley, Los Angeles, and London: University of California Press, 1997).

Borodkin, Leonid, 'Trud v GULAGe: mezhdu prinuzhdeniem i stimulirovaniem', in *Gulag: Ekonomika prinuditel'nogo truda*, eds. L. Borodkin, P. Gregorin, and Oleg Khlevniuk (Moscow: Rosspen, 2005).

—— and Simon Ertz, 'Forced Labour and the Need for Motivation: Wages and Bonuses in the Stalinist Camp System', *Comparative Economic Studies* 47 (2005).

Boterbloem, Kees, *The Life and Times of Andrei Zhdanov, 1896–1948* (Montreal: McGill-Queen's University Press, 2004).

Brandenberger, David, *National Bolshevism: Stalinist Mass Culture and the Formation of Modern Russian National Identity, 1931–1956* (Cambridge and London: Harvard University Press, 2002).

Brooks, Jeffrey, *Thank You, Comrade Stalin! Soviet Public Culture from Revolution to Cold War* (Princeton, NJ.: Princeton University Press, 2000).

Brown, Kate, 'Gridded Lives: Why Kazakhstan and Montana Are Nearly the Same Place', *American Historical Review*, 106: 1 (2001).

—— *A Biography of No Place. From Ethnic Borderland to Soviet Heartland* (Cambridge, MA.: Harvard University Press, 2003).

Bucher, Greta, 'Struggling to Survive: Soviet Women in the Postwar Years', *Journal of Women's History* 12: 1 (2000).

—— *Women, the Bureaucracy and Daily Life in Postwar Moscow, 1945–1953* (Boulder: East European Monographs, 2006).

Buckley, Mary, 'Why be a shock worker or a Stakhanovite?', in *Women in Russia and Ukraine*, ed. Rosalind Marsh (Cambridge: Cambridge University Press, 1996).

—— *Mobilizing Soviet Peasants. Heroines and Heroes of Stalin's Fields* (Lanham: Rowman & Littlefield Publishers, 2006).

Burawoy, Michael, 'From Sovietology to Comparative Political Economy', in *Beyond Soviet Studies*, ed. Daniel Orlovsky (Washington: The Woodrow Wilson Center Press, 1995).

Burton, Christopher, 'Medical Welfare During Late Stalinism. A Study of Doctors and the Soviet Health System, 1945–53'. Ph.D. diss. (Chicago: The University of Chicago, 2000).

—— 'Vseokhvatnaia pomoshch' pri stalinizme? Sovetskoe zdravookhranenie i dukh gosudarstva blagodenstviia, 1945–1953', in *Sovetskaia sotsial'naia politika: stseny i deistvuiushchie litsa, 1940–1985*, eds. Elena Iarskaia-Smirnova and Pavel Romanov (Moscow: Variant, Centre for Social Policy and Gender Studies, 2008).

Cardona, Euridice and Roger D. Markwick, ' "Our Brigade Will Not Be Sent to the Front": Soviet Women under Arms in the Great Fatherland War, 1941–45', *Russian Review* 68 (2009).

Caroli, Dorena, 'Bolshevism, Stalinism, and Social Welfare (1917–1936)', *International Review of Social History* 48 (2003).

Carr, E. H. *The Bolshevik Revolution, 1917–1923*, 3 vols. (London: Macmillan, 1950–53).

—— *The Interregnum, 1923–1924* (London: Macmillan, 1954).

—— *Socialism in One Country, 1924–1926*, 3 vols. (1958–1964).

—— *Foundations of a Planned Economy, 1926–1929*, 3 vols., with R. W. Davies (London: Macmillan, 1969–78).

—— *The Russian Revolution from Lenin to Stalin (1917–1929)* (London: Macmillan, 1979).

Chatterjee, Choi and Karen Petrone, 'Models of Selfhood and Subjectivity: The Soviet Case in Historical Perspective', 67: 4 *Slavic Review* (2008).

Chumachenko, Tatiana A., *Church and State in Soviet Russia. Russian Orthodoxy from World War II to the Khrushchev Years* (Armonk, NY, and London: M. E. Sharpe, 2002).

Clark, Katerina, *The Soviet Novel. History as Ritual*. 3rd edn. (Bloomington and Indianapolis: Indiana University Press, 2000).

—— *Petersburg, Crucible of Cultural Revolution* (Cambridge and London: Harvard University Press, 1995).

Clements, Barbara Evans, 'Later Developments: Trends in Soviet Women's History, 1930 to the Present', in *Russia's Women. Accommodation, Resistance,*

Transformation eds. Barbara Evans Clements, Barbara Alpern Engel, and Christine D. Worobec (Berkeley, CA: University of California Press, 1991).

Cohen, Stephen F. *Bukharin and the Bolshevik Revolution: A political Biography, 1888–1938* (New York: A. A. Knopf, 1973).

—— 'Bolshevism and Stalinism', in *Stalinism. Essays in Historical Interpretation*, ed. Robert C. Tucker (New York: W. W. Norton, 1977).

—— 'Bukharin, NEP, and the Idea of an Alternative to Stalinism', in his *Rethinking the Soviet Experience: Politics and History Since 1917* (New York: Oxford University Press, 1985).

Edward D. Cohn, 'Disciplining the Party: The Expulsion and Censure of Communists in the Post-War Soviet Union, 1945–1961.' PhD diss., The University of Chicago, 2007, 540–51.

Coleman, Heather J. 'Becoming a Russian Baptist: Conversion Narratives and Social Experience', *Russian Review* 61: 1 (2002).

—— *Russian Baptists and spiritual revolution, 1905–1929* (Bloomington: Indiana University Press, 2005).

Colton, Timothy J. *Moscow. Governing the Socialist Metropolis* (Cambridge and London: Belknap Press, 1995).

Confino, Michael, 'The New Russian Historiography and the Old—Some Considerations', *History and Memory* 21: 2 (2009).

Conquest, Robert, *The Harvest of Sorrow: Soviet Collectivization and the Terror-Famine* (New York and Oxford: Oxford University Press, 1986).

—— *The Great Terror. A Reassessment* (New York and Oxford: Oxford University Press, 1990).

Conroy, Mary Schaffer, *Medicines for the Soviet Masses During World War II* (Lanham: University Press of America, 2008).

Conze, Susanne, 'Weder Emanzipation noch Tradition. Stalinistische Frauenpolitik in den vierziger Jahren', in *Stalinismus. Neue Forschungen und Konzepte*, ed. Stefan Plaggenborg (Berlin: Arno Spitz, 1998).

—— *Sowjetische Industriearbeiterinnen in den vierziger Jahren. Die Auswirkungen des Zweiten Weltkrieges auf die Erwerbstätigkeit von Frauen in der UdSSR, 1941–1950* (Stuttgart: Franz Steiner Verlag, 2001).

Corley, Felix, *Religion in the Soviet Union: An Archival Reader* (Houndmills, Basingstoke: Macmillan, 1996).

Cottam, K. J., 'Soviet Women in Combat During World War II: The Rear Services, Partisans and Political Workers', *Soviet Armed Forces Review Annual* 5 (1981).

Daniels, Robert V. *The Conscience of the Revolution: Communist Opposition in Soviet Russia* (New York: Simon and Schuster, 1969).

——'The Left Opposition as an Alternative to Stalinism', *Slavic Review*, 50:2 (1991).

Danilov, A. A. and A. V. Pyzhikov, *Rozhdenie sverkhderzhavy. SSSR v pervye poslevoennye gody* (Moscow: Rosspen, 2001).

David, Michael Z. 'The White Plague in the Red Capital: The Control of Tuberculosis in Russia, 1900–1941'. PhD diss. (Chicago: University of Chicago, 2007).

David-Fox, Michael, 'Multiple Modernities vs. Neo-Traditionalism: On Recent Debates in Russian and Soviet History', *Jahrbücher für Geschichte Osteuropas* 54: 4 (2006).

——, Peter Holquist, and Marshall Poe (eds.), *The Resistance Debate in Russian and Soviet History* (Bloomington: Slavica Publishers, 2003).

Davies, R. W., *The Socialist Offensive. The Collectivisation of Soviet Agriculture 1929–1930* (London: Macmillan, 1980).

——'The Socialist Market: A Debate in Soviet Industry, 1932–33', *Slavic Review* 43: 2 (1984).

——*Soviet History in the Gorbachev Revolution* (London: Macmillan, 1989).

——*Crisis and progress in the Soviet economy 1931–1933*. vol. 4, 'The industrialisation of Soviet Russia' (London, Basingstoke: Macmillan, 1996).

——*Soviet History in the Yeltsin Era* (New York: St Martin's Press, 1997).

——, Mark Harrison, and S. G. Wheatcroft (eds.), *The Economic Transformation of the Soviet Union, 1913–1945* (Cambridge and New York: Cambridge University Press, 1994).

——and Stephen G. Wheatcroft, *The Industrialization of Soviet Russia 5. The Years of Hunger: Soviet Agriculture, 1931–1933* (Houndsmills and New York: Palgrave Macmillan, 2004).

Davies, Sarah, *Popular Opinion in Stalin's Russia. Terror, Propaganda, and Dissent, 1934–1941* (Cambridge, New York, and Melbourne: Cambridge University Press, 1997).

——and James Harris (eds.), *Stalin. A New History* (Cambridge: Cambridge University Press, 2005).

Depretto, Jean-Paul, 'Stratification without Class', *Kritika: Explorations in Russian and Eurasian History* 8: 2 (2007).

Deutscher, Isaac, *Stalin, a political biography* (London and New York: Oxford University Press, 1949).

Dunham, Vera S., *In Stalin's Time. Middleclass Values in Soviet Fiction.* Enlarged and updated edn. (Durham and London: Duke University Press, 1990).

Dunn, Ethel and Stephen D. 'Religion as an Instrument of Culture Change: The Problem of the Sects in the Soviet Union', *Slavic Review* 23: 3 (1964).

Duskin, Eric, *Stalinist Reconstruction and the Confirmation of a New Elite, 1945–1953* (New York: Palgrave, 2001).

Easter, Gerald M. *Reconstructing the State. Personal Networks and Elite Identity in Soviet Russia* (Cambridge and New York: Cambridge University Press, 2000).

Edele, Mark, 'Strange Young Men in Stalin's Moscow: The Birth and Life of the Stiliagi, 1945–1953', *Jahrbücher für Geschichte Osteuropas* 50: 1 (2002).

—— 'Soviet Veterans as an Entitlement Group, 1945–1955', *Slavic Review* 65: 1 (2006), 113–16.

—— 'More Than Just Stalinists: The Political Sentiments of Victors, 1945–1953', in *Late Stalinist Russia. Society between Reconstruction and Reinvention*, ed. Juliane Fürst (London and New York: Routledge, 2006).

—— 'Soviet Society, Social Structure, and Everyday Life. Major Frameworks Reconsidered', *Kritika: Explorations in Russian and Eurasian History* 8: 2 (2007).

—— *Soviet Veterans of the Second World War. A Popular Movement in an Authoritarian Society, 1941–1991* (Oxford: Oxford University Press, 2008).

—— 'Veterans and the Village: Red Army Demobilization and Postwar Demography', *Russian history/Histoire russe* 36: 2 (2009).

—— and Michael Geyer, 'States of Exception: The Nazi-Soviet War as a System of Violence, 1939–1945', in *Beyond Totalitarianism. Stalinism and Nazism Compared*, eds. Michael Geyer and Sheila Fitzpatrick (Cambridge and New York: Cambridge University Press, 2009).

Edelman, Robert, 'A Small Way of Saying "No" Moscow Working Men, Spartak Soccer, and the Communist Party, 1900–1945', *The American Historical Review* 107: 5 (2002).

Ellman, Michael, 'The 1947 Soviet Famine and the Entitlement Approach to Famines', *Cambridge Journal of Economics* 24: 5 (2000).

—— 'Stalin and the Soviet Famine of 1932–33 Revisited', *Europe-Asia Studies* 59: 4 (2007).

—— and S. Maksudov, 'Soviet Deaths in the Great Patriotic War: A Note', *Europe-Asia Studies* 46: 4 (1994).

Engelstein, Laura, *The Keys to Happiness. Sex and the Search for Modernity in Fin-De-Siecle Russia* (Ithaca and London: Cornell University Press, 1992).

Engerman, David C., 'The Ironies of the Iron Curtain. The Cold War and the Rise of Russian Studies in the United States', *Cahiers du Monde russe* 45: 3–4 (2004).

—— *Know Your Enemy. The Rise and Fall of America's Soviet Experts* (Oxford: Oxford University Press, 2009).

Erickson, John, 'Red Army Battlefield Performance, 1941–45: the System and the Soldier', in *Time to Kill. The Soldier's Experience of War in the West 1939–1945*, eds. Paul Addison and Angus Calder (London: Pilimco, 1997).

Fainsod, Merle, *Smolensk under Soviet Rule* (New York: Vintage Books, 1958).

Feher, Ferenc, Agnes Heller, and György Markus, *Dictatorship over Needs* (Oxford: Basil Blackwell, 1983).

Fieseler, Beate, 'Die Invaliden des "Grossen Vaterländischen Krieges" der Sowjetunion—Eine politische Sozialgeschichte 1941–1991' (Habilitationsschrift, Ruhr-Universität Bochum, 2003).

Figes, Orlando, *The Whisperers. Private Life in Stalin's Russia* (New York: Metropolitan Books, 2007).

Filtzer, Donald, *Soviet workers and Stalinist industrialization. The formation of modern Soviet production relations, 1928–1941* (Armonk, NY: M. E. Sharpe, 1986).

—— 'The Standard of Living of Soviet Industrial Workers in the Immediate Postwar Period, 1945–1948', *Europe-Asia Studies* 51: 6 (1999).

—— *Soviet Workers and Late Stalinism. Labour and the Restoration of the Stalinist System after World War II* (Cambridge, New York, Melbourne: Cambridge University Press, 2002).

Finkel, Stuart, 'An Intensification of Vigilance. Recent Perspectives on the Institutional History of the Soviet Security Apparatus in the 1920s', *Kritika: Explorations in Russian and Eurasian History* 5: 2 (2004).

Fitzpatrick, Sheila, 'Cultural Revolution in Russia 1928–32', *Journal of Contemporary History* 9: 1 (1974).

—— (ed.), *Cultural Revolution in Russia, 1928–1941* (Bloomington: Indiana University Press, 1978).

—— *Education and Social Mobility in the Soviet Union 1921–1934* (Cambridge, London, New York, and Melbourne: Cambridge University Press, 1979).

—— 'Postwar Soviet Society: The "Return to Normalcy", 1945–1953', in *The Impact of World War II on the Soviet Union*, ed. Susan J. Linz (Totova, NJ: Rowman & Allanhead, 1985).

—— 'New Perspectives on Stalinism', *Russian Review* 45: 4 (1986).

—— 'War and Society in Soviet Context: Soviet Labor before, during, and after World War II', *International Labor and Working-Class History* 35 (1989).

—— *The Cultural Front. Power and Culture in Revolutionary Russia* (Ithaca and London: Cornell University Press, 1992).

—— 'The Great Departure: Rural-Urban Migration, 1929–33', in *Social Dimensions of Soviet Industrialization*, eds. William G. Rosenberg and Lewis Siegelbaum (Bloomington, IN.: Indiana University Press, 1993).

—— *Stalin's Peasants. Resistance and Survival in the Russian Village after Collectivization* (Oxford: Oxford University Press, 1994).

—— 'Supplicants and Citizens: Public Letter-Writing in Soviet Russia in the 1930s', *Slavic Review* 55: 1 (1996).

—— 'Intelligentsia and Power. Client-Patron Relations in Stalin's Russia', in *Stalinismus vor dem Zweiten Weltkrieg. Neue Wege der Forschung*, ed. Manfred Hildermeier (Munich: R. Oldenbourg Verlag, 1998).

—— *Everyday Stalinism. Ordinary Life in Extraordinary Times: Soviet Russia in the 1930s* (New York and Oxford: Oxford University Press, 1999).

—— (ed.), *Stalinism. New Directions*, ed. Sheila Fitzpatrick (London and New York: Routledge, 2000).

—— 'Happiness and Toska: An Essay in the History of Emotions in Pre-War Soviet Russia', *Australian Journal of Politics and History* 50: 3 (2004).

—— *Tear off the Masks! Identity and Imposture in Twentieth-Century Russia* (Princeton and Oxford: Princeton University Press, 2005).

—— 'Social Parasites. How Tramps, Idle Youth, and Busy Entrepreneurs Impeded the Soviet March to Communism', *Cahier du Monde russe* 47: 1–2 (2006).

—— 'Revisionism in Soviet History', *History and Theory* 46 (2007).

—— 'My Father's Daughter: A Memoir by Sheila Fitzpatrick', in *Against the Grain. Brian Fitzpatrick and Manning Clark in Australian History and Politics*, eds. Stuart Macintyre and Sheila Fitzpatrick (Melbourne: Melbourne University Press, 2007).

—— 'Revisionism in Retrospect: A Personal View', *Slavic Review* 67: 3 (2008).

—— *The Russian Revolution*. 3rd edn. (Oxford: Oxford University Press, 2008).

——, Alexander Rabinowitch, and Richard Stites (eds.), *Russia in the Era of NEP. Explorations in Soviet Society and Culture* (Bloomington and Indianapolis: Indiana University Press, 1991).

Freeze, Gregory L., 'The Stalinist Assault on the Parish, 1929–1941', in *Stalinismus vor dem Zweiten Weltkrieg: Neue Wege der Forschung*, ed. Manfred Hildermeier (Munich: Oldenbourg, 1998).

Fürst, Juliane, 'Prisoners of the Soviet Self?—Political Youth Opposition in Late Stalinism', *Europe-Asia Studies* 54: 3 (2002).

—— 'Not a Question of Faith—Youth and Religion in the Post-War Years', *Jahrbücher für Geschichte Osteuropas* 52: 4 (2004).

—— (ed.), *Late Stalinist Russia. Society between Reconstruction and Reinvention* (London and New York: Routledge, 2006).

—— 'Between Salvation and Liquidation: Homeless and Vagrant Children and the Reconstruction of Soviet Society', *Slavonic and East European Review* 86: 2 (2008).

Gaddis, John, *We Now Know. Rethinking Cold War History* (Oxford and New York: Oxford University Press, 1997).

Gatrell, Peter, *A Whole Empire Walking. Refugees in Russia During World War I* (Bloomington, IN: Indiana Unversity Press, 2005).

Geiger, H. Kent, *The Family in Soviet Russia* (Cambridge, MA.: Harvard University Press, 1968).

Gentes, Andrew, 'Katorga: Penal Labour and Tsarist Siberia', *Australian Slavonic and East European Studies* 18: 1–2 (2004).

—— 'Vagabondage and Siberia. Disciplinary Modernism in Tsarist Russia', in *Cast Out. Vagrancy and Homelessness in Global and Historical Perspective*, eds. A. L. Beier and Paul Ocobock (Athens: Ohio University Press, 2008).

Getty, J. Arch, 'State and Society under Stalin: Constitutions and Elections in the 1930s', *Slavic Review* 50: 1 (1991).

—— 'Afraid of Their Shadows: The Bolshevik Recourse to Terror, 1932–1938', in *Stalinismus vor dem Zweiten Weltkrieg. Neue Wege der Forschung*, ed. Manfred Hildermeier (Munich: R. Oldenbourg Verlag, 1998).

—— ' "Excesses Are Not Permitted": Mass Terror and Stalinist Governance in the Late 1930s', *The Russian Review* 61: 1 (2002).

——, Gabor T. Rittersporn, and Viktor Zemskov, 'Victims of the Soviet Penal System in the Pre-War Years: A First Approach on the Basis of Archival Evidence,' *The American Historical Review* 98: 4 (1993).

——and Roberta T. Manning (eds.), *Stalinist Terror. New Perspectives* (Cambridge and New York: Cambridge University Press, 1993).

——and Oleg V. Naumov, *The Road to Terror. Stalin and the Self-Destruction of the Bolsheviks, 1932–1939* (New Haven and London: Yale University Press, 1999).

——, Oleg V. Naumov, and Nadezhda V. Muraveva, *Yezhov. The Rise of Stalin's 'Iron Fist'* (New Haven and London: Yale University Press, 2008).

Getzler, Israel, 'Lenin's Conception of Revolution as Civil War', *Slavonic and East European Review* 74: 3 (1996).

Geyer, Michael and Sheila Fitzpatrick (eds.), *Beyond Totalitarianism. Stalinism and Nazism Compared* (Cambridge: Cambridge University Press, 2009).

Gill, Graeme, *The Origins of the Stalinist Political System* (Cambridge and New York: Cambridge University Press, 1990).

Glantz, David M. and Jonathan House, *When Titans Clashed. How the Red Army Stopped Hitler* (Lawrence, Kansas: University Press of Kansas, 1995).

—— *Colossus Reborn. The Red Army at War, 1941–1943* (Lawrence: University Press of Kansas, 2005).

Gleason, Abbott, ' "Totalitarianism" in 1984', *The Russian Review* 43: 2 (1984).

—— *Totalitarianism. The Inner History of the Cold War* (New York, Oxford: Oxford University Press, 1995).

Goldman, Wendy, *Women, the State, and Revolution: Soviet Family Policy and Social Life, 1917–1936* (Cambridge: Cambridge University Press, 1993).

—— *Women at the Gates. Gender and Industry in Stalin's Russia* (Cambridge: Cambridge University Press, 2002).

—— *Terror and Democracy in the Age of Stalin. The Social Dynamics of Repression* (Cambridge and New York: Cambridge University Press, 2007).

Gorlitzki, Yoram, 'Ordinary Stalinism: The Council of Ministers and the Soviet Neopatrimonial State, 1946–1953', *The Journal of Modern History* 74: 4 (2002).

—— and Oleg V. Khlevniuk, 'Stalin and His Circle', in *The Cambridge History of Russia. Vol III: The Twentieth Century*, ed. Ronald G. Suny (Cambridge and New York: Cambridge University Press, 2006).

—— and Oleg Khlevniuk, *Cold Peace. Stalin and the Soviet Ruling Circle, 1945–1953* (Oxford and New York: Oxford University Press, 2004).

Gorsuch, Anne E. *Youth in Revolutionary Russia: Enthusiasts, Bohemians, Delinquents* (Bloomington, IN: Indiana University Press, 2000).

Graham, Loren R. *The Ghost of the Executed Engineer. Technology and the Fall of the Soviet Union* (Cambridge and London: Harvard University Press, 1993).

Granick, David, *Management of the Industrial Firm in the USSR. A Study in Soviet Economic Planning* (New York: Columbia University Press, 1954).

Graziosi, Andrea, 'G. L. Piatakov (1890–1937): A Mirror of Soviet History', *Harvard Ukrainian Studies* 16 (1992).

—— *The Great Soviet Peasant War. Bolsheviks and Peasants, 1917–1933* (Cambridge, MA.: Harvard University Press, 1996).

Green, Rachel, ' "There will not be orphans among us": Soviet orphanages, foster care, and adoption, 1941–1956', PhD diss. (Chicago: The University of Chicago, 2006).

Gregory, Paul R., *The Political Economy of Stalinism. Evidence from the Soviet Secret Archives*. (Cambridge, New York, and Melbourne: Cambridge University Press, 2004).

——and Andrei Markevich, 'Creating Soviet Industry: The House That Stalin Built', *Slavic Review* 61: 4 (2002).

Gronow, Jukka, *Caviar with Champagne. Common Luxury and the Ideals of the Good Life in Stalin's Russia* (Oxford and New York: Berg, 2003).

Gross, Jan T., *Revolution from Abroad. The Soviet Conquest of Poland's Western Ukraine and Western Belorussia*. expanded edn. (Princeton and Oxford: Princeton University Press, 2002).

Grossman, Gregory, 'The "Second Economy" of the USSR', *Problems of Communism* 25: 5 (1977).

Hachten, P. Charles, 'Property Relations and the Economic Organization of Soviet Russia, 1941–1948'. PhD diss. (Chicago: The University of Chicago, 2005).

——'Separate Yet Governed: The Representation of Soviet Property Relations in Civil Law and Public Discourse', in *Borders of Socialism. Private Spheres of Soviet Russia*, ed. Lewis Siegelbaum (New York and Houndsmills: Palgrave Macmillan, 2006).

Hagenloh, Paul M., ' "Chekist in Essence, Chekist in Spirit": Regular and Political Police in the 1930s', *Cahiers du Monde russe* 42: 2-3-4 (2001).

——*Stalin's Police. Public Order and Mass Repression in the USSR, 1926–1941* (Baltimore: The Johns Hopkins University Press, 2009).

Halfin, Igal, *From Darkness to Light. Class, Consciousness, and Salvation in Revolutionary Russia*. (Pittsburgh, PA: University of Pittsburgh Press, 2000).

——*Terror in My Soul: Communist Autobiographies on Trial* (Cambridge, MA.: Harvard University Press, 2003).

Harris, James R., *The Great Urals: Regionalism and the Evolution of the Soviet System* (Ithaca, NY.: Cornell University Press, 1996).

——'Was Stalin a Weak Dictator?', *The Journal of Modern History* 75 (2003).

Harrison, Mark, *Accounting for War: Soviet Production, Employment, and the Defence Burden, 1940–1945* (Cambridge: Cambridge University Press, 1996).

—— 'The USSR and Total War. Why Didn't the Soviet Economy Collapse in 1942?', In *A World at Total War. Global Conflict and the Politics of Destruction, 1937–1945*, eds. Roger Chickering, Stig Förster, and Bernd Greiner (Cambridge: Cambridge University Press, 2005).

Haslam, Jonathan, *The Vices of Integrity. E. H. Carr 1892–1982* (London and New York: Verso, 1999).

Healy, Dan, 'Sexual and Gender Dissent. Homosexuality as Resistance in Stalin's Russia', in *Contending with Stalinism. Soviet Power & Popular Resistance in the 1930s*, ed. Lynne Viola (Ithaca and London: Cornell University Press, 2002).

Heinzen, James, *Inventing a Soviet Countryside. State Power and the Transformation of Rural Russia, 1917–1929* (Pittburgh, PA: University of Pittsburgh Press, 2004).

—— 'Informers and the State under Late Stalinism. Informant Networks and Crimes against "Socialist Property", 1940–53', *Kritika: Explorations in Russian and Eurasian History* 8: 4 (2007).

—— 'Korruptsiia v GULAGe: dilemmy chinovnikov i uznikov', in *Gulag: Ekonomika prinuditel'nogo truda*, eds. L. Borodkin, P. Gregorin, and Oleg Khlevniuk (Moscow: Rosspen, 2005).

Hellbeck, Jochen, *Revolution on My Mind. Writing a Diary under Stalin* (Cambridge MA., and London: Harvard University Press, 2006).

Heller, Klaus and Jan Plamper (eds.), *Personality Cults in Stalinism— Personenkulte im Stalinismus* (Göttingen: V & R unipress, 2004).

Hessler, Julie, 'Postwar Normalisation and Its Limits in the USSR: The Case of Trade', *Europe-Asia Studies* 53: 3 (2001).

—— *A Social History of Soviet Trade. Trade Policy, Retail Practices, and Consumption, 1917–1953* (Princeton and Oxford: Princeton University Press, 2004).

Hirsch, Francine, *Empire of Nations: Ethnographic Knowledge and the Making of the Soviet Union* (Ithaca: Cornell University Press, 2005).

Hoffmann, David L., *Peasant Metropolis. Social Identities in Moscow, 1929–1941* (Ithaca and London: Cornell University Press, 1994).

—— *Stalinist Values. The Cultural Norms of Soviet Modernity, 1917–1941* (Ithaca and London: Cornell University Press, 2003).

Holquist, Peter, ' "Information Is the Alpha and Omega of Our Work": Bolshevik Surveillance in Its Pan-European Context', *The Journal of Modern History* 69 (1997).

——*Making War, Forging Revolution. Russia's Continuum of Crisis, 1914–1921* (Cambridge and London: Harvard University Press, 2002).

Holzman, Franklyn D., *Soviet Taxation: The Fiscal and Monetary Problems of a Planned Economy* (Cambridge, MA.: Harvard University Press, 1955).

Hosking, Geoffrey, *A History of the Soviet Union 1917–1991*. Final edn. (London: Fontana Press, 1992).

Husband, William B. *'Godless Communists'. Atheism and Society in Soviet Russia 1917–1932* (DeKalb: Northern Illinoi University Press, 2000).

Iazhborovskaia, Inessa, Anatolii Iablokov, and Valentina Parsadanova, *Katynskii sindrom v sovetsko-pol'skikh i rossiisko-pol'skikh otnosheniiakh* (Moscow: Rosspen, 2009).

Inkeles, Alex, *Public Opinion in Soviet Russia. A Study in Mass Persuasion* (Cambridge, MA.: Harvard University Press, 1967).

——and Raymond Bauer, *The Soviet Citizen. Daily Life in a Totalitarian Society* (Cambridge, MA.: Harvard University Press, 1961).

Ivanova, Galina, *Labor Camp Socialism. The Gulag in the Soviet Totalitarian System* (Armonk, NY, and London: M. E. Sharpe, 2000).

Jahn, Hubertus, *Geschichte des Bettelns in Rußland von den Anfängen bis heute* (Paderborn: Ferdinand Schöningh Verlag, 2010).

Jasny, Naum, *Soviet Industrialization, 1928–1952* (Chicago: University of Chicago Press, 1961).

Johnson, Robert Eugene, *Peasant and Proletarian: the Working Class of Moscow in the Late Nineteenth Century* (Leicester: Leicester University Press, 1979).

Jones, Jeffrey W., ' "People without a Definite Occupation". The Illegal Economy and "Speculators" in Rostov-on-the-Don, 1943–1948', in *Provincial Landscapes. Local Dimensions of Soviet Power, 1917–1953*, ed. Donald J. Raleigh (Pittsburgh, PA: University of Pittsburgh Press, 2001).

Kappeler, Andreas, *Russland als Vielvölkerreich. Entstehung. Geschichte. Zerfall* (Munich: C. H. Beck, 1993).

Keller, Shoshana, 'Trapped between State and Society: Women's Liberation and Islam in Soviet Uzbekistan, 1926–1941', *Journal of Women's History* 10: 1 (1998).

Kelly, Catriona, *Children's World. Growing up in Russia 1890–1991* (New Haven and London: Yale University Press, 2007).

—— *Comrade Pavlik. The Rise and Fall of a Soviet Boy Hero* (London: Granta Books, 2005).

—— *Refining Russia. Advice Literature, Polite Culture, & Gender from Catherine to Yeltsin* (Oxford and New York: Oxford University Press, 2001).

Kenez, Peter, *The Birth of the Propaganda State: Soviet Methods of Mass Mobilization, 1917–1929* (Cambridge and New York: Cambridge University Press, 1985).

——, *Cinema and Soviet Society, 1917–1953* (Cambridge: Cambridge University Press, 1992).

Kern, Gary, *The Kravchenko Case. One Man's War on Stalin* (New York: Enigma Books, 2007).

Kharkhordin, Oleg, *The Collective and the Individual in Russia. A Study of Practices* (Berkeley, Los Angeles, and London: University of California Press, 1999).

Khlevniuk, Olev V., 'The Objectives of the Great Terror, 1937–1938', in *Soviet History, 1917–53. Essays in Honour of R. W. Davies*, eds. Julian Cooper, Maureen Perrie, and E. A. Rees (New York: St Martin's Press, 1995).

—— *In Stalin's Shadow. The Career of 'Sergo' Ordzhonikidze* (Armonk, NY and London: M. E. Sharpe, 1995).

—— *Politbiuro. Mekhanizmy politicheskoi vlasti v 1930-e gody* (Moscow: Rosspen, 1996).

—— 'The Reasons for the "Great Terror": the foreign-political aspect', in *Russia in the age of wars, 1914–1945*, eds. Silvio Pons and Andrea Romano (Milano: Geltrinelli, 2000).

—— 'The Economy of the OGPU, NKVD, and MVD of the USSR, 1930–1953. The Scale, Structure, and Trends of Development', in *The Economics of Forced Labor: the Soviet Gulag*, eds. Paul R. Gregory and Valery Lazarev (Stanford, CA: Hoover Institution Press, 2003).

—— *The History of the Gulag. From Collectivization to the Great Terror* (New Haven and London: Yale University Press, 2004).

—— *Master of the House. Stalin and His Inner Circle* (New Haven and London: Yale University Press, 2009).

King, Francis, 'The Russian Revolution and the Idea of a Single Economic Plan 1917–28', *Revolutionary Russia* 12: 1 (1999).

Kingston-Mann, Esta, 'Transforming Peasants in the Twentieth Century: Dilemmas of Russian, Soviet and Post-Soviet Development', in *The Cambridge History of Russia. Vol. III: The Twentieth Century*, ed. Ronald G. Suny (Cambridge: Cambridge University Press, 2006).

Kizenko, Nadieszda, *A Prodigal Saint. Father John of Kronstadt and the Russian People* (University Park, PA: The Pennsylvania State University Press, 2000).

Klier, John, and Shlomo Lambroza (eds.), *Pogroms. Anti-Jewish Violence in Modern Russian History* (Cambridge and New York: Cambridge University Press, 1992).

Kornai, Janos, *The Economics of Shortage*. 2 vols. (Amsterdam: North-Holland Publishing Co., 1980).

Kostyrchenko, Gennadii, *Out of the Red Shadows: Anti-Semitism in Stalin's Russia* (Amherst, NY.: Prometheus Books, 1995).

—— *Tainaia politika Stalina. Vlast' i antisemitism* (Moscow: Mezhdunarodnye otnosheniia, 2003).

Kotkin, Stephen, *Magnetic Mountain. Stalinism as a Civilization* (Berkeley, Los Angeles, and London: University of California Press, 1995).

—— '1991 and the Russian Revolution: Sources, Conceptual Categories, Analytical Frameworks', *The Journal of Modern History* 70: 2 (1998).

—— 'Modern Times: The Soviet Union and the Interwar Conjuncture', *Kritika: Explorations in Russian and Eurasian History* 2: 1 (2001).

—— 'The State—Is It Us? Memoirs, Archives, and Kremlinologists', *The Russian Review* 61: January (2002).

Krylova, Anna, 'The Tenacious Liberal Subject in Soviet Studies', *Kritika. Explorations in Russian and Eurasian History* 1: 1 (2000).

—— 'Stalinist Identity from the Viewpoint of Gender: Rearing a Generation of Professionally Violent Women-Fighters in 1930s Stalinist Russia', *Gender & History* 16: 3 (2004).

—— 'Identity, Agency, and the "First Soviet Generation"', in *Generations in Twentieth-Century Europe*, ed. Stephen Lovell (Houndsmills, Basingstokes: Palgrave Macmillan, 2007).

Kuhr, Corinna, 'Children of "Enemies of the People" as Victims of the Great Purges', *Cahiers du Monde russe* 39: 1–2 (1998).

Kuntsman, Adi, '"With a Shade of Disgust": Affective Politics of Sexuality and Class in Memoirs of the Stalinist Gulag', *Slavic Review* 68: 2 (2009).

Kuromiya, Hiroaki, *The Voices of the Dead. Stalin's Great Terror in the 1930s* (New Haven and London: Yale University Press, 2007).

——'The Soviet Famine of 1932–1933 Reconsidered', *Europe-Asia Studies* 60: 4 (2008).

Lebina, N. B., *Povsednevnaia zhizn' Sovetskogo goroda: normy i anomalii 1920/1930 gody* (St Petersburg: Kikimora, 1999).

Ledeneva, Alena V., *Russia's Economy of Favours. Blat, Networking and Informal Exchange* (New York and Cambridge: Cambridge University Press, 1998).

——, '*Blat* and *Guanxi*: Informal Practices in Russia and China', *Comparative Studies in Society and History* 50: 1 (2008).

Lenoe, Matthew E., *Closer to the Masses: Stalinist Culture, Social Revolution, and Soviet Newspapers* (Cambridge, MA.: Harvard University Press, 2004).

——*The Kirov Murder and Soviet History* (New Haven: Yale University Press, 2010).

Lévesque, Jean, 'Exile and Discipline: The June 1948 Campaign Against Collective Farm Shirkers', *The Carl Beck Papers in Russian & East European Studies* 1708 (2006).

Lewin, Moshe, 'The Disappearance of Planning in the Plan', *Slavic Review* 32: 2 (1973).

——*Russian Peasants and Soviet Power. A Study of Collectivization* (New York and London: W. W. Norton & Co., 1975).

——*The Making of the Soviet System. Essays in the Social History of Interwar Russia* (New York: The New Press, 1994).

Lincoln, W. Bruce, *Red Victory. A History of the Russian Civil War* (New York and London: Simon and Schuster, 1989).

Lindenmeyr, Adele, *Poverty Is Not a Vice. Charity, Society, and the State in Imperial Russia* (Princeton, NJ.: Princeton University Press, 1996).

Lovell, Stephen, *Summerfolk. A History of the Dacha, 1719–2000* (Ithaca and London: Cornell University Press, 2003).

——'Soviet Russia's Older Generations', in *Generations in Twentieth-Century Europe*, ed. Stephen Lovell (Houndsmills, Basingstokes: Palgrave Macmillan, 2007).

——, Alena Ledeneva, and Andrei Rogachevskii (eds.), *Bribery and Blat in Russia. Negotiating Reciprocity from the Middle Ages to the 1990s* (New York: St Martin's Press, 2000).

McDermott, Kevin, *Stalin* (Houndsmills, Basingstoke: Palgrave Macmillan, 2006).

Madison, Bernice Q., *Social Welfare in the Soviet Union* (Stanford, CA.: Stanford University Press, 1968).

Maier, Robert, *Die Stachanov-Bewegung 1935–1938. Der Stachanovismus als tragendes und verschärfendes Moment der Stalinisierung der sowjetischen Gesellschaft* (Stuttgart: Franz Steiner Verlag, 1990).

Malia, Martin, *The Soviet Tragedy. A History of Socialism in Russia, 1917–1991* (New York: The Free Press, 1994).

—— 'Revolution fulfilled. How the revisionists are still trying to take ideology out of Stalinism', *TLS* 15 June 2001.

Manley, Rebecca, *To the Tashkent Station. Evacuation and Survival in the Soviet Union at War* (Ithaca and London: Cornell University Press, 2009).

Manning, Roberta T., 'Women in the Soviet Countryside on the Eve of World War II, 1935–1940', in *Russian Peasant Women*, eds. Beatrice Farnsworth and Lynne Viola (Oxford: Oxford University Press, 1992).

Markevich, Andrei, 'Soviet Urban Households and the Road to Universal Employment, from the End of the 1930s to the End of the 1960s', *Continuity and Change* 20: 3 (2005).

Marples, David R., 'Ethnic Issues in the Famine of 1932–1933 in Ukraine', *Europe-Asia Studies* 61: 3 (2009).

Martin, Terry, 'The Origins of Soviet Ethnic Cleansing', *The Journal of Modern History* 70, no. 4 (1998).

—— *The Affirmative Action Empire. Nations and Nationalism in the Soviet Union, 1923–1939* (Ithaca and London: Cornell University Press, 2001).

Markwick, Roger D., *Rewriting History in Soviet Russia. The Politics of Revisionist Historiography, 1956–1974* (Houndsmills, Basingstoke: Palgrave, 2001).

Massell, Gregory J., *The Surrogate Proletariat: Moslem Women and Revolutionary Strategies in Soviet Central Asia, 1919–1929* (Princeton NJ.: Princeton University Press, 1974).

Mawdsley, Evan, *Thunder in the East. The Nazi-Soviet War 1941–1945* (London: Hodder Arnold, 2005).

—— and Stephen White. *The Soviet Elite from Lenin to Gorbachev. The Central Committee and Its Members, 1917–1991* (Oxford and New York: Oxford University Press, 2000).

Mayer, Arno J., *The Furies. Violence and Terror in the French and Russian Revolutions* (Princeton, NJ.: Princeton University Press, 2000).

Medvedev, Roy, *Let History Judge: The Origins and Consequences of Stalinism* (London: Macmillan, 1972).

Merl, Stephan, *Sozialer Aufstieg im sowjetischen Kolchossystem der 30er Jahre? Über das Schicksal der bäuerlichen Parteimitglieder, Dorfsowjetvorsitzenden, Posteninhaber in Kolchosen, Mechanisatoren und Stachanowleute* (Berlin, Duncker & Humblot, 1990).

——, *Bauern unter Stalin: die Formierung des sowjetischen Kolkhossystems, 1930–1941* (Berlin: Duncker & Humblot, 1990).

Merridale, Catherine, 'The 1937 Census and the Limits of Stalinist Rule', *The Historical Journal* 39: 1 (1996).

—— *Night of Stone. Death and Memory in Russia* (London: Granta Books, 2000).

—— *Ivan's War. Life and Death in the Red Army, 1939–1945* (New York: Metropolitan Books, 2006).

Millar, James R. 'The Little Deal: Brezhnev's Contribution to Acquisitive Socialism', *Slavic Review* 44: 4 (1985).

—— and Alec Nove, 'A Debate on Collectivization: Was Stalin really necessary?', *Problems of Communism* 25 no. 4 (1976).

Miner, Steven Merritt, *Stalin's Holy War. Religion, Nationalism, and Alliance Politics, 1941–1945* (Chapel Hill and London: The University of North Carolina Press, 2003).

Mironov, B. N., *Sotsial'naia istoriia Rossii perioda imperii (XVIII – nachalo XX v.). Genezis lichnosti, demokraticheskoi sem'i, grazhdanskogo obshchestva i pravovogo gosudarstva.* 2 vols. (St Petersburg: Dmitrii Bulanin, 2000).

Mitrofanova, A. V. (ed.), *Rabochii klass SSSR nakanune i v gody Velikoi Otechestvennoi voiny 1938–1945 gg.* vol. 3 (Moscow: Nauka, 1984).

Moine, Nathalie, 'Le miroir de statistiques. Inegalites et spheres privée au cours du second stalinisme', *Cahiers du Monde russe* 44: 2–3 (2003).

Montefiore, Sebag, *Stalin. The Court of the Red Tsar* (New York: Vintage Books, 2003).

Moon, David, *The Russian Peasantry 1600–1930. The World the Peasants Made* (London and New York: Longman, 1999).

Morrissey, Susan, *Heralds of Revolution. Russian Students and the Mythologies of Radicalism* (New York and Oxford: Oxford University Press, 1998).

Moskoff, William, *The Bread of Affliction. The Food Supply in the USSR During World War II* (Cambridge: Cambridge University Press, 1990).

Murphy, Kevin, *Revolution and Counterrevolution. Class Struggle in a Moscow Metal Factory* (Chicago: Haymarket Books, 2007).

Musial, Bogdan, *'Konterrevolutionäre Elemente sind zu erschießen'. Die Brutalisierung des deutsch-sowjetischen Krieges im Sommer 1941.* 2nd edn. (Berlin and Munich: Propyläen, 2001).

Nagle, John D., 'A New Look at the Soviet Elite: A Generational Model of the Soviet System', *Journal of Political & Military Sociology* 3: 1 (1975).

Naiman, Eric, *Sex in Public. The Incarnation of Early Soviet Ideology* (Princeton, NJ.: Princeton University Press, 1997).

Naimark, Norman, *The Russians in Germany. A History of the Soviet Zone of Occupation, 1945–1949* (Cambridge, and London: The Belknap Press of Harvard University Press, 1995).

Nakachi, Mie, 'Replacing the Dead: The Politics of Reproduction in the Postwar Soviet Union, 1944–1955'. PhD diss. (Chicago: The University of Chicago, 2008).

——'N. S. Khrushchev and the 1944 Soviet Family Law: Politics, Reproduction, and Language', *East European Politics and Societies* 20: 1 (2006).

Naumov, V. P., 'Sud'ba voennoplennykh i deportirovannykh grazhdan SSSR. Materialy Komissii po reabilitatsii zhertv politicheskikh repressii', *Novaia i noveishaia istoriia*, 2 (1996).

Neuberger, Joan, *Hooliganism. Crime, Culture, and Power in St. Petersburg, 1900–1914* (Berkeley, Los Angeles, and London: University of California Press, 1993).

Northrop, Douglas, *Veiled Empire. Gender & Power in Stalinist Central Asia* (Ithaca and London: Cornell University Press, 2004).

Nove, Alec, 'Was Stalin Really Necessary?' *Encounter*, 18:4 (1962)
—— 'The "Logic" and Cost of Collectivization', *Problems of Communism* 25: 4 (1976).
——*An Economic History of the USSR 1917–1991*. New and final edn. (London: Penguin, 1992).
—— *The Stalin Phenomenon* (London: Weidenfeld & Nicolson, 1993).
Oja, Matt F., 'From *Krestianka* to *Udarnitsa*. Rural Women and the *Vydvizhenie* Campaign, 1933–1941', *The Carl Beck Papers in Russian & East European Studies* 1203 (1996).
Osokina, Elena, *Za fasadom 'stalinskogo izobiliia'. Raspredelenie i rynok v snabzhenii naseleniia v gody industrializatsii 1927–1941* (Moscow: Rosspen, 1999).
—— *Our Daily Bread. Socialist Distribution and the Art of Survival in Stalin's Russia, 1927–1941* (Armonk, NY, and London: M. E. Sharpe, 2001).
Parrish, Michael, *The Lesser Terror. Soviet State Security, 1939–1953* (Westport, Connecticut and London: Praeger, 1996).
Payne, Matthew J., *Stalin's Railroad: Turksib and the Building of Socialism* (Pittsburgh, PA: University of Pittsburgh Press, 2001).
Pechenkin, A. A., 'Byla li vozmozhnost' nastupat'?' *Otechestvennaia istoriia* 3 (1995).
Pennington, Reina, *Wings, Women, and War. Soviet Airwomen in World War II Combat* (Lawrence: University Press of Kansas, 2001).
Peris, Daniel, '"God Is Now on Our Side": The Religious Revival on Unoccupied Soviet Territory During World War II', *Kritika: Explorations in Russian and Eurasian History* 1: 1 (2000).
Pethybridge, Roger, *The Social Prelude to Stalinism* (London and Basingstoke: Macmillan, 1974).
Petrone, Karen, *Life Has Become More Joyous, Comrades: Celebrations in the Time of Stalin* (Bloomington, IN.: Indiana University Press, 2000).
Pikhoia, R. G., *Sovetskii soiuz: istoriia vlasti 1945–1991* (Novosibirsk: Sibirskii khoronograf, 2000).
Pipes, Richard, *The Formation of the Soviet Union: Communism and Nationalism, 1917–1923*, rev. edn. (Cambridge and London: Harvard University Press, 1964).

—— *The Russian Revolution 1899–1919* (London: Collins Harvill, 1990).

—— '1917 and the Revisionists', *The National Interest* (Spring 1993).

—— *Vixi. Memoirs of a Non-Belonger* (New Haven and London: Yale University Press, 2003).

Pisiotis, Argyrios K., 'Images of Hate in the Art of War', in *Culture and Entertainment in Wartime Russia*, ed. Richard Stites (Bloomington and Indianapolis: Indiana University Press, 1995).

Plaggenborg, Stefan, and Jean-Paul Depretto, 'La recherche sur le stalinisme en Allemagne', *Le Mouvement social*, 196 (2001).

Pleshakov, Constantine, *Stalin's Folly. The Tragic First Ten Days of World War II on the Eastern Front* (Boston and New York: Houton Mifflin Co., 2005).

Poliakov, Iu. A. (ed.), *Naselenie Rossii v XX veke. Istoricheskie Ocherki.* 3 vols. (Moscow: Rosspen, 2000–2005).

Polian, Pavel, *Ne po svoei vole…Istoriia i geografiia prinuditel'nykh migratsii v SSSR* (Moscow: OGI, 2001).

Popov, V. P., 'Gosudarstvennyi terror v sovetskoi Rossii. 1923–1953 gg. (istochniki i ikh interpretatsiia)', *Otechestvennye arkhivy* 2 (1992).

Priestland, David, *Stalinism and the Politics of Mobilization. Ideas, Power, and Terror in Inter-war Russia* (Oxford: Oxford University Press, 2007).

Pyzhikov, Aleksandr V., 'Sovetskoe poslevoennoe obshchestvo i predposylki khrushchevskikh reform', *Voprosy istorii*, no. 2 (2002).

Rees, E. A. (ed.), *The Nature of Stalin's Dictatorship. The Politburo, 1924–1953* (Houndmills: Palgrave Macmillan, 2004).

Rendle, Matthew, 'The Problems of "Becoming Soviet": Former Nobles in Soviet Society, 1917–41', *European History Quarterly* 38: 7 (2008).

Rieber, Alfred J., 'The Sedimentary Society', in *Between Tsar and People. Educated Society and the Quest for Public Identity in Late Imperial Russsia*, eds. Edith W. Clowes, Samuel D. Kassow, and James L. West (Princeton, NJ.: Princeton University Press, 1991).

Riegel, Klaus-Georg, *Konfessionsrituale im Marxismus-Leninismus* (Graz, Vienna and Cologne: Styria, 1985).

Rigby, T. H., *Communist Party Membership in the USSR 1917–1967* (Princeton, NJ.: Princeton University Press, 1968).

—— *Lenin's Government: Sovnarkom 1917–1922* (Cambridge and New York: Cambridge University Press, 1979).

—— 'Early Provincial Cliques and the Rise of Stalin', *Soviet Studies* 33, no. 1 (1981).

—— 'Was Stalin a Disloyal Patron?', *Soviet Studies* 38: 3 (1986).

Rimmel, Lesley A., '*Svodki* and Popular Opinion in Stalinist Leningrad', *Cahiers du Monde russe* 40: 1–2 (1999).

Rittersporn, Gabor T., *Stalinist Simplifications and Soviet Complications. Social Tensions and Political Conflicts in the USSR 1933–1953* (Chur: Harwood Academic Publishers, 1991).

Roberts, Craig Paul, '"War Communism": A Re-Examination', *Slavic Review* 29: 2 (1970).

Rosenberg, William, Diane P. Koenker, Ronald G. Suny (eds.), *Party, State, and Society in the Russian Civil War. Explorations in Social History* (Bloomington and Indianapolis: Indiana University Press, 1989).

Roslof, Edward E., *Red Priests: Renovationism, Russian Orthodoxy, and Revolution, 1905–1946* (Bloomington, IN: Indiana University Press, 2002).

Rossman, Jeffrey J., *Worker Resistance under Stalin. Class and Revolution on the Shop Floor* (Cambridge and London: Harvard University Press, 2005).

Rowney, Don K., *Transition to Technocracy. The Structural Origins of the Soviet Administrative State* (Ithaca and London: Cornell University Press, 1989).

Sanborn, Joshua A., *Drafting the Russian Nation. Military Conscription, Total War, and Mass Politics, 1905–1925* (DeKalb, Illinois: Northern Illinois University Press, 2003).

Scammell, Michael, *Solzhenitsyn. A Biography* (London: Hutchinson, 1984).

Service, Robert, *Stalin. A Biography* (Cambridge, MA.: Harvard University Press, 2005).

Shearer, David R., *Industry, State, and Society in Stalin's Russia 1926–1934* (Ithaca and London: Cornell University Press, 1996).

—— 'Social Disorder, Mass Repression, and the NKVD During the 1930s', *Cahiers du Monde russe* 42: 2-3-4 (2001).

—— 'Elements near and Alien: Passportization, Policing, and Identity in the Stalinist State, 1932–1952', *The Journal of Modern History* 76: 4 (2004).

—— *Policing Stalin's Socialism. Repression and Social Order in the Soviet Union, 1924–1953* (New Haven and London: Yale University Press, 2009).

Shlapentokh, Vladimir, *Public and Private Life of the Soviet People. Changing Values in Post-Stalin Russia* (New York and Oxford: Oxford University Press, 1989).

Siegelbaum, Lewis H., *Stakhanovism and the Politics of Productivity in the USSR, 1935–1941* (Cambridge: Cambridge University Press, 1988).

—— *Soviet State and Society between Revolutions, 1918–1929* (Cambridge, New York and Melbourne: Cambridge University Press, 1994).

—— ' "Dear Comrade, You Ask What We Need": Socialist Paternalism and Soviet Rural "Notables" in the Mid-1930s', *Slavic Review* 57: 1 (1998).

—— (ed.), *Borders of Socialism. Private Spheres of Soviet Russia* (New York: Palgrave Macmillan, 2006).

—— *Cars for Comrades: the Life of the Soviet Automobile* (Ithaca: Cornell University Press, 2008).

Skarovskij, Michail V., 'Die russische Kirche unter Stalin in den 20er und 30 Jahren des 20. Jahrhunderts', in *Stalinismus vor dem Zweiten Weltkrieg: Neue Wege der Forschung*, ed. Manfred Hildermeier (Munich: Oldenbourg, 1998).

Slezkine, Yuri, *Arctic Mirrors. Russia and the Small Peoples of the North* (Ithaca and London: Cornell University Press, 1994).

——, 'The Soviet Union as a Communal Apartment, or How a Socialist State Promoted Ethnic Particularism', *Slavic Review* 53, no. 2 (1994).

—— 'How I Became Multicultural', in *Intellectuals and the Articulation of the Nation*, eds. Ronald Suny and Michael Kennedy (Ann Arbor: The University of Michigan Press, 1999).

—— *The Jewish Century* (Princeton, NJ.: Princeton University Press, 2004).

Smith, Mark B., 'Individual Forms of Ownership in the Urban Housing Fund of the USSR, 1944–64', *Slavonic and East European Review* 86: 2 (2008).

Smith, S. A., 'The First Soviet Generation: Children and Religious Belief in Soviet Russia, 1917–41', in *Generations in Twentieth-Century Europe*, ed. Stephen Lovell (Houndsmills, Basingstokes: Palgrave MacMillan, 2007).

Sokolov, Andrei, 'Forced Labor in Soviet Industry: The End of the 1930s to the Mid-1950s. An Overview', in *The Economics of Forced Labor: the Soviet Gulag*, eds. Paul R. Gregory and Valery Lazarev (Stanford CA: Hoover Institution Press, 2003).

Solomon, Peter H., *Soviet Criminal Justice under Stalin* (Cambridge, New York, and Melbourne: Cambridge University Press, 1996).

Starr, S. Frederick, *Red and Hot. The Fate of Jazz in the Soviet Union 1917–1980* (New York and Oxford: Oxford University Press, 1983).

Steinberg, Mark, *Proletarian Imagination. Self, Modernity, and the Sacred in Russia, 1910–1925* (Ithaca and London: Cornell University Press, 2002).

Stites, Richard *Revolutionary Dreams. Utopian Vision and Experimental Life in the Russian Revolution* (New York and Oxford: Oxford University Press, 1989).

—— *Russian Popular Culture. Entertainment and Society since 1900* (Cambride, and New York, and Melbourne: Cambridge University Press, 1994).

Suny, Ronald G., *The Baku Commune, 1917–1918: Class and Nationality in the Russian Revolution* (Princeton, NJ.: Princeton University Press, 1972).

—— 'Toward a Social History of the October Revolution', *The American Historical Review* 88: 1 (1983).

—— *The Revenge of the Past. Nationalism, Revolution, and the Collapse of the Soviet Union* (Stanford, CA.: Stanford University Press, 1993).

—— *The Soviet Experiment. Russia, the USSR, and the Successor States* (New York and Oxford: Oxford University Press, 1998).

Taubman, William, *Khrushchev. The Man and his Era* (New York and London: W. W. Norton & Co., 2003).

Thurston, Robert W., 'Fear and Belief in the USSR's "Great Terror": Response to Arrest, 1935–1939', *Slavic Review* 45: 2 (1986).

—— *Life and Terror in Stalin's Russia 1934–1941* (New Haven and London: Yale University Press, 1996).

Tomoff, Kiril, *Creative Union: The Professional Organization of Soviet Composers, 1939–1953* (Ithaca, NY.: Cornell University Press, 2006).

——, Julie Hessler, and Golfo Alexopoulos (eds.), *Writing the Stalin Era: Sheila Fitzpatrick and Soviet Historiography* (Houndsmills and New York: Palgrave Macmillan, 2010).

Tucker, Robert C., *Stalin as Revolutionary, 1879–1929: a study in history and personality* (New York: Norton, 1973).

—— 'Stalinism as Revolution from Above', in *Stalinism. Essays in Historical Interpretation*, ed. Robert C. Tucker (New York: W. W. Norton & Company, 1977), 77–108.

—— *Stalin in Power. The Revolution from above 1928–1941* (New York and London: W. W. Norton & Company, 1992).

Tumarkin, Nina, *The Living & the Dead. The Rise and Fall of the Cult of World War II in Russia* (New York: BasicBooks, 1994).

Vail, Peter, and Aleksandr Genis, *60-e. Mir sovetskogo cheloveka* (Moscow: Novoe literaturnoe obozrenie, 2001).

van Ree, Eric, *The Political Thought of Joseph Stalin. A Study in Twentieth-Century Revolutionary Patriotism* (London and New York: Routledge Curzon, 2002).

Varese, Federico, 'The Society of the vory-v-zakone, 1930s–1950s', *Cahiers du Monde russe*, vol. 39: 4 (1998).

Veidlinger, Jeffrey, *The Moscow State Yiddish Theater. Jewish Culture on the Soviet Stage* (Bloomington and Indianapolis: Indiana University Press, 2000).

Verbitskaia, O. M., *Rossiiskoe krest'ianstvo: ot Stalina k Khrushchevu* (Moscow: Nauka, 1992).

Viola, Lynne, *The Best Sons of the Fatherland. Workers in the Vanguard of Soviet Collectivization* (New York and Oxford: Oxford University Press, 1987).

—— *Peasant Rebels Under Stalin. Collectivization and the Culture of Peasant Resistance* (Oxford: Oxford University Press, 1996).

—— 'Popular Resistance in the Stalinist 1930s: Soliloquy of a Devil's Advocate', *Kritika* 1: 1 (2000).

—— 'The Role of the OGPU in Dekulakization, Mass Deportations, and Special Resettlement in 1930', *The Carl Beck Papers in Russian & East European Studies* 1406 (2000).

—— (ed.), *Contending with Stalinism. Soviet Power and Popular Resistance in the 1930s* (Ithaca and London: Cornell University Press, 2002).

—— 'The Cold War in American Soviet Historiography and the End of the Soviet Union', *The Russian Review* 61: 1 (2002).

—— *The Unknown Gulag. The Lost World of Stalin's Special Settlements* (Oxford and New York: Oxford University Press, 2007).

——, V. P. Danilov, N. A. Ivnitskii, and Denis Kozlov (eds.), *The War against the Peasantry, 1927–130: The Tragedy of the Soviet Countryside* (New Haven, CT: Yale University Press, 2005).

von Geldern, James, *Bolshevik Festivals, 1917–1920* (Berkeley CA: University of California Press, 1993).

—— 'Life in-Betweeen: Migration and Popular Culture in Late Imperial Russia,' *Russian Review* 55: 3 (1996).

von Hagen, Mark, *Soldiers in the Proletarian Dictatorship. The Red Army and the Soviet Socialist State, 1917–1930* (Ithaca and London: Cornell University Press, 1990).

Weiner, Amir, *Making Sense of War. The Second World War and the Fate of the Bolshevik Revolution* (Princeton and Oxford: Princeton University Press, 2000).

—— (ed.), *Landscaping the Human Garden. Twentieth-Century Population Management in a Comparative Framework* (Stanford, CA.: Stanford University Press, 2003).

—— 'Something to Die for, a Lot to Kill For: The Soviet System and the Barbarisation of Warfare, 1939–1945', in *The Barbarization of Warfare* ed. George Kassimeris (New York: New York University Press, 2006).

Werth, Nicolas 'Un état contre son peuple. Violence, répressions, terreurs en Union soviétique', *Le livre noir du communisme. Crimes, terreur, répression*, ed. Stéphane Courtois et al. (Paris: Robert Laffont, 1997).

—— *Cannibal Island. Death in a Siberian Gulag* (Princeton and Oxford: Princeton University Press, 2007).

Wheatcroft, Stephen, 'The Scale and Nature of German and Soviet Repression and Mass Killings, 1930–45', *Europe-Asia Studies* 48: 8 (1996).

—— 'Towards Explaining the Changing Levels of Stalinist Repression in the 1930s: Mass Killings', in *Challenging Traditional Views of Russian History*, ed. S. G. Wheatcroft (Houndsmills, Basingstoke: Palgrave Macmillan, 2002).

Wirtschafter, Elise Kimerling, *Social Identity in Imperial Russia* (DeKalb: Northern Illinois University Press, 1997).

Wolff, David, and Gael Moullec, *Le KGB et les pays Baltes 1939–1991* (Paris: Belin, 1999).

Wynn, Charters, *Workers, Strikes, and Pogroms. The Donbass-Dnepr Bend in Late Imperial Russia, 1870–1905* (Princeton, NJ.: Princeton University Press, 1992).

Youngblood, Denise J., *Russian War Films. On the Cinema Front, 1914–2005* (Lawrence: University Press of Kansas, 2007).

Zaleski, Eugene, *Stalinist Planning for Economic Growth, 1933–1952* (London and Basingstoke: Macmillan, 1980).

Zima, V. F., *Golod v SSSR 1946–1947 godov: proiskhozhdenie i posledstviia* (Moscow: Institut Rossiiskoi istorii RAN, 1996).

Zubkova, Elena, *Russia after the War. Hopes, Illusions, and Disappointments, 1945–1957*. Transl. by Hugh Ragsdale (Armonk, NY and London: M. E. Sharpe, 1998).

—— *Poslevoennoe sovetskoe obshchestvo: politika i povsednevnost' 1945–1953* (Moscow: Rosspen, 2000).

—— 'The Soviet Regime and Soviet Society in the Postwar Years: Innovations and Conservatism, 1945–1953', *Journal of Modern European History* 2: 1 (2004).

—— *Pribaltika i Kreml'. 1940–1953* (Moscow: Rosspen, 2008).

Zubok, Vladislav and Constantine Plashakov, *Inside the Kremlin's Cold War. From Stalin to Khrushchev* (Cambridge, MA.: Harvard University Press, 1996).

INDEX

Pipes, R. 212, 223, 224, 228–9
planning 194–5, 196–8, 200, 204,
 207, 208, 209–10
plenipotentiaries 103, 106, 114,
 207
Podlubnyi, S. F. 62–3, 168–9
Poland 8, 42, 52, 155–6; *see also*
 revolution from abroad
Poles 42, 49, 134, 153, 172,
 174, 188
police 19, 44, 48, 52, 61, 62, 63, 64,
 65, 67, 77, 79, 89–90, 102, 103,
 108–11, 121, 131, 134, 138,
 143, 184, 247 n. 22
 numbers 109
Politburo 48–9, 77, 90, 101, 101–2,
 120, 166
polygamy 94–5, 146, 147;
 see also family; divorce;
 gender
Popper, K. 225
popular opinions 141, 154
Poskrebyshev, A. N. 79
posters 136
post-modernism 214, 215
post-revisionism 220, 222, 224–5,
 236–41
POWs, *see* prisoners of war
prisoners of war, *see* repatriation;
 veterans; Order No. 270
prisons 41, 61, 205; *see also*
 concentration camps;
 GULAG; special settlers
pro-natalism 76, 81
propaganda, *see* ideology; posters;
 newspapers; cinema; novels;
 music; poetry
property 75, 76, 86–7, 200–1
propiska, *see* residence permit
Provisional Government 99
prostitution 56, 90
pusher, *see* tolkach

Pushkin, A. S. 170
Putin, V. V. 233, 234

quicksand society, *see* society

Radek, K. B. 48
radio 63, 154, 157
rationing 8, 18, 200, 207
Red Army 18–19, 22–5, 32, 44, 46,
 52, 90, 94, 102, 105, 109,
 130–1, 145–6, 156, 160, 188–9,
 198–9; *see also* demobilization
religion 38–9, 43, 48–9, 66, 74, 75,
 83, 115–16, 127–8, 131, 138,
 142, 143–53, 177, 193–4
 Marxism-Leninism as a 77, 86,
 88, 91, 125, 128, 146, 148, 161
 see also ideology
repatriation 43, 53, 60–1, 72
repression, *see* terror
residence permit 63, 78
resistance
 against collectivization 18, 44–7
 against Red Army 32
 against Bolshevik power 38
 historiographical discussion
 about 238–40
respectability 69, 88–90, 92–3,
 169–71, 191–2
revisionism 214, 217–22, 224, 225,
 231, 237–8
revolution 39, 41, 49–50, 75, 136
 of 1905 6, 99, 130, 141
 of February 1917 6, 99, 129
 of October 1917 6, 30, 38, 55, 76,
 99, 103, 107, 127, 129, 159, 172
 cultural 7, 47, 221
 from abroad (1939–41) 8, 52,
 155–6
 world 38
 see also French Revolution;
 revolution from above